MAGALIESBERG

R EYE

WONDERFONTEIN SPRUIT

BANK EYE

VENTERSPOST
EYE

Syanite Dykes forming walls to the Dolomite water compartments

KRUGERSDORP

GEMSBOKFONTEIN
EYE

RANDFONTEIN

esburg

Coach

Route

D0850558

The Wonderfontein 'Valley of the Eyes'

GOLD THEIR TOUCHSTONE

'Men have a touchstone whereby to try gold
but gold is the touchstone whereby to try men.'

Thomas Fuller,
The Holy State and the Profane State 1642

Gold
Their Touchstone

Gold Fields of South Africa 1887–1987

A Centenary Story

Roy Macnab

Jonathan Ball Publishers
Johannesburg

First published in 1987 by
Jonathan Ball Publishers
P O Box 548
Bergvlei 2012

ISBN 0 86850 140 9

Design and phototypesetting by Book Productions, Pretoria
Printed and bound by National Book Printers, Goodwood, Cape

Contents

List of Illustrations

Endpapers by Arthur Stead: The Wonderfontein 'Valley of the Eyes'

Colour section between pages 100 and 101

Shaft sinking at Kloof No 4 shaft
Original share certificate for 50 Paardekraal G M Co. shares (Africana Museum)
The Gold Fields coat of arms
A touchstone, some 2000 years old (Musée des Antiquités, Saint Germain-en-Laye)
Mural by Jan Juta of Simon van der Stel with visiting Hottentots, the Castle, Cape Town
    (South Africa House, London)
O'okiep: Carolusberg Mine, 1985
Copper smelting, 1985
Rope raise at East Drie No 5 subvertical shaft, 1985
Saldanha Bay from which is exported the mined treasure of Black Mountain
Black Mountain: an Aladdin's cave at Aggeneys
Ancient stamp mill, Rooiberg
Ancient fire-set, Rooiberg
Stone cottage at Luipaardsvlei, once lived in by Rhodes and Rudd
Northam, 1986: platinum mining in the bushveld.

Colour section between pages 212 and 213

Coalbrook Colliery
Guest cottages at West Driefontein
Instruction at Gold Fields training centre at Kloof
Peter Ngobeni, sprinter
Scene at Gold Fields Resource Education Centre, Pilanesburg National Park
Pella Church, restored by The Gold Fields Foundation, and serving the Black Mountain
    community
Robinson Deep Mine, 1935-6: watercolour by Walter Battiss (Africana Museum)
Chris Shaft, 1936: graphite on paper by W H Coetzer (Africana Museum)
'Simmer & Jack Saterdag Middag 1919': watercolour by J H Pierneef (Africana Museum)
Sub Nigel locomotive: painting by David Shepherd
Gold Fields' new building in downtown Johannesburg: exterior and interior
Gold Fields of South Africa: location map of main operations

vi

Black and white illustrations

Preface

This is a tale told on the occasion of a celebration. It is a book to mark one hundred years of activity in South Africa of the country's oldest mining house, Gold Fields. It is not the first book to be written about the company Rhodes and Rudd founded in February 1887; it will certainly not be the last. An official history of Gold Fields appeared as long ago as 1937. Thirty years after that came another, *Gold Paved the Way,* where the late A P Cartwright described the worldwide activities of the British company, Consolidated Gold Fields, including those in South Africa. Since that time Gold Fields of South Africa has emerged as an independent South African company. My task has been to tell for the first time the story of that company and at the same time to give an account of the endeavours in this country of Gold Fields men in the long years when these were still being directed from London. Mine is exclusively the story of Gold Fields in Southern Africa over the past century. The interpretation of the events it contains and the opinions it expresses are my own; they are not necessarily shared by the company itself.

Many people have helped me to make the book. Men from the Gold Fields past, as well as the present, have accompanied me through the world of mining, to which I came as a stranger and which proved to be ever more fascinating the better I got to know it. I am grateful to Robin Plumbridge, the GFSA chairman, for having suggested my journey in the first place. He sensibly took the precaution of providing me with a guide and mentor in the person of his former deputy chairman, Peter van Rensburg. Without him I would certainly have found myself derailed somewhere along the West Wits Line. As it was, he indicated where I should put down the boreholes for my research. Thanks to him the cores often came up with high grade historical material as if I had dipped my pen in the richness of the Carbon Leader.

In London, at Consolidated Gold Fields, Don Barton, for so long that company's link-man with South Africa and his colleague in the archives, Peter Kirby, helped me locate South African material. I am grateful also for the help given me in England by Richard Kitzinger and by Alan Rudd, at 83 the last surviving son of the co-founder. At Oxford, the library staff of Rhodes House were particularly helpful. In South Africa the early archival material is located in the Gold Fields Collection of the Cory Library at Rhodes University. Here Mr Berning and his staff helped to make my stay in Grahamstown fruitful while the hospitality given me by the Vice Chancellor, Professor Henderson, insured that it was also enjoyable. At Barlow Rand in Johannesburg Maryna Fraser found valuable material for me among the records of Rand Mines and Central Mining. John Lang, although busy at the time with his own history of the Chamber of Mines, nevertheless found time to help me with my own researches in the Chamber's archives. He also kindly allowed me to read the text of his story of the Krugerrand. I am similarly grateful to John Wentzel who let me see the text of his history of the family law firm, Webber Wentzel, so long associated with Gold Fields. Tony Fleischer made available to me the private papers of his father, Spencer Fleischer, and the journal kept by his mother which provided a valuable insight into the life of the Gold Fields community of forty and fifty years ago. Ian Mackenzie, whose family has had a long connection with Gold Fields, some of it chronicled in *Mackenzie Saga* by A N Wilson, also took a kindly interest in my task. Harald Krahmann provided me with interesting material on his father, Dr Rudolf Krahmann, while the octogenarian geologist, Robert Pelletier, despite the accumulation of years, had clear memories of Gold Fields in the early 1930s. To Arthur Stead, who received me hospitably at his Simonstown home, I am specially grateful not only for having lent his artistic talents to the creation of the endpapers of this book but also for giving me the benefit of his many years at Gold Fields, for whose history he has a special feeling. I am also indebted to Gail Nattrass for being so helpful about tin and about Rooiberg in particular.

So many people whose careers were landmarks down the Gold Fields years, such as the former chairman, Ian Louw, and former deputy chairman, Robin Hope, to name only two, allowed me to profit from their Gold Fields experience. I am grateful to all of them, too numerous to name, for the time they gave me in answering my questions. At 75 Fox Street over many months the company secretary, Don Dykes, and his assistant Brian Nattrass, made me feel so much at home that I almost acquired delusions of grandeur and began to imagine myself a Gold Fields man. Helene Mendes and her staff in Public Affairs, Gail Human in the library, Pam Conticini and her Registry staff, were tireless in their efforts to locate material even when it sometimes meant a special journey to Luipaardsvlei to mine among its dusty files for historical tailings. When my text was finished, Pat Hill generously passed on word of it to her word processor. Others, including Tim Bett and Robert Smith, patiently spent hours checking facts and figures. Twin angels of mercy, Pat Kirkland and Myrtle Elsworthy, were always at hand with tea and sympathy.

To Gail Behrmann and Andrew Lanham, the Gold Fields photographer with the eye of an artist, I am particularly indebted for their strenuous efforts to locate and procure illustrations for the book. For some of these acknowledgement is due to the Africana Museum, the Barnett Collection at *The Star* and that newspaper's own photographic library, to J F Wolmarans for sinkhole photographs, to *Die Transvaler* and the *Financial Gazette* for cartoons, to the Rudd House collection at Kimberley, to South Africa House, London, for the Simon van der

Stel mural, to the public libraries of Johannesburg and Germiston, and the Musée des Antiquités Nationales, Saint Germain-en-Laye, France, for the touchstone illustration.

In general, I have used the monetary and measurement systems in practice in South Africa at the time events took place there. South Africa's currency consisted of pounds and shillings until February 1961 when the Rand was introduced with a value of ten shillings. In 1971 the metric system replaced the British Imperial system of measurement in South Africa.

ROY MACNAB   *November 1986*

Prologue

Gold Fields of South Africa was founded in London during the celebrations in the British capital of the Golden Jubilee of Queen Victoria, whose great Empire covered a quarter of the land mass of the earth. A quarter of the world's peoples were her subjects. As the British Empire approached its zenith, its greatest proponent, Cecil John Rhodes, in co-founding a goldmining company in 1887, might almost have been offering it as a salute to a celebration.

A century later Gold Fields has the distinction of being the oldest mining house in South Africa, the only one born in the Nineteenth Century, soon after the discovery of gold on the Witwatersrand, that has survived intact to the present day. Its contemporaries, though maintaining their names in one form or another, were absorbed by later organizations. In 1887 Gold Fields of South Africa was a foreign company operating in the South African Republic; today in the Republic of South Africa it has the same nationality as the country where its work is done.

With a capitalization of more than R10 billion and employing nearly 100 000 people, the South African company is larger, more muscular than the British company, Consolidated Gold Fields, from which it sprang and with whom it maintains an adult, fruitful relationship. The British company is still the biggest minority shareholder in Gold Fields of South Africa, for whom in the long years in which the latter was growing to maturity in Southern Africa it provided both capital and direction.

The company has a continuity and a sense of history that go far beyond the name it bears, which is the original name given to it by Rhodes and Rudd at its birth in 1887. It was transferred to the company in South Africa a decade or so before it acquired its independence in 1971. The story of the company tangles with that of South Africa itself. There is in its current activities a continuity that stretches far back into our national history. At its O'okiep copper mine in Nama-qualand, for instance, it realizes an ambition that goes back some 300 years when Simon van der Stel, Governor of the Cape, impressed by the copper ornaments of the Hottentots, took a prospecting party there in 1685. It was the first such mining expedition in South African history. In the Transvaal, at Rooiberg, it continues the tin mining activities of an antique age, those performed by the ancients from some unrecorded time who left behind traces of their primitive

1

industry. And at Union Tin, too, in the first years of this century, one of the great figures of Afrikaans and world literature, Eugene Marais, as a mine doctor, took *The Road to Waterberg* and, studying the natural world around the mine, wrote the classic studies for which he is celebrated. And there is Deelkraal, youngest of the Gold Fields gold mines but situated on what is perhaps the oldest farm in the Transvaal; Deelkraal, so named because here in 1837 in the Gatsrante, the Voortrekker leaders, Hendrik Potgieter and Gert Maritz, divided up the cattle, which they had at first lost to the Matabele and then later retrieved after the Battle of Vegkop. Gold Fields, after a century, is part of the warp and woof of South Africa itself.

This continuity applies, in a different way, to its present-day activities. Gold Fields was founded as a mining company and a century later it remains essentially what it originally set out to be. From this it derives both its strength and its limitations. Other great companies founded centuries ago in the British Empire have turned to other things. In Canada, for instance, the historic Company of Adventurers of England Trading into Hudson Bay – the famous fur traders of 1670 – now runs department stores! In South Africa there are mining houses whose income is augmented by the growing of oranges or the running of fishing fleets. Gold Fields, in the main, sticks to its last; it is a mining house. Its traditional caution, its innate conservatism, may have lost it an opportunity now and again during the past century, and even the circumstances of its greatest achievement, the discovery and development of the West Wits Line, were almost out of character. Yet these qualities, allied to an old-fashioned trait inherited from its Victorian past, an integrity in doing business, have made Gold Fields the survivor that it is. Its contribution to the wealth and the development of South Africa has been immense. Today it provides ten percent of the gold of the free world and its great mines, such as Driefontein Consolidated and Kloof, will be producing wealth for the nation well into the Twenty-first Century.

The story of Gold Fields' activities in South Africa reflects South Africa itself. The company's growing independence from London, for instance, followed South Africa's own course along the road to national independence. The company's evolution was conditioned by what happened to South Africa, by events that took place here, dramatic and violent as these were from time to time: three wars, rebellion, revolution, bloody strikes. As the years passed, the 'very English company', in the words of a German admirer, became increasingly South African in spirit and sentiment. The day of the resident director, like that of the colonial Governor, eventually came to an end. In 1971, when Gold Fields of South Africa became an independent company, an Afrikaans newspaper, announcing the fact remarked, with obvious satisfaction, that the head of Rhodes's old company was a *boereseun*, underlining the fact that the first chairman of the South African company was an Afrikaner.

What follows, then, is an account of how a great mining company, born of a British parent in the heyday of empire, grew to adulthood in a South Africa that was itself growing up at the same time, went through the same growing pains

2

endured by the country itself, merging its own romantic story with that of the nation of whose activity it forms a part.

Just ten years before the advent of modern South Africa, with the arrival at the Cape of Jan van Riebeeck, a British writer, Thomas Fuller, wrote in his book, 'The Holy State and the Profane State' in 1642: 'Men have a touchstone whereby to try gold but gold is the touchstone whereby to try men.' He was echoing a statement believed to have been made by Chilon in 560 BC but he could well have been writing about the men of Gold Fields since for 100 years these have been tested – as men – by gold. And no doubt gold will continue to be their touchstone as the company, from the confidence of strength and the accumulation of years, faces the problems that are assuredly coming to it with another century.

Rhodes and Rudd : A Personal Company 1887 - 1892

At the beginning of 1887 the City of London, the financial centre of the world, heard for the first time the name, The Gold Fields of South Africa. It was a splendidly grandiloquent, all-embracing name for the company that was registered on 9 February that year to exploit the newly discovered gold of the Witwatersrand. The name is perhaps an indication of the size of the ambitions and the future intentions of the two men who were its founders. They were Cecil Rhodes who was thirty-three and Charles Rudd, who was nine years older; they had been partners since 1873 in business at Kimberley, where within a year they would succeed in amalgamating the diamond mines under the flag of their own company, De Beers. If one day they were to repeat with gold on the Rand what they had achieved with diamonds at Kimberley – and within a few months Rhodes was proposing to some of his Kimberley colleagues an amalgamation of their claims and interests on the Rand – then The Gold Fields of South Africa might well have been an appropriate name for such a wide umbrella of interests.

Rudd had sailed from the Cape for England the previous November less than a year after the pegging of the first claims on the Witwatersrand and now in February 1887 he was busily at work in London. Rhodes meanwhile was in Pretoria, sweating in the mid-summer heat as he wrote letter after letter, sent cable after cable, to his partner with advice as to what he should be doing with what Rhodes called their 'prospecting company'. Everything depended on Rudd's mission to London to raise money for the development of the properties they had been acquiring along the Witwatersrand during the previous few months and for which they had paid out of their own pockets. 'I hope you may succeed with Company', he wrote early in February 1887. 'With our judgement it is sure to be a success ....' Their judgement had certainly proved successful thus far. It was in some ways a curious partnership. The two men had much in common, their background for instance, but in character they were very different, one from the other. Rudd was a product of the English gentry and had been educated at Harrow and Trinity College, Cambridge, the same élite establishments attended by Rhodes's father, the Rev Francis Rhodes of Bishops Stortford. The vicar had sent some of his own seven sons to famous public schools, Herbert to Winchester, Frank to Eton but Cecil had gone down-market to the local grammar school, a fact which had to be compensated for, he felt later, by obtaining a

Promise fulfilled C.J. Rhodes

Cecil John Rhodes, the imperial statesman who was co-founder of The Gold Fields of South Africa. His international celebrity and place in history have tended to overshadow his partner, though at Gold Fields Rudd was the more active of the two. This signed portrait was Rhodes's favourite.

Charles Dunell Rudd, co-founder in 1887 of The Gold Fields of South Africa – 'your company', as Rhodes, his partner, used to say.

degree at Oxford. Thanks to Rudd who had kept their diamond business going while his partner was attending his terms at Oxford, Rhodes finally achieved his ambition. Rudd and Rhodes had come to South Africa for the same reason, each hoping to regain his health, Rudd in 1865, Rhodes five years later. Their later colleagues, Jameson and Beit, had similar health reasons for coming to South Africa. Rhodes had gone farming with his brother Herbert in Natal. Rudd was also in Natal, hunting with that historical curiosity, John Dunn, who took numerous Zulu wives, founded the Dunn clan and became a Zulu chief. Rudd before his health broke down showed promise of becoming a great athlete but this was an ambition that was realized in a later generation when his grandson Bevil Rudd became an Olympic champion. Rhodes had some success as an oarsman at Oxford and was elected a member of Vincents Club, home of Oxford Blues; sporting prowess was also to be one of the qualifications for a Rhodes scholarship at Oxford.

In 1887 when Rudd and Rhodes entered the gold arena of an unknown Rand they already had behind them an impressive track record on Kimberley's tough diamond fields.

Everything had begun to happen quickly, once Kimberley had been convinced that reports coming from the Witwatersrand of the presence of gold barely sixty kilometres from the Transvaal capital, Pretoria, meant more than the advent of another Barberton or Pilgrim's Rest. In July 1886 a Kimberley produce merchant, Fred Alexander, while passing through Potchefstroom had run into a prospector named Jan Bantjies who had arrived from the Rand with some rich pannings and was trying to raise money to buy a small prospecting battery. Alexander was immediately interested, went back to the Rand with Bantjies, collected some further samples and returned to Kimberley in some excitement. In the hope of interesting the diamond men of Kimberley in the prospects for gold on the Rand, he demonstrated his samples to a group of people which included Rhodes and Rudd, their associate, the lawyer Caldecott, Hermann Eckstein, the colleague of Beit and Wernher, and also J B Robinson.

The Diamond Fields Advertiser, reporting on the demonstration of 17 July, said it really looked as if there was something in these reports from the Rand since Mr J B Robinson was leaving for the Transvaal that Sunday. Robinson had reason to be in a hurry; he needed to recoup his fortunes, which, he maintained, had been ruined by Rhodes and Beit, though it was Beit who put up the £20 000 to enable Robinson to go to the Rand and set up the Robinson Syndicate. Robinson's quick reaction paid off. He moved fast with his cash box – there was always a handy £5 000 to tempt a hesitant farmer – he bought wisely and on a big scale and stole a march on Rhodes whom he detested all his life.

Rhodes and Rudd decided to move only after their friend, Caldecott's brother-in-law, an Afrikaner physician named Hans Sauer, had himself gone to the Rand to take its pulse, and had come back with some specimens. Dr Sauer had gone to the Rand on the advice of a fellow physician, Dr Bird, who had already abandoned his consulting rooms in Potchefstroom to seek his fortune on the Rand.

Left: *J B Robinson,
here shown with his
'lucky' pith helmet,
would never co-operate
with Gold Fields
because of his hatred
for Rhodes, but in the
1950s his grandson
became a director of a
Gold Fields company.*
Right: *Dr Hans
Sauer, who went with
Rhodes, Rudd and
Caldecott on their first
purchasing expedition
to the Rand in 1886.
Sauer Street, on
which Gold Fields
offices abut, is named
after him.*

There his name is commemorated by the Bird Reef running through one of Gold Fields' earliest properties, Luipaardsvlei. Sauer mounted the coach that was going to the Transvaal only to find J B Robinson already sitting there; on being questioned, Robinson said he was going to Pretoria; Sauer, also concealing his destination, said he too was going to the Capital. The coach stopped at Potchefstroom for the night but when it continued the next day neither Robinson nor Sauer was on it. Discovering each other at the Royal Hotel each admitted he was really going to the Rand and after hiring a two-wheeler Cape cart they completed their journey together.

In a few days Sauer was back in Kimberley convinced that he had just visited the new El Dorado where fortunes would be made. He told Caldecott who sent him to Rhodes. Once more Rhodes and Rudd attended a demonstration; this time they brought along two Australian miners who knew something about goldmining and they crushed and panned Sauer's offerings. This time the partners acted, Rhodes asking Sauer to go back to Witwater, as he called it, on the coach the next day and to secure for him options from the farmers. He wrote out a cheque for £200 for Sauer as an advance – 'the most remunerative that

Rhodes ever signed', he recorded later 'for he amassed a far greater fortune out of the Witwatersrand gold mines than he ever did out of diamonds'. Rhodes, like Robinson, thought it prudent to hide his incipient interest in the Rand from the watchful eyes of others in the diamond industry at Kimberley. 'Everyone knows you returned only the day before yesterday', he told Sauer, 'it is better not to excite curiosity.' Sauer accordingly arranged to pick up the coach twenty kilometres outside Kimberley. To his amazement when it stopped to pick him up, he found Rhodes and Rudd already installed inside. On reflection they had decided to go to the Witwatersrand themselves. It was in more than one way an historic journey for on that day for the first time the coach did not go straight on to Pretoria but from Potchefstroom made a detour, taking a rough track over what is now East Driefontein to the Rand. In due course Rhodes, Rudd and Sauer arrived where Colonel Ignatius Ferreira had parked his wagon a stone's throw from where today, a century later, Gold Fields of South Africa has its Johannesburg headquarters.

'Within a fortnight of our arrival', Sauer wrote later, 'Ferreira's camp began to assume the aspect of a busy place; tents and tented wagons covered a wide area and here and there primitive reed and clay shanties appeared.' Every day vehicles of every sort deposited new arrivals and the camp grew ever larger. There was no accommodation; people made do as best they could. It was mid-winter on the Transvaal highveld, a little less severe than usual that year, but nevertheless offering little comfort to those who had come from distant places and who warmed themselves with the thought that this time it really was the real thing. There had been gold discoveries in the Transvaal before and in 1871 the Boer Government, chronically short of funds, had actually offered a reward for the discovery of a new field. At the beginning there had been *Eersteling* – Firstborn – up near Potgietersrus; later Pilgrim's Rest and Barberton in the Eastern Transvaal had produced the first gold rushes but in the end there was disappointment. Excitement had been intense but it was short-lived. A few made fortunes but some of the Kimberley people had burned their fingers and had become wary. South Africa had still to throw up its California, its Western Australia, its Canadian Klondike. But during that July and August of 1886 those like Rhodes, Rudd and Sauer, soon to be joined by Caldecott, those who had abandoned the relative comfort of their homes at Kimberley for the bleakness of the Witwatersrand in winter, were right. They were standing on the greatest goldfield the world has ever known and Rhodes with that curious intuition that he possessed seemed to sense it when he told Rudd: 'You have got the biggest gold reefing in the world under your feet.'

Little by little, as time went on, prodded and probed with borehole and shaft, the Witwatersrand revealed its true and unique nature. The 500 kilometre crescent that is today known as the golden arc is the north-western edge of a vast basin. The gold deposits along this arc were concentrated there in ancient times when particles of gold were washed down rivers from mountains into a sea. The particles of gold sank on the sea-shore nearest the river mouths, together with pebbles and mud and other debris. The grains of gold, mixed with the pebbles and mud, formed a series of layers that looked like modern concrete. Over the ages these conglomerates were covered with molten rock and the sea or basin was filled in as the surface of the old volcanic world crumpled. The pebbles and gold from the sea-shore of antiquity became packed into hard rock, lying in thin layers deep below the surface. What became known as the Main Reef – the exposed rim of one of the layers in this ancient basin – was what had been discovered in 1886.

How had it happened? In Ferreira's camp one heard several names. There were the Struben brothers, Fred and Henry, sons of a Ladysmith magistrate, there was Jan Bantjies who had run into Fred Alexander and whose pannings had first interested Kimberley. Above all, there were the two Georges – George Harrison and his partner George Walker. A century after it all happened discussion and debate about details of the discovery go on still. Barely five months before Rudd and Rhodes reached the Rand, Harrison and Walker had been digging stone to build a house for Widow Oosthuizen at Langlaagte some fifteen kilometres west of the centre of present-day Johannesburg. Harrison had had goldmining experience in Australia and one Sunday walking over the farm he noticed the reef outcrop, that tell-tale strip of gold-bearing rock with its white pebbles sandwiched together like pieces of pork in a rough country paté. Harrison and Walker had been down on their luck; they had urgent need of work and had been pointed in the direction of Widow Oosthuizen by Fred Struben and his brother who were some fifteen kilometres away on the farm Wilgespruit in the valley north of Florida. Here on 18 September 1884 the Strubens had discovered gold and two years later were working what they called the Confidence Reef, digging out the gold-veined quartz. Harrison took a sample of the outcrop from Langlaagte back to the Strubens who put it through their mill. There was the gold; the Witwatersrand had been born. What Harrison had found was the Main Reef, large and apparently infinite; what Struben had at Confidence Reef was small and finite and in due course there was no more quartz to be found. Struben was the first to discover payable gold on the Witwatersrand in 1884 but what Harrison had uncovered was the reef upon which the century-old Witwatersrand gold industry has been built.

What Harrison and Walker had unearthed at Langlaagte in February 1886 was of interest not only to the thousands of fortune-seekers who soon turned up from all parts of the world where Johannesburg now stands; the Boer Government of Paul Kruger was also taking it very seriously. Colonel Ferreira, who came from Pretoria, went to see Kruger who was a friend of his, with a petition to the Government urging it to proclaim a public digging. Rhodes and Rudd were among the several hundred claim-holders who gathered on the farm Turffontein on 5 August to hear from the Government representatives, Christiaan Joubert from the mines department and Johann Rissik, the surveyor, what the Republican authorities intended to do. In the crowd they could see the white pith helmet of J B Robinson who was soon to have a major share of the choicest properties among the farms that formed part of the public diggings proclaimed by the Government the following month. These included Langlaagte, where Harrison had parted with his discoverer rights for £10. On the antique maps of Africa where he had made his discovery there appeared the words *hic sunt leones* which turned out to be tragically true for the discoverer of the Witwatersrand; he was eaten by a lion, but he is gratefully commemorated by the South African mining industry who erected a monument to his memory.

Robinson had an advantage over the Rhodes party; he had his companion Marcus but he was really a loner. He made his own decisions, right or wrong, and acted quickly. Rhodes, Rudd, Sauer and Caldecott could never agree among themselves about what they should buy. They moved along the Rand as far as Rietfontein – near the present Jan Smuts airport. This they eventually bought, together with Witkopjes, from the farmer du Preez; Rhodes left his partners there and made his way back along the Rand picking up other properties, Klein Paardekraal and a share in Roodepoort. It was rather a hit-and-miss affair. Rhodes's methods of acquiring claims were delightfully haphazard, say his biographers Lockhart and Woodhouse, a mixture of hard business and relaxation. Competition for properties was keen; everyone was trying to get a slice of the action but where to go for it, what to buy? It was a gamble from which the farmers profited. Rhodes thought the prices were far too high; Rudd was sus-

The earliest document in the Gold Fields archives, an invoice from a firm of Potchefstroom merchants for goods supplied to Rhodes and Rudd for their expedition to the Rand in the winter of 1886.

picious and cautious, expecting to be tricked. Sauer blamed him for letting opportunities slip through his fingers when they might have secured claims on
what became the rich Central Rand. Others were doing better. Beit had appeared
on the scene and took what Rhodes had rejected. The partners argued among
themselves. Caldecott was not sure about Sauer. He asked his aide John Scott,
who became a secretary at Gold Fields and a judge in Rhodesia, to keep an eye on
him. 'I am anxious to know what Sauer is about', he told Scott on 18 August and
went on, 'You might offer to keep a proper record of his transactions which is
the only way that I can see that much good will come from his operations.'
Caldecott, on the other hand, annoyed Rhodes. 'Caldecott is terrible', he tells
Rudd. 'He does nothing and pays nothing.' In due course the lawyer quit and
went back to Kimberley and the law. The expenses of that first pioneering expedition to the Rand in 1886 are set out in the first document in the archives of
Gold Fields. It is an invoice for £235 for stores and supplies issued by a pair of
Potchefstroom merchants, Jacobsohn and Kauffman. The invoice throws light
on what was required in those days for such an expedition. There are some
curious items including two gallons of Cape brandy (thirty shillings), useful no
doubt to facilitate transactions among the farmers as to keep off the effects of
winter on the highveld; there was a case of whisky, too, followed by fruit salts,
castor oil and various kinds of paper!

If Rudd and Rhodes during that Transvaal winter of 1886 ended up with a
rather indifferent collection of properties, it was possibly because they were not
as lucky or as adventurous as men such as Robinson, Beit and others of the
Kimberley fraternity, who were now spending the money they had made from
diamonds in the hope of making even more out of gold. Moreover, they were
discouraged by those who might have known better, men such as Gardner
Williams, the American mining expert at De Beers who, according to Sauer, had
said: 'If I rode over these reefs in America I would not even get off my horse to
look at them. In my opinion they are not even worth hell room.' For this monu-
mental misjudgement the good-natured Williams was teased for the rest of his
life. The engineer Pauling was another of Rhodes's associates who believed the
Main Reef ore would never provide a worthwhile yield. He told Rhodes he had
made a mistake in buying Luipaardsvlei. Yet Luipaardsvlei, a low-grade producer, was a name that survived in the annals of Gold Fields, as sturdy as the little
stone house that Rudd and Rhodes built there and which exists still. Rietfontein,
too, among the early properties, figures there, for both properties, though they
went elsewhere for thirty years or more, returned to Gold Fields ownership in
the end. And Middelvlei that Rhodes bought almost prophetically out beyond
Randfontein, another Robinson gem – where there was no sign of the reef but
which existed like a marker for the future, where one day the riches of the West
Wits Line would make the fortune of the company that he and Rudd had
founded.

What Rhodes grasped very quickly, however, was the way the Rand would
develop. There was no room for the small prospector, the individual digger, as-

sociated with alluvial diggings, a folksy figure in a broad hat, shaking gold from a pan. Capital in large quantities would be necessary, capital that only a properly constituted company could provide, capital to buy and install the mining machinery on the farms where the outcrop had been detected. And they would have to have it quickly to exploit their investment if it were not to be wasted. 'Send out machinery so that we can pay dividends', was one of the messages Rudd received from Rhodes after reaching London. In all his activities, in all his letters and telegrams there is that atmosphere of haste, the breathlessness of a man in a hurry, as if Rhodes knew he would never reach the age of fifty and had to complete everything in half the usual time. Right at the beginning he was talking of the amalgamation of the claims on the Rand and he had even persuaded Robinson to discuss it though the talks came to nothing. Rhodes had hurried back to Kimberley to be at the bedside of young Neville Pickering, probably the only love of his life, who was dying. The talks were never resumed.

The Rand in any case could never be his sole preoccupation. There was, of course, Kimberley and in 1887 his amalgamation plans for De Beers had reached a crucial stage. And always in his mind was that vision of the world that lay beyond the Limpopo in the north, in a territory that would one day bear his own name. The partners talked things over; there would have to be a division of labour. In 1909, on an impulse, Rudd jotted down on a couple of pieces of hotel writing-paper some notes about his life and on one of them he wrote: 'Agreed with Rhodes that the diamond affairs should be left in his hands and that I should manage the goldmining.' So that was why it was Rudd and not Rhodes who took ship for England in November 1886. Armed with Rhodes's full power to act for him, he was to raise the money and to float the company, The Gold Fields of South Africa, which Rhodes in talking or writing to Rudd always referred to as 'your company'. The Gold Fields of South Africa was thus primarily the creation of Rudd, though they became joint managing directors and participated equally in the rich profits that were derived from the interests they acquired on the Rand. In the eye of posterity Rudd has been overshadowed by Rhodes's enormous international celebrity, by his place in the history of the British Empire; it is a bust of Rhodes the imperial statesman that dominates, alone, the entrance hall of the Gold Fields offices in Johannesburg, though it was Rudd who controlled its early life.[1] Rhodes is to Rudd what Rolls is to Royce in another great commercial partnership; Royce was the genius whose engineering skill perfected the famous car that all the world refers to as a Rolls.

In 1887 neither Rhodes nor Rudd was well-known outside the diamond circles of Kimberley or in Cape Town where each was a member of the Cape Parliament, but Rudd through his brother Thomas had an excellent entrée to the City of London and very quickly he was able to achieve everything he had hoped for.

The company was registered on 9 February 1887 with an authorized capital of £250 000 in 230 000 shares of £1 and 200 Founder shares of £100. The first issue was of 125 000 shares at par, 25 000 being reserved for issue in South Africa. Of the balance 70 000 shares had been taken firm and 30 000 were offered to the public by a prospectus dated 16 February. The prospectus described the purpose of the company as 'acquiring and dealing with certain auriferous and other mineral properties, interests and rights in South Africa and also for carrying on general exploration with a view to making further investments of a similar nature'. The prospective investor is also informed that the promoters are C D Rudd and C J Rhodes 'who have already purchased auriferous properties to the extent of £25 000 and secured many valuable refusals; but opportunities for favourable investment of capital appear so greatly to exceed private means that the public are now invited to join us in the enterprise'. And so they did, with alacrity, the issue being over-subscribed and the list of shareholders 'comprised between 400 and 500 as good names as were generally found'.

How had it all been done? Who were the people who put up the money to launch The Gold Fields of South Africa? Thomas Rudd, who became the company's first Chairman, was the key figure. He was a director of a joint stock bank in the city, a fellow director of which was William Arbuthnot, member of a family distinguished then as now in the world of merchant banking. Through the Arbuthnot connection investors in Gold Fields were represented by the appointment to Thomas Rudd's board at Gold Fields of Sir Richard Pollock, a former civil servant in India where he had helped to put down the Indian Mutiny in 1857 and was now a director of the Southern Mahratta Railway. More than 14 000 shares were taken up by Scottish interests. Accountants, bankers, lawyers, even judges from Glasgow and Edinburgh, parted with their money for an interest in Gold Fields activities on the Rand and from time to time these Scottish shareholders would have a strong word to say about them.

Hatton Garden diamond merchants, as might be expected, bought shares and the name of Anton Dunkelsbuhler figures in their list for 300, a fact that might well have been of interest to a young man who was soon to join the firm from Germany and whose name would figure in the history of Gold Fields and other places – Ernest Oppenheimer.

A significant group of backers for the new company were brokers and jobbers from The London Stock Exchange, where *The Economist* noted that May, there was an upsurge in mining stock activity; these brokers and jobbers who specialized in mining shares, took more than 8 000 Gold Fields shares. These various financial interests were represented on the first board. With Thomas Rudd and Pollock were John James Hamilton from the Stock Exchange and they were joined by two men who knew South Africa and were friends of the promoters, William Farmer who had business interests there and Leigh Hoskyns, later Sir Leigh Hoskyns, a barrister who had been a magistrate in the courts of Griqualand West and like Rhodes was the son of a clergyman. In fact his clerical father was one of the first shareholders; Leigh Hoskyns also had the distinction of outliving all the other members of the original board and was a director at the time of his death in 1923. The first secretary of the company was H E M Davies, destined in due time to succeed Thomas Rudd as Chairman, and, financial wizard that he was, to play a major part in the fortunes of the company in the early days. It was

from Davies's firm of City accountants that the company's business was conducted, although the board met for the first time in Thomas Rudd's own office at 63 Queen Victoria Street, near the Mansion House railway station.

It was typical of the industrious and vigorous age in which the company was born that the first statutory meeting of the newly registered The Gold Fields of South Africa should have been held on a Saturday, which in the modern business world has ceased to be a working day. It was at noon on 19 March 1887, and, although much else was happening in England on that day, there was an eager and enthusiastic collection of people who assembled at the City Terminus Hotel in Cannon Street in the heart of the City of London to hear what C D Rudd Esq MLA of Kimberley had to tell them. They might well have preferred to have been out on the Thames tow path at Hammersmith, for that day the Oxford and Cambridge boat crews were out practising for their annual encounter. There had been news from South Africa in *The Times* – it concerned the Zulus. 'They complain that all the good country has been taken from them and what is left is not habitable. The Zulus are determined to appeal to the Queen direct.' The lady in question was at Osborne on the Isle of Wight with Prince and Princess Henry of Battenberg, preparing for the round of engagements that had been arranged to

Left: *Thomas Rudd, brother of C D Rudd, and the first chairman of The Gold Fields of South Africa, 1887. His City of London contacts enabled the company to find its first shareholders.*

Right: *Herbert Davies, first company secretary, succeeded Thomas Rudd as chairman in 1896. His financial wizardry made money for the company as well as for himself.*

15

mark the fact that she had been on the throne for fifty years. The papers were full of Queen Victoria's golden jubilee which those attending the meeting at the City Terminus Hotel might have felt was being appropriately celebrated by themselves in creating a new gold company. In Germany the Kaiser Wilhelm I, whose son was married to one of Victoria's daughters and who in 1871 from the Palace of Versailles had sent a message of goodwill to the President of the South African Republic, W M Pretorius, was going to be ninety. The Prince of Wales, who before long would describe Rhodes as 'a wonderful character, so lucid in his explanations', was on his way to the birthday celebrations. In Russia a plot to kill the Czar had been uncovered.

'Foggy at first, possibly clearing later' was the London weather report for Saturday, 19 March 1887. This was also a fairly accurate description of the report that Charles Rudd had to make to the shareholders of Gold Fields at their first meeting since he was able to give them only a hazy idea of what the company, which had taken over the founders' interests on the Rand, really owned. He himself did not know. All he knew was that Rhodes, who was becoming increasingly excited about the Rand, was still in the market and determined not to be outdone by others from Kimberley who were still buying, the Frenchman Jules Porges, for instance, who had launched Wernher and Beit on to the South African scene. 'The belief in Randt (sic) is increasing daily. Porges is here and has invested heavily. Robinson has given £16 000 for a property called Randfontein beyond Witpoort', he had informed Rudd in London. 'If you get your syndicate formed telegraph me a credit as I am daily missing things for lack of money. The opinion is steadily growing that the Randt is the biggest thing the world has seen. You must trust me with a credit if our prospecting company is formed. Cable it to Pretoria.'

Rudd in London had been getting messages thick and fast from Rhodes in South Africa; he passed on the news to the shareholders that Saturday noon. You must trust us, seemed to be the message he was trying to get across to them and they seemed prepared to do that. It is really a kind of personal company, he explained, financial backing for the Rhodes-Rudd partnership. The partners had certainly got themselves a fine deal, nearly everything Rhodes had asked for when he set out in a letter to Rudd what needed to be done in London. 'Your business will be', he wrote, '1. to get as much money as you can. 2. order large quantities of machinery. 3. draw a trust deed with wide powers. 4. obtain a good remuneration or else the company is not worth working for.' Rhodes, being in a hurry, never had time for false modesty. 'The people you are arranging with must remember that in dealing with us they are dealing with no ordinary representatives, that we have the whole thing at our fingers' ends ...'

Rudd seems to have communicated this strong sense of self-confidence to the shareholders that March Saturday in 1887; the backers of the company at its formation would have no means of controlling Rhodes and Rudd who had achieved their personal company. They had complete control of its activities in South Africa and even in London Charles Rudd, with his brother as chairman

16

and two friends on the board, would be able to direct its course. It had been a skilful operation. Rudd and Rhodes had handed over their properties on the Rand at cost and received their founders' shares; they would only make profits if the company itself prospered; therefore it was in their own interest to keep the shareholders happy. Of the ten South African mining companies, many of them with outlandish names, registered in London that year, The Gold Fields of South Africa was the only one where Vendor's Interest was entered as nil; in all the others the vendors had demanded in cash and scrip up to seventy-five percent of the money subscribed. It was not surprising, therefore, as one financial writer was to say, that Gold Fields was the most popular company in the City of London.

The agreement between the company and the founders would give the latter three-fifteenths of any profits the company made. In addition, instead of being paid managerial salaries or directors' fees, they would have a further two-fifteenths of the profits for the work they would do for the company as joint managing directors. Rudd and Rhodes undertook to the company that one or the other of them would always be in South Africa to attend to company business, for the shareholders, too, were depending entirely on the ability of the managing directors to deliver the profits. The time would come when the shareholders would realize just how much they had given Rudd and Rhodes and their dissatisfaction would express itself in insisting on another arrangement, but at their inaugural meeting there had been not a word of criticism.

Rudd, with every reason to be satisfied with the success of his mission, was back in Kimberley by May. With one director back in South Africa, the other prepared to leave for London, but it was not with the intention of going to make the acquaintance of the company's directors or shareholders. Rhodes achieved much in a busy life but he never managed to attend a meeting of Gold Fields shareholders. Travelling to England that July he was wearing his De Beers hat and his American consultant Gardner Williams was with him. They were on their way to see the Rothschilds to get the backing they needed for that final step towards the amalgamation of the diamond fields and they succeeded. There were no watertight doors between Rhodes's interests. Gold Fields, like it or not, would soon be involved in the fortunes of De Beers and both in due course in that third and overriding interest, the Chartered Company in what Rhodes was to call 'my country' – Rhodesia. That was why he had been so insistent about Rudd getting the trust deed from Gold Fields when the company was formed. For him it was an instrument of power.

Back in Kimberley, Rudd was catching up with Rhodes's shopping activities, though his partner had kept him well informed while he had been away in London. A letter in April had told him: 'Porges got back yesterday from Barberton. I gather from him he will buy again on Randt in which he thoroughly believes. He has with Robinson driven up all prices and it is very difficult to purchase anything worth having.' Again, in that curious, almost uneducated language that he used, he tells Rudd: 'Barberton has smashed up but Witwater is all right. I bought one good property for the company viz D van Wyk for £40 000 and £20 000 in scrip.' This was Luipaardsvlei.

Meanwhile in London the Gold Fields shareholders were getting an independent view of what their managing directors were doing in South Africa on their behalf. The weekly London journal *South Africa* was publishing a series of articles by its editor E P Mather, later to be gathered into a book, about the author's impressions of the goldfields and their prospects. 'My object in continuing my journey westward from Roodepoort', he wrote one week, 'was merely to see some of the country which the Cape capitalists Messrs C D Rudd and C J Rhodes and Caldecott had been purchasing at long figures. These gentlemen have bought some heavy interests on the Rand and they have handed these interests over at cost price to the shareholders of a company with the very clumsy and inconvenient title of "The Gold Fields of South Africa". What prices they paid may be gathered from the prospectus of the company which sets forth the capital at a quarter of a million.' Mather goes on to say that 'the Main Reef seems to turn at Roodepoort. There is no direct continuation apparent. The Botha Reef which runs for a long distance has a large body and carries fair gold. Mr C J Rhodes on behalf of a London company paid £40 000 in cash and £30 000 (sic) in scrip for a farm on which this reef runs. The immense purchase was made on very shallow tests and it remains to be seen whether this clever speculator has not ventured too much on surface indications or what they would call in America "grass roots".' However, Mather later took a closer look at this property, Luipaardsvlei, and Gold Fields shareholders would have been relieved to hear that 'a twenty stamp battery is at work at the company's property but other mills aggregating 140 stamps are now in course of erection and the other plant and general appointments are of a very complete and superior character ...'.

Gold Fields was off the mark; it had begun to produce though Luipaardsvlei, contrary to general belief, was not the first of its mines to do this. This distinction belonged to the Banket company which had been formed to work claims on the farms Roodepoort to Witpoortje. In February 1887 Rhodes wrote to Rudd: 'The crushing of fifty tons though apparently not good to my mind was satisfactory ... we took the takings and found them full not only of gold but also of quicksilver.'

The first efforts by Gold Fields to mine gold in South Africa did not, however, match the success of the company's flotation in London. It was soon apparent that their properties were inferior to those of some of their competitors. The Robinson Mine, for instance, had produced an astonishing 4 000 ounces from 700 tons of ore in November 1888, though this was an exceptional result. Mediocre results from mining subsidiaries such as Luipaards Vlei – a low-grade producer and gold fetching only about £4 an ounce – did not, however, prevent Gold Fields going ahead in its first three years; it invested money in the more successful operations being conducted by others on the Central Rand. There was at first more speculation than mining going on in the early days of the Rand and Gold Fields succeeded in doubling its capital and in paying its shareholders divi-

18

dends. In a six-week period in 1889, for instance, it shifted £300 000 worth of stock in a rising market. 'Fortuitous, fluky, random, hit and miss' are some of the meanings offered by Roget's Thesaurus for the word 'speculation'. In those first days Gold Fields rode the swings and roundabouts of speculation as well as any, if not better than most.

A particularly harsh view of the situation was taken at this time by a distinguished visitor to South Africa and Rhodesia. This was Lord Randolph Churchill, the father of Winston Churchill, who for a handsome fee had undertaken to write articles for the popular Press in London, later published in a book. 'In the early days of the Rand gold field', he wrote, 'folly and fraud reigned supreme. The directors and managers were, as a rule, conspicuous for their ignorance on all matters of practical mining. The share market was their one and only consideration, the development and proper working of the mines being in many cases absolutely neglected.' Lord Randolph's ill-humour was in part due to the fact that he was already mortally ill; he upset most of the people he met, including members of the Rand Club who had given him hospitality, but his critical view of affairs did not prevent him acquiring a few gold interests of his own.

In any event, it was soon apparent, as far as Gold Fields was concerned, that the managing directors still had their hearts in diamonds, in Kimberley. To their astonishment the people who had given their money in 1887 to found a gold-mining company discovered in June the following year that the company had more money in diamonds than in gold; £141 000 in diamonds, only £98 000 in other properties. Rudd and Rhodes were within their rights, they had that wide trust deed from Gold Fields as they had from De Beers and as far as Rhodes was concerned both companies were merely instruments for the implementation of his wider political ambitions for the British Empire; he could not see what the Gold Fields shareholders had to complain about. But they did, vociferously, at the meeting in 1888 when neither Rhodes nor Rudd was present and Thomas Rudd in the chair had to calm them down, explaining that the company had been set up not to work any particular mine but to deal in mines and mining shares. Gold mines and gold shares, the shareholders retorted, insisting that the De Beers shares should be sold and they would not be mollified even when told that the diamond shareholding stood at a profit of £50 000. Moving Gold Fields money into diamonds at Kimberley – De Beers shares hit £46 – had been good business but its real significance was as a demonstration of Rhodes's and Rudd's independence, of what in fact they had meant by the 'personal company'.

However, despite the fears and suspicions of shareholders about Kimberley, Gold Fields, whose birth had been registered in London, quite clearly had been born a Transvaler, in the place that had first been known as Randjeslaagte but now, as the last decade of the Nineteenth Century approached, was known to the world as Johannesburg. Here Gold Fields put down its pioneering roots a century ago; here it was to grow with the city and the country to which all its activities belonged. Early on, Gold Fields displayed the panache that has marked

19

1887: Gold Fields had its first office in Saratoga Avenue, Doornfontein.

its career, in choosing to have its first office in the smart residential area of Doornfontein – Parktown had not yet emerged – in the newly named Saratoga Avenue; it was a typical building of the period, long and low with a wide verandah. By Cape cart it took about fifteen minutes to 'downtown' Johannesburg where the primitive Stock Exchange was operating at the corner of Commissioner and Simmonds Streets, near where Gold Fields itself would one day be located.

In the beginning, however, the main Gold Fields office in South Africa was in Cape Town. This suited Rhodes in particular for in 1890 he became Prime Minister of Cape Colony; Rudd, too, was a member of the Assembly, his wife was a member of an old Cape family, the Chiappinis and they acquired in Fernwood a beautiful home at Newlands. In Johannesburg Rudd had accommodation on the premises at Doornfontein – the building with its stables had cost, according to the 1888 report, just over £1 105. To look after the office a young man named Harry Currey had been detached from his duties as Rhodes's secretary. Rhodes had told Rudd: 'I have young Currey instead of Grimm. He is quicker and can write a good letter.' Currey was soon exercising his literary skills in informing the directors in no uncertain language about his difficulties and frustrations in Johannesburg; mine managers who were speculating, wives who

20

Fernwood, *Rudd's Cape home.*

were gossips, no information or guidance was coming from London and he was in the dark most of the time; his letters earned him a sharp reprimand from London and Currey could not wait to get back to Kimberley. Meanwhile an accountant, Francis Lowrey, had been brought in to help and in due course he took charge of the office.

The men in Doornfontein office might have felt they had reason to complain but their difficulties were nothing compared with those faced by the men who pioneered the gold mines, who got down to the arduous business of extracting their gold. Transport was inadequate – the railway only arrived in 1894 – water was not easily obtainable, fuel was scarce and monopolies tolerated by a corrupt Government raised the price of dynamite. By the end of 1888 there were forty-four mines with a capitalization of £7 million and they were producing gold worth more than £1 million. In the early days mining was confined to the oxidized ore of the outcrops, that is to say, where the gold-bearing rock was close to the surface. The true geological nature of the Witwatersrand ore was not immediately understood, nor consequently that it would demand a new and unique manner of mining and treatment. In 1887, the year in which Gold Fields was founded, South African production was a mere 1,2 tons of gold, less than one percent of world production but within five years it had risen to 30 tons, was

Harry Currey, who was running Gold Fields office in Johannesburg in 1888 and was reprimanded for writing rude letters to London. In due course he became a member of the Union Parliament; his son, Ronald Currey, was a famous headmaster of St Andrews, Grahamstown, a school which at one time produced both the chairman and deputy chairman of GFSA.

worth £4,5 million and represented fifteen percent of world production. By 1910, on the formation of the Union of South Africa, this country was providing just over a third of the world's gold. Before the end of the century the Rand would have replaced the United States as the world's premier producer. But before that could happen the mining houses, and not least Gold Fields, would have to go through some traumatic experiences.

It was Charles Rudd who was to have the first of these and it was an experience that almost ended his days. The gentle Rudd who had come to South Africa to try to regain his health and who had found at Kimberley that his business trans-

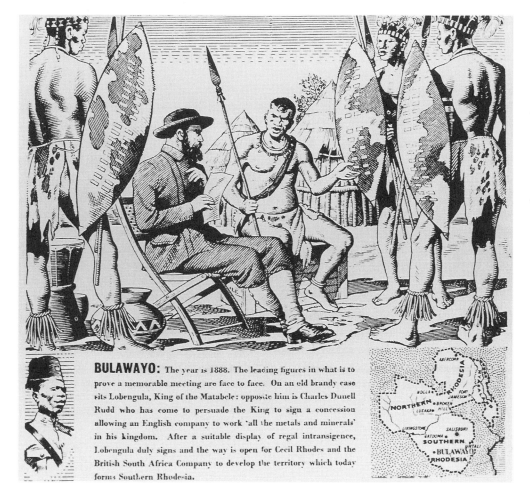

BULAWAYO: The year is 1888. The leading figures in what is to prove a memorable meeting are face to face. On an old brandy case sits Lobengula, King of the Matabele: opposite him is Charles Dunell Rudd who has come to persuade the King to sign a concession allowing an English company to work 'all the metals and minerals' in his kingdom. After a suitable display of regal intransigence, Lobengula duly signs and the way is open for Cecil Rhodes and the British South Africa Company to develop the territory which today forms Southern Rhodesia.

'Lobengula treated us exceedingly well,' said Mr Rudd in an interview … 'We always found him very fair and he often gave us a very patient hearing' (from The Cape Argus, *19 November 1916).*

'The king where the fields lay was not a savage potentate of the ordinary type but an intelligent man' (Thomas Rudd to shareholders, 1888).

actions were hampered by an inability to do his share of the drinking that was an unavoidable part of every business deal, was about to be cast by Rhodes in the role of Victorian hero, as if he were a General Gordon or a Sir Richard Burton. Early in 1888 Currey in the Doornfontein office received a letter from him saying that he and Rhodes had talked about their affairs and 'we have come to the conclusion that our best chance of a big thing is to try and make some terms with Lobengula for a concession for the whole of his country. Rhodes has arranged for such Imperial support as can be granted and it is thought best that I should start with an expedition at once'.

Rhodes having completed the amalgamation of the diamond fields at Kimberley, was ready for his most ambitious move so far to extend the interests of the British Empire. To obtain from Lobengula, the son of a one-time Zulu general Moselikatse, in his kingdom of Matabeleland beyond the Limpopo, the mineral rights of the territory, was to be the important first step and it was Rudd who was destined to take it. In due course he was to say that he had done it for Gold

Fields and when much later he had to deal with some recalcitrant shareholders who did not seem to appreciate what he had done for them, he had no hesitation in saying petulantly: 'We do a great deal for the company. I went to Lobengula over the concession at the risk of my life ...' It was true. The tremendous triumph for Rhodes and Rudd in obtaining the concession that led to the creation of the British South Africa Company and of Rhodesia almost ended in disaster for Rudd. He later recorded what happened after Lobengula, bought off with a load of rifles and the promise of a gunboat on the Zambesi, had signed the all-important document. Saying good-bye to his companions 'Matabili'[2] Thompson and Rochfort Maguire, 'I then started from the King's Kraal with this concession and I tried to go quickly with it down the country; but in crossing the desert I was seized with illness. I suffered intensely from thirst and thought I was dying. I managed to crawl to an ant-bear hole and I dropped the concession down the hole and on top of it I dropped £3 500 in specie belonging to this Company – money which I had with me in the cart at the time. I was found by some natives of Khama's country, carried to a mud-hut and kindly treated by them and afterwards the concession was rescued by Major Goold-Adams, who is now in command of a column in Matabeleland.'

In due course the news reached London and on 24 November 1888 Gold Fields issued a special statement which made their managing directors the heroes of the hour. 'I have much pleasure in informing you that telegraphic advices are to hand that Mr C D Rudd has obtained an exclusive Mining Concession over the entire Dominion of Lobengula which the Board believes comprises Matabeleland and Mashonaland.' Thomas Rudd, feeling that his brother's achievement might be underrated thought it necessary to explain that 'the king where the fields lay was not a savage potentate of the ordinary type but an intelligent man'.

The Rudd Concession, as it was henceforth known, ensured the Gold Fields managing director a place in history but it is the wrong place. As the American historian, J G Galbraith, has commented: 'It is ironic that Rudd should be remembered in relation to the Concession that led to the British South Africa Company. The company was the vehicle for the soaring ambition of Rhodes, Rudd had no interest in painting maps red; as time went on he betrayed more and more irritation with the megalomania of his partner, and the first fissures which in 1896 became a complete break, appeared about the time of the Concession that has linked his name to Rhodes.'

Excitement among the Gold Fields shareholders about the Concession was to be short-lived; it was a much more complicated affair than had at first been thought. Other parties interested in Lobengula's territory had been busy and Rhodes had to buy them out. Rudd told the shareholders: 'Do not run away with the idea that you were entitled to or that we anticipated that you would have the whole of the Matabele Concession.' Rudd had crossed the Limpopo on the understanding that Gold Fields would get a half share in the Concession; this was whittled down to twenty-eight percent. However, when the British South Africa Company was formed with a Royal Charter, after the official acceptance of the Rudd Concession, Gold Fields shareholders came in for a very sizeable block of shares and all their misgivings evaporated. They readily agreed that Gold Fields capital should be increased by creating 120 000 new shares at £1 'to develop the Matabele Concession lately obtained'. When Rudd and Rhodes proposed that the shares should be issued at £3, they dug in their toes and insisted on obtaining them at par. Rhodes was furious. His anger almost drove him from Gold Fields for good; it also drove a wedge between him and Rudd. He wrote to his partner: 'I think The Gold Fields of South Africa have behaved disgracefully. I am thinking of resigning but shall await your decision. I always said you made a mistake in giving them up the Concession and I must add I think I ought to have been consulted. We might have had the best people in England. I have no intention of working for these fellows for the balance of my life. A more ungrateful crew I have never come across. I do not think I shall attend the yearly meeting... the one point you forget was that, though you obtained the Concession, I may have to spend my life in developing it and you have handed me over to a crowd I will not work for.' These were hard words and when Rhodes came to London later in the year he again expressed his views forcibly. He was as good as his word; he did not attend the Gold Fields meeting that year, nor for that matter in any other year, but the Gold Fields secretary, Herbert Davies, who had now joined the Board, established a good relationship with Rhodes and eased the company back into his good books.

Rhodes may have felt unappreciated by his shareholders but he was beginning to receive adulation and expressions of admiration from all sides; he was entering the most successful period of his life. He was about to become Prime Minister of the Cape; the Pioneer Column would be going north to create the country that would bear his name. He was becoming an international figure. In another year he would dine with Queen Victoria at Windsor; in 1894 he was there again and this time the Queen wrote in her diary: 'I had a long conversation with Mr Rhodes. He said he had had great difficulties but that since I had seen him last he had added 12 000 miles of territory to my Dominions.' The Royal Family even became directly involved in his business activities; the Prince of Wales's son-in-law, the Duke of Fife, joined the board of the Chartered Company. Rhodes was riding on the crest of the wave. His ambitious dreams were everywhere taking shape. His intoxication with the British Empire knew no bounds. On a journey across the veld with his friend Lord Grey, they lay encamped under the stars. The peer slept in his tent but in the middle of the night he was suddenly awakened by Rhodes.

'What's happening, Rhodes, what's the matter?', he asked alarmed, suspecting the camp was on fire.

'Have you ever thought, Grey', Rhodes said to him, 'what a wonderful thing it is to be an Englishman?'

Lord Grey, uncertain as to his friend's sobriety or sanity, went back to sleep. In any event, in this new period of his life Rhodes had little time for the affairs of Gold Fields, although when it suited him and that time was coming, the company, quite unwittingly, would be used, almost disastrously, to further his unbridled political ambitions in the Transvaal.

Fortunately for Gold Fields Charles Rudd continued to give his undivided attention to the company and at the annual meeting of shareholders his honest and frank appraisal of company affairs became an event to which all looked forward. In November 1889, after his success with Lobengula and while the attention of shareholders was concentrated in the north, he thought it a convenient moment to confess that their interests on the Rand, the original reason for the creation of the company, had been a disappointment. He and Rhodes had believed the large reefs of low-grade ore would pay rather than the small reefs of high-grade. 'We based our investments on that theory but our theory was wrong and Mr Rhodes and I felt we had not done as well as men of our experience and knowledge might have done on the Witwatersrand.'

In order to invest first in diamonds at Kimberley and then in what it was hoped would be the treasure-house of Matabeleland, Gold Fields' investment on the Rand was progressively reduced until only one-fifth of it remained. At the beginning of 1891 in a letter to Lowrey in Johannesburg Rudd said: 'I have already written to you that we have so far decided to concentrate all our forces in Mashonaland – both capital, engineers, Currey, and everything else that can be brought to bear are to be sent up there in April. Rhodes wants me to go up there with him in August after Parliament. This being the case it is useless to pretend that we desire new business on the Rand because we have not the capital for it...' Later Lowrey had a hint from Currey that they were thinking of closing the Johannesburg office and running the Rand interests from Cape Town as an economy. The Gold Fields of South Africa began to look increasingly like a misnomer. Systematically, though at the same time profitably, they had whittled down their Rand interests until all that remained was a holding of some 57 000 shares in Luipaards Vlei where they had previously had more than 200 000 shares. Once more the money was going into De Beers. As it turned out the company in withdrawing from the Rand had done the right thing even if for the wrong reasons. The withdrawal had more to do with Rhodes's interests in Kimberley and his schemes for the north than with the mediocre performance of its indifferent Rand properties. Nevertheless, the withdrawal for whatever reason had been made in the nick of time; goldmining on the Witwatersrand had by the time the 1890s arrived hit a major snag: pyritic ore, below the oxidized zone. To extract the gold from pyritic ore would be a much more difficult and costly process since it would have to be taken from the sulphides and the old method they had been using on the Rand, removing the gold by amalgamation with mercury, would not work. The mining community took fright; people were saying the Witwatersrand, after all, was only an old river bed. The market collapsed and with it the fortunes of companies and individuals. There was deep gloom at the Rand Club and *The Star* reported that no fewer than 169 members had failed to pay their subscription. 'Grass will grow in the streets', predicted Percy FitzPatrick. The Rand after all looked like becoming another Barberton.

The Cape Bank among others went under, taking Francis Lowrey's £1 000 savings with it and prompting him to write to Rhodes: 'I fear I must ask you not to call on me to reduce my salary for the next two to three months as I had nearly £1 000 in the Cape Bank .... my present capital consists of thirty shillings ready and a parcel of unsaleable scrip.' It was an unhappy situation for the Gold Fields manager to find himself in. However, another bank that would play a big part in the future of Gold Fields, the Standard Bank, had the courage to open a new branch in Johannesburg. Lowrey went along and as he reported 'drank prosperity to it in bad language. Surely this irony of fate was never more strikingly exemplified, one bank smashed and then another tottering and a third indulging in opening orgies all on the same day'.

The crisis fortunately did not last long. There was one man on the Rand who was doing something about it. His name was John Jack, a Scotsman whose partner was a German, August Simmer, and together they gave their name to one of the great mines in the Gold Fields Group. In 1936, when he was an old man, Jack wrote to the chairman of the company describing what action he had taken all those years before. 'I enclose you herewith under registered cover the first certificate and trial of Rand banket ore taken from the late Primrose Mine, Germiston in 1889 by me personally and given to J S McArthur in Glasgow. I watched the process personally in McArthur's laboratory in Glasgow and on receipt of the result, as per enclosed certificate, I at once said to McArthur "You have what will lift Johannesburg". I gave him a letter of introduction to the late Mackie Niven and another to the late Edmund Brayshaw. He proceeded to the Rand with these introductions and started the great cyanide extraction on the Rand.' The McArthur Forrest cyanide process, in overcoming the problem of pyritic ore not only saved the Rand from ruin; it also enormously improved prospects for mining profits by giving the mines a much bigger return per ton of ore mined.

Engineers on the Rand who were actually conducting operations in the mines were becoming much more knowledgeable about the particular nature of mining there. A new expression was being heard. Deep Levels. The reef dipped down from the outcrop at an angle of twenty-five degrees or more and for all they knew it went on indefinitely into the earth and, with shafts driven down to depths, its gold could be tapped along the way. When the time came for Gold Fields to return to the Rand in all seriousness, it was with the conviction that its future lay in deep-level mining. Before that could happen, however, the company would have to go through a bad patch, its fortunes reaching a deep level of their own, with shareholders chastising their managing directors themselves growing uneasy about each other as the gap between their respective priorities widened.

In 1891 company prospects looked grim. There were profits of £16 000 but no dividends. So much of its money was tied up in diamonds in Kimberley but De Beers slumped badly on the news that a new diamond pipe, the Wesselton Mine, had been discovered near Kimberley and might seriously threaten their hold on the diamond industry. Shareholders were also becoming worried by their investment in Rhodes's schemes for the future Rhodesia. Money was being swallowed up at an alarming rate and now they were being asked to increase the company's capital in order to take over the goldmining interests of Heany and Johnson. What real evidence was there of rich gold reefs beyond the Limpopo? At the November meeting some of the shareholders accused the board of being 'no more than puppets in the hands of Mr Rhodes'. It was hardly the best moment for Rhodes to try to secure a place on the board for his brother, Captain Ernest Rhodes, late of the Royal Engineers. 'A gentleman may be capable without belonging to that family', commented a shareholder with some acerbity. Rhodes was not there nor was Charles Rudd and once again it was left to Davies to smooth things over. Ernest Rhodes joined the board and before long he would be making his way to Johannesburg to take charge there as the first resident director.

Meanwhile, a feeling had been growing among shareholders that the old agreement that the company had with Rudd and Rhodes was no longer tenable. The company's capital was now twice what it had been when the agreement had been made in 1887 but they were still entitled to their three-fifteenths share of the profits on their founders' shares and another two-fifteenths as payment for the work they did for the company. The first rumble of discontent came from Johannesburg itself. The correspondent there of the London journal *South Africa*, referring early in 1890 to the publication of the Gold Fields report said, 'it seems strange that not a word of friendly criticism has been vouchsafed to them by the home Press. It does not appear to have struck the English financial journalists that the remuneration given to the managing directors and the profits accruing to the founders' shares are out of all proportion to the reserve fund and the amount distributed among the ordinary shares in dividends'. They were drawing some £30 000 each but the commentator in Johannesburg did not think much of their performance, referring to the 'motley list of companies in which they had bought shares as "investment"'. The upshot of all this was that Rudd and Rhodes would have to accept a new agreement. By that time, however, the company had taken a new form and even a new name. It was going back to the Rand to mine the deep levels; outcrop mining had become a thing of the past, and Gold Fields was ready to part with the last of its outcrop holdings.

The key figure in bringing about the change in Gold Fields strategy and who finally won Rudd round to his way of thinking was Percy Tarbutt, a London mining engineer who had been present when Rudd addressed the first meeting of Gold Fields in March 1887. From being a shareholder he soon became a consultant to the company and went out to South Africa to look at Luipaardsvlei and other Gold Fields claims. Tarbutt, like the American Hamilton Smith, was one of the first to recognize that deep levels would be the future pattern of mining on the Witwatersrand though at first – and fortunately for his own pocket – few followed him. Suggesting to Rhodes that he should peg claims to the south of the rich Robinson Mine, he received an emphatic no, whereupon he asked if he

himself and his partner Arthur Boucher might take up claims on their own account. 'A fool and his money are easily parted', Rhodes is said to have replied, 'peg if you want to.' Tarbutt went ahead, pegging his deep-level claims and his company, African Estates Agency, acquired a half share in Village Main Reef for £25 000, in due course parting with it to Gold Fields for £300 000, after its manager, the American J S Curtis, had shown that he knew what he was talking about when he struck the Main Reef at 517 feet.

Although Gold Fields itself had largely withdrawn from the Rand, its first secretary, Herbert Davies, a board member in 1889, had maintained his own interests there through his companies, the South African Gold Trust and Agency and the African Gold Share Investment Company which held gold shares for dividends. In this way Davies had kept contact with Tarbutt's activities on the Rand. Tarbutt's associate Curtis spoke to his fellow American, Hennen Jennings, who was working for the so-called Corner House, the group of Kimberley men with Rand interests, Hermann Eckstein, Beit, Wernher, Lionel Phillips. They, too, soon became interested in deep-levels and under Phillips's leadership were soon 'pegging the deeps'. In due course under the name Rand Mines these deep-levels were put to work. It was through Beit that Rhodes and Rudd in particular was soon to be as enthusiastic as any. No man among the mining mag-

Rhodes and Beit. 'Little Alfred' was Rhodes's financial genius. From their friendship grew a tradition of co-operation between Gold Fields and Rand Mines.

29

nates had a greater influence on Rhodes than Alfred Beit when it came to business matters; as another Corner House man, Sir Percy FitzPatrick, writer and politician, was to say: 'There can be no doubt whatever that Beit was Rhodes's financial genius.' Another of Beit's associates, William P Taylor, claimed to have introduced the two men in Kimberley in 1879 when Rhodes, then twenty-six, had said: 'I am going to control the whole diamond output before I am much older.' And to that Beit, who was also twenty-six, replied: 'That's funny. I have made up my mind to do the same. We had better join hands.' And they did, establishing a real bond between them, sharing their opportunities and thereby creating an atmosphere in which their respective companies – Rand Mines and Gold Fields for instance – could co-operate and this co-operation between their companies continued even after they had disappeared from the scene. Rhodes followed Beit along the business trail to the benefit of his fortune; Beit in turn became his ardent supporter in all his great imperial schemes, fulfilling a role there that Rudd, despite the famous Concession, was unwilling to take on. There was, however, more than sentiment behind Beit's approach to Gold Fields through Rhodes and Rudd to bring the company in with his own to develop the deep levels. Beit and his associates grouped their own ten deep-level interests under the roof of Rand Mines, the first deep-level company, and he persuaded Gold Fields to come in with a substantial participation. 'Rhodes's brains are not to be despised and if we had interests apart there would always be friction,' he wrote in 1892. At about this time Rudd was telling Currey that he had just dined with Beit, commenting: 'There is no doubt that his deep-levels scheme will be a grand one and very popular'.

[1] Rudd, however, is recognized in a set of portraits of the partners hanging at the entrance to the main Gold Fields board room in Johannesburg.
[2] Thompson always insisted on this spelling.

CHAPTER TWO

Deep Levels : High Hopes
1892 – 1895

Working behind the scenes in London to enable Gold Fields to make an impressive re-entry on the Rand stage as the curtain went up on a new act in the drama, the start of deep-level mining, was H E M Davies and Percy Tarbutt. Tarbutt had addressed a meeting of Davies's company, the African Gold Share Investment Company and *South Africa* had reported his saying, with considerable foresight: 'You will find the ore sufficient to keep 2 000 head of stamps at work night and day for 100 years.' And he went on: 'There is no doubt that the Witwatersrand is a permanent district and will last our lifetime and that of our children.' Before long, he maintained, they could produce a million ounces of gold a year. And, thought Davies, listening to him, Gold Fields must be there. He designed a new company – the Consolidated Gold Fields of South Africa – since it amalgamated the original Gold Fields of South Africa with Tarbutt's company on the Rand, the African Estates Agency and the two London companies that Davies himself had formed, the South African Gold and Trust Agency and the African Gold Share Investment Company. In this new arrangement the old agreement that Rudd and Rhodes possessed, and which had caused dissension, would have to be changed. The founder share provisions which had preference over dividends in the allocation of profits would have to go. And they did. Instead Rhodes and Rudd were given 80 000 shares for their founder rights plus a further 25 000 shares at par for cash. It was not a bad deal when one considers that their interest amounted to a fifth of the capital of the new company which was £1 250 000. Before long Rhodes and Rudd each had a shareholding worth £1 million and in less than four years Rhodes would tell a British parliamentary enquiry that he had made between £300 000 and £400 000 a year out of the company. The new company may not have been the 'personal company' of Rhodes and Rudd any longer but one might have thought so when one saw what they made out of it. Tarbutt and Davies had not done badly either, being awarded 369 000 shares for their own little companies.

The all-important question was – would the shareholders accept the new arrangement? They were called to a special meeting on 8 August 1892 to consider it. Rudd was not very sanguine. The meeting the previous year had been the most discordant on record. Rudd wrote pessimistically to Currey: 'The fact is our total Mashonaland holding is discredited, our De Beers depreciated and the deep-level interests are looked upon as speculative and visionary and with an utter absence of confidence and speculation generally, it is only by artificial means that the shares are kept at their present level.' Rudd may have been going through a bad patch as he sometimes did. He had already written to Currey from the Berkeley Hotel in London: 'I am somehow endlessly busy here tho' I hardly know what particular work or pleasure I get through. Anyway I get to bed about 1 am and up at 8 am and never seem to have a moment's leisure.' Rudd had talked about 'artificial means' to keep the level of share prices up. Such means might well have been employed to keep the level of shareholder confidence up since the circular they received ahead of the meeting – signed by the secretary H D Boyle but no doubt prepared by Davies – told a different story from Rudd's letter to Currey, written a fortnight earlier. 'The latest advices from Mashonaland are highly satisfactory', the circular affirmed. 'The position of the De Beers Consolidated Mines Limited was never so good as it is now and there is every prospect of increasing dividends.' However, the company meeting had as its principal object to consider the Witwatersrand, which the circular said, echoing Tarbutt, 'bids fair to eclipse all the gold-producing districts of the world … the board feeling convinced that South Africa will shortly excel all other countries in the production of gold and being anxious to maintain the leading position of the company and to enable its management to keep pace … with the great financial houses with whom it has become associated in many of its large investments on the Witwatersrand, have resolved to create an ample share reserve for this purpose'.

Charles Rudd need not have had any qualms about the shareholders. When he got up to speak to them they gladly accepted the whole scheme and gave a gentle cheer on hearing the founders' shares had been abolished. They were gratified to know that Rudd's 'plunge' into deep-level shares earlier in the year had already produced a profit of more than £70 000.

There were cheers and unanimous votes all round. The euphoria was reminiscent of scenes in Johannesburg a few weeks earlier. There on 9 July flags had been flown from the Rand Club as a salute to the fact that for the first time the Rand's gold output, as revealed by the June figures, had exceeded 100 000 ounces. 'The Century at Last' was the headline over the editorial in *The Star* that evening and the Stock Exchange had emptied earlier than usual as everyone went to the club to celebrate in the usual way. And Gold Fields shareholders leaving the Terminus Hotel's great hall on 8 August 1892 seemed to be equally as happy. They were turning their back on Gold Fields' first five groping years. Under a new name and with a clear purpose the company was back on the Rand ready to play its part in the creation of South Africa's great mining industry now that its true nature, mining at depth, had been finally understood. The new era that Gold Fields was now entering would be dominated by the engineers and the technicians upon whose skills in working the unique Witwatersrand series the shareholders' profits would now depend, and it was perhaps significant that Percy Tarbutt joined the board as this new era began.

KNIGHT'S REEF

Start of a new mine: Knights Deep, 1895.

The first three years in which Consolidated Gold Fields of South Africa, from its inception in August 1892, operated on the Rand saw the company's assets and wealth expand in a manner that went far beyond the hopes of those who had sanctioned its new form and its increased capital. Everything, at last, seemed to be going right and before long even the reserve shares had been issued as Gold Fields took full advantage of the deep-levels boom that was building up, going strongly through 1894 and well into the following year. The company's co-operation with other mining houses, its participation in their activities, was proving a valuable strategy; before long the 35 000 shares it had in Rand Mines were worth nearly a quarter of a million pounds, a profit of nearly £6 a share.

Gold Fields profits were not the only thing showing substantial growth as the 1890s progressed; the Rand itself and the town of Johannesburg were unrecognizable from the days of Ferreira's camp seven or eight years earlier. The organization of the mining industry, which in 1889 had its own Chamber of Mines, was taking the shape that distinguishes it from mining industries elsewhere. The system of mining groups was evolving, each mining house having its own

33

family of subsidiary mining companies that operated the mines. It was a system dictated by the nature of mining on the Rand, where deep levels, unlike the earlier outcrop mines that could be worked on small capital, required an investment of millions which no individual mine by itself could raise. So the mining finance houses, the Corner House in the lead, Gold Fields just behind and others in their turn, began to exercise their special functions, to provide and advance the enormous sums that were required while underground developments were proceeding at individual mines in the group. It was often a lengthy and expensive period before a mine could be brought to profitable production. While capital was being spent on an enormous scale there was never any certainty of final success in overcoming the great technical difficulties, gaining access to deeper levels, pumping water out, pumping air in, maintaining a rate of extraction that would make the mine viable. Gold Fields like the others had to have both faith and patience, sometimes for a long time; in the case of one of their famous mines, Sub Nigel, there was a wait of seventeen years.

By the mid-nineties when the various mines were producing, as they did in 1894, almost £7 million worth of gold and by the end of the decade one-quarter of the world's gold, ten clearly defined groups controlled the Rand mining industry. In importance Gold Fields was second only to the Corner House where the Eckstein brothers, Wernher, Beit and Phillips had concentrated their efforts. This was the group with which Gold Fields had the closest relationship through their participation in Rand Mines. But as time went on there were joint endeavours with other houses, all of whom discussed their mutual problems and interests under the roof of the Chamber of Mines whose first president had been Hermann Eckstein. Each group was dominated by strong personalities whose names became household words in South Africa and who were referred to as Randlords, an expression first heard at a Gold Fields meeting when Tarbutt's friend Cecil Quentin, on hearing that Gold Fields had 25 000 shareholders, exclaimed 'Twenty-five thousand Randlords and Randladies'.

Apart from Rhodes and Rudd and the Corner House personalities there was Barney Barnato, who had been slow to come to the Rand but now had his Johannesburg Consolidated Investment Co (JCI as it is still known today though its ownership has changed); there was the Sigismund Neumann group, while the Albu brothers, George and Leo who, like Neumann, Beit and Wernher, the Ecksteins' had come from Germany, had created what they were to call General Mining, which like Barnato's company would go elsewhere into different ownership. Another German, Adolf Goertz, had a group which would one day become Union Corporation. There was George Farrar at the head of a mixed Anglo-French group, destined one day to become part of Gold Fields. Another Gold Fields friend, Abe Bailey, was busy with his South African Townships, while Kruger's Jewish friend Sammy Marks and his partner Lewis had their African and European Investment Co. And of course there was the loner J B Robinson. The Robinson syndicate had been formed when Beit put up the money to enable Robinson to go to the Rand to buy farms and claims. Hermann

Eckstein had managed it at first, putting together the companies to develop such properties as the Robinson Mine, Langlaagte and Randfontein. It was eventually dissolved when Beit decided they would get on better without the difficult Robinson and this they did in setting up the company, H Eckstein and Company. Among all these companies Gold Fields stands out at this time by its essentially British character – one of its managing directors even found time to be Prime Minister of the British colony of the Cape and to organize the further expansion of the British Empire. It was making its way on the Rand with British capital. In fact one reason why Beit wanted Gold Fields in on his Rand Mines scheme was to have some British money working for him; his own funds had come mostly from France and Germany. However, Gold Fields, 'the very English company', in the words of a German admirer, was operating in the Boer republic of the Transvaal and in an atmosphere dominated by influences and interests from the continent of Europe. Just how cosmopolitan Johannesburg was may be judged from the census of 1896 which disclosed, for instance, that 3 000 Russians were working there, a number which by 1899 had reached 7 000, according to the Chief Rabbi of Johannesburg. There were Germans, French, Americans, Scandinavians and others. These were the Uitlanders from all corners of the earth and as the decade wore on, they would become increasingly a thorn in the Boer flesh, their presence in Kruger's domain leading in the end to open conflict.

Before politics began to cloud the air and to threaten in particular the fortunes of Gold Fields, the company passed through a period of tremendous development, when, having committed itself to deep-levels, it quickly increased its interests, either alone or in co-operation with other houses, establishing among them a position of prominence and an enviable reputation. Marshalling its various deep-level claims, it floated in 1893 Gold Fields Deeps and then, together with the Corner House and the Neumann group, it acquired a line of deep-level claims to the south of the first deep-level mines. Gold Fields and the Corner House together owned nearly all the potential mining ground on the Central Rand, the area in which Rudd and Rhodes had missed out first time round in 1886. Even before this took place, a list of Gold Fields holdings, issued in May 1893, looked impressive – Village Main Reef at the top of the list, 85 000 shares worth £351 000; Rand Mines, Crown Reef, City and Suburban, New Rietfontein and Luipaards Vlei, Geldenhuis. Development had to be paid for and shareholders were frequently being asked to increase the capital. They did not seem to mind. Profits were being made, at this stage still largely through clever share-dealing, an activity at which Herbert Davies was particularly adept. In 1893 there was a ten percent dividend. The original £1,25 million capital in £1 shares in 1892 was re-organized in 1894. Split in half, part stayed in ordinary shares, the rest in six percent preference shares. At the same time the capital was increased to £1 875 000 by the creation of a further 625 000 preference shares. Two years later, following further changes in the arrangements with Rhodes and Rudd, the capital became £1 975 000 and the following year, with a further

725 000 ordinary shares, capital was well past the £2 million mark, going up to £2 750 000. By 1898 Gold Fields' capitalization stood at £3 250 000, the market having absorbed yet another 550 000 new ordinary shares. Gold Fields was approaching the end of the century as a considerable company. By this time it was in control of three mines whose names are among the most famous in the history of South African goldmining, and which were to become the mainstay of the company's fortunes until the discovery of a new generation of mines more than thirty years later. These were the Robinson Deep (1894), the Simmer and Jack (1896) and the Sub Nigel, registered in 1895, the celebrated Gold Fields trio, popularly known as Faith, Hope and Charity.

This was the period when Gold Fields as a company was acquiring its nuts and bolts, as it were, the wherewithal to actually produce gold as opposed to just dealing in gold shares and properties. And the dominant figure in the Gold Fields workshop was one of the most remarkable mining engineers ever to work in South Africa. He was an American named John Hays Hammond, who had put aside a considerable business in the United States to come to the Rand to work for Barney Barnato. However, feeling that his genius was not properly appreciated at JCI he was willing to be snapped up by Rhodes for Gold Fields at an enormous price which made him the highest salaried man in the country. His achievements as a mining engineer committed to deep-levels amply justified this, and, judging by his autobiography, Hammond thought so, too.

In the cosmopolitan Johannesburg of the 1890s the American mining contingent was impressive. Barnato had got on to Hammond through the American managing director of De Beers, Gardner Williams; J S Curtis, who had been manager at Langlaagte, was already doing some impressive engineering at Village Main, where Gold Fields acquired three-quarters of the shareholding. Hennen Jennings at the Corner House was another of the Americans who was active in the technical development of the deep-level mines, although it was Hamilton Smith, whose detailed and astonishingly prophetic report in 1893 – 'the southern outcrop of the basin has not yet been determined but it is probably in the Orange Free State...' – made him the first to realize the full significance of the dip in the reefs. It was the policy of those cautious, hence immensely successful financiers, the Rothschilds, to obtain expert technical advice before committing their funds. In coming to South Africa whether with Rhodes or Beit, they first obtained the impressions of American mining experts. Hamilton Smith was one of these. He, possibly concerned about the cost of getting down to the reef at depth, appears to have backtracked after his initial enthusiasm. According to Hammond, the Rothschilds had been advised by Smith to stay out but he, Hammond, talked them into changing their minds. Publicity for Smith's pessimistic view of the cost of the deep-levels might have upset the prospective investor and at one stage Rudd, hearing that *The Times* was going to publish an article about deep-levels by Hamilton Smith, got in touch with the Editor to see if he could prevent it. At the time the Rand boom was at its highest.

So Hammond with a two-year contract that would give him £12 000 a year, an enormous salary in those days, three times what the chairman earned, went to work as Gold Fields' consulting engineer in Johannesburg. Cecil Rhodes had been responsible for putting him there and Hammond always felt he could deal with Rhodes direct if he so felt. It was, however, Ernest Rhodes, not Cecil Rhodes, who was the resident director in Johannesburg; this was however no problem for the American who felt he could always persuade Ernest to do whatever he suggested. Lowrey had departed to work for the company in Rhodesia. He had not thought much of Ernest Rhodes's appointment: 'Captain Rhodes is going to boss us here as Resident Director...' he had written to Currey in May 1893, and Charles Rudd, still with Cecil Rhodes in overall charge in Southern Africa, was not particularly enthusiastic either. 'As to Ernest Rhodes, I must say he is most anxious to help and is very good at figures but I have not yet made up my mind whether he is really clever and reliable in his judgement in our class of work. He goes too much like a bull at a fence for me and is, I think, too sanguine and speculative.'

The nature of mining on the Rand was changing and John Hays Hammond came to accelerate the process of change; change was going on, too, in the company's affairs. New homes were being acquired, in London as in Johannesburg, and new faces were appearing in each of them. In London, 8 Old Jewry, in the heart of the City, had become the new premises of Consolidated Gold Fields of South Africa following the re-organization of the company in 1892, and would remain so until after the First World War. In 1894 in Johannesburg Ernest Rhodes and Hammond were in an equally impressive building, very different from the elongated pondokkie in Doornfontein. Here they had a modern three-storey building on the corner of Simmonds and Fox Streets which looked as if it had been picked up by crane in London and lowered where the old camp of tents had been seven years earlier. Gold Fields had acquired a new address in London and in Johannesburg but the original telegraphic address continued to be used for almost a century, the celebrated 'Giovano' which Rhodes and Rudd used as a kind of shorthand in letters and telegrams when they wished to refer to the company. Giovano is a corruption of the Italian name Giovanni, the Italian form of Johannes, and a happy choice of telegraphic address for a company devoted to gold with which the name Giovanni had an ancient connection. Giovanni was the first name of the Doge of Venice, Giovanni Dandolo, who in 1284 had introduced the best known gold coin of those times, the Venetian Ducat, which became the Krugerrand of the Middle Ages. 'Giovano' had first been used in telegrams by the Johannesburg office but later it was adopted throughout the company and used not only by Gold Fields of South Africa but also by its associated company Consolidated Gold Fields in London.

Johannesburg had been taking shape in bricks and mortar; the Corner House was another architectural landmark and the new Rand Club became yet another. FitzPatrick's fear of grass in the streets had not been realized, they were now macadamized. In London, although Thomas Rudd was still Chairman, Herbert Davies, his deputy, was the man who really ran the day-to-day affairs of the

company and he appointed to assist him as company secretary J C Prinsep, destined to play a long and leading role in the office at 8 Old Jewry. A young lad recently out of his public school, Marlborough, also joined the staff and put his foot on the bottom rung of the Gold Fields ladder and climbed it steadily until at the outbreak of the Second World War he reached the top and became the chairman. He was Herbert Porter. In Johannesburg Ernest Rhodes took on two assistants, Edward Birkenruth and George Richards. Hammond was also doing a little empire-building of his own, bringing into his office some outstandingly able engineers, including H H Webb who became his successor both in London and in Johannesburg. Webb finally followed him home to America, having helped to found the School of Mines in Johannesburg, which in due time became part of the University of the Witwatersrand.

Hammond, who was referred to by Julius Wernher rather unkindly though not entirely untruthfully, as a 'windbag', claimed to be the founder of deep-level mining on the Rand but in fact others were in the field before his arrival. His compatriot J S Curtis had been the first to hit the headlines when, using a diamond drill for the first time, he struck the Main Reef at depth at Village Main, prompting *The Star* to say that he 'has placed the vexed question of the continuity and increasing richness of the Main Reef beyond dispute'. Village Main, largely owned by Gold Fields, had become the proving ground for deep-level mining, thanks to Curtis, and in so doing, according to *The Star*, it had assured

38

Herbert Porter, who joined Gold Fields in London as a boy from school in 1889 and stayed for 55 years. He had been chairman of the company for five years when he died in 1944. In 1937 he represented London at the celebration in Johannesburg of the silver jubilee of the company.

the future of the Rand. It is historically appropriate that Village Main, nearly a century later, barely a kilometre from the centre of modern Johannesburg, is still a going concern and though in different ownership, it is reassuring for that curious continuity that distinguishes the Gold Fields story that a Gold Fields director still sits upon its board.

Curtis had made his reputation as a pioneer of well-directed boreholes. Hammond whose name, like that of Curtis, would also be associated with mines as historically famous as Village Main, made a reputation for himself, and hence for Gold Fields, as a sinker of shafts. He greatly accelerated the speed at which shafts were sunk. In a short time the monthly average of 70 feet had been doubled; soon it was 250 feet and so it went on. Gold Fields got into the habit of breaking records and never got out of it; even after Hammond's day it continued to mark up shaft and tunnelling records, as will be seen.

Hammond had learned his mining skills in one of the best mining schools in the world, at Freiberg in Saxony, and in the United States he had built up a highly successful consultancy business, not only in mining engineering but in management as well. He was a real professional; he was fascinated by the particular nature of goldmining on the Rand, by the problem of going ever deeper, by the question of how far one might eventually go in efforts to tap that descending reef in deep-level mines. 'One of the first of these mines we developed', Hammond recorded, 'was the Robinson Deep. I had estimated that we would strike the reef on a certain date at about 1800 feet. We did strike it within a few feet of the depth and within a few days of the time I had set. Deep-level mining received a great impetus from this "remarkable guess" while I gained an unearned reputation as a prophet.' It was not, perhaps, as undeserved as he suggests. Many of Hammond's forecasts, with the passage of time, have turned out to be true. In 1899 after he had left South Africa he was saying that mining there at a depth of 8 000 feet was a possibility; on arrival on the Rand he had talked about a depth of 5 000 feet and at that time he forecast that by the end of the century the Rand would be producing gold worth £20 000 000; at the time he was speaking this was the value of world production. Hammond, who died in 1936, had seen his Robinson Deep become the deepest mine in the world within his lifetime and it held that record for many years.

The American's forceful personality and inexhaustible self-confidence showed in everything he did. He was not content merely to develop existing properties but was busily looking for others. 'I told Rhodes frankly that I had a very poor opinion of his properties but I felt that with his backing, I could acquire some other mining interests to level up his investments', he was to write later. He claimed that Rhodes had given him the green light and that he was responsible for spending 'many hundred thousand pounds'. During the period in which Ernest Rhodes and Hammond were running Gold Fields business in Johannesburg, the company's capitalization, as has been seen, expanded quite remarkably, though others, notably Charles Rudd, would dispute that all the credit for this lay with Hammond. Nevertheless, it is true that many of Ernest

Rhodes's letters to London would begin 'Mr Hammond recommends…'

During 1894, the year in which Robinson Deep was registered, the Simmer and Jack company decided to increase its capital by issuing 25 000 new shares. Gold Fields saw its opportunity and came in with an offer to combine some of its own deep-level claims with those of Simmer and Jack; in effect, it was in today's language a take-over bid. The capital would be increased to £250 000 instead of the £110 000 of the original Simmer intention and Gold Fields would take up 98 000 shares as its vendor interest. It was an ambitious scheme that prompted one Simmer director to comment that Gold Fields was showing 'a wonderful amount of pluck in investing so much money in deep levels'. The deal went through and in the newly constituted Simmer and Jack with its 900 claims, Gold Fields had got the biggest company on the Rand; three subsidiaries then emerged as products of Hammond's planning. Simmer and Jack West, Simmer and Jack East and Rand Victoria. The last-named was in due course to capture the imagination of miners everywhere and to put the Rand firmly on the world map when it put down a borehole a mile from the outcrop which then intercepted the Main Reef at 4 571 feet.

Simmer and Jack, which under Gold Fields direction was to have an enormous future, had already by the time Gold Fields came on the scene, a romantic past. August Simmer, the German, and John Jack, the Scot, were an unlikely pair to have their names immortalized by an historic mine; they ran a store out at Lake Chrissie in the Eastern Transvaal where a number of Scots had settled with the blessing of the Boers. The latter were inclined to think that of all those who came from the British Isles, the Scots were the nicest to dislike. One of these Boers, a farmer named Meyer from Elandsfontein, near where Johannesburg stands today, was in the habit of coming to Lake Chrissie to seek winter grazing. If he had not run up debts at the Simmer and Jack store, these two would never have entered the world of mining. To balance the debts they in due course acquired a half interest in Meyer's farm Elandsfontein. In September 1886 they received a tip-off that prospectors were swarming unlawfully over the property; Jack, who had sensibly got the mineral rights with his half interest in the farm, grabbed his horse and rode 240 kilometres to investigate. It was the same quick response to crisis he would show in 1889 when he went to see McArthur in Glasgow about the cyanide process. Jack reached the farm in the nick of time, pegged out the claims he was entitled to on the mynpacht, which straddled the Main Reef, and which he registered just a couple of hours before the farm Elandsfontein became the first property, together with Driefontein, to be selected when the Government proclaimed the Public Diggings on 20 September 1886.

Simmer and Jack, the name on the store, was transferred to the potential mine; at the same time Jack, remembering the farm near Glasgow where he had grown up, gave its name, Germiston, to the township that was to develop on the mynpacht. Simmer and Jack, the German and the Scot, were often thought to be twins, so alike they looked, each bearded, each dressed in the same clothes from the same peg in their store but they were very different in character. The Scot,

excited by the new prospects of a fortune through mining, was in a hurry to develop the mine; Simmer would have been happy to sell out and in due course, when the slump came and despite Jack's part in resolving the crisis over pyritic ore which had caused the panic, Simmer had his way. The pair had parted with their interest by the time Gold Fields came on to the scene and in due time made their names familiar in stock exchanges round the world. A century later although no longer in the Gold Fields stable, they are still being quoted in the pages of the *Financial Times* in London and in November 1985 a Johannesburg paper carried the headline: 'Simmer's taxed income up'.

Robinson Deep and Simmer and Jack had been gathered into the Gold Fields fold but now Hammond's restless energy was leading him towards what was probably his greatest service to Gold Fields in the 1890s. He was looking eastward towards the Heidelberg district, to Nigel, in particular, some fifty kilometres away and before long he was pressing the company to buy up as many claims as it could on the dip of the outcrop where the Nigel mine had been producing since 1886. Tarbutt, now a director of the company, and his colleague

42

All aboard the tailings wheel: Simmer and Jack, 1897.

TAILINGS WHEEL 38-0 DIA
-1-197 S&L.P

33

Quentin, had already taken a good look at Nigel and had bought large holdings. It was these holdings that Hammond recommended the company to buy and once more they took his advice. The name Sub Nigel was conferred casually, almost haphazardly. Gold Fields' lawyers, Solomon and Thompson which became the firm Webber Wentzel, who to this day still serve Gold Fields, had written to Ernest Rhodes about registering Sub Nigel, and asked him 'whether the foregoing is the title you have decided upon for the new company'. The letter, preserved in the Gold Fields collection, has a note scrawled almost languidly in Ernest Rhodes's hand, instructing his office to send a reply 'Sub Nigel will do'. And Sub Nigel did, somewhat lazily at first, but by 1928 with sufficient vigour as to make it the richest producer in the world.

Sub Nigel's past had been as romantically unusual as that of Simmer and Jack. During the nineteenth century the romantic novels of Sir Walter Scott were read as eagerly in the Transvaal as they were in the author's native Scotland. The father of F W Reitz, President of the Orange Free State and State Secretary under Kruger in the Transvaal, had been a personal friend of Scott; F W Reitz translated the poems of the Scottish poet Robert Burns into Afrikaans and his son, Deneys Reitz, carried on the literary tradition as author of the classic, *Commando*, relating his experiences during the Anglo Boer War. Dr Jameson used to imagine himself as Ivanhoe or Quentin Durward, romantic notions that led him into adventures that had nothing to do with medicine and landed him and Gold Fields in considerable trouble. One of Scott's fans in Pretoria was A P Marais, who owned a farm called Varkensfontein in the Heidelberg district near the Blesbok Spruit. Marais had been reading Scott's novel, *The Fortunes of Nigel*, about a man who lost his inheritance. In 1888 Marais almost lost his. He had interests in a number of mining syndicates and was always on the look-out for new opportunities. He had sent a prospector to Varkensfontein but the man spent more time with his bottle than his pick axe. Meanwhile parties of fortune-hunters from Natal, making their way to the Rand, would leave the coach at Heidelberg and then strike out, often across Marais's property, to reach their destination. One day a group of these travellers picked up the outcrop of a reef and in a short time, having plied Marais's man with questions and whisky, they were on their way to Pretoria. Here they explained to Marais they were keen on agricultural pursuits and would like to buy his farm for £1 000. Marais, however, was not so easily deceived; at no stretch of the imagination was the farm worth £1 000; they had obviously found something there. He mounted his horse to go and have a look and as he rode, he thought of the swindle of which he was meant to be the victim. It reminded him of Nigel and there and then he decided that Nigel would be the name of the mine which he suspected would be the future of Varkensfontein. What the drunken prospector had missed, what the itinerant miners had found, was oxidized ore that they had crushed easily and in their pan they had detected its heavy tail of gold.

Very soon the Nigel Mine came into existence but, as claims were pegged in profusion around the so-called Nigel Reef, many other companies emerged which also made Nigel part of their corporate name. Of these the original mine, however, was the only one that made any profits. For a long time the Nigel Reef was thought to be a freak, an isolated deposit of rich ore; no-one at that stage imagined that the Main Reef would be detected on what became the Far East Rand. However, those far-seeing deep-level enthusiasts, Tarbutt, Quentin and Boucher who specialized in pegging claims on the dip to the south of the richest mines, had acquired their interests near the original Nigel mine and it was these claims that Hammond persuaded Gold Fields to buy and which subsequently became Sub Nigel, registered on 7 August 1895 with a capital of £350 000 in £1 shares. Three years later J H Curle, a mining engineer who wrote about mining and was mining editor of *The Star*, commented: 'In the 1895 boom the Consolidated Gold Fields took up extensive interests in the district. Thousands of claims were acquired at high prices. The Nigel Deep, Nigel Central Deep and Sub Nigel were floated and the district rose in the estimation of the district.' Curle himself obviously had little enthusiasm for what Gold Fields had done nor indeed for the Nigel district; he did not realize then, any more than did Gold Fields, that Sub Nigel was an investment that would have to be put on one side until it was ripe. It was a long time maturing but when it eventually bore fruits these were manifold.

Hammond, manipulating the pliable Ernest Rhodes had, in his forceful way, added greatly to Gold Fields' possessions on the Rand but everything he had done, everything he wanted to do, cost a lot of money. This was an aspect of Gold Fields business that did not worry him unduly; it did, however, worry Rudd who could see that the company's purchases, at Hammond's behest, would require tremendous expenditure if they were to be brought to production and create dividends for shareholders. Although he admired Hammond's skills and even his qualities as a man, he began to feel that the American was overstepping the mark, that he was exceeding his role as consulting engineer. Hammond, it seemed, was trying to run the company. It was, however, Davies in London who became incensed. He wrote to Ernest Rhodes in November 1894 referring to Hammond's suggestion that they should sell Rietfontein. 'We note Hammond's remarks in explanation of advising us to sell. This only emphasises what I have always said that engineering and finance should not be combined. It would be ridiculous for us in London to instruct Hammond in regard to shaft-sinking and I contend it is equally ridiculous for a Consulting Engineer upon the Rand to take a market view and judge what stocks should or should not be sold and the sooner the two functions are separated, the better it will be for the company.' Hammond, interfering in a sphere in which Davies was obviously the expert, share-dealing, had touched a raw spot. 'Owing to our change in policy in realising outcrops in favour of Deep Levels our profits this year will be very large and to these profits Hammond will not have contributed anything material either in the way of work or advice.' Davies, as Deputy Chairman, was not satisfied with Ernest Rhodes's management in Johannesburg and told him: 'We shall never get into really good working order in regard to Sales and Purchases until you make your Consulting Engineers and Mine Managers report personally and regularly on changes in mines under their control and you transmit the same to London at your discretion with any comments as to local markets and influences.'

If Hammond were interfering in the company's investments, it was because he had a vested interest. Under his arrangements with Cecil Rhodes he was allowed stock options at par in Gold Fields flotations and to make the most of this privilege he had started to tell the company how to play the market. Stock options for mining engineers were a common form of remuneration at the time. Ernest Rhodes also came in on the act and both he and Hammond operated on the local Stock Exchange for themselves. It was possible in Johannesburg for local mine officials to exploit price differences and launch stock manipulations to the disadvantage of operators in the City of London.

It was all very well for Davies in London to try to put a little backbone into Ernest Rhodes in Johannesburg to get Hammond under control, but it was still Charles Rudd down in Cape Town who had an overall responsibility. Rudd, however, was slow to realize that Hammond and Ernest Rhodes were undermining his position.

Hammond did not like Rudd and as long as he had direct access to Cecil Rhodes, he was not going to bother himself with Rudd. In fact, he wrote to Cecil Rhodes: 'As I have frequently told you I am not an admirer of Mr Rudd and would prefer to work for your brother and yourself for a very much smaller compensation than I would expect from Mr Rudd.' As long as Hammond could control Ernest Rhodes he had nothing to worry about. As he recorded in his memoirs, 'Rhodes would say "If Ernest agrees and you don't hear to the contrary, go ahead!" Ernest always agreed and I never heard to the contrary. We made rapid progress.'

Hammond's autobiography is a large tome. Rudd, more modestly, wrote his in 1909 on two pieces of hotel writing paper and there he stated that during the 1890s he spent six months of every year in South Africa and six months in England. Most of his six months in South Africa would be spent at the Cape; he never really enjoyed going to the Rand. Rhodes had once written to Davies about him: 'I think myself he is suffering from a little reaction after visit to Randt and very likely has got one of those terrible sick headaches to which he is liable.' His experience at the Rand Club would certainly not have improved his migraine. He was blackballed. Charles Leonard, who in Currey's time had done some legal work for the company, appears to have been responsible. Currey himself wrote: 'That cad Leonard when pressed for his reasons for blackballing Mr Rudd said it was due to his action in some old diamond transaction with … of all people in the world! He, however, made it infinitely worse by saying at a public meeting of the club that no man had ever been blackballed by the club against whom there was not a very serious social or commercial charge.' Rhodes was to have the same experience, not in Johannesburg but in London where he was blackballed at the Travellers Club, a club which has reciprocity with the Rand Club. His

46

sponsors at the Travellers were none other than the Prince of Wales, the Duke of Fife and Earl Grey, all of whom, as custom dictates, resigned when their candidate was refused.

There is a particular irony about Rudd's experience at the Rand Club, when one considers the kind of man he was. It was the personal traits in his own character, his integrity, his honesty and straight-dealing that right from the start he conferred upon the company he had helped to create, laying the foundation of the reputation that Gold Fields continues to enjoy to this day. It was precisely because he felt Hammond should understand the way Gold Fields did business that he wrote to Ernest Rhodes: 'You must clearly understand that nothing in the nature of what you suggest can possibly be carried out by this company.' Ernest Rhodes, prompted by Hammond, had suggested a course of action at Village Main from which they might take personal advantage. 'The Village is one of those companies for which we are not only actually but morally responsible and any large sales preceding the shutting down of the mill would do enormous harm to the company and absolutely preclude the possibility of meeting shareholders on a fair platform later on or asking for an increase in capital. Any money consideration in such a matter as this goes for nothing. I am sure that Cecil will agree with me in thinking that the company's prestige must be put before any consideration of actual profit, and I think you would do well to explain this to Hammond so that he will understand the basis clearly on which we wish to work.'

If business were not being conducted in Johannesburg in the manner that Rudd thought desirable, he had perhaps only himself to blame if he continued to believe that Gold Fields' interests on the Rand, which in two years had doubled in size, could still be supervised from Cape Town. It was perhaps only when at the end of 1895, as will be seen, when Gold Fields was at the centre of dramatic political events in Johannesburg, that Rudd down at Cape Town really realized how he had betrayed himself through his own lack of vigilance. Meanwhile, the independence being shown by Hammond and Ernest Rhodes and the exception taken to it by Rudd and Davies, provided an early manifestation of what would become more apparent as the years went by, a sensitivity about who really wagged the company tail, London where the capital came from or Johannesburg where the mines were. Back in September 1889 Harry Currey had seen it coming when he wrote: 'If the powers that be in London and those in South Africa are each going to paddle their own canoe irrespective of one another, it seems to me to be only a matter of time when the crash will come.' In 1895 Rudd and Davies pulled rank and London declared that company policy was made at 8 Old Jewry. In future all share transactions would take place on the London Stock Exchange and not in Johannesburg; what's more, there would be no more options for managers or staff which in the past had allowed them to make a penny or two on the side.

Strained relationships within the company were also seen sometimes in relationships between the company and other mining houses. Early on Cecil

Rhodes fell out with Hermann Eckstein which prompted Wernher to ask Beit to mediate between them; he may well have succeeded since the Corner House (Eckstein's name rendered into English – *eck*, corner; *stein*, stone) and Gold Fields continued to be partners in various fruitful schemes. One of these was the Vierfontein Syndicate of 1893 when Eckstein and Gold Fields co-operated in a scheme to supply water to the town and the mines, a scheme which set the pattern for the future in drawing a distinction between water for domestic purposes and water for industry, the forerunner of the Rand Water Board.

Gold Fields participated in another syndicate that had been formed on Eckstein's initiative and one which had far-reaching consequences for the development of residential Johannesburg. This was the Braamfontein Syndicate, an embryo property company, since in due course it converted its Braamfontein farm into some of Johannesburg's smartest suburbs. On 10 March 1893 the directors of the company, who included Francis Lowrey for Gold Fields, resolved that 'the township beyond the jail' should be called Park Town and in view of the fact that the trams would shortly be going beyond Hospital Hill, Park Town – soon to be written Parktown – was to be the first of the company's townships to be developed. Others followed – they were called Westcliff, Forest Town, Arcadia. From the top of the ridge at Parktown one looked down upon the plantation known as Sachsenwald, once the property of Beit's cousin Lippert, who had been a rival of Rhodes and Rudd for the Lobengula Concession. It was Francis Lowrey's privilege, as a director, to take his friends on shooting parties and picnics in the Sachsenwald forest and to go riding in the 'drives' between the trees of what is now the suburb of Saxonwold. Gold Fields was helping to make Johannesburg, a process it was to intensify a decade later when it created its own property company.

Water supplies, residential townships – this was not all. It also pioneered the use of electricity. The General Electric Power Company was founded as a Gold Fields subsidiary with a capital of £200 000 and with plant on the Simmer and Jack mine, from which it supplied power to other mines and also to such townships as Germiston, which was said to glow more brightly than the metropolis itself, since Johannesburg relied on a small power station in Parktown. Gold Fields was literally blazing a trail which in due course led it to the Victoria Falls Power Company, which in its turn became a successful investment for Gold Fields.

In 1893 another name appeared which was to assume great importance for the company. On 6 March that year Apex Mines was registered with a capital of £50 000. Of the 44 500 vendor shares, Gold Fields received 37 500 in exchange for freehold rights over the farm Rietfontein. Three years later two shafts were sunk and at just under 100 feet coal was found. In due course Apex Mines had two sections, one for coal and the other for gold. In the end it was Apex coal that assumed a lasting significance.

Sir George Farrar came on the Apex scene and assumed the dominant role when it became part of the Anglo-French group but in the end, after many years, it came back to Gold Fields but it is sometimes forgotten that when it all began so long ago, Gold Fields was there. When the articles of association of Apex Mines were re-drafted in 1896, the documents stated 'and the first directors shall be Edward Birkenruth, George Farrar and William Dalrymple'.

Of all the joint ventures that Gold Fields participated in at this time, none was more profitable than its co-operation with the Corner House in launching Rand Mines even though it parted with its shareholding too soon. It made a profit of half a million pounds but if it had waited it could have made twice as much as the shares reached £50. Later Julius Wernher, who made the biggest individual fortune on the Rand, more than £10 million and was the most careful of financiers, was to criticize Gold Fields' management 'as they do things too much in the happy go lucky style – their responsibilities in developing all their properties are enormous and in bad times few will care to join them with money to help'. There were, however, certain schemes which the Corner House, or at least Lionel Phillips, suspected Gold Fields would not be willing to join. In the middle of 1894 Phillips was trying to get £10 000, not to float a new company, but rather what looked like a secret society whose object would be to try to influence the voters in the coming Transvaal elections in order to topple Kruger and replace him with Piet Joubert who would be more friendly towards the mining houses. Phillips wrote to Beit that the only doubtful people were the Gold Fields.

'I doubt if Gold Fields would provide money without instructions from home,' he said.

Phillips was right. Nevertheless, in the light of what was to happen late the following year there is something quaintly ironic in his picture of a pussy-footing Gold Fields.

Phillips had not been keeping up with Rhodes. Charles Rudd had and he became convinced that Gold Fields was becoming too heavily committed to Rhodes's endeavours in Rhodesia and ought to review its interests there. At the shareholders' meeting in 1893 he had, however, made a spirited defence of his partner.

'The man who has saved Mashonaland and all the northern parts of South Africa for the British Empire is Cecil Rhodes,' he declared resoundingly.

The Matabele rebellion having been successfully put down, Rhodes had gone back to the Cape from the north and been received as a hero. At a civic banquet attended by 300 he had said, 'it was fortunate to have an idea and to be able to call upon funds in support of that idea'. But for how long? Both De Beers and Gold Fields had been subsidizing the Chartered Company. Gold Fields, with a resignation threat from Rhodes, had unhappily agreed to advance £500 a month. When the subsidy had been renewed in 1894 the company had been given as a sop the right to 250 claims in Matabeleland which they could develop or not as they pleased. The following year, however, Rudd and Davies decided that Gold Fields would channel no more money into Rhodes's hinterland and Rhodes was told by letter that the company 'would not go into any more of these mixed up companies and would sell gradually all the scrip they held in them as well as

49

Charter shares'. Gold Fields' brief attempt to go it alone in Rhodesia with properties on its own account, acquiring it was said, the 'skim milk' at top prices, for which Francis Lowrey was blamed, had been as disillusioning for the company's shareholders as their participation in the affairs of the BSA Company.

During 1894, whatever irritations that may have existed between London and Johannesburg or between London and Salisbury disappeared in the great enthusiasm that investors round the world were showing for the Rand where a tremendous boom was building up. It was as if suddenly the world had woken up to the fact that the Rand was different from all places where gold had been found, not only in the extent of the goldfield but in its regularity and its permanence. The Rand's significance as the greatest source of gold the world had ever seen was that it had emerged just at the very moment that gold was most needed. World production of gold had been declining for forty years; commodity prices were everywhere going down and the world economy looked distinctly seedy. But the western world needed gold since it had come very close to possessing a single monetary system based on the international gold standard. This standard had not been an artificial invention but had been developing steadily throughout the nineteenth century, partly because Britain, the world's leading industrial country, had adopted gold as the monetary basis of the pound sterling following the Napoleonic wars. France too had adopted the gold standard and Germany in the 1870s. By the time gold had been discovered on the Witwatersrand in 1886, it had become the basis of international payments among the leading industrial nations of the world. And in the 1890s the mere knowledge that gold was always on the way to London in those weekly consignments in Sir Donald Currie's ships of the Union Castle Line, and that the Bank of England could 'tap' this regular flow if necessary, helped to give the world its confidence in sterling. But throughout the 1890s the Banque de France in Paris was also accumulating gold on a steady basis as part of its monetary policies. In 1898 the trade statistics of the German Empire indicated for the first time that the South African Republic had provided Berlin with just under £2 million worth of gold. A combination of economic and psychological influences, and the sudden awareness of the true significance of the Rand, sent shareholders in the City of London, rentiers in France, banks in Germany scrambling for Africa's gold as their governments had been scrambling for Africa itself.

While in South Africa Gold Fields was pushing ahead, though not without difficulty, in the task of being a producer of gold through the mines it controlled, at the same time the significance of the company was becoming increasingly important internationally. By 1895 the number of its shareholders had reached 10 000; the previous year for the first time lady shareholders had been at the annual meeting and the following year, as an indication of the widening circle of shareholders, the directors' reports were published in French and German as well as English. Soon an office was opened in Paris. The international nature of that unique family, the Rothschilds – there are English, French and German-speaking branches of the family – had ensured a European link for Rhodes's interests, whether in De Beers or Gold Fields. At the same time Gold Fields' close links with Jules Porges, whose company on his own retirement had become Wernher, Beit & Co, also ensured a strong French interest in Gold Fields; in fact the time would come when French shareholders would ask for special representation on the Gold Fields board. In 1895 the French banker Albert Kahn was in touch with Davies in London and Julius Wernher about a participation in Village Main. Like his namesake, Rodolphe Kahn, Albert Kahn made a fortune out of his South African dealings. A bachelor like Rhodes, whom he greatly admired, he spent his money on promoting international friendship, the *Autour du Monde* travelling fellowships being inspired by the Rhodes Scholarships.

Rudd and Davies exploited to the full this international interest in the company. The big share boom of 1894-95 gave them the opportunity to build up its financial resources for the development of the deep-levels and for their new strategies. The outcrop interests were sold off at a large premium – between 1893 and 1895 they got rid of 350 000 shares. There is no doubt that their skill in the London stock markets and in the organization of the company's finances in general ensured the means by which Gold Fields' mining operations could continue – literally – at ever deeper levels. Their impatience with what might seem like extravagance on Hammond's part or Ernest Rhodes's managerial inadequacy in employing funds is, in this light, understandable. In a letter to Ernest Rhodes, Rudd provided an idea as to how they operated. He and Davies 'with other friends' arranged the purchase of not less than 80 000 shares to keep up ordinary share values when a Gold Fields capital increase and stock conversion was going through late in 1894. Acting for the company, they made considerable sums of money for it with their share-dealings; but they also operated for themselves, quite separately, and made their individual fortunes.

On 6 November 1895 the shareholders met as usual at their hotel in Cannon Street; it was more a celebration than an annual stock-taking. Thomas Rudd, as chairman, got to his feet and, to the excitement of the shareholders, he said: 'I am in the proud position of announcing to you today a realised profit certainly larger than any ever anticipated when we founded this company and larger than any ever realised by any limited company in the City of London...' The Stock Exchange boom had enabled the company to show an appreciation of no less than £9 million on their mining stocks; the company had made an enormous profit for the year and was proposing to pay a dividend of 100 percent, making 125 percent for the whole year on the ordinary shares. £200 000 was going into reserve and more than a million pounds was being carried forward. It was an extraordinary financial situation where the reserve fund and the unappropriated profit together were nearly equal to the authorized capital of the company. Gold Fields might well have had 10 000 happy shareholders to enjoy the record profits of 1895 but its biggest shareholders, because of the early agreements between the founders and the company, were Rudd and Rhodes and in that year some £500 000 was due to them. Some sections of the financial Press referred to 'this millstone round the company's neck'. It still seemed as if 'a personal company'

51

fitted the description of Gold Fields and not a few of those 10 000 shareholders began to feel that their company could not go on indefinitely being tied to the personal fortunes of Rhodes and Rudd, let alone inflating them to such a degree. A change was coming, but that it should come within a month of that euphoric annual general meeting in London and in such dramatic circumstances that had nothing to do with profits and everything to do with politics in South Africa, was to stagger the world. The company history of Gold Fields was about to tangle with the national story of South Africa itself. Gold Fields might have been registered in London and directed from there, its shareholders in 1895 distributed among the capitals of Europe and its shares sold on their stock exchanges, but its real life was in South Africa and it was events in that country that would give it the character that it possesses today.

CHAPTER THREE

Blood and Thunder
1895 – 1902

'The political disturbance at the commencement of the year 1896 caused a not inconsiderable interruption to the development of the mining industry on the Witwatersrand…' Thus wrote the directors in their report for 1896. This was all the company, deciding to keep its eyes tightly shut, was prepared to say about one of the most celebrated episodes in South African history and one in which the company's name was deeply involved – the Jameson Raid.

The boom on the Rand during 1894 and 1895 and the euphoria it had created had thrown up a smokescreen hiding the deteriorating political situation in the Transvaal and, from the eyes of the Gold Fields board in London, the activities of some of its employees in Johannesburg. Rhodes, Prime Minister of Cape Colony, no doubt felt his enormous Gold Fields earnings that year had arrived most conveniently for his political schemes; he was hard at work on what he was to call 'the revolution'. In June 1894 Lionel Phillips had written to Beit: 'The Gold Fields people urged me to go down to Cape Town and talk over matters with Rhodes.' To do that, he thought, would be to arouse the suspicions of the Kruger Government. Anyway, he asked, 'Should I be wise to trust Rhodes's advice?' Kruger's hostility to Rhodes was well known. Rhodes himself had written to Davies from Madeira about his problems: 'the other difficulty is the worthy Kruger and his unfortunate hostility to myself'. Very soon Lionel Phillips was to become one of the principal actors in Rhodes's evolving intrigue and Beit himself would be called upon to help pay for it. By this time Rhodes was convinced that Kruger stood four-square across his own grandiose plans for a great federation of Southern Africa as part of the British Empire. Kruger was boxed in with British territories all about him, except in the east; Rhodes had tried to buy Lourenço Marques from the Portuguese and when that failed was prepared to send Dr Jameson and the BSA Police to seize Beira, but this was stopped by the British Government, who were concerned not to upset Britain's oldest ally, the Portuguese, nor the Germans who tended to nod kindly towards the Boers. Rhodes was further frustrated when the Netherlands Railway provided a line from Delagoa Bay to Pretoria and Kruger was less reliant on the British colonies to the south and their ports.

Kruger felt threatened, not only by Rhodes's plans outside the Transvaal but also by mounting pressures inside his country, where Uitlanders now outnumbered Boers and were demanding votes and other things. Kruger had imagined the working of the Rand mines to be short-lived. The foreigners would come but after a while they would surely depart again, having first, through taxation, filled the empty coffers of his Treasury. But that was not to be. The Uitlander population continued to grow and showed no interest in departing. If, as was being said, the mines might last another sixteen years, then the foreigners would have to wait fourteen years to qualify for a vote, Kruger reckoned. Leaders of the mining industry, however, were growing increasingly impatient with the Boer administration which they considered corrupt and inefficient. Their list of grievances grew. A Reform Committee was set up. The situation was ripening for Rhodes's conspiracy. He and Jameson met Gold Fields consulting engineer, John Hays Hammond in Rhodesia and decided that an armed revolt organized in Johannesburg could bring Kruger down. The mining houses could not do it by themselves; in any case not all of them would support such action. It would be necessary to have a British force to march in on the pretext that British lives in Johannesburg were in danger. This would be Dr Jameson's role; at the head of a contingent of the BSA Police he would go in and help the Reformers to establish a new Government in place of Kruger. To do this Jameson's force would have to be conveniently nearby and in due course they were encamped at Pitsani inside the border of Bechuanaland (today's Botswana) with the Transvaal. Rhodes was confident he would have the tacit approval of the British High Commissioner at the Cape, Sir Hercules Robinson, whose name had already been suggested as someone to succeed Thomas Rudd as chairman of Gold Fields.

Rhodes, planning his revolution for the Rand, saw his own company, Gold Fields, as the obvious centre for operations and before long he had dispatched his military brother, Colonel Frank Rhodes DSO, as his personal representative there. The company lawyers, Solomon and Thompson, drew up a legal document which refers to the appointment of Colonel Rhodes 'to represent Consolidated Gold Fields in the South African Republic'. Rudd was later to protest that he had not been properly consulted, had never approved of the Colonel's appointment nor recognized his authority in Johannesburg. Rhodes's reasons for sending his brother to the Rand had nothing to do with goldmining; in the guise of a managing director of Gold Fields he was to use his military training to organize the armed revolt. He would have the enthusiastic support of Hammond who, being an American, felt he belonged to a nation that knew all about revolutions. Ernest Rhodes, meanwhile, sensibly decided to clear out while the going was good. He asked Rudd if he might go to England on home leave and by mid-October had gone, never to return. He had sought to reassure Rudd in Cape Town that during his absence everything in Johannesburg would go on well. 'Frank will be with me for a fortnight here and Richards and Hammond know the whole working of this office thoroughly.' He added, 'I am very pleased to get home.' In a month or so he would be even more so.

Cecil Rhodes in sending his military brother to the Johannesburg office had

cynically and recklessly usurped the company for his political ends. Soon the plotters were meeting regularly in the Gold Fields building; before long guns and ammunition were being brought into the country disguised as mining machinery and stores, and they were being hidden on Gold Fields property, such as the Simmer and Jack mine. Gold Fields was not alone in the plot. Rhodes, in the flotation of his revolution was offering participation to other mining groups. Phillips, Beit and FitzPatrick from the Corner House were in, so was the Farrar group with George Farrar one of the ringleaders; when a wagon carrying his safe

Enrolling Volunteers at the
Gold fields office. Johannesburg -

was intercepted in due course, it was found to be stocked with arms and ammunition. Abe Bailey, too, was there and the list included a mining engineer named Robert Fricker who later became head of Gold Fields activities on the Rand, having first cooled his heels in Pretoria Gaol like all the other conspirators, when the muddled plot and the botched raid ended in the great fiasco of Jameson's ride and its ignominious end. 'It is still a puzzle that so many able men could have been drawn into so muddled a plot', commented Rhodes's biographers Lockhart and Woodhouse. Charles Rudd put it even more emphatically. 'They could only have been arranged by a madman', was his comment on the plans for the Rand revolution inspired by his partner.

What happened in the last days of December 1895 are well known. Jameson, waiting at Pitsani, carried a letter signed by the Reform Committee leaders asking him to intervene on the Rand. He was, however, not to move until word came from Johannesburg that they were ready for him. The Committee, hesitant, undecided, procrastinating, never gave the word. They were getting cold feet and had sent their leader, Charles Leonard, and Frederic Hamilton, the

Editor of *The Star*, to see Rhodes and to get an assurance from him that Jameson would not move without a clear instruction to do so from the Reform Committee. Jameson, however, got tired of waiting; it was after all very hot at Pitsani; he 'took the bit between his teeth' on 29 December, crossed the border and began to ride for Johannesburg.

Once the news was out that Jameson was on his way, the Reform Committee in Johannesburg was galvanized into action and their headquarters, the Gold Fields building at the corner of Simmonds and Fox Streets, became the focal point of everyone's attention. Outside in the street there was a constant crowd before the building, while inside, the Reform Committee met in permanent session debating what to do. As Leonard was still at the Cape, Phillips was in charge and soon he had turned the Gold Fields offices into the seat of the provisional government of Johannesburg. A dramatic account of these days as 1895 ended and 1896 began, when Johannesburg was administered from the Gold Fields building, is contained in the diary of Mrs John Hays Hammond. On New Year's Eve, 1895, she wrote: 'The streets are alive at a very early hour and the

For two days at the end of 1895, at the time of the Jameson Raid, Johannesburg was 'run' by the Reform Committee at its headquarters in the Gold Fields offices. Here the crowd surges round the door at Gold Fields to read the latest proclamation posted up by Percy FitzPatrick, the committee secretary.

57

excitement increases. The Reform Committee sits in perpetual session in the offices of the Gold Fields. They are appointing sub committees for the safeguarding and comfort of the town.

'In order to silence rumours in regard to the hoisting of the English flag, Mr Hammond after some difficulty secured a flag of the Transvaal and took it into the committee room this morning. The entire body of men swore allegiance with uncovered heads and upraised hands. The flag now floats from the roof of the Gold Fields.' Mrs Hammond, however, neglected to add that it was flying upside down which would normally have been considered an insult if it had been done deliberately.

Soon the crowd in the street, which had been watching the *Vierkleur* flying over the roof of the building, had their attention diverted to the door of the Gold Fields offices; a notice signed by Percy FitzPatrick was being posted up and the crowd moved closer to see what it said. 'Notice is hereby given that this Reform Committee adheres to the National Union Manifesto and reiterates its desire to maintain the independence of the Republic. The fact that rumours are in course of circulation to the effect that a force has crossed the Bechuanaland border, renders it necessary to take active steps for the defence of Johannesburg and preservation of order...'

'Active steps' meant the issue of arms and ammunition and this now took place from the Gold Fields offices; among those who watched it taking place were detectives from the Johannesburg Police who later gave evidence in court. Detective Andries Smorenberg watched arms being brought in from the mines which were handed out at the Gold Fields offices. Detective Joseph van Dyk told how the distribution of arms had been supervised by Colonel Bettington.

'Was Trimble there?', the detective was to be asked in court.

'Yes.'

'The same Trimble who was formerly Chief Detective of Johannesburg?'

'Yes.'

When the crisis had started the Government in Pretoria had asked Colonel Trimble to take charge in Johannesburg but Trimble soon became an enthusiastic supporter of the revolt.

The Government in Pretoria was not quite sure how to handle Johannesburg; Jameson on the other hand could be dealt with by the Boer commandos. Pretoria put out an olive branch to the Reformers and talks were held; Eugene Marais, who was later to become internationally famous as writer and poet and was then editor of *Land en Volk*, was sent from Pretoria with Abraham Malan, General Piet Joubert's nephew, to talk to the Reformers. Marais made a second visit and this time was met at Park Station by Abe Bailey in his carriage; Marais, blindfolded, was taken through the noisy streets and into the Gold Fields office, which he said later he recognized despite having been taken there blindfolded. The talks came to nothing. The Reformers thought they were winning. Mrs Hammond wrote in her diary: 'Mr Phillips had just addressed the crowd collected around the Gold Fields waiting for news.... one voice called out "And how

about Jameson?" Mr Phillips answered "I am instructed by the Reform Committee to state to you, as I did to the Government, that we intend to stand by Jameson. Gentlemen, I now call upon you to give three cheers for Dr Jameson". There was prolonged and enthusiastic cheering.' A detective in the crowd was later to say that, with the expected arrival of Dr Jameson, ladies were waiting with flowers to greet him.

Hays Hammond himself recorded: 'About daybreak on Thursday January 2, Colonel Rhodes and I who had been sleeping on the floor in my office, were awakened by the arrival of bugler Valle of Dr Jameson's force....Jameson was progressing slowly but surely on his way to Johannesburg. Valle thought he would be there in a few hours.'

The Reform Committee, among others, had been trying to stop Jameson, however, to get him to go back. In Cape Town Rhodes was appalled at what he had done. He told Schreiner, a member of his Cape Cabinet: 'Yes, yes, it is true. Old Jameson has upset my apple cart....twenty years we have been friends and now he goes in and ruins me.' Nothing could now stop Jameson, however, except the Boers and this they did effectively. Despite his earlier boasts of taking

Left, Eugene Marais, the Afrikaans poet and writer, who in 1895 as editor of the Pretoria newspaper, Land en Volk, *tried to mediate between the Pretoria authorities and the Reformers. He was led blindfolded into the Gold Fields building by Abe Bailey (right). In the 1930s Bailey's company was one of the first to take an interest in Gold Fields' West Wits project.*

the Transvaal with half a dozen revolvers and a sjambok or two, he was stopped at Doornkop near Krugersdorp by the Boers under Commandant (later General) Piet Cronje and after some mild skirmishing he and his men were made prisoners.

'When the news of Jameson's surrender was confirmed this evening', Natalie Hammond wrote in her diary, 'the surging crowd around the Gold Fields became an excited and dangerous mob. Pressing thickly together in their frenzy, they began to mutter threats against the Reform Committee; plans were made to blow up the Gold Fields where the Reformers sat in session. Several gentlemen essayed to speak from the windows but were received with howls and curses from the stormy tumult below.' It was left to Sam Jameson, Dr Jim's brother, to speak to the crowd. 'It was oil on troubled waters', wrote Mrs Hammond. However, the game was up. Simpson, the Gold Fields surveyor, offered to prepare horses to enable the ringleaders to ride to safety across the Natal border but the offer was refused. They did not consider they were in danger.

Edward Birkenruth, who with George Richards had had nothing to do with the conspiracy, got off a letter to Davies in London. 'We have none of us had much sleep for a week and it is quite pitiful to see Colonel Rhodes and those on whom most of the responsibility has fallen.' Colonel Rhodes, Hammond and the rest of the Reformers, like Jameson and his troopers, would soon have plenty of time to catch up on their sleep; there was nothing much else to do once they had been locked up in the Pretoria Gaol to await trial.

Meanwhile messages were flying fast and furiously between Gold Fields' offices in London, Cape Town and Johannesburg when it was realized with horror what Rhodes had done to the company. Rudd, like Rhodes, was in Cape Town. He had been planning to go to the Rand, but Rhodes, no doubt wanting him out of the way at the crucial time of the uprising, had asked him to postpone the visit until after the New Year. 'The news that our company was taking a prominent part in the political movement came upon me like a thunder clap and I only gathered it from the conflicting Press telegrams on the 2nd when I wired you.' Rudd informed London, 'I have been assured that none of our company funds have been employed in aid of the movement but at the same time I see by the Press telegrams that they appear to have largely contributed.' In fact, as later became clear, Gold Fields money in considerable quantity had been paid in cheques, signed by Colonel Rhodes and deposited by the Reform Committee's secretary, Raymond Schumacher of the Corner House, in an account at the Standard Bank called the Development Concession Account which was in reality the revolution account.

Rudd informed London he was preparing to leave for the Rand at once and he cabled the British representative in Pretoria, Sir Graham Bower, for an assurance that he would have no problems at the Transvaal frontier. In due course he received a guarded message via Government House in Cape Town who were to 'inform the owner of Fernwood that it would not be prudent to try to enter Johannesburg'. Gold Fields in London had informed Rudd that they were being

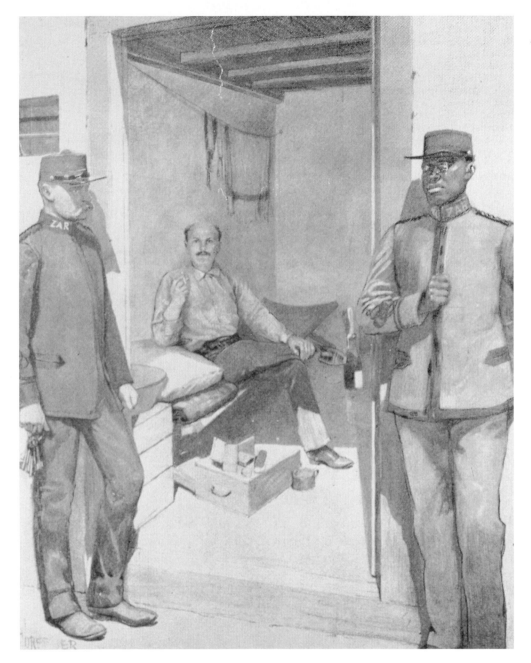

inundated with enquiries and asked him if they should go and see Chamberlain, the Colonial Secretary, or the Boer Consul-General in London, Montagu White, to assure them that Gold Fields knew nothing about the political activities of its employees in Johannesburg. Should they get in touch with Kruger direct? In due course, the board in London put out a Press statement that employees of the company had acted without authority.

But it was on Charles Rudd that the company was now relying to try to salvage the company's name and its future, since the disgrace of the co-founder. And Rudd had been caught napping. Davies might well have recalled a letter he had once written to Rhodes: 'Rudd's enthusiasm oozed away on …. turning his back upon the scene of operations – he told me here that this always was so with him.' Rudd began by writing a stiff note to the hapless Colonel Frank Rhodes: 'I think you will admit that I have been hardly dealt with in these matters and that the affairs of the Company have been taken completely out of my hands. After discussion with Cecil I shall write again re powers.' This letter of 5 January 1896 suggests that the partners met in Cape Town after Jameson's disastrous ride but there is no record of this. According to Matabili Thompson, Rhodes would not see Rudd who then asked Thompson to get Rhodes to cancel his brother's power of attorney. 'At last, late one afternoon, I got the assurance from Rhodes that he had cancelled Frank's power of attorney. I carried the information to Rudd at night on horseback.' Another message goes off to Birkenruth in Johannesburg from Rudd.

'Colleague has revoked all powers granted by him in South Africa re Company, appointing me sole representative.' As Rudd had been officially warned not to go to the Rand he sent Major Henry Sapte. Sapte had joined the company in 1892, having previously been military secretary to the High Commissioner, Sir Henry Loch, and he had been working for Gold Fields in Rhodesia. Now he and Birkenruth had the difficult task of getting Gold Fields back into its legitimate business which was mining for gold on the Rand. And this in the strained atmosphere of Johannesburg after the abortive uprising. Birkenruth and Richards felt that Rudd had let them down. 'You have tacitly allowed us to recognize Colonel's authority as your joint representative', they told Rudd by telegram. 'We emphatically repudiate all responsibility.' Richards resigned and in due course Rudd received a cable from London 'Board presume you have accepted G Richards's resignation. Unless you see good reason to the contrary all employees, including Hammond, charged at Pretoria, should be suspended pending trial.' Rudd then had to inform London: 'Hammond threatens if suspended to damage Gold Fields, C J Rhodes, C D Rudd as far as possible. For myself personally I have no fear at all as to the result but as regards C J Rhodes probably, it is almost certainly to affect political position in England and as regards Gold Fields it means total disorganization of engineering works.' But Hammond continued to serve Gold Fields even while in Pretoria Gaol, from where he communicated advice as to what should be done on the mines. He was, after all, a professional.

Cecil Rhodes was down but he was by no means out. He had resigned the Premiership of the Cape, and from the board of the Chartered Company. Early in February his solicitor in London, Hawksley, sent a message to the Gold Fields secretary, Prinsep, that if Gold Fields felt that 'the hostility of the Transvaal to Mr Rhodes was detrimental to the Company then he would resign'. Gold Fields meanwhile had asked Rhodes to come to London for a chat and in mid-January he took ship for England. There were others over there who wanted to talk to him, including members of the British Parliamentary Committee that was set up to enquire into the Jameson Raid. In due course their report was to say: 'Mr Rhodes occupied a great position in South Africa; he was Prime Minister of Cape Colony and beyond all other persons, should have been careful to abstain from such a course as that which he adopted. As Managing Director of the BSA Company, as director of De Beers Consolidated and The Gold Fields of South Africa, Mr Rhodes controlled a great combination of interests; he used his position and those interests to promote and assist his policy.' But no longer, as far as Gold Fields was concerned. The Raid had wrecked the old arrangement whereby he and Rudd had been appointed managing directors. Herbert Davies once more set to work to reform the company as it picked itself up after the Raid. Although Rudd offered no public comment on what his partner had done, their old relationship could never be the same, and Rudd was determined that Rhodes's domination of the company had to cease. In the first place his two brothers would have to go. Ernest Rhodes resigned from the Gold Fields board after Rudd had told Davies that if Ernest Rhodes stayed, then he would go. Meanwhile Thomas Rudd gave up the chairmanship of the board and Davies took over, Charles Rudd having said that he himself did not want it.

In March 1896 Davies called a special meeting of shareholders to consider new proposals about Rhodes and Rudd. Both had resigned as managing directors but were willing to continue as directors and on new terms. They were no longer to receive two-fifteenths of the profits. They were entitled to a share of the company's capital, however, and Davies suggested that they should have 100 000 shares as a final settlement of their claims on the company. To provide these the company would have to increase its capital to £1 975 000. The shareholders agreed to the new arrangements although they were reminded by one of their number that these new shares were worth £1 200 000 which, no one could deny, was a great deal of money. Considering what Rhodes's recklessness and Rudd's lack of vigilance had cost the company, the shareholders were being extremely magnanimous. However, public opinion in Britain about the Jameson raiders and the plotters of the Reform Committee was changing and turning them into heroes, a development which prompted Rudd in an official letter to the board to comment somewhat acidly that 'the proposal of the British aristocracy to turn President Kruger into the "Buffalo Bill" of the London season along with Dr Jameson, is hardly likely to soothe the Boer or satisfy the Hollander official'. In the same letter Rudd is concerned about getting company business going again on the Rand where Major Sapte has been holding the fort in Rudd's absence. The military symbolism is intentional since Rudd obviously did not like the military appearance of the Johannesburg office. 'One is met constantly by alleged promises by the "Captain" and the "Colonel" which have been hung up by the "Major"!' Birkenruth, at least, had no military title! Hammond, however, was still the key figure.

'No doubt when Mr Hammond is about again, matters will become even more pressing…I am inclined to suggest to Mr Hammond a general meeting in London towards the end of May and make him responsible for carrying on the mining operations of the company with the staff he doubtless dominates.' Such comment about plans for Hammond is astonishing; Rudd makes it sound as if Hammond was down with a mild cold whereas of course he and the other plotters were in Pretoria Gaol waiting to be tried for their lives. Indeed, by the time May arrived, Gold Fields' consulting engineer had been sentenced to death, though later reprieved. Hammond had been ill, not with a cold but with dysentery, and had been allowed by the Boer authorities to go to the Cape to recover. While he was there stories began to circulate that the plotters would be lynched, that a grisly antique had arrived in the Transvaal, the old beam from which the Boer rebels had been hanged by the British at Slagtersnek in 1815, and people drew their own conclusions. Natalie Hammond feared for her husband if he were to return to the Transvaal to face trial. She consulted her friend James Rose-Innes, the future Chief Justice of the Union, and recorded: '"If you think his going back is a needless throwing away of a valuable life" I began with a timid hope beginning to grow in my heart, "I will chloroform him and have him taken to sea". Mr Rose-Innes leaned forward and took my hand gently in his. "Mrs Hammond, your husband is doing the right thing in going back – if he were my own brother I would say the same" and I accepted his decision.'

Hammond, Frank Rhodes, Phillips and Farrar were all sentenced to death at the Pretoria trial but were reprieved and later released on paying fines of £25 000 each. The other plotters, including Robert Fricker, were fined £2 000. Jameson was handed over to the British authorities and tried in the British courts in London where he served a short sentence at Wormwood Scrubs prison. In due course he was to be honoured with a baronetcy, becoming Sir Leander Starr Jameson. Returning to South Africa, he took over his friend Rhodes's old job as Prime Minister of the Cape. During the Pretoria trial, Advocate J G Dickson of Solomon and Thompson, maintained a watching brief for Gold Fields and in due course he reported to the company that 'nothing of importance has been adduced against the company; nor does there seem to be any desire on the part of the Prosecution (as far as I have heard) to implicate the company *qua* company'. Davies had placed £5 000 at the disposal of the Johannesburg office to help with expenses to do with the trial and later Johannesburg sold surplus stores to raise money to help pay the Reformers' fines. Further funds were made available so that the offices, and a damaged stairway, which had suffered during the time they were occupied by the Reform Committee, could be done up.

Hammond ceased to work for Gold Fields on the Rand. The luck which had saved him from the gallows was not yet exhausted. He had booked passages to England in the *Drummond Castle* for himself and his family but cancelled them when he found he needed a little extra time in Johannesburg to clear his desk for his successor there, H H Webb. The ship sailed without him and sank off Ushant with very few survivors. In due course when Hammond reached London he re-negotiated his contract with Gold Fields and became the head consulting en-

Op het Hoog Gerechts Hof van den Z A Republiek

Aan den Cipier of Opsichter van de Gevangenis voor het

District

Pretoria

N ADEMAAL de hieronder genoemde gevangenen op dezen dag respectievelijk en behoorlijk voor dit Hof veroordeeld zijn wegens de misdrijven hieronder gemeld, en wegens genoemde misdrijven door genoemd Hof veroordeeld zijn om de afzonderlijke straffen te ondergaan respectievelijk achter hunne namen geplaatst; zoo dient deze om u te gelasten, in naam van het Gouvernement der Zuid-Afrikaansche Republiek, de genoemde verschillende gevangenen in uwe bewaring te ontvangen en hen daar veilig te houden totdat zij de gezegde straffen zullen hebben ondergaan of anderszins daarvan op wettige wijze zullen ontslagen zijn.

Namen der gevangenen.	Vonnis.	Wegens welk misdrijf gevonnist.
1) Lionel Phillips	Doodvonnis	Hoog verraad
2) George Farrar	Doodvonnis	Hoog verraad
3) Francis Rhodes	Doodvonnis	Hoog verraad
4) John Hays Hammond	Doodvonnis	Hoog verraad

Gegeven onder mijne hand te Pretoria

dezen 28ste dag van April 1896.

Getuige:—

van den gezegden

Griffier van het Hof

Charles Sheldon's impression of the courtroom scene in Pretoria at the trial.

gineer at 8 Old Jewry with responsibilities world-wide.

In London, the departure of Ernest Rhodes, at the insistence of Charles Rudd, left a vacancy on the board and the company looked around for a suitable replacement. In the current difficult circumstances it was important to find someone, perhaps a public figure with an established reputation whose presence on the board would guarantee the status of the company in the eyes of the world. They chose a man who combined a number of qualities that made him an admirable choice in British eyes. Above all, he had captained England at cricket and was now the President of the MCC. He had been Governor of Bombay and been a junior minister in various Tory Governments, serving at the War Office and the India Office. He was a man with all the forcefulness of the Victorian autocrat that he was and perfectly fitted the thundering great title that he had inherited – he was the fourth Baron Harris of Seringapatam, of Mysore and of Bevoir in the County of Kent. In 1896, in becoming a director and vice-chairman, Lord Harris, as a former captain of England, began a distinguished innings at Gold Fields which was to last for thirty-three years. In choosing Harris as vice-chairman, Davies had already his own successor in mind. Harris was not a figure entirely from the outside. In fact, he had connections with some of the discredited figures involved in the Jameson Raid. Colonel Frank Rhodes had been his military secretary when he was Governor of Bombay and Dr Rutherfoord Harris, Secretary of the Chartered Company, who had made a considerable contribution to the botching of the Jameson Raid, was his cousin. He had also known Cecil Rhodes since the 1880s.

As President of the MCC, he had seen the England side led by his friend and fellow peer, Lord Hawke, arrive in South Africa just as the troubles started. Sir Frederic Hamilton recorded how, as Editor of *The Star*, he was present with Rhodes at Groote Schuur soon after the news had come that Jameson was riding towards Johannesburg, and Rhodes had said to him: 'I have invited Hawke and the English cricketers to lunch and they will be here in half-an-hour. God knows what I can say to them with this on my mind!' Lord Hawke had been advised by Abe Bailey, as President of the Wanderers, to come on to Johannesburg – the game of cricket had priority over revolutions and that kind of thing – but when the cricketers arrived at Park Station, Bailey was not there to meet them; he was in Pretoria Gaol. The match went on and the South African batsman Tom Routledge dispatched the bowling of the MCC to all corners of the Wanderers.

One of the first tasks that Lord Harris undertook for Gold Fields was to sign a letter to President Kruger in the hope that it might clear the Transvaal air a little and improve the atmosphere of the place in which the company had its operations, South Africa. On 24 August 1896 Major Sapte in Johannesburg wrote a note to the State Secretary, Dr W J Leyds, asking for an appointment as, he said, he had an important communication to bring him. It was the Gold Fields letter, in the composing of which Charles Rudd had had a hand.

'The first intimation which the Board had of the events in question', the State President read, 'was derived from telegraphic intelligence published in the English newspapers. The Board neither countenanced, authorized nor approved any of the proceedings which can be regarded as inimical to the peace of the Republic.' The Board, Kruger read on, did not know the Reform Committee was using its offices. It had published statements in the London newspapers to that effect. 'As soon as it came to the knowledge of the Board that sums of money amounting to about £70 000 had been contributed out of the company's funds towards the expenses of the political movement (which contributions were unauthorized) repayment of the sums so advanced was immediately demanded and obtained. The books of the company will bear out this statement.' Lord Harris finally expressed the hope to the State President that 'friendly relations between the Government of the South African Republic and the Board of the Consolidated Gold Fields of South Africa Limited will continue to exist to the benefit of the Transvaal Government and the company's shareholders'.

Whether Kruger felt better disposed towards Gold Fields as a result of this letter is not known. For him it was probably still Rhodes's company and an idea of what he thought about that may be gained from the experience of an Afrikaner who joined Gold Fields in Johannesburg and gave it more than thirty years of loyal service. His name was W S Smits and in order to join Gold Fields in 1896,

Willem Sebastian Smits, for many years Gold Fields property expert. Kruger boxed his young Boer ears for joining 'Rhodes's company' in 1896. As a Transvaal burgher on commando he had reluctantly to go to war with his chairman, Lord Harris, assistant Adjutant-General of the Imperial Yeomanry. After the war he helped develop the Gold Fields townships of Dunkeld and Illovo, and in the 1930s assembled the farming properties that came to make up the West Wits Line. He had the unusual distinction of having given his name to the road in Dunkeld – Smits Road – where his boss Guy Carleton Jones had his home.

he gave up his post as Assistant Mining Commissioner in Johannesburg. His resignation of this post brought a summons from the State President in Pretoria. Kruger asked him what he meant by deserting the service of the Republic for that of Mr Rhodes. Young Willem Smits said he wanted to better himself. Kruger berated him furiously for some minutes then ended up by giving him a friendly box on the ears. Since Kruger's strength was such that he was capable of holding down a wounded buffalo by his horns, Smits departed with stinging ears, he recounted later, and the hope that in going to Gold Fields he would find a gentler master.

Throughout 1896 in the wake of the events with which the year had started, Gold Fields had to struggle with problems; apart from the question of re-establishing relations with the Government of the Republic where it operated, it was having to cope with the economic consequences of the Raid which, having successfully let out the air from Rhodes's ballooning ambitions for the empire, had also deflated the gold share boom very smartly. Gold Fields shareholders who had seen their shares go to over £19 suddenly found they were worth little more than £7. Nothing too bad could be said about Rand gold shares that a few months earlier had been the darlings of the market. The bears gave Gold Fields their particular attention and rumours starting in Paris were doing the rounds to the effect that the deep-levels policy to which the company was committed had been a gross error because the sums needed to bring the mines to production would be enormous. Gold Fields, however, determined to maintain its optimism and having made a profit of £1 million declared a dividend at the same level as the previous year, despite the financial storms that were blowing up, a fact which caused some to feel that the hand-out had been rash.

The collapse of the boom had left the company not only with problems in its finances, but in its operations as well. Davies had made money for the company with his dealings in shares and in properties; this together with money raised by fresh issues of capital financed the buying and developing of new properties. The deep-level properties had issued enough capital to enable them to get shafts to the reef; after that they hoped to pay for equipment with the issue of the reserve shares. In November 1895 Simmer and Jack had established a world record in sinking an incline shaft 127 feet during the month. But Rudd was warning Johannesburg against trying to get a mine such as Simmer to produce before it had been really developed – it would be more expensive in the long run. 'Do not dream of starting in a small way, keep the lesson of Village and its forty stamp mill before you and do not sanction any start until the property is thoroughly developed and capable of beginning and going on with the full complement of stamps.' And he was to remind those conducting operations: 'Every shilling a day saved in our Simmer and Jack big mill represents £25 000 a year.' It required courage to give such advice at a time when Gold Fields, out of the outcrops which were the dividend payers, had only deep-levels, which were not yet producers and which needed more capital from the shareholders to enable them to become so. Simmer and Jack alone needed £350 000. Gold Fields' financial position early in 1897 looked desperate and ugly stories were doing the rounds that the company was in debt to the banks and would not last another six months. None of this was true and at a special meeting in May, Lord Harris in the chair because Davies was ill, put the record straight in a forthright way. Charles Rudd defended his personal position with his usual skill. He told them frankly his own private fortune was involved in Gold Fields. 'I therefore stand here today as one of yourselves – up to the neck.' Rudd declared his optimism in the Rand – it would produce £1 000 million worth of gold; there was work for another fifty years. These prophecies like most of those made by Rudd at the

annual general meetings in the early days, were to come true. The shareholders rallied round and put up more capital. The share market took heart from such a brave show of confidence at Gold Fields and prices began to go up again. But then 1897 was rather a special year in London and a deflated share-market would not have been appropriate for the occasion.

Queen Victoria was about to celebrate her Diamond Jubilee amid scenes of the greatest emotion and fervour. In the decade that had gone by since her Golden Jubilee, which was also the first ten years in the life of The Gold Fields of South Africa, the British had really come to appreciate the significance of their Empire 'on which the sun never set'. On 22 June 1897, the Queen's subjects, giddy with patriotic excitement, flocked to London from countryside and suburb to celebrate her Diamond Jubilee. Throughout the night the railways poured a jubilant throng into the capital, while thousands more tramped in from outlying districts to line the richly decorated procession route. Avid schoolboys and frail survivors of the Charge of the Light Brigade in the Crimean War in 1854, cockney costers, London Bobbies – all prepared by their presence to offer Victoria proof of their allegiance. Lord Harris was not in his office at Gold Fields that day. He had a special part to play in the procession as the Queen's standard-bearer. As vice-chairman of Gold Fields, he might have taken a special interest in one of the crowned heads of Europe who was there with him. This was Victoria's grandson, Kaiser Wilhelm II, who had sent President Kruger a telegram of congratulations on having subdued Dr Jameson and the raiders. This had caused the eclipse, temporarily, of the man who, more than any other had personified the great British imperial sweep of the 1890s: Cecil Rhodes, co-founder of Lord Harris's company.

The financial difficulties which Gold Fields had experienced after the Jameson affair also affected its relations with other mining houses, notably Rand Mines. The relationship between the Corner House and Gold Fields had taken a knock over Rhodes's recklessness which had involved both Phillips and Beit and had cost a lot of money, leaving Julius Wernher wringing his hands, since he thoroughly disapproved of the way his company had become involved. Now, when Gold Fields, because of financial problems, withdrew from an undertaking given earlier to provide funds for mines in which the two houses had joint interests, Wernher was angry. 'There is no thought of our *financing* the Gold Fields', he wrote. 'They will have to pay heavily for any help they get…we shall not forget their conduct, you may be sure.' At the same time, if Gold Fields were in trouble, the astute Wernher was not averse to picking up anything that might drop from the Gold Fields table. 'The Gold Fields Company alone will offer food enough for all the hungry not to speak of others of course.' A few months later, after Gold Fields had increased its capital once again, Wernher wrote: 'The Gold Fields will get their new money but it will not last long and in six months they will be in a worse fix and may have to realise assets at what they fetch – we shall not forget their conduct.'

Wernher's wishful pessimism was not to be realized. Gold Fields once more hung on by the skin of its teeth until solid progress with development began to be made. Robinson Deep, soon to become with Simmer and Jack a main source of income for Gold Fields, had hit rich ore with its shafts and, to raise money for equipment, had issued debentures. Rudd himself set an example and took up £50 000 worth for his own account. By March 1899 Robinson Deep was showing an annual profit of £142 000, crushing with 100 stamps soon to be increased to 200. Simmer and Jack, crushing with 280 stamps, was coming along with a monthly profit of £30 000 and there were others on the way, all of them providing evidence that Gold Fields was completing the transition from a speculative to a development orientated company, one that would provide rich dividends for its shareholders from the profitable production of its mining subsidiaries. For companies like Gold Fields and the Corner House poised as they were late in 1899 to carry the South African gold mining industry confidently into the Twentieth Century, the outbreak of war in South Africa could not have come at a worse time.

The Kruger Government in Pretoria had sent an ultimatum to the British Government in London requiring that a satisfactory answer to the demands it contained should be received before or upon Wednesday, 11 October 1899, not later than five o'clock in the afternoon. If no such satisfactory answer was forthcoming, Pretoria would regard the action of Her Majesty's Government as a formal declaration of war. At ten forty-five on the evening of 10 October Joseph Chamberlain in London cabled Milner, the British High Commissioner in Cape Town, that Britain was unable to accept the Boer demands. Conyngham

Greene, the British Agent in Pretoria, was instructed to ask for his passport, and Britain and the South African Republic, to be joined by its sister state, the Orange Free State, were at war.

The ultimatum contained four important demands: the settlement of the differences between Britain and the South African Republic by a friendly course of arbitration; the instant withdrawal of British troops on the Republican frontier; the removal, within a reasonable time, of all military reinforcements that had arrived in South Africa since 1 June 1899; and that Her Majesty's troops at present on the high seas should not be landed at South African ports.

These demands unsatisfied, on 11 October Boer commandos crossed over from the Transvaal to invade Natal and before long were besieging the British forces in Ladysmith, including Colonel Frank Rhodes and Dr Jameson. They also struck westwards and did the same at Kimberley where Cecil Rhodes himself was trapped in the siege. Mafeking was also surrounded. Gold Fields, a British controlled mining house in the South African Republic, was also caught in the middle. Mining operations on the Rand closed down. Sapte had already returned to London. Birkenruth removed himself to Cape Town and advised his Hanover Square tailor in London, who was making a new suit for him, that if war broke out he should send it to a different address. His colleague F M Watson was left in Johannesburg to keep an eye on things as long as it was possible. Watson's messages to Birkenruth at this time reflect the excitement and the tensions in Johannesburg as the Anglo–Boer War began. W S Smits, being an Afrikaner and a burgher of the Transvaal, would soon be at war with his own chairman, since Lord Harris assumed the post of Assistant Adjutant-General of the Imperial Yeomanry. 'Smits has had orders to hold himself in readiness', Watson informed Birkenruth 'and I think that after a little while he will not be around the Gold Fields much. He has had to buy a horse this morning.' The Gold Fields horses had been commandeered by the Boers but Watson had managed to get his own away safely to the Cape. Uitlanders who were British subjects were getting out as quickly as they could; others who were not were taking their time and some even went off to fight for the Boers. Among these was an assayer on Rand Mines, an Irish nationalist named John McBride[1], who put together an Irish Brigade to fight the British. 'We don't know exactly where we stand here', Watson complained to Birkenruth, 'this beloved Government issues one thing today and another thing tomorrow. One day it is said they will rush us all out of the country and the latest this morning is that all British subjects must get a permit to remain in the country.' Watson decided it was time to go and locked up the office. There was no more activity on the mines; the pumps were not working and the shafts were flooded. The black miners had returned to their tribal homes.

What was remarkable when the war was over was the relative ease with which the mines and the mining companies were able to resume where they had left off. Managers returned to their offices to find the cash and documents just as they had left them. And most of the mining companies in their first reports after the

war paid tribute to the discipline and honesty of the men of the commandos who might easily have looted the offices and wrecked the mines. Special credit was due to such Boer leaders as General Louis Botha, who sensibly resisted the urgings of hotheads among the Boers who wished to destroy the mines, which they saw as the source of their troubles. The young and mentally deranged Judge Kock, following the death of his father, General Kock in the battle of Elandsfontein in Natal, assumed the title of General himself and, with 100 men, rode to Johannesburg determined to wreck the mines and destroy 'Rhodes's building', the offices of Gold Fields. By a clever ruse, the Boer military governor of the town, F E T Krause, himself later to become a judge, succeeded in separating Kock from his men, arrested him and then sent his men on a wild goose chase to the Geldenhuis mine. In June 1900 Krause had the dismal duty of surrendering his town to Lord Roberts who then went on to raise the Union Jack over the Boer capital, Pretoria. Kruger departed for Europe and the Boers went over to guerrilla warfare, remaining in the field until May 1902. In 1901 the mining companies were required by General Lord Kitchener to provide mine guards at their properties. Some 1 500 men were required and Gold Fields had to make a contribution of £17 500 towards the costs of these special arrangements. Mines on the East Rand were considered to be particularly vulnerable and Gold Fields succeeded in getting some powerful naval searchlights from Simonstown which

73

were mounted at Nigel Deep, the Jupiter Mine and at Simmer and Jack East, where one exceptionally powerful light was rigged up at the top of the 100 foot high Louise shaft headgear.

Gradually mining operations were started again, despite numerous difficulties and in particular the shortage of African labour. The black miners who had gone home while the white men fought their war seemed in no great hurry to come back. By March 1902 Robinson Deep and Simmer and Jack were crushing again and Gold Fields was back in business but things were slow; Rand production in 1902 was only half that of 1899.

Changes meanwhile were going on at Gold Fields. Birkenruth had gone back to London and joined Sapte, his old colleague from Johannesburg. Sapte's main achievement on the Rand had been the building of the Main Reef Road from Roodepoort in the west to Boksburg in the east, some forty-five kilometres. While manager of Gold Fields in Johannesburg, he had been appointed chairman of the Witwatersrand Road Trust, a joint stock company set up in December 1896 to lay and control what was first called the Witwatersrand Road. He had to overcome the opposition of the Volksraad to the road. His Gold Fields connection – it was less than a year since the Jameson Raid – could hardly have endeared him to the Boers. However, by July 1897, having spent some £12 000 on the road, he persuaded some members of the Volksraad to drive along it. They were won over. The Main Reef Road turned out to be one of the major improvements on the Rand in the early days and continues to be an important highway.

Sapte had become Joint Secretary in London with Prinsep. Birkenruth, on the other hand, joined the board which was the first time that Gold Fields had a man with South African experience as a director in London other than the founders. A new team was assembling at 8 Old Jewry. Several familiar faces were no longer there. Herbert Davies had died in July 1899 and been succeeded by Lord Harris as chairman. Another warrior from the past, Sir Richard Pollock, who had helped to put down the Indian Mutiny, had died, so had W M Farmer. Of the original board Sir Leigh Hoskyns and J J Hamilton were still there. At Rhodes's insistence Rochfort Maguire, whose formidable intellect had won him a fellowship at that intellectual Olympus, All Souls College, Oxford, and who had gone with Rudd to see Lobengula, joined the board.

Oxford had a very important place in Rhodes's own life; it was natural that he should press Gold Fields to have an Oxford luminary on its board. 'Have you ever thought', he once said to Bishop Alexander, 'how it is that Oxford men figure so largely in all departments of public life? The Oxford system in its most finished form looks very unpractical yet wherever you turn your eye – except in science – an Oxford man is at the top of the tree.' Rhodes, in committing his fortune to the creation of the Rhodes Scholarships, helped to keep it that way and in due course South Africans who went to Oxford with these scholarships came also to the top of the Gold Fields tree, one of them presiding over Gold Fields of South Africa in its centenary year.

Although as business partners Rhodes and Rudd had drifted apart in the years

74

following the Jameson Raid, yet they continued to be in touch as fellow directors of Gold Fields and as friends. Rhodes still had something to say about company matters. In 1897 he was writing about Turffontein Estates: 'If we succeed in getting a tramway and business matters improve on the Rand, I have no doubt the revenue will reach £19 000.' In the same year he tells his secretary, Lewis Michell, about his holding of Rietfontein shares – 'another 17 500 represented by the sale of stores for the revolution and which I paid for'. Gold Fields were holding the shares as well as another 17 500 'in my favour'. And he writes to Davies urging Gold Fields activity in the North. 'I fully understand your chief interests are Johannesburg but the North should not be entirely neglected and a company in which you would put your interests would be the right solution. As I take such an interest in the North you would find me personally devoting my judgement to it and after my lifelong experience I think that is worth something.' In 1901 Gold Fields grouped its Rhodesian interests into the Consolidated Exploration and Development (Rhodesia) Company. In September 1900, Rudd wrote to Rhodes: 'You and I believe in nothing that we do not see something of ourselves.' Rudd was writing in particular about the administration of their affairs in Rhodesia but he was really expressing the basic philosophy that had guided them in the creation of Gold Fields of South Africa as 'a personal company'. Their letters were always formal as was the custom of those times. Always 'Dear Rhodes' and 'Very sincerely yours, C D Rudd'. But from time to time there was a glimmer of humanity, almost of intimacy that throws a little light on a long and unusual friendship. Rudd had begun to worry about Rhodes's health. 'I hope you are keeping strong and have got rid of the rheumatic pains – better up country than near the coast.' And Rhodes, the bachelor, had helped Rudd with family affairs, finding a place on the De Beers board for his son Percy who was to occupy it for fifty-nine years, and even, surprisingly, to provide some help with a love affair. 'I have taken a good deal of trouble. Women's pride is a funny thing but it is alright. The nuisance is she has always been in love with your boy but it may make a happy life for two people.'

Rhodes's time was running out. For much of 1901 he was in Britain with Jameson. In August he went to Scotland and met Winston Churchill who, as a war correspondent, had been captured by Louis Botha but, escaping from his Pretoria prison, had eventually reached Cape Town via Lourenço Marques and Durban, and had stayed at Groote Schuur. He wrote to Rhodes: 'I was sorry not to have seen you in South Africa but the Boers interfered with most people's arrangements.' In January 1902 Rhodes made up his mind to return to South Africa in order to be present at the trial of a Polish woman, Princess Radziwell, on a charge of forging letters concerning himself. Jameson thought a Cape summer would kill Rhodes and as his physician advised him not to go. But it was no use. 'Rhodes insists on going at all risks', Jameson said. Two months later he was dead.

The year 1902 saw not only the end of the Anglo-Boer War and the start of a new chapter in South Africa's history; it saw also the end of the Rhodes-Rudd era at Gold Fields and a new turn in the story of the company. Cecil Rhodes died in his cottage at St James on 26 March 1902 and was buried in the Matopo Hills of Rhodesia; at the Gold Fields annual meeting Rudd paid a moving tribute to his old partner. Soon he was mourning another death, that of his brother Thomas Rudd, and before the year was out he had announced his own retirement from the company he and Rhodes had founded fifteen years earlier, under Thomas Rudd's chairmanship. Charles Rudd went off to live on his estate in Scotland and died in 1916; over the years, though he was no longer at Gold Fields, he not only maintained a lively interest in its affairs but discussed these, often critically, in letters to Harris, Birkenruth and Sapte. In January 1916, shortly before his death, Birkenruth was seeking his advice on a problem to do with Simmer Deep debentures. For Rudd, perhaps, the personal company had never ceased to exist. 'Your company', Rhodes had called it in talking to him about Gold Fields. And so it might have seemed right till the end.

[1] He was shot by a British firing squad in Dublin in 1916 after the Easter Rising of that year.

CHAPTER FOUR

The Crucible
1902 – 1924

By the time peace had returned to South Africa with the Treaty of Vereeniging on 31 May 1902, the mines were already trying to catch up on the lost production of two idle years. Crushing had started early in 1902 and by September of that year forty-one mines were operating. At the end of the following year 276 000 ounces of gold had been produced by sixty-two mines. Gold Fields was relying on its main producers, Robinson Deep and Simmer and Jack; Knights Deep, which had been scheduled to start operating in June 1900, was producing in 1903, and in November that year Edward Birkenruth told shareholders that they were hoping to receive an income of £400 000 a year from these mines. The previous year the shareholders had received a dividend of twenty-five percent and Gold Fields appeared to be moving ahead confidently into the new post-war era. Rudd in his final speech to them in 1902 had spoken about Gold Fields profits: 'These profits were made by buying cheaply or marking out deep-level areas which were afterwards capitalized and now form our subsidiary companies and why should not a vast amount of money still be made in the Transvaal in the same way?'

In the decade that followed, from 1903 until 1913, two of these subsidiaries, Robinson Deep and Simmer and Jack provided £982 000 in dividends on an issued capital of £4 million; and after 1907 Knights Deep, having overcome some early water problems, became equally profitable, though in the end it was to run out of luck before it ran out of ore. These were the winners in the Gold Fields stable; most of the others never got beyond the starting line; in that same decade Sub Nigel on the East Rand, which was to find greatness much later, together with the Jupiter and Simmer Deep on the Central Rand, produced dividends to the value of £145 000 and by 1913 they had a combined capital of £3 300 000. Gold Fields' problem was that it had too much on its fork at the same time. In the booming mid-1890s under Hammond's influence, it had created too many subsidiaries, and in 1906 it had to pass its dividends in order to support them financially. A more efficient way to manage these would have to be found. The solution was amalgamation and several mining houses began to reorganize their properties in this way. Gold Fields formed Simmer Deep by combining some 1 000 claims on South Rose Deep, South Geldenhuis, Rand Victoria and Rand Victoria East. Gold Fields, like the other mining houses with deep-levels, was

beginning to understand that the best way to run these was to have a large plant and a large area for extensive development, where poor areas could be offset by good. Simmer Deep was an early result of this thinking. Similarly, Jupiter absorbed Simmer and Jack West and in this way both these made their modest contribution to Gold Fields profits. But these were difficult times on the Rand for the mining houses, not least for Gold Fields which described 1906 as 'the worst year this industry has ever had'.

There was an acute shortage of black mine labour and of new capital as well as political uncertainties in the new British colony of the Transvaal. In the mines, yields declined at depth and so many of Gold Fields' properties turned out to be low-grade with ore values averaging a little above 5 dwt to the ton. These were testing times for the mine technicians; they now had tube mills for grinding the ore and down below a new type of light drill to dig it out. Management, too, was becoming sharper and it says much for the skill and ingenuity of both that

78

Gold Fields was able to get its cost-per-ton figure down to the lowest average on the Rand. In a very hard school, often with inferior properties, the company was learning efficiency as a recipe for survival. In London a cautious financial policy was being followed despite the criticism that dividends were being withheld and that too much was going to reserve – at one stage this reached £2 million, but the board was right in its caution and its prudence allowed it to get through the difficult years that led up to the First World War.

The company missed paying a dividend in 1903 and again in 1906 but otherwise there was always something for those who had backed their faith in the Rand with their money. In the historic year of 1910 which saw the biggest amalgamation of all, that of the four British colonies of South Africa, to form the Union of South Africa as a dominion under the Crown, they received a celebratory thirty-five percent for the second year running. London, from which Gold Fields was controlled, was still the principal centre for raising finance for new mining ventures and the largest amount of all was raised there for the South African mining industry. In that historic year of 1910 the overseas investment, still largely British, in the South African mines was equivalent in value to the entire steel industry of the United States, and in 1913 South Africa was providing nearly forty percent of the world's gold, worth more than £93 million. Such

Robert Fricker, joint manager with Chaplin at Gold Fields after the Anglo-Boer War. As a Reformer he had been gaoled in Pretoria following the Jameson Raid. The two managers were never at cross purposes, as this Johannesburg signpost might suggest.

79

progress as this had been achieved in the most difficult circumstances, both economic and political. The contribution made by Gold Fields had much to do with the three men who directed its affairs in Johannesburg during those years that linked one conflict, the Anglo-Boer War, to the next, the Great War.

Early in 1896, just as the Reformers, having paid their fines, were leaving the Pretoria Gaol, a young man not yet thirty arrived in Johannesburg with his wife. He had come to South Africa with a vague idea of going on to Rhodesia in search of his fortune, but arriving on the Rand he decided to take a three-month temporary job at Gold Fields. His name was Drummond Chaplin. Like Charles Rudd and Rhodes's father he had been to school at Harrow, from where he had gone on to Oxford and made a name as a cricketer. He was also a barrister and, with his social background, he was sure to know the best people everywhere and to have the right introductions. He was destined to leave his mark on Gold Fields, for having caught the eye of the Transvaal Governor, Lord Milner, directing the reconstruction of the former Boer republic from *Sunnyside* in Johannesburg's northern suburbs, he would soon be caught up in its politics and inevitably Gold Fields would follow after. However, it did not happen at once. When his three-month stint at Gold Fields was over, he did some legal work for a while until meeting Francis Younghusband of *The Times* who persuaded him to join that London newspaper and go to Russia as its correspondent.

In April 1901, however, Chaplin was back in Johannesburg. Dr Jameson once said with his customary flair for confusing imagination with truth that it was Rhodes himself, who had met Chaplin in Kimberley, who had selected him for a career in Gold Fields. However it was Edward Birkenruth, whose house in Johannesburg the Chaplins had occupied, who approached Chaplin in London and asked him if he would care to go back to the Rand. Birkenruth told him that he could combine his duties at Gold Fields with his work for *The Times*. Chaplin did not think the two jobs were compatible and chose Gold Fields. He was appointed joint manager at £2 000 a year. 'It is rather difficult to know what to do', he had written to his mother. 'On the one hand I am not particularly anxious to go back to Johannesburg and though the salary is a good one to begin with, we should not be rich bearing the prices and the place in mind, the chief attraction is of course the possibility of it leading to a very good income.'

Chaplin's fellow manager and his senior was Robert Fricker, the mining engineer from Mitcham in Surrey and one of the gaoled Reformers. Although very different from each other, Chaplin with his quick intelligence and Fricker with his technical knowledge combined to make an efficient office. In due course Chaplin welcomed a fellow cricketer to the staff when Douglas Christopherson arrived. The seventh son in a family of ten boys he was a member of the most remarkable cricketing family of those times. Under the captaincy of their father, Derman Christopherson, the family fielded an entire team. They were friends and neighbours in Kent of the president of the MCC; since he was also chairman of Consolidated Gold Fields, Lord Harris had soon persuaded at least two of the cricketers to join the company. Stanley Christopherson, who had played for

England in 1884, gave up stockbroking to join the Gold Fields board. Douglas, having taken part in suppressing the Matabele rebellion, joined Gold Fields in Johannesburg. Here, in due course, he was to take charge for fifteen years, finally returning to London to take a seat on the board next to his brother.

In 1895, it had been Rhodes's personal recklessness that had pitched Gold Fields, a mining finance house, into Transvaal politics. After the Anglo-Boer War during the period known as the Reconstruction, leading up to Responsible Government in 1907, all the mining houses, through the Chamber of Mines, became part of the power structure, political, economic, social that was determining the future of South Africa. Because of its overwhelming position as a creator of wealth, the mining industry and its leaders on the Rand were bound to have a major say in the taking of decisions. Without their financial resources no attempt to reconstruct the Transvaal after the devastation of war could have succeeded. Milner was determined from the start that the mining houses were going to play a leading role in helping him to implement his political policies. He had his own chosen lieutenants who came to be known as the Milner Kindergarten, young men from Oxford and Cambridge, but he soon picked out the 'rather exceptional Chaplin' and saw in him someone who might play an outstanding role. He nominated him a member of the Town Council saying it would be 'a splendid political training for him'. When the Colonial Secretary, Joseph Chamberlain, arrived on the Rand to take a look at the situation for himself, Milner placed Chaplin next to him at dinner. As a result Chamberlain was taken to see the Robinson Deep mine; through Chaplin Gold Fields was becoming prominent in the public eye. The young American who was Mrs Chamberlain was taken to see how the Gold Fields mineworkers lived, Mrs Chaplin telling a friend somewhat mockingly that a top storey had been hurriedly added to one of the houses 'and is therefore now worthy of receiving so distinguished a guest'. Chamberlain wanted the mines to guarantee the first £10 million of a £30 million loan that was needed to get the Transvaal on its feet. Gold Fields put itself down for £1 million. 'As we have a reserve fund of a million Consols we shall simply change it into this loan, which will be at four percent – it will be very good business for us', Chaplin told his mother, probably unaware that a member of the Colonial Secretary's family, his brother Arthur Chamberlain, had owned more than 900 Gold Fields shares.

Following Chamberlain's visit, Chaplin, who had a prominent part in it, was approached by George Farrar who wanted Chaplin to succeed him as President of the Chamber of Mines, a position which, according to Chaplin himself, was 'the most conspicuous position outside the Government in the Transvaal'. Beit, too, pressed the young Gold Fields manager to accept but Chaplin hesitated because he did not wish Fricker, who had been Deputy-President in 1902, to be offended by a signal honour for a junior colleague. In 1905, with Fricker's explicit agreement, Chaplin did become the first Gold Fields man to head the Chamber of Mines. He would have done so the previous year had he not gone down with enteric. The Chaplins had already had their home leave in Europe

and when Chaplin in 1904 asked London if he could make another trip overseas, he was told it would have to come out of his leave. Chaplin refused to accept this and got his way, as he was now beginning to do in most things. There was no doubt that Chaplin was making his mark in Johannesburg. 'Mr Chaplin has won his laurels everywhere', wrote *Men of our Times* in 1905. Gold Fields profited from this. Chaplin had panache and, in persuading Gold Fields to do things in style, he conferred upon the company a characteristic it has maintained to this day.

Soon Chaplin had persuaded Gold Fields to build him a house; it would be no ordinary house since the distinguished architect Herbert Baker was selected to design and build it. In his own memoirs, Sir Herbert Baker described how he had been travelling by boat to England. Rhodes was on board and so was Birkenruth and Baker sat next to the latter at table. That, he maintained, was how eventually he received the Gold Fields commission to build the house for Chaplin's use. Typically, Chaplin arranged for the Governor, Lord Milner, to lay the foundation stone. He also spent some of his own money to pay for various refinements that made the house Marienhof one of the finest built by Baker in what by now had become the smartest part of Johannesburg, Parktown. Baker was to write: 'The house did truly express the different characters of Drummond and Marguerite Chaplin, he calm, reserved, scholarly, she restless, insatiable, ever asking for the moon.' Later, after Chaplin had left Gold Fields in 1914 to become Administrator of Southern Rhodesia, the house was sold to Ernest Op-

penheimer, who changed its name to Brenthurst, the home of the Oppenheimers ever since.

Everybody who was anybody was entertained by the Chaplins at Marienhof and Gold Fields actually encouraged their hospitable instincts, in the belief that it was good for business. Colonel Frank Rhodes, back in London in 1901 after his misadventures in South Africa, had gone along to 8 Old Jewry and told the directors that Gold Fields did not compare with its competitors when it came to entertaining and he apparently convinced them that lavish entertainment would do the company nothing but good. Chaplin and Fricker[1] were given special allowances in order to provide it.

Gold Fields had not confined its interest in property to Marienhof. In December 1901 it presented a new property company to the Rand. It had formed the African Land and Investment Company with a capital of £300 000 and £200 000 debentures in the belief that with the war in the Transvaal over, the Rand would go ahead and Johannesburg would expand, land values at the same time increasing with the size of the town. To the north of Johannesburg they acquired large properties, Dunkeld and Illovo and in due course these were laid out as townships where one-acre plots were sold for £136. Progress, however, was slow and the chairman of the company, Robert Fricker, was concerned about paying the interest on the debentures. Gold Fields was prepared to pay it themselves if it were necessary. 'The failure on the part of Gold Fields to protect a debenture of this sort so recently issued would absolutely spoil our credit for

George Bompas (left) and Edward Melvill, like W S Smits, ran the African Land and Investment Company which laid out Illovo and Dunkeld, today smart northern suburbs of Johannesburg. In 1959, African Land and Investment was given the historic name Gold Fields of South Africa as a vehicle for bringing together all the southern African interests of Gold Fields.

any future operations in the way of obtaining money', he was informed by Stanley Christopherson from London. In the event it was not necessary and Edward Melvill, managing director of the company, was in due course to express an optimism that was to be amply justified. 'There is no doubt that the favourite suburbs are extending towards the north, along the saddle from Parktown towards Rosebank, Dunkeld, Melrose and Illovo. As soon as the electric trams now under consideration are completed in that direction and businessmen be placed in quick and easy communication with Johannesburg, villa residences will spring up and the favourite acre plots, instead of the confined 100 x 50 stands will attract the richer section of the public.' He was quite right. They did, but Melvill did not stay long enough to see it happen. His place was taken by W S Smits, who, having survived commando service against the British Yeomanry of Lord Harris, was back at Gold Fields, his loyalty to the company being specifically praised by Harris in a speech to shareholders in London. Others came to work for the company including George Gwinneth Bompas, who became its secretary. Bompas, like all the others who worked for Gold Fields in the first years of this century, achieved immortality when the company decided to name the highways and byways of Dunkeld and Illovo after its

employees; hence Fricker and Chaplin Roads, Christopherson, Bompas, Melvill and Smits Roads in Dunkeld, and in Illovo, Rudd Road and Harries Road after the company's land surveyor Will Harries. The scores of people who take their cars along these elegant, tree-lined roads on every Johannesburg day, though they may not think of it as they do it, are driving along the avenues of Gold Fields' own South African history.

During 1903 Drummond and Marguerite Chaplin were indulging their sophisticated and civilized tastes on a grand tour of Europe. The faithful Fricker keeps him regularly informed of what goes on at Gold Fields. 'At the office from nine to six every day without a morning off, one stands a chance of getting stale, especially under the worrying and depressing influences now prevailing.' He also tells Chaplin: 'John Grenfell has gone north, turning off first to Phalaborwa to see some old workings.' Fricker, though he could not know it, was in fact announcing what turned out to be an historic journey for Colonel Grenfell, having looked at the ancient diggings at Phalaborwa, went on to discover copper at Messina and to launch a great mining industry there.

Chaplin in Paris received another letter from Fricker with highly significant news about their own affairs at Gold Fields. It concerned the activities of Edward

Pullinger, who with his brother had established a reputation for putting down their boreholes in the right places. Pullinger, Fricker told Chaplin, 'struck what is most probably the Randfontein reef on Gemsboksfontein south of Middelvlei proving his theory that the formation continued its southerly course ... this has sent up Middelvlei to twenty-two shillings here but I think the reef will miss the ground, traversing our two big blocks of ground to the East of the mynpacht.' A week later Fricker writes again: 'I think it is quite probable that our claims on Middelvlei will turn out well after all. As you know, Pullinger struck it very rich in his borehole to the South and judging from the lie of the country the reef should run into our ground leaving the Middelvlei mynpacht to the West.' The excitement was premature – by about thirty years! When Pullinger tried to sink a shaft a few years later, water poured in and drowned his hopes. When in due time Gold Fields came to appreciate the significance of Pullinger's pioneering effort, it preserved the old shaft as an historical curiosity on its Venterspost mine where it arouses the interest of the visitor to this day. A while after Fricker wrote his letter to Chaplin in Paris, Lord Harris was announcing in London a contribution of £1 000 to the Rhodes Memorial that Sir Herbert Baker was designing on the slopes of Table Mountain. 'There is no company in South Africa which should be more appreciative of the services of the late Mr Rhodes to South Africa than this', he said, 'his knowledge of what it was doing, however far away he might be in other affairs, was always extremely clear.' If Harris had had Middelvlei in mind, which he had not, he might also have said 'clairvoyant' for by one of those quirks of history the rather useless property that Rhodes had bought back in 1886 actually marked the area where Gold Fields was destined to make its greatest contribution to mining in South Africa.

In 1905 Drummond Chaplin, having returned from yet another trip overseas, took over the Presidency of the Chamber of Mines in time to cope with the biggest problem in its history, the highly controversial and divisive issue of employing Chinese labour on the mines.

The shortage of unskilled labour was the most pressing problem facing the industry after the Anglo-Boer War. African labourers were not returning to the Rand in sufficient numbers to enable the mines to operate at full strength. While the war was still going on, Gold Fields had foreseen the problems with which they would be faced when the mines started operating again. Lionel Phillips, writing from London to the Corner House, said he had had a meeting with Harris, Birkenruth and Sapte to discuss the labour shortage. 'They are', he said, 'in general in favour of united action.' Birkenruth had told him, in the manner of a Biblical parable: 'If five persons look each for a man, they are more likely to be supplied than if one person looks for five.' Phillips had been told at Gold Fields that they had already by their own exertions secured about 6 000 Africans 'to be brought direct to the mines when the roads are clear'. They would need the first three months to put their own arrangements into operation after which they would be ready to co-operate with other houses in a joint effort. This joint effort was to lead to the creation of the Witwatersrand Native Labour Association. A great effort was made by the mining houses to tackle together the problems that were common to each of them. Even J B Robinson, then living in London in the splendour of his Park Lane mansion, Dudley House, had a meeting with Lord Harris who felt encouraged by this further evidence of unity in the industry.

If the mines on the Rand failed because of a lack of sufficient men to run them, then South Africa itself could have no future. The Imperial Government therefore sanctioned the importation of 50 000 Chinese, recruited mainly in North China. In the limited time they spent on the Rand they were able to save the industry. Lord Harris had tried to persuade Chamberlain to allow the importation of Indian labour for the mines but this had been refused. He and Gold Fields then became among the loudest champions of Chinese labour; as *The Star* had reported, before Chamberlain's visit to the Rand, only Fricker among the mining leaders was calling publicly for Chinese labour; after the visit all the mining leaders, except FitzPatrick, were calling for it, although most of them would probably have agreed with the sentiments of George Farrar, who, in his presidential address to the Chamber in 1904, had said: 'No one regrets more than I do that it is necessary to go outside the continent of Africa for our labour supply.' The mining houses, however, seemed to be the only people who wanted the Chinese. They were already becoming a political football both in Britain and in the Transvaal, in both of which elections were about to take place. In Britain the Liberals came to power in the 1906 general election which had seen demonstrations in Hyde Park against what the placards called 'Chinese Slavery in South Africa'. In the Transvaal, Responsible Government was about to be granted to the colony and the Afrikaners, represented by the *Het Volk* party of Generals Botha and Smuts, were as opposed to Chinese labour as was the Liberal Party in Britain; each determined to send the Chinese home though for different reasons.

Botha and Smuts looked like being in opposition to the mining leaders who put up candidates for their own Progressive Party, which aimed to prevent the Boers from regaining at the polls what they had lost in the war. Chaplin was in the forefront; he liked Botha, who used to come and play tennis at Marienhof but Chaplin distrusted his charm and feared for the mining industry if he were to become the first Prime Minister which he assuredly did. Lionel Phillips at the Corner House was as politically ambitious as Chaplin, but in London Sir Julius Wernher and the Board of Wernher, Beit, remembering the Jameson Raid, prevented their man in Johannesburg from standing for the Transvaal Parliament. Chaplin, on the other hand, became the member for Germiston. In his own chairman, Lord Harris, he had another politician. 'I do not know that I would not have been a Cabinet Minister if I had not come to Gold Fields,' he once told his shareholders. Unlike Wernher, Harris threw himself wholeheartedly into the politics of the Transvaal, where at the beginning of 1904 he himself, together with his wife and fourteen-year-old son, George[2], arrived in Johannesburg on a four-month stay. With a seat in the House of Lords, he was a member of the British Parliament and before long he was using his powerful and influential voice to promote the cause of Chinese labour.

87

Chinese miners in their compound, Simmer and Jack, circa 1904.

Interviewed by the journal, *South Africa,* he maintained that the introduction of Chinese labour on the Rand would allow the industry to expand and thus offer increased opportunity for white skilled labour, white unemployment being one of Lord Milner's problems. 'There are about 4 000 stamps waiting to be dropped when sufficient labour has been procured,' he told the Press, 'but the introduction of 80 000 Coloured labourers – even if they could be introduced at once – would not mean that all those stamps could all be introduced immediately, but a very large proportion, between 3 000 and 4 000, I should say, could be started and that would make a tremendous difference to the output.' He was right. Within a year of their arrival, the Chinese had doubled the output on the mines. At the end of 1905 some 45 000 Chinese had arrived and Gold Fields had one of the biggest allocations. Together with Rand Mines and Farrar's Anglo-French group, they accounted for 71,5 percent of them, more than 4 000 being employed at Simmer and Jack. Sub Nigel was unable to employ any as it lay outside the area designated for Chinese labour. Birkenruth followed his

88

chairman, Lord Harris, to the Rand and Chaplin took him out to see how the Chinese workers were getting on. He reported to London: 'I went out yesterday to look at one of the mines where they are employed and was immediately impressed with their extraordinary adaptability and the perfect order maintained.'

When he arrived back in London from Johannesburg, Lord Harris was appalled at the lurid and sensational way that the question of Chinese labour was being presented in Britain and he used every occasion that he could to air his own views. At a dinner of the Imperial South Africa Club, presided over by the young Duke of Westminster, who as ADC to Lord Roberts had hoisted the Union Jack over Pretoria, and where the guest of honour was the Colonial Secretary, Alfred Lyttleton, Harris made a forthright speech in defence of Chinese labour on the Rand. He could not understand, he said, why the Cape Colonial Government had misgivings when they themselves had a population – the Cape Malays – who had come originally from the East. When the Colonial Secretary spoke, he offered comforting noises for the mining companies. Nothing, he said, would

Chinese miners at Luipaardsvlei, 1906. More than a third of the imported Chinese worked on Gold Fields mines.

be achieved in South Africa unless the great gold industry could be developed.

Later that year Harris was appealing to Gold Fields shareholders to play their part in the propaganda war, a forerunner of what would happen many, many years later in another labour context. 'Wherever you have the opportunity – and you have many opportunities; there are between 20 000 and 30 000 of you with an average holding of eighty-six ordinary shares – to implore the people of this country to leave the Transvaal to push its great industry on without interruption.' He gave them a glowing account of what he had seen in South Africa. 'I cannot say it is all due to us, but we have had a large part in it. That immense stretch of forty miles of chimneys on the veld, hundreds of miles from where the railhead was when they had begun to be erected, is a very remarkable sight … it is a godsend – the discovery of this gold – to South Africa; it is essential to its welfare.'

Harris had returned to London convinced that Gold Fields should continue to play a political role in the manner of Chaplin and Fricker. 'I think this company must realize,' he said, 'that it cannot divest itself of the responsibility of assisting in the administration of the local and even perhaps of colonial affairs. It will probably mean an increase of the staff in Johannesburg. Time devoted to public duties is time spent away from the office and therefore if office work has got to be done, there may have to be more men to do it.' Two years later shareholders had heard Charles Rudd say, 'Unfortunately Lord Milner whatever his wishes and convictions may be and whatever his personal energies and his knowledge of the country may be, is after all and must be, influenced and more or less controlled by people 6 000 miles away and through them, by party politics and political prejudices.' This, too, was a truth that would become relevant in the affairs of Gold Fields half a century or so later.

Those administering the affairs of Gold Fields, whether in London or in Johannesburg, were airing a new philosophy; in the early days the creation of wealth for the mining houses was the major if not the only motivation for mining operations. Little regard was given to the interests of the host territories where the mines were situated. Mining men had been the civil arm of much of Britain's colonial expansion that had helped to open up the unknown world, but when control from London was diminished and later removed, the mining men had to come to terms with, even become involved with, those who acquired political control where the mines were. This was Chaplin's experience and quite clearly he had in Lord Harris a chairman who would support him in his efforts to influence the political and social climate in which Gold Fields was operating.

Lord Harris had visited South Africa at the beginning of 1904. His influence was wide; he had contacts at the highest levels in British public life, including the Royal Family; he was an ADC to King Edward VII and later that same year he learned with satisfaction of the visit to one of Gold Fields' mines of two members of the King's family, his sister Princess Helena, accompanied by her daughter, Princess Victoria. They had been at Robinson Deep. The daughter and granddaughter of Queen Victoria had come to South Africa on a pilgrimage. Princess

Helena, better known as Princess Christian, had lost a son, Prince Christian Victor, during the Anglo-Boer War. The Prince had died of illness and in November 1900 had been buried in the Pretoria cemetery. When his mother arrived in South Africa she was distressed to learn that two attempts had been made to disturb the grave and remove the Prince's remains. The identity of those responsible was never established; one theory was that as the body of President Kruger was on its way back from Europe for burial in the cemetery, there may have been some who could not accept the idea of President Kruger and Queen Victoria's grandson being buried in the same ground. The two Princesses, having visited Pretoria, then came on to Johannesburg to spend three days with Lord Milner during which they drove out in their carriage to be received at Robinson Deep. Later they went on to Rhodesia to see the grave of Cecil Rhodes, co-founder of the company that owned the mine.

Not long after this Royal visit, Lord Milner started to pack his bags. His term as Governor and High Commissioner during which Chaplin had maintained good relations with him, was ending and in 1905 Lord Selborne arrived to take his place. His particular task would be to try to bring about the unification of Britain's four colonies in South Africa, the Cape, Natal, Transvaal and Orange River Colony, to form the British dominion of the Union of South Africa. Chaplin did not get on with him.

Selborne was very demanding and would go to the mining houses for money for his own projects, claiming that his own treasury was empty. He was asking for money for student hostels. 'Chaplin is very angry with Lord Selborne,' Phillips tells Wernher, 'as he appealed to the Gold Fields and they declined to contribute whereupon he wrote a letter asking whether they had any objection to his approaching the London Directors direct. They of course replied that they had no objections but Chaplin regards it as a great affront that Lord Selborne should go behind them here and has written urging Lord Harris not to contribute.'

Selborne then wanted the mining houses to help him tackle the question of white unemployment which was creating social problems for the administration. Again Phillips to Wernher: 'The Gold Fields have been most refractious, Fricker wrote me a letter saying they were prepared to take their share of the first 400 men at four shillings a day but could not find room for any more. He is a very obstinate man. I explained very carefully to Chaplin and made him realize, I think, that such an attitude is very impolitic. They have now arranged, I believe, to use the share of unemployed they are taking to make a road and will place the ordinary contract price at their disposal.' Gold Fields was also doing its part in providing employment by building more houses and this time Lord Selborne seems to have been impressed, noting: 'I find upon enquiry that during the period Consolidated Gold Fields spent £81 983 upon 186 houses for married men – a further fifty houses being rented on their mines.'

In 1907 Chaplin received a message that, as he told his sister, he was to rush to London for three weeks 'to discuss the labour question while Botha is there'.

Lord Harris, chairman of Consolidated Gold Fields for more than thirty years, as Johannesburg saw him during his stay in 1904. England's cricket captain in the 1870s, later President of the MCC, he always found places at Gold Fields for good cricketers such as the Christophersons. He is even believed to have found a position in the mining house for a Lords groundsman.

General Botha was going to London to attend the Colonial Conference, the Empire get-together that was the forerunner of the Commonwealth Conferences of today. Botha seems to have sensed the anxiety of the mining houses about his own attitudes towards their industry and at a dinner at the Savoy Hotel attended by the South African community in London he assured them that it was untrue that he would oppress them on coming to power. He was as true as his word and the time would come when he would even be accused of being in league with them. However, one thing was quite clear. With a Liberal Government in power in Britain and *Het Volk* controlling the Transvaal, the days of Chinese labour on the mines were numbered. The departure of the Chinese did not proceed as rapidly as was expected, however, and the last of them did not leave until 1910. Their departure did not unduly dislocate the industry. African miners had worked beside them in the stopes and had profited from their example. Birkenruth had noted how well they got on together. Despite the Chinese exodus, the momentum in production was not lost.

Labour problems of a different kind, however, were looming. White workers were organizing, on the mines as in other industries, to protect their rights and advance their interests, not only before the mine-owners, their employers, but in relation to workers who were not white. A noisy 'all white' socialism with strong Australian influences was being preached; Australian ex-Servicemen who had stayed behind after the Anglo-Boer War were said to be playing a part. In a memorandum to the Chamber of Mines in 1905 Lord Selborne referred to 'an increase in Trade Union influence on the Australian model'. Labour as a movement was in the ascendant throughout the Western world in the early years of the century. A great social upheaval had followed the recognition of trade unions in Britain in 1871 and the principle of collective bargaining was no longer challenged there. In South Africa where the majority of the white miners were still immigrants – in 1904 only five percent, for instance, were Afrikaners – it was only to be expected that the new socialist teaching would find a following. In any case miners from Britain arrived to raise a clarion call for trade unionism in the goldmining industry and had helped to create the Transvaal Miners' Association (the TMA) in 1902. The new socialism on reaching the Rand became strongly colour-conscious. The slogan sweeping the world, 'Workers of the World Unite', applied exclusively to white workers when it was proclaimed in South Africa. This became increasingly evident once the white miners started to believe that the mining houses would sacrifice their interests if it suited them, cutting their costs by employing cheaper black labour.

In 1902, H H Webb, who had succeeded Hammond as Gold Fields' consulting engineer in Johannesburg, sent to London a costs analysis which showed clearly how Gold Fields could best effect economies. White salaries amounted to 34,5

Gold Fields took the field for their match against Rand Mines in Johannesburg in 1904 with a very famous cricketer in their side. Captain of England and President of the MCC, Lord Harris, seated centre and wearing a large hat, was also chairman of the company. The Corner House, not to be outdone, had as their captain a member of staff who was a famous Springbok, G A Faulkner, seated fourth from right.

93

percent of costs, black wages and food 24,5 percent, explosives 12 percent, coal 8,6 percent and sundries 20,4 percent. Webb then asked permission to begin training blacks for semi-skilled and responsible work so that they could replace the lowliest white workers 'though we will have to pass through a succession of strikes to reach this point'. To suggest that there might be something wrong with this line of thought, whereby a skilled black miner might be paid less than a skilled white miner with consequent benefit to company profits, would be to impose the moral values of a later age in regard to race that did not exist at this time. But the attitudes of 1902 would produce in due course the 'equal pay for equal work' slogan. Webb was right about the strikes. And the first one of any consequence occurred at a Gold Fields mine, Knights Deep, in 1907.

The mine management had given instructions that in future white miners would have to oversee the work being done by three rock drills instead of the usual two; this meant inevitably the employment of fewer white miners and consequently a reduction in costs at the mine. The miners objected and went on strike and they were supported by their colleagues in other mines. Some 300 of them went to Pretoria expecting a sympathetic reception from General Botha, who was sending the Chinese home, but they got no satisfaction and in due course the strike collapsed. The dislocation of mining activity that it had caused, bringing out 6 400 men, is significant not for economic reasons, though it involved £1 million in wages, but because it highlighted a kind of incipient class warfare on the Rand. The strike leaders determined to build on their experience at Knights Deep in 1907 and as time went on they increased their membership until by November 1911 their journal, *Worker*, was able to write: 'The TMA have scooped in quite a number of new members particularly at the Simmer and

94

Jack. This is particularly gratifying as this mine, owing to the Chaplin influence, has always been a weak link in the labour chain.'

Drummond Chaplin, according to his biographer B K Long, 'got on excellently with his men in his company's mines but always at a certain distance'. Chaplin's patrician instincts would never allow any kind of familiarity or fraternizing with the miners in his employ; George Farrar, on the other hand, would put on a cloth cap and go among them as if he were one of them. One of the leaders of the labour movement who developed a particular hostility towards Chaplin, whom he suspected had interfered with his own plans, was Colonel W A Creswell, who later was to become a Minister of Labour in the Union Government. Creswell's solution to the labour problems on the mines – and as manager at Village Main Reef he had studied it closely – was to employ only white miners, skilled and unskilled. No need for blacks or Chinese. Creswell's scheme was supported by *The Times* in London and for a while he persevered with his experiment at Village Main but it had to be abandoned in the end. It did not make economic sense.

The labour problems simmered on, a worry for Gold Fields as for the other houses, who were particularly concerned about the real grievances of mineworkers about their health and welfare in the highly disagreeable environment in which they had to earn their living. The introduction of rock drills had increased the danger of lung diseases, the dreaded miner's phthisis, and thousands of pounds were spent in trying to alleviate the situation. Medical experts from other countries were imported. Sir Almroth Wright, Surgeon-General Gorgas of Panama and A J Orenstein, one of the great names in mining medicine, appeared on the scene. Within a year the dust content in the air at Simmer and Jack and at Robinson Deep was reduced to one-tenth of its previous level. Nevertheless, it was a terrible reflection on the conditions of mining on the Rand when in 1913, as labour strife broke out once again, a Labour Party pamphlet disclosed that of the seventeen men who had formed the strike committee following the Knights Deep stoppage in 1907, no fewer than twelve had subsequently died of phthisis.

The misfortunes of 1907 were followed by a happier year for Gold Fields, the best since the end of the war. Fricker, who was appointed to take charge of the company's interests in West Africa, left for London where he was able to provide encouraging news from the producing mines. Simmer and Jack turned in profits of more than £683 000; Robinson Deep £467 000, Knights Deep £271 000. Simmer East and Nigel Deep were also producing profits, though Nigel Deep was about to be absorbed by Sub Nigel which itself was preparing to make a modest start with a tube mill and thirty stamps. The attitude shown by the Botha Government in the Transvaal towards labour unrest had restored the confidence of the mining houses, share prices were beginning to rise and despite the departure of the Chinese, output had been maintained and dividends were being paid. During 1908 the National Convention was being held and progress was being made by Lord Selborne towards the goal of union. Busily engaged as Selborne's secretary was Dougal Malcolm, in due course to become a director of Gold Fields and as Sir Dougal Malcolm president of the BSA Company. In South Africa the political and economic barometer looked set fair. Lord Harris, in his speech to shareholders in 1909, seemed almost to be bored with the lack of excitement in the situation or was he looking for a way to present to them as casually and in as matter of fact a way as possible a change in policy?

'I do not think you would be altogether satisfied with the sweet simplicity of a Rand mining share,' he told them, 'mining there has become so prosaic. Mining on the Rand is an absolute certainty. You want a bit of a gamble? Well, we think we can find you that somewhere else in the world.'

Consolidated Gold Fields of South Africa was already changing its investment strategy. 'We are a South African company,' Lord Harris had said once but now he was turning it into an international company, the multi-national corporation of tomorrow. Interests had been acquired in West Africa where Fricker took charge. The company went into North America under the influence of Hammond who had finally returned home permanently to the United States, his place in London being taken by H H Webb. It even became interested in Siberia. Its interests were usually in gold mining – 'what we understand best' as Harris had said – but they included such other industries as electric power production.

Many of these new interests were acquired in 1909 when Harris described the directors' report as 'the best ever offered to shareholders' but it was a report that gave no indication that they anticipated difficulties in the way ahead. But within a year or two gold shares were going out of fashion; in 1911 the Gold Fields share price had fallen from £6 to just over £3; the market seemed to have particular doubts about the company's future, despite its obviously sound financial position, with a reserve of £2 million, but its main income producers, Robinson Deep and Simmer and Jack, had been milling away for fifteen years, and, it was thought, must come to a stop before long. The grade of ore in the Gold Fields subsidiaries was falling, costs were rising, what kind of long-term future could it have in South Africa?

Lord Harris in a frank talk to shareholders had said: 'Some years ago the directors had a somewhat academical but very serious and interesting discussion as to whether Gold Fields was to be a company with a terminable or, so far as mundane things go, was it to have an interminable existence, and we came to the conclusion that what the investing public would expect of such a company as Gold Fields was that it should be interminable but we are a company which habitually invests in properties which have terminable lives.' It seemed in 1911 that Consolidated Gold Fields in London, in order to ensure that it had an interminable life, was looking to a wider world beyond its terminable properties in South Africa. Among those who gained the impression that Gold Fields was losing interest in the Rand was the London office of Wernher, Beit where the able but somewhat arrogant Louis Reyersbach was playing a dominant role after service with the company in South Africa. Early in 1911 he wrote to a colleague in Johannesburg, the equally able Raymond Schumacher who had come a long way since the days of the Reformers' trial when he told the judge that he had acted as Colonel Rhodes's secretary. Reyersbach told Schumacher that Birkenruth was leaving for the Cape on that week's boat and went on to say: 'The Gold Fields appear to be rather pessimistic about the Rand and are not inclined to embark on new ventures there. The profit for their last financial year when analysed is shown to be made almost entirely out of sales of Crown Mines and City Deeps and, in all, their commitments in the Transvaal have decreased by over one and three-quarter millions in three years. From a conversation I had with Webb, he is by no means optimistic as I would have expected about Shamva and does not think the present capitalization is at all justified for anything Rhodesian.' Shamva was one of the properties north of the Limpopo, the Falcon mine was another, that Gold Fields had brought to production and in 1911 the Gold Fields Rhodesian Development Company had been formed to look after these interests, taking the place of the Rhodesian Exploration and Development Company formed a decade earlier at Rhodes's suggestion.

Reyersbach again wrote to Schumacher about Gold Fields' attitude to the Rand as he perceived it. A year had gone by. It was August 1912 and Gold Fields was still parting with shareholdings on the Rand. Reyersbach wrote: 'The Gold Fields this week have been trying to sell City Deeps. After bargaining for several days I have bought from them 20 000 shares ... I propose to apportion 14 000 to the Rand Mines and to keep the remainder for ourselves.' Ourselves was no longer Wernher, Beit. Both these gentlemen were now dead and the company in London changed its name to the Central Mining and Investment Corporation with Sir Lionel Phillips as its senior member. By August 1912 Reyersbach was convinced that Gold Fields was going to quit South Africa. 'Evidently their policy is to gradually clear out of all but a few things which they manage themselves, then to reduce their Johannesburg office considerably and to await an opportunity of disposing of the remainder of their Transvaal assets. So clearly does this policy seem to be laid down that, whenever prices at which they have decided to sell are obtainable they appear openly in the market regardless of consequences and they may therefore for some time to come be rather a disturbing factor unless in one way or another, which I cannot quite make up my mind at present, a combination be formed to buy them out.' Reyersbach may have had good grounds for thinking that Gold Fields was pulling out; whatever may have been in the minds of its directors nothing was committed to paper. There may also have been an element of wishful thinking in Reyersbach's opinion, distorted by the fact that his own company was now wearing Crown Mines as a feather in its cap, an amalgamation of mines on the Central Rand that for decades was the greatest name in South African mining, the largest single gold producer in the world. But Reyersbach had been mistaken. 'A combination be formed to buy them out' – that, some sixty years after he wrote those words in relation to Gold Fields, was to be the fate of his own proud company, Rand Mines. In Somerset Maugham's enduring phrase, 'the dog it was who died', Gold Fields once more clung on, reduced perhaps to a handgrip on the Rand, then with the passage of time building a bridgehead until in another generation it would acquire the richest fields ever known and a mine that would eclipse the Crown Mines. But all this lay in the future.

By 1913 the Union of South Africa had been in existence three years and in that year Sir Herbert Baker, who had built Marienhof for Chaplin, completed his masterpiece, the Union Buildings high up on Meintjeskop in Pretoria as the seat of government for a single South Africa, presided over by General Botha and largely dependent for its housekeeping money on the gold mines of the Witwatersrand. All the mining houses had supported the creation of the Union and some of the mining leaders were now members of the Union Parliament, whose sessions were being opened by the first Governor-General, Viscount Gladstone. Lord Selborne, his task over, had returned to England. Among these mining personalities was Drummond Chaplin who was joined in the House of Assembly by Lionel Phillips, George Farrar and Percy FitzPatrick, who had sensationally defeated Louis Botha himself at the polls. In due course Harry Currey, who had looked after the Gold Fields office in Johannesburg in the late 1880s, was also there.

Milner had written to Chaplin's sister saying that Gold Fields should encourage her brother to remain in the Union Parliament and should make arrangements to facilitate political life for him. Chaplin, he said, could hardly be expected to continue in Parliament doing 'very disagreeable work at considerable personal sacrifice'. Jameson had been along to see Lord Harris in London about the importance of keeping Chaplin in Parliament. Harris, however, needed no convincing and Gold Fields felt it could only be to the advantage of the company to have one of their own men, politically experienced but at the same time knowledgeable about mining finance and management, able as a member of Parliament to influence whatever legislation might be enacted in regard to the mines. Harris was anxious to make company arrangements that would suit Chaplin and in due course Birkenruth arrived in Cape Town with the suggestion that Chaplin should be a member of the London board but be resident director in South Africa. Chaplin, however, felt it was not possible to serve on the London board while resident in South Africa, the age of air transport not yet having arrived as the solution to such a problem.

Both Birkenruth and Jameson wrote from Cape Town to Gold Fields with flattering reports on the work that Chaplin was doing in Parliament. He had, said Jameson, 'very great influence' with Smuts and, as a result, the mining industry as a whole was gaining an importance in national affairs.

In May 1913, the Parliamentary session over, Chaplin arrived back in his office at Gold Fields in Johannesburg just as serious labour troubles on the mines erupted, producing a crisis not only for the Government, since the strike soon turned to violence and bloodshed, but for the mining houses as represented by men such as Chaplin, Phillips and Farrar who were members of the Legislature.

It was a paltry dispute at the New Kleinfontein mine near Benoni that started it all, a tiny match that lit a big fire. The failure of the 1907 strike following the Knights Deep dispute had rankled ever since among the trade union leaders, who had been building up their strength and were looking for a chance to test it. In New Kleinfontein they saw that chance. The new manager at the mine in order to improve efficiency had, among other things, changed the working hours of five underground workers. When these refused to accept the changes, he sacked them. Thereupon three surface workers resigned out of sympathy. Their union, the Amalgamated Society of Engineers, began negotiations with the mine management for their reinstatement but no agreement could be reached. The dispute then developed into an out and out confrontation between organized labour and the mining industry and on 4 July 1913 a general strike started. One of the first group of miners to throw in their weight with the strike came from Knights Deep; Gold Fields and Chaplin in particular were deeply implicated. Work on the mines had ceased and white miners were marching on Johannesburg determined to hold a meeting and ignoring the ban the Government had already placed upon such a meeting. The *Worker* had already referred to 'a war which must bring the South African public and in particular the Union Parliament to its senses and its knees'.

The strike started on a Friday; a week-end of violence lay ahead. British troops under General O'Brien had to be brought in to help the police; there were scuffles and clashes in Market Square and among the casualties were eighty-eight policemen. Towards the end of the afternoon there was a lull and some of the police were withdrawn but after nightfall it started again. Many of the strikers had renewed their courage with a drink and a hooligan element took over, bent on destruction. A fire was started at Park Station, then the offices of *The Star* were blazing; the mining houses, the police had heard, would be the next target. The situation was getting out of hand; shops, particularly where guns and ammunition were sold, were being looted. As the night wore on the violence subsided but the next day, Saturday, it started up again. There was a report that a band of strikers was on its way from the East Rand in order to burn down the Rand Club, 'the haunt of the capitalist classes'. That morning the courageous though perhaps foolhardy Chaplin was in his office as usual. 'I did not expect him to come back alive so violent were the strikers' attitudes,' Marguerite Chaplin said later. In the course of the morning Chaplin received a message from the Prime Minister asking him to meet him and General Smuts that afternoon at the Carlton Hotel. Botha and Smuts drove over from Pretoria but waited at Orange Grove until it was clear what the situation was in central Johannesburg. It was there that Chaplin, together with Phillips and Farrar, met the two Generals and, having discussed the crisis, they decided that the two Government leaders would have to meet the strikers. Botha and Smuts drove courageously to the Carlton Hotel and with a crowd milling angrily outside, they met the strike leaders and somewhat ignominiously accepted their demands. Smuts was the Minister of Mines and later he told Parliament: 'We signed because the police and Imperial forces informed us that the mob was beyond their control. If quiet was not restored anything could happen in Johannesburg that night. The town might be sacked; the mines permanently ruined.'

In the battle to protect the Rand Club earlier that day when the gallant Colonel Stallard and other members helped the local police forces to keep the attackers at bay, a celebrated incident took place where the central actor – and finally the victim – was a Gold Fields miner. He was one of the strike ringleaders and worked at Knights Deep, one of the company's three main producers. His name was J L Labuschagne. When it was all over and Judge Wessels, in the course of his official enquiry, was trying to determine how Labuschagne met his death, he was told by George Apson, the last man to speak to him, how it happened. Labuschagne, he said 'took his position about twenty yards from Simmons the jewellers and chucking his cap in the road and pulling his coat halfway down his back and facing the soldiers said "Come on, shoot". At this the crowd cheered to the echo, when suddenly a volley of bullets came tearing up the street. The crowd went running in all directions …. when we picked him up he was stone dead.'

In May 1973 *The Star* published an eye-witness account by E F Grote of what happened from the troops' point of view. 'Then came the man, a six-footer, out of the crowd and stood in the middle of Commissioner Street next to the lamp-post, his jacket open, hitting his chest and shouting to the soldiers "Don't shoot women and children. Shoot me." A young officer walked down the ranks and with his little rod tapped one of the soldiers on the shoulder, calmly saying, "Give him all he asked for!" The soldier stepped down in the street and on his knee, aimed his rifle, fired, and the man tottered and crumpled in a heap beside the lamp-post.'

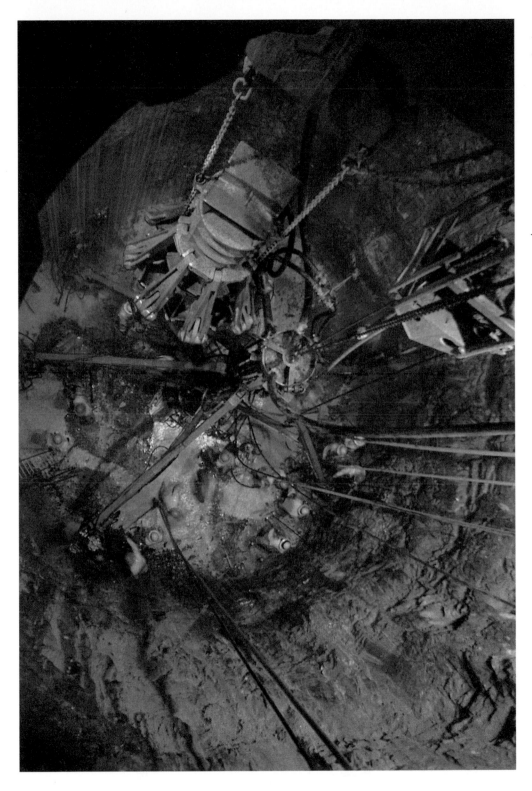

'We are, perhaps, the most romantic of industries. We are too devoted to our strange and ancient craft to want to do anything else'
Rudolph Agnew to the Royal Society of Arts, 11 May 1983

Shaft sinking at Kloof No. 4 shaft: boom rig operating on shaft floor with cactus grab slung above, 1985

Top: Original share certificate made out to Harry Caldecott for 50 Paardekraal G M Co. shares, signed by Harry Currey, December 1887

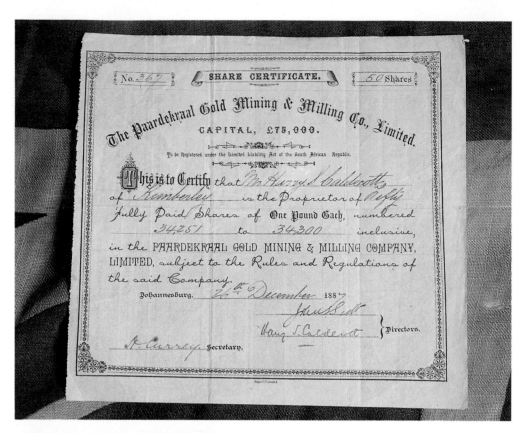

Left: A golden coat of arms, presented to the independent Gold Fields of South Africa by Consolidated Gold Fields, London, 1 July 1971

Right: Touchstones, black and flint-like, are still used today as in antiquity to test the quality of gold by rubbing the stone with the metal. This touchstone, found at Choisy-au-Bac, north of Paris, is about 2 000 years old. Near it were found a little gold bar ingot and gold ring

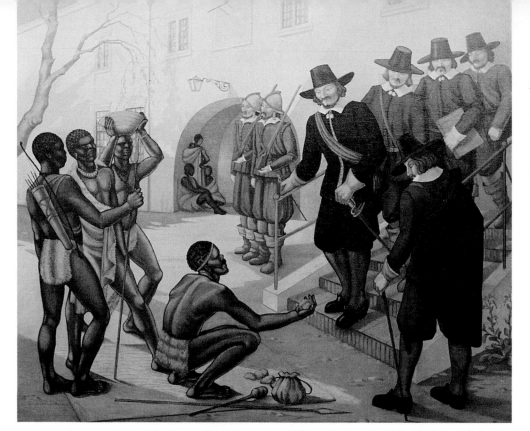

Top: *Simon van der Stel's prospectors pioneered O'okiep in 1685, having seen the copper ornaments worn by Hottentots visiting the Castle in Cape Town. This mural by Jan Juta is in South Africa House, London*

Left: *O'okiep today: Carolusberg Mine, 1985*

Right: *Copper smelting, 1985*

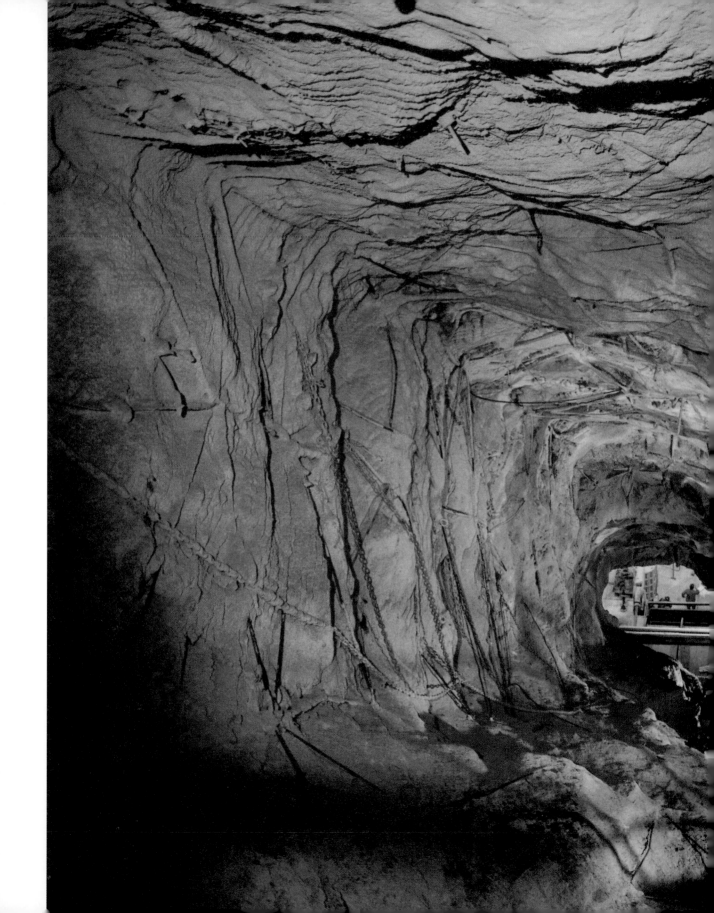

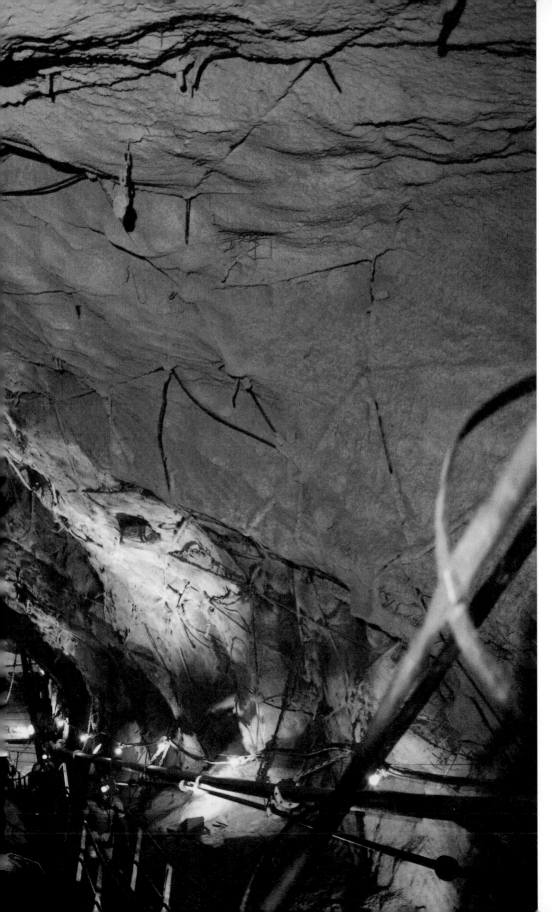

*Rope raise at East
Drie No. 5 subvertical
shaft, 1985*

Saldanha Bay from which is exported the mined treasure of Black Mountain

Black mountain: an Aladdin's cave at Aggeneys

Top left: *At Rooiberg an ancient stamp mill provides modern sculpture for a modern mine with an ancient tradition*

Top right: *Also at Rooiberg: tin-miners of an antique age left their mark, as in this ancient fire-set*

Left: *The stone cottage where Rhodes and Rudd lived for a time at Luipaardsvlei, where it was a landmark for some 80 years*

Northam, where in 1986 Gold Fields announced a bold new project to mine platinum. This lone rig, a beacon of light in the bushveld dawn, stands as a symbol of faith in a bright future

There was evidence that Labuschagne, like many others that night, had been drinking. In the Knights Deep report that year there is no mention of the dramatic and untimely end of one of their miners. His death, however, highlighted a new factor in the make-up of the white mining community, the fact that he was an Afrikaner. In 1904 only five percent of white miners had been Afrikaners but in 1907 following the dispute at Knights Deep, Afrikaners had been brought in as strike-breakers and then had stayed on; at the time of Labuschagne's death in 1913, some seventy percent of the white miners were Afrikaners. Yet the trade union activists, those who were urging them into action not only against the mining houses but against an Afrikaner led Government, were immigrants. It was significant that when further trouble broke out at the beginning of 1914, just six or seven months later, none of the strike leaders had been born in South Africa, a fact which prompted General Smuts, still smarting from his defeat in July 1913, to rid himself of the problem by bundling them on to a ship and sending them to Britain.

In the middle of 1913 and in the midst of all his problems at Gold Fields during the strike, Chaplin was having to make a personal decision about his career. Roderick Jones, who had been a war correspondent in South Africa and as Sir Roderick Jones became head of Reuters, was staying with the Chaplins at Marienhof when Chaplin received the offer of the post of Administrator of Southern Rhodesia. They discussed it at length. Marguerite Chaplin was not at all enthusiastic about moving to Rhodesia, Chaplin 'was not dissatisfied with his treatment from Gold Fields but wanted more scope'. He would have to think about it.

Miners' Strike, 1913: death of a Gold Fields miner. J L Labuschagne, a striking miner from Knights Deep, stands at the corner of Loveday and Commissioner Streets and invites the troops – 'Shoot me!' They complied.

Meanwhile conditions in South Africa were as unfavourable as the report presented to shareholders that year by Lord Harris. 'In the many years I have been addressing you,' he said, 'we have had some very bad times to face but I doubt if we ever had a year in which disappointments have been so numerous and the blows have come from so many different directions.' Harris was referring not only to events in South Africa that year but to the calamities that had attended the company's excursions 'somewhere else in the world'. Gold Fields was having to cope with a massive depreciation in its investments of some £1,4 million. It had to transfer £1 million from reserve and take the rest from profits; and yet it still managed to give the shareholders a ten percent dividend. Stock markets round the world had been alarmed by the near revolution that had hit the Rand; gold shares there, it seemed, were subject to 'political risk', a phrase that would be used ever after in relation to investment in South Africa. By the beginning of 1914 Gold Fields shares, which had been worth £8 in 1903, had fallen to just under £2.

'I don't at all like the state of affairs here,' Chaplin was writing to his friend and fellow politician, John X Merriman, one time manager at Langlaagte, then Prime Minister of Cape Colony, who had refused the post of Finance Minister in the Botha Government. 'It seems to me that we might be in the thick of another row at any time. There is a vast amount of intimidation going on and it is even extended into cricket and similar matters – no scabs allowed to play cricket much less work! We are short of forty or fifty thousand natives on the mines. The strike thoroughly upset them and the next thing will be that they will combine in order to get more pay. Meanwhile not a shilling is to be got in London for anything here and really if you look at the position of affairs in the country, can you wonder … it is ridiculous to expect them to incur the enormous expenditure involved in developing these low-grade mines for a low return unless they are confident that the Government is reasonably efficient and the public reasonably sympathetic.' While Chaplin was writing, his colleague from the Corner House, Sir Lionel Phillips, was lying dangerously ill in hospital, having narrowly survived an attempt on his life by a gunman who had wounded him in the street while walking from his office to the Rand Club. The attempted assassination had nothing to do with the strike but was committed by a man with a grievance against Phillips's company. Nevertheless it was an episode that did little to restore the confidence of the outside world in the Rand.

On the strike Merriman had come out with a really hard-hitting statement which, read now more than seventy years later, has a lasting ring of truth about it. 'The true manual workers of this country are the native and Coloured people – these are the people who do the hard manual work in this country and those men who came out on strike were the supervisors and aristocrats of labour. Small care or regard have they for the true and ill-considered worker.' Merriman's words illustrate what has been true of South Africa over the centuries, that the country is not one stage on which one national drama is enacted, but a collection of stages on which several dramas, sometimes unrelated, go on at the same time. At this time, 1913, the great class war that was already in progress in Europe, the struggle of the workers for economic and political power which they would wrest from the capitalists and the magnates, was being acted in South Africa on a whites-only stage – white miners versus white mine-owners.

On another whites-only stage the Boer–British drama was still going on; the armed conflict of 1899-1902 had brought to an end the Boer republics but not Afrikanerdom and by 1913 a resurgent Afrikaner nationalism was seeking to end British Imperial influence in South Africa which was being exercised, it believed, through the mining houses and their powerful voice, the Chamber of Mines. The grievances on the one hand of white Bolshevik miners against British capitalism and on the other hand the grievances of Afrikaner nationalists against British Imperialism united these two on the same stage and in the strangest alliance against the mining houses ever seen in South Africa, Bolsheviks and born-again Boers in the same bed! The result of this development, as will be seen, was the armed revolt on the Rand in 1922. However, before this could happen, the whole world would go up in flames. But these were some of the background influences, the peculiarly South African circumstances that were shaping, perhaps unconsciously, the career of the company in South Africa, the pre-natal influences moulding the embryonic Gold Fields of South Africa of the future.

The outbreak of war in Europe on 4 August 1914 with Britain, France and Russia in alliance against the German and the Austrian Empires had repercussions of a particular kind in South Africa. As a British dominion, South Africa was automatically at war with Britain's enemies, but the degree of its participation would be decided by the Union Government. The Prime Minister, General Botha, before he could play any part in the World War would first have to deal with civil violence and incipient civil war. The general strike that had started with a dispute involving railwaymen at the beginning of 1914 had been vigorously dealt with. General De la Rey, a legendary leader from the Anglo-Boer War, had gone in with a detachment from the Union Defence Force and threatened to blow the leaders of the trade unions out of their headquarters at Trades Hall. When the strike collapsed, General Smuts had the leaders sent to Durban where they were put aboard the *SA Umgeni* which sailed for Britain.

The outbreak of the European War later that year provided that other party of grievance-bearers, the Boer faction that wanted the republics back, to take their chance and go into action. General De la Rey was one of the first casualties. He was shot by accident near Johannesburg when the car in which he and General Beyers, the head of the Defence Force, were travelling failed to stop at a road block that had been set up by the police to catch a gang of criminals known as the Foster Gang. Were the two generals on their way to join a rebellion against the Union Government? This started in due course and Beyers, having resigned from the Union Defence Force, was among them; he was drowned trying to escape across a river. Another hero of the Boer War, General De Wet, was captured by the troops of Botha and Smuts who arrived on the scene in buses. The revolt collapsed and Botha was then ready to accede to the British Government's request and march against the German troops in South West Africa, then a German colony. This Botha did personally, being the last Prime Minister in history to go into battle at the head of his troops, though on sighting the Germans he is said to have shouted excitedly '*Daar kom die Engelse*' a natural mistake for a Boer General who only a few years earlier had been in action against the British Army. In that South West African campaign Gold Fields lost a good friend and the Rand mining industry a colourful leader. Major Sir George Farrar, who had won a DSO in the Anglo-Boer War, was with Botha's forces in South West Africa when he was killed in a rail accident in the territory.

With the disturbances in South Africa during the opening stages of the World War now over, the mines on the Rand despite a shortage of skilled miners – some seventeen percent left to go to the war – and the difficulty of obtaining mining supplies, particularly dynamite, cyanide and zinc from abroad, settled down to play their own important part in the war, to supply the gold that was needed to pay for the Allied effort to defeat Germany. The Bank of England throughout the war bought the entire gold output from South Africa but at a fixed price of 77/9d an ounce; this price had been acceptable in 1914 but as time went on costs increased on the Rand; Britain then went off gold, the purchasing power of the pound decreased and in the end some of the low-grade mines were facing extinction. Despite all this, the mines together, between 1915 and 1918, were able to produce gold to the value of more than £152 million.

Douglas Christopherson directed Gold Fields' affairs in Johannesburg throughout the war years; Chaplin in 1914, the year that Robert Fricker died, finally accepted to go to Rhodesia as Administrator to the delight of Dr Jameson. As Sir Drummond Chaplin he was to return to the Union later and to the South African Parliament in 1924 but never again to Gold Fields. He did, however, build himself another Marienhof, the magnificent Noordhoek[3] at the Cape and, predictably, it was the Governor-General who laid the foundation stone. Christopherson obtained two assistants in Christopher Hely-Hutchinson, whose family had provided a Governor of Natal, and were close friends of the Chaplins; and Leslie Brown, but neither spent long in Johannesburg. Both were soon in the Army, Brown eventually coming back to the office as a colonel with a DSO and Hely-Hutchinson with an MC. Eighteen others won decorations for gallantry; they were among the 952 Gold Fields men in South Africa who went to the war and more than sixty never returned.

Christopherson, short-handed, struggled on as best he could and went seven years without home leave. In 1915 he managed to get the Jupiter mine going again; this had had to close in October 1913 due to labour shortages and high costs but by 1915 conditions had sufficiently improved to allow crushing to begin again that September. His main achievement that year, however, was at Robinson Deep. Here, in a deal with Central Mining, with Booysens Estate and South Deeps, the Robinson Deep claim area was considerably increased. A new company, Robinson Deep Ltd was formed with a total area of 557 claims and its

success was further evidence that the only way to work the low-grade ore profitably was to work it on as large a scale as possible. The new claims added to Robinson Deep enabled a new shaft, suitably named the Chris shaft after Douglas Christopherson, to be sunk to a vertical depth of 4 250 feet, the deepest shaft on the Rand at the time. Later the first sub-vertical shaft in the history of South African mining was sunk, being taken from 3 800 feet to 5 600 feet.

Named as a trustee of this new company was Charles Wentzel, a Rand lawyer whose firm Webber Wentzel, successor to Solomon and Thompson, would continue its long and enduring association with Gold Fields. Wentzel and Christopherson were firm friends who enjoyed to pull each other's leg in public. On one occasion at a dinner Christopherson had to propose a toast to Gold Fields; the cricketer in him came to the surface and, referring to the company's integrity, he spoke of its sporting capacity, its sporting outlook on life; Gold Fields, he maintained, was a group of sportsmen. Wentzel in replying said he was sure Christopherson was right. 'No group that was anything but a group of sportsmen would accept the bills that our secretaries send to your Group.' 'Nor,' he added 'would they swallow the law which I gave to them.' There was, however, a sequel when Gold Fields did query the bill coming from Webber Wentzel. Ben Friel was the partner in the law firm dealing with the complaint, Gold Fields having suggested, with slight sarcasm, that Friel had made a mistake with the

Triumvirate of the Twenties. Douglas Christopherson (centre), resident director in Johannesburg, with William Mackenzie (left) and Guy Carleton Jones. The three, seen here looking at a model of the Chris Shaft, named after the resident director, engaged Rudolf Krahmann to test his theories which led to the discovery of the West Wits Line.

105

noughts in the figure that he had charged. Friel immediately wrote back to Gold Fields, having added a further nought, saying 'Thank you for drawing my attention to my mistake.' Gold Fields, however, served an ace in the next game, once more a complaint about the size of the bill. Friel telephoned Gold Fields and said, 'Charles Wentzel would have charged much more', to which came the sizzling reply from Gold Fields, 'but we resent having to pay a Wentzel fee for a Friel opinion'.

In 1915 Gold Fields demonstrated its sporting instincts in a practical way and as a result the mining industry on the Rand has benefited ever since. In that year the Chamber of Mines received from the Gold Fields consulting engineer, C D Leslie, a memorandum in which he set out a scheme whereby all white employees would receive holidays on full pay up to a maximum of £1 a day. The scheme was not extended to black miners since their employment conditions were different; they worked between four and twelve months on the mines then returned to their tribal homes for a period of months. Thanks to what was regarded at the time as a progressive initiative on the part of Gold Fields, all underground and surface workers on the mines by 1917 were enjoying at least fourteen days' paid holidays a year. The President of the Chamber, Evelyn Wallers of Rand Mines, declared with pride that the industry was ahead of any other industry in the world in granting paid holidays to daily-paid workers. Its magnanimity even included those who had been on strike in 1913 and 1914; for the purposes of the scheme they had not broken their service.

Leslie, as consulting engineer at Gold Fields, did not confine his efforts for the mining industry to improving working conditions with holidays-with-pay. Although himself a technical man, he was strongly convinced of the human factor in mining. He was largely responsible for persuading the Union Government to set up Miners' Training Schools; these became so popular that their accommodation became inadequate and Leslie decided to open another school for fifty apprentices at Robinson Deep. Leslie was continuing the work of a predecessor, H H Webb, who back in 1902 had persuaded the company to give a lead in training; it also made an annual award of forty guineas and a gold medal to the Institution of Mining and Metallurgy in London to encourage research into the problems of mining, particularly deep-level mining. In March 1917, again with prompting from Gold Fields, the Government accepted an Honorary Scientific and Technical Committee 'to investigate and advise with reference to industrial development and research within the Union'. When, many years later, the chairman of Gold Fields of South Africa took his place on the Council for Scientific and Industrial Research (C S I R) in Pretoria, the chair had been warmed for him all those years before by C D Leslie. It was a tragedy for Gold Fields when this enlightened engineer, like George Farrar in South West Africa, lost his life in a railway accident in Moçambique in 1920.

Douglas Christopherson, ably served by Leslie and by his consulting metallurgist W A Caldecott, was also keeping his eye on the East Rand and renewing his hopes for Sub Nigel in a practical way by increasing its claim area. He acquired from Ludwig Erlich claims on the Grootfontein property on the northern boundary of the mine, some 383 claims in exchange for 43 420 Sub Nigel reserve shares. In 1921 Gold Fields transferred 500 Grootfontein claims to the Sub Nigel subsidiary for 130 000 shares, increasing its holding in this East Rand mine to 240 000 shares. Christopherson was declaring and redeclaring his faith in Sub Nigel but a few years had still to go by before he could begin those regular telegrams to London announcing ever more exciting results. These eventually enabled the Gold Fields holding in the mine to earn more than £7 million in dividends.

One of the main events stirring the interest of the mining houses during the First World War occurred during 1915; this was a major take-over which was to have a curious sequel for Gold Fields some seven years later. In 1915 J B Robinson who had become Sir Joseph Robinson, Bart decided at the age of seventy-five to give up his interests on the Rand and Solly Joel, in charge of the old Barnato company JCI, had bought him out for four-and-a-half million pounds. It was the biggest deal in Rand history up till that time. When Joel's accountants examined Robinson's books they found that the old buccaneer had secretly acquired land which he subsequently sold to his own companies through the agency of a trust company that he controlled. In one case land and options that he had bought for £60 000 had been sold to his own Randfontein shareholders for £275 000. The upshot of these revelations was that JCI sued Robinson for £462 000 and during protracted proceedings in the courts Robinson ended up losing some half a million pounds and hearing from the Chief Justice of the Union some highly publicized home truths as to his character.

Even more significant than the Robinson affair of 1915 was the birth the following year of a brand new mining house that was destined among other things to acquire control of JCI. With the seizure by the Custodian of Enemy Property of German and Austrian investments on the Rand, worth some 125 million US dollars, large blocks of shares passed into new hands. A pair of these hands belonged to Ernest Oppenheimer, himself born in Germany but now the wartime Mayor of Kimberley and a rising star in the mining firmament. With the aid of interests on Wall Street he was able to found a new mining house which he called the Anglo American Corporation of South Africa. Its original purpose was to develop new properties on the East Rand, but before long it had built up a wide range of mining interests which included, not only gold, but diamonds and copper. The Anglo American Corporation was to grow in time to be the biggest and most powerful corporation in South Africa and indeed a giant by world standards. From time to time, as will be seen, its great shadow would fall upon the activities of Gold Fields and not always to the comfort of its elder.

The First World War, as it progressed, produced strong anti-German feeling in Johannesburg as elsewhere in the British Empire and there was irrational prejudice against people and companies with German names. Such names were consequently changed. Even the British Royal Family, descended from the

Hanoverians, gave up their German family name and became the House of Windsor and their kinsmen, the Battenbergs, became the Mountbattens. In these circumstances appeared in 1918 another new name in South African mining, a company called Union Corporation, the new name for the company founded by Adolf Goertz under his own name in 1897, and although registered in England, seven of its directors were Germans. German names were going out of fashion on the Rand and yet curiously enough so many of the Germans who had helped to create its mining industry had become English baronets – Julius Wernher, son of a German General, father of a British General, Otto Beit, Little Alfred's brother, Sigismund Neumann, Frederick Eckstein, George Albu, and in due course, some of the Oppenheimer family.[4]

In Johannesburg even some of the familiar place names were anglicized. Francis Lowrey's favourite picnic spot, the tree-lined Sachsenwald, became the salubrious suburb of Saxonwold.

Within a year of the end of the Great War, even Gold Fields had acquired a new name though that had nothing to do with any German connection; there was none. The company's affairs at the highest level were directed by those who belonged to the British Establishment, the House of Lords and the Council of the MCC, where Stanley Christopherson succeeded Lord Harris as chairman. Harris, back in 1914, had brought another cricketer on to the Gold Fields board, a member of the Kent XI. Since he was also a member of the House of Lords he was doubly qualified to be a director of Gold Fields. This was Lord Brabourne, who spent the war years looking after Gold Fields' affairs in the United States, and eventually for a short period before his death would become chairman of the company; his son would also be a director of Gold Fields until appointed to Harris's old job, Governor of Bombay.[5]

When in 1919 New Consolidated Gold Fields came into existence it did so in order to reflect a change of direction in company strategy. As Harris said later: 'We found a few years ago that we were unable to undertake work outside of mining in South Africa without the directors becoming personally liable.' Gold Fields in London had decided to diversify, to go into industry, property – mining might be abandoned altogether – but when the lawyers examined the articles of association of the company formed in 1892, they came to the conclusion that the directors were not legally free to use the company's capital in any way they saw fit. The way round this restriction was to form a new company; so New Consolidated Gold Fields Limited was formed as the operating company of Consolidated Gold Fields of South Africa which would hold all the shares in the new company and receive by way of dividends all its profits. Both companies would have the same capital, the same directors, the same offices and personnel, in fact there would be no practical changes at all. It was in the direction of company policy that change was to be found.

Gold Fields was going to invest in industry, not just the mining industry of the Rand, which, in any case, was on its knees in the first two or three years following the Armistice. Britain, in agreement with its Allies and in order to pay for the war, had decided to abandon the fixed price of gold which was some £4 an ounce; gold was allowed to be sold freely in the market and in this way it earned a premium of sixteen shillings an ounce. This premium was the difference between the sterling price of gold and the price it earned in countries still on the gold standard, such as the United States. Without this premium some twenty-four of the thirty-nine mines would by 1921 have been working at a loss. By 1920 the premium had risen to £2 an ounce and the value of South African production had risen sharply to £42 million. The advantages from the premium were, however, short-lived; sterling rose in value, mining costs shot up alarmingly, the price of gold fell from 120 shillings to ninety-seven shillings in 1921 and again to ninety-four shillings in 1922. There seemed little hope for the low-grade mines and Gold Fields had to close down Simmer Deep and Jupiter. Then in September 1920 that unlucky mine Knights Deep had a disastrous fire which caused its permanent closure. This valuable dividend-earner – £1 287 000 since 1916 – was lost. All Gold Fields had now were Faith, Hope and Charity, Robinson Deep and Simmer and Jack and an enlarged Sub Nigel now showing profits. There was not enough in the Gold Fields kitty to pay a dividend either in 1921 or 1922. Some of the shareholders were not taking kindly to the disastrous decline in their company's fortunes; the Press had some unkind cartoons and everyone was blaming the directors. Harris said he had received a letter which suggested 'we are a lot of old fossils and suggests that as I have retired from first-class cricket I might also retire from the chairmanship of the company'. Harris, however, was made of sterner stuff. His correspondent had no doubt forgotten how, captaining England in Australia in 1879, he had had to deal with the Australian mob that invaded the pitch at Melbourne to express its dissatisfaction with an umpire and how Harris had defended the unfortunate man, himself being hit over the head with a stick. With Gold Fields on a sticky wicket, Harris had no intention of declaring his innings. 'I suppose,' he said, at the 1920 meeting, 'that if there was anyone who doubted the wisdom of the change by which we were given full power to invest outside South Africa and in other industries beside mining, they must acknowledge that we were right after the catastrophes of the last twelve months.' He went on to say: 'Mr Rhodes and Mr Rudd cannot be held to blame because they made a bad shot at what lay underground.... they had to depend upon the theory of mining of the experts of the day who had absolutely no experience anywhere in the world of such a formation as that of the Witwatersrand.'

Were the Rudd-Rhodes chickens coming home to roost? By 1921 it might have seemed so. It was the worst year in the company's history, the first and only time that company accounts revealed a deficit - £111 000. On the market Gold Fields shares were down to 13/6d. Lord Harris referred to the 'terrible figure of depreciation of £492 000'. Even Robinson Deep owed the company more than £222 000. 'On the doors of 8 Old Jewry,' announced one recalcitrant shareholder with a dramatic flourish 'there are thirty-five companies' names – and all are in liquidation.'

Harris was not unaware of the pity of it all. 'To us who have worked so long on the basis of this being a great South African gold mining house and to many of its oldest shareholders it must, I think, be a subject of regret that circumstances have defeated us and that the volume of our interests in South African gold mining cannot, unless new areas are found, in all probability increase.' That was the key phrase – 'unless new areas are found'. They were, and their discovery was to give new life to Gold Fields and in the very year that saw life itself extinguished in its valiant old chairman of the 1920s, Lord Harris.

In these unpromising times – in 1920 – a new and distinguished name from the world of journalism joined the Board of New Consolidated Gold Fields in London. Chaplin had come to the company from *The Times*; so did Geoffrey Dawson, in fact straight from the Editor's chair which he had vacated after a disagreement with the paper's proprietor, Lord Northcliffe. Dawson was already familiar with Gold Fields in Johannesburg; under the name Geoffrey Robinson he had been a member of the Milner Kindergarten. After serving as Milner's secretary, he became Editor of *The Star* in October 1905, when Milner returned to Britain. By supporting Chinese labour in his editorials, he would have endeared himself to Harris and Chaplin. Meanwhile his predecessor at *The Star*, Frederic Hamilton, had begun a close association with Gold Fields, having set up in London together with Ludwig Erlich a company with mining interests in South Africa. This was the HE Proprietary Company (H for Hamilton, E for Erlich) which had a joint interest in Luipaards Vlei with Gold Fields for a long time and much later, after sixty years became part of Gold Fields of South Africa.

About the time Dawson joined the Board in London, William Mackenzie was appointed in Johannesburg to assist Christopherson, and in particular to look after the new industrial and commercial interests which, according to the new policy of the company, Gold Fields was to acquire. Mackenzie had come across from the Standard Bank, then known as the African Banking Corporation, and was a member of a remarkable family that for more than a century has succeeded in having one foot in Scotland and the other in South Africa; in 1985 his brother's son, Ian Mackenzie, was chairman of the Standard Bank of South Africa when Gold Fields acquired an important stake in it. William Mackenzie, who would in due course succeed Christopherson in Johannesburg, had shown some courage in joining Gold Fields when he did for its fortunes had reached a low ebb. However, it was the kind of situation in which all the Mackenzies in various generations have thrived. He set about his task with gusto as the company looked around for suitable investments outside mining.

Lord Harris had expressed the view that South Africa, having had to improvise during the war, had made a start with manufacturing industries. 'There are very strong indications,' he said, 'that industrial business in that country is going to develop rapidly and that South Africa will become more and more self-contained and by degrees more and more capable of exporting its raw or manufactured produce .... we did not wish to be behind in the opportunity of investment in industrials....' The industries that came under Mackenzie's direction

110

included an engineering and construction business, a furniture factory, a brick and tile works, a rubber factory, a soap and oil manufacturing concern and the building of a sugar mill. With Hugh le May the company had made arrangements to participate in a project to build a floating dock at Lourenço Marques (now Maputo) and to construct the famous Polana Hotel there.

Some of these industrial projects were more successful than others. The question of whether to diversify, to balance mining with other activities, has been a recurring theme for discussion in Gold Fields boardrooms, in London as in Johannesburg.

The initiative has more often than not come from London where Consolidated Gold Fields, from a vantage point high up in the financial centre of the world, has continued to take a global view ever since the days when Lord Harris urged shareholders to go 'somewhere else in the world'. Gold Fields of South Africa, on the other hand, from its vantage point in Johannesburg, looks out of its windows and sees gold mines and other mines on its doorstep, and although from time to time it has sent out scouting parties into the industrial backyards of others in search of opportunity, the site of mine dumps is a constant reminder of its first and abiding interest.

By 1922 it was politics once more, rather than mining or industry, that was uppermost in the minds of those directing the affairs of Gold Fields in Johannesburg as it was for most other people there at that time. For sixty-seven terrible days it was not so much the problem of saving the mines as of preserving themselves since politics had turned to revolution, with miners' commandos, armed and trained, in open battle with the armed forces of the State. General Smuts, who during the previous troubles in 1913 and 1914 had been Minister of Mines, was now in ultimate charge as Prime Minister. His South African Party had won the general election in 1921. General Botha had died prematurely in 1919 and Gold Fields had sent a contribution for the memorial that was being erected to him in Pretoria. Smuts had spent the last two years of the Great War as a member of the British War Cabinet and Afrikaner nationalists believed that he had sold the Boer birthright to the British. Some of them, including General Hertzog and Dr E G Jansen, the future Governor-General, had even gone to the Peace Conference at Versailles in the hope of getting back the republics. They had been turned away, even by Lloyd George who, having been pro-Boer in 1900, was now Britain's Prime Minister. For the trade unions in South Africa, increasingly, and quite legally, influenced by the Communist Party which rejoiced in the success of the Bolsheviks in Russia, Smuts's victory at the polls appeared as a particular challenge to themselves. It seemed to show the continuing strength of British capitalism in the country which they believed not only controlled the mining industry but called the political tune.

However, the so-called mining capitalists were having a hard time. When the gold premium evaporated, those running the mining houses said they would not be able to carry on mining operations unless wages, and hence costs, were cut. The trade unions flatly refused to accept this and a strike, reminiscent of 1913,

111

was declared. This time it was to be much more serious and its repercussions far-reaching. In fact it was to be the prelude for a new departure for South Africa, along a path from which it has never strayed and willy-nilly Gold Fields would inevitably have to follow.

At first, trade unionists and the Chamber of Mines tried to settle their differences by negotiation. There had been an agreement known as the Status Quo Agreement, made in 1918. This re-established the colour bar, or job reservation, as it had existed at the outbreak of the Great War. During the war the places of miners who had gone into the Services had been partly filled by Afrikaners but not in sufficient numbers and the mine managers had relaxed the rules so that work formerly done by white miners was being performed by blacks. With the war over, the unions insisted on the return to the status quo. At the end of 1921, faced with economic difficulties, the Chamber announced it was ending the Status Quo Agreement; on the same day white workers in the coal mines were told their wages had been cut. On New Year's Day, 1922, the coal miners went on strike, and the gold miners, after holding a ballot, followed. By 9 January 1922 the mines had closed down except for essential services. Work also stopped in engineering works and power stations along the Rand. Some 22 000 men were idle.

Two months later, in early March, they were still out but it did not look as if the strike was going to succeed. The unions made approaches to the Chamber for further talks but were rudely rebuffed. The union leaders were then thinking of holding another ballot to determine whether they should return to work. At that point the body of Communist extremists among the strikers led by Percy

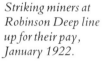

Striking miners at Robinson Deep line up for their pay, January 1922.

112

1922 Revolt. A Black voorloper leads a procession of miners whose banners proclaim: 'Workers of the World unite for a White South Africa'.

Fisher, and known as the Council of Action, decided to take over the strike which they feared might collapse. They cut across the union leaders, appealing directly to the strikers in their commandos. He urged them to go into action and at that point the Government acted, too, declaring martial law and calling up the troops. Many of those in the strike commandos were Afrikaners some of whom had been in touch with the rebel Boer Generals, J J Pienaar and Wessel Wessels and been sympathetically received. Fisher's Bolsheviks wanted a Transvaal Republic outside the Union, so did the extremist Afrikaner nationalists. In the end the striker commandos that went into action presented some odd scenes; a column might be led by the Red Flag while behind it the strikers were singing the old Boer Volkslied. Another group carrying a banner 'Workers of the World Unite for a White South Africa' would be singing the Communist 'The Red Flag'.

The striker commandos were well armed. Having started with a variety of weapons including bicycle chains, knobkieries, crowbars and of course explosives, they then got hold of guns which seemed to exist in private possession in large quantities on the Rand. Some equipment even came from Government sources since some of the strikers were actually called up for service when martial law was proclaimed. They drew their uniforms and arms from the Commissariat and these then found their way to the commandos.

Particularly valuable to the commandos were miners who had had military experience during the war. One of these, a young South African who not long out of Michaelhouse had gone to France and returned with a DSO and an MC, was working at the Modderfontein mine. Many years later he was the first South

African to become resident director of Gold Fields in Johannesburg. His name was Spencer Fleischer and he recorded what happened in 1922. 'Nominally I was a striker though my sympathies were not with them. They organized themselves into platoons and companies and drilled and tried to get me to assist them because of my military experience. I refused and they sent a contingent of fifty men to fetch me at New Modder but I heard about it and dodged them. My parents were then at Van Ryn and had had quite a scrap and I went there on my motorcycle. I was fired on by the strikers and then "captured" by the burghers who would not allow me to get in touch with my parents, despite my pass and special constable certificate. The OC burghers could not read!' Fleischer was the only South African who, having been a striker in 1922, eventually became President of the Chamber of Mines. There was another 1922 striker who also had that distinction; he was Canadian, working at the time on Sub Nigel. His name was Stowe McLean and he became chairman of General Mining in due time.

The striker commandos gained early success particularly on the East Rand; they cut communications, attacked mines and police stations and there were some ugly and unnecessary clashes with black miners. However, when General Smuts himself arrived on the Rand and his colleague of the East African campaign of 1916, General Sir Jacobus van Deventer, took charge of Government troops, the rebel commandos had little chance of survival. Even the South African Air Force, still in its infancy, was brought into action and the archives of this distinguished corps record how it bombed the Johannesburg suburb of Fordsburg, where Fisher and his colleague Spendiff had made their headquarters in Market Square and where a sniper with a rifle shot down one of the planes. Van Deventer, having pushed the strikers off Brixton Ridge, assembled his artillery near where the Hertzog Tower now stands and soon the guns were hitting targets in Fordsburg. Fisher and Spendiff refused to surrender and shot themselves. The battles ended and Johannesburg and the mines eventually got back to work again but there had been considerable loss of life. The Armed Forces alone lost 230 men killed, twice as many as had been lost in the South West Africa campaign during the war. Of 853 people brought to trial, forty-six were charged with treason and murder. Of these, eighteen were convicted and sentenced to death. Four were executed, the rest reprieved. 1922 remains one of the most bizarre and dramatic episodes in South African history.

For sixty-seven days events on the Rand had held the headlines in the world Press with predictable consequences for share prices of South African mining houses. Gold Fields, like the others, had suffered as a result of a fall in production of its mining subsidiaries. Simmer and Jack, in particular, had been hit. There was no dividend from Gold Fields that year and even the payment of dividends on preferential shares had to be delayed. But the mines were starting to produce again and since in the end the miners had had to accept lower wages, even the low-grade producers were able to remain in business.

The 1922 upheaval was in fact a watershed in South Africa's evolution and that

Colonel Spencer Fleischer was called away from Sub Nigel by General Smuts (right) to command the Mines Engineering Brigade in World War II. He was the first South African to become resident director of Gold Fields in Johannesburg, 1947-1953. During the Royal visit to South Africa in 1947, he was decorated with the CBE by King George VI, having previously received from King George V the DSO and MC for gallantry in the trenches in France during World War I. A reluctant striker in 1922, he was the only South African striker to become President of the Chamber of Mines.

of its gold mining industry. The strike had turned into a rebellion against British Imperial influence in South Africa and the Chamber of Mines with its strong British financial connections. In this way it had combined the ambitions of right-wing Afrikaner nationalists with those of left-wing Labour organizers. But the destruction of the striker commandos in which these ambitions were merged was not the end of the affair nor of these particular ambitions. It had ended the unconstitutional and illegal attempt by Afrikaner nationalism with the Labour movement to achieve their ends. Smuts's handling of the 1922 revolt, and the dissatisfactions that it had engendered, provided promising political ground for Afrikaner nationalists and the Labour Party to defeat what they regarded as British Imperial influence and British capitalist influence at the polls in electoral collaboration.

This time they would seek to win constitutionally at the polls what had been lost unconstitutionally at the barricades. And this time they succeeded. At the general election of 1924 South Africa acquired its first Nationalist Prime Minister in General Hertzog who arrived in the Union Buildings with the support of the Labour Party in the Pact Government. He appointed to his Cabinet the former manager at Village Main, Chaplin's old enemy, Colonel Cresswell who found Sir Drummond Chaplin, back from Rhodesia, sitting opposite him in the new Parliament. From 1924 onwards the political influence of the mining houses and their so-called magnates was reduced and would never be the same. Gold would continue to play an essential role in South African affairs; from then on the personalities of the gold mining houses would be a power behind the scenes but would never again dictate the political or economic direction of South Africa.

Lord Milner had seen it all with a remarkable understanding of South Africa. He wrote from London to Lionel Phillips soon after the first election for the Union Parliament in 1910 and he said: 'People here are apt to regard "Hertzogism" as just a regrettable eccentricity. It is a pity, they feel, that there should still be some Boers so retrogressive and fanatical, but after all they are just an unfortunate and exceptional survival which does not matter very much.

'I take an entirely different view. In my opinion Hertzogism represents the real permanent type. It is only what you have got to expect – what I, for my part, always expected. It is not Hertzog who is the exception or the eccentricity. It is Botha and Smuts in their more liberal moments. They are the "sports" and it is not Hertzog and men of his type but the more enlightened Boers who will toe the line.

'Botha himself would always, I think, prefer to be conciliatory and reasonable but whether he is strong enough to make his own natural disposition prevail – whether indeed any man is or could be strong enough to dominate the intense racialism and passion for race-ascendancy of the Boers (the natural growth of two centuries of isolation and a life-and-death struggle with barbarism) – is another question.'

The year 1922 had been a year in which old scores had been settled in South Africa though these not finally until the general election of 1924, as has been seen.

116

But another old score was settled in 1922, in London. Rhodes had been in his grave twenty years and more but his old enemy J B Robinson was still around and in that year, though eighty-two years of age, very much in the public eye. The chairman of Gold Fields, Rhodes's old company with whom Robinson would never co-operate, took it upon himself, as if he carried a proxy from the past, to put a barrier across Robinson's path. That path was leading Sir Joseph Robinson, Bart into the House of Lords. He had arrived in the mail boat with members of his family from Cape Town and the official *London Gazette* had announced his elevation to the peerage as Lord Robinson. Over my dead body, seems to have been the reaction to the news from Lord Harris determined to have the buccaneer blackballed from that most exclusive of clubs, the British House

In June 1922 Lord Harris, the Gold Fields chairman, made a strong attack on J B Robinson in the House of Lords to prevent a peerage being conferred on 'the old buccaneer'. Sir Joseph Robinson, with his son and two daughters, is seen here arriving at Southampton in the mail boat from Cape Town. The official London Gazette *had announced that he was to become Lord Robinson of Wynberg, but as a result of Lord Harris's action and the debate that followed, Robinson asked leave to decline the honour.*

of Lords. On 22 June 1922, he quit his office at Gold Fields in the City and made his way to Westminster, where in the House of Lords he delivered himself of a speech on the Robinson peerage which was to have sensational results.

Harris had not acted precipitately but had discussed with fellow peers, particularly those with South African connections, what he intended to do. The *London Gazette* had announced the peerage for Robinson as head of the Robinson Banking Corporation. Harris pointed out that no such bank existed; it had ceased operations in 1907; he asked also what were the 'national and imperial services' that Robinson, according to the *Gazette*, had rendered. He reminded the House of the circumstances (already referred to) of the court case involving Robinson and JCI, and repeated the words of the Chief Justice of the Union: 'It is wholly inconsistent with the obligation of good faith that the defendant should have made for himself these profits by the method which the evidence discloses.' Robinson, in Harris's view, was not, therefore, the kind of man to have in the Lords. 'These are facts,' boomed Harris 'and surely these facts were not before the Prime Minister when he recommended Sir Joseph Robinson for distinction at His Majesty's hand? Surely the Prime Minister must have been misled and consequently His Majesty misled?' The debate was resumed a week later and was notable for some hard comments on Robinson by two men who had held high office in South Africa, Lord Buxton, Governor-General during the Great War, and Lord Selborne.

Robinson, whatever his faults may have been, behaved with dignity throughout this humiliating experience. He wrote a letter to the Prime Minister, Lloyd George, and this was read out in Parliament. 'I have read with surprise,' wrote Robinson 'the discussion which took place yesterday in the House of Lords upon the proposed offer of a peerage to myself. I have not as you know in any way sought the suggested honour. It is now sixty years since I commenced as a pioneer the task of building up the industries of South Africa. I am now an old man to whom honours and dignities are no longer matters of much concern. I should be sorry if any honour conferred upon me were the occasion for such ill-feeling as was manifested in the House of Lords yesterday and while deeply appreciating the honour which has been suggested, I would wish, if I may without discourtesy to yourself and without impropriety to beg His Majesty's permission to decline the proposal.'

So the matter was dropped. Robinson returned to the Cape where he died in 1929. King George V was incensed by the manner in which the granting of honours had somehow got out of control. The Robinson peerage was only one of several examples; it was suggested that suitable back-handers were being passed to the Prime Minister to facilitate matters, though Robinson was to say with obvious satisfaction that the whole thing had not cost him a penny. However, the question of granting of titles and honours to South Africans would soon become academic. One of the first acts of the first Nationalist Prime Minister, General Hertzog, was to end the granting of British titles, symbols of British Imperialism, to South Africans.

The somewhat controversial action taken by the chairman of Gold Fields in 1922 in putting down the founders' old opponent, J B Robinson, had nevertheless tied up a loose end from the company's past. But as the story is one that never stands still, even while a drama is in progress, such as the events of 1913 and 1922, on the South African stage, new players appear in the wings ready to carry the story on into the future. In 1913 in the midst of the troubles of that year Guy Carleton Jones arrived in the wings of the Gold Fields stage having rejected the advice of John Hays Hammond not to leave his native Canada for South Africa. Then, in 1922, in the midst of the troubles, a young professional soldier, educated at Wellington and the Royal Military College, Sandhurst, and a member of Colonel Frank Rhodes's old corps, the Dragoons, arrived in South Africa. His name was Percy Hammond.[6] Carleton Jones would in due course have John Hays Hammond's old job at Gold Fields, and much else, and later on Percy Hammond would occupy Colonel Rhodes's old chair. In so doing, they added further links in the Gold Fields continuity chain.

Carleton Jones, a mining engineer of genius, was at the South African end but in London two other mining engineers whose names would become part of South African mining history also appeared in the Gold Fields wings. One was John Agnew, a New Zealander, who became a director in 1922 and later was the

John Agnew, left, chairman of Gold Fields, 1933-1939, the first mining engineer to hold that position; he found the labour to launch the West Wits Line.

Robert Annan, the Scottish mining engineer, who became chairman of Consolidated Gold Fields in London in 1944 and retired in 1960 when he was 75. He died in 1981 at the age of 96, commemorated by the Annan Shaft at Doornfontein.

119

first engineer to become chairman; he also had the distinction of founding a family dynasty within the company, to which he was followed not only by his son but also by his grandson, each mounting the ladder to the top. The other engineer who also became chairman was Robert Annan who joined the company in 1930. His father had been a director many years earlier. John Annan, a partner in the firm of accountants Annan and Dexter, one of the earliest on the Rand (a reminder of which is Annan House in Fox Street, Johannesburg) became a director of Gold Fields in 1907 in unusual circumstances. Lord Harris was having problems with those faithful but difficult Scottish shareholders who had been among the company's first financial backers; they had formed a committee to look after their interests and had appointed Annan as their professional spokesman. Annan had so impressed Harris that he was invited to join the Board but within a year of his appointment he had died during a visit to the United States.

With John Agnew and Robert Annan in London and Guy Carleton Jones in South Africa, the Gold Fields *dramatis personae* was changing its character, as the play itself was about to change and the great central episode in the company's story, the discovery of the West Wits Line, was about to be enacted. The age of the amiable amateurs, the aristocrats and cricketers was fading; the era of the chairman-engineer was beginning and that was as it should be since gold mining in South Africa was about to acquire a new dimension and there would no longer be any place for that old British distinction between gentlemen and players.

---

[1] Fricker did this in another fine Parktown house, *Gateways,* which was demolished in 1972.

[2] He became the 5th Lord Harris on the death of his father in 1932. He himself died in 1984 at the age of 95.

[3] In 1986 the home of John Wiley, Minister of the Environment in the South African Government.

[4] Sir Ernest Oppenheimer survived a German torpedo which in 1918 sank the *Galway Castle* on which he was a passenger. He was fished out of the sea.

[5] His son, the present Lord Brabourne, is the husband of Countess Mountbatten of Burma.

[6] He is commemorated by Hammond Road, Turffontein.

CHAPTER FIVE

If Fortune Favours the Bold
1924 – 1939

The discovery early in the 1930s of the West Wits Line was made at exactly the right time not only for Gold Fields but also for South Africa. South Africa, like the rest of the world, was in the grip of the Great Depression. After a brief period of relative prosperity about 1925, the world economy began to slow down and by the 1930s had almost come to a standstill. Men and machines were everywhere idle. In America the great stock exchange crash on Wall Street in 1929 had echoed round the world like a thunderclap. Some 1 700 banks had gone under and thirty-seven million Americans had no work. From the United States Lord Brabourne had come back to London and become chairman of the company on the retirement of Lord Harris in 1929. In 1931 he grimly told shareholders: 'We have tried in the past to minimize risk by geographical distribution of our investments but that has failed us for depression and depreciation have been worldwide and no country has escaped them ... there is hardly a company in Great Britain or in the United States which has not had to suffer from the fall in profits and diminution or passing of dividends. In these circumstances can you be surprised that we have not escaped the storm?'

By the end of the 1920s Gold Fields had so reduced its interests in South Africa that nearly half its investments were located elsewhere. One by one its industrial undertakings, including those on which it had hopefully embarked in South Africa, were folding under the weight of the Depression; the company was surviving because of the income that it derived from its Transvaal gold mines, 'our mainstay', as Harris had called them. These were Robinson Deep, Simmer and Jack but, above all, Sub Nigel. In the 1920s Sub Nigel was like a lamp that seemed to burn ever brighter as it kept alive the hope that better times lay ahead. By 1928 it had become the richest gold producer of its time, achieving a peak grade of 19,7 dwt a ton milled and it held this record until 1963 when Free State Geduld sprinted past with 21,19 dwt. Gold Fields' shareholders were told in 1926: 'The outstanding feature of our mining investments is the almost sensational appreciation of our investments in the Sub Nigel mine....we hold 240 000 shares.' The dramatic change in the fortunes of Sub Nigel had taken place during the stewardship of its young Canadian mine manager, Guy Carleton Jones who, with the geologist Dr Leopold Reinecke, had finally mastered the puzzle of the 'pay-shoots' in which gold occurs on the East Rand. To get at the gold one has to follow the often erratic course of the shoots which, running roughly north-west to south-east, are broken up by faults; rich ore suddenly gives way to barren ground, and in this game of hide-and-seek the problem is where to pick up the rich shoots again. In due course Reinecke and Carleton Jones located the so-called Main Shoot; it ran from the surface workings of the Old Nigel Mine to a depth of 5 800 feet and the values it showed tended to increase at depth. Once found and followed, this Main Shoot ensured the riches of Sub Nigel and the survival of Gold Fields which needed its dividends to keep its head above water in 1931. During that dark period, 1927 to 1932, Sub Nigel dividends ranged from thirty-seven-and-a-half percent to seventy-five percent. And after that for several years they soared well above 100 percent. By that time, however, Carleton Jones was busy with something else.

In 1925 he had been called to Johannesburg as assistant consulting engineer, and although his devotion to Sub Nigel never diminished, his restless and energetic mind had already begun to tackle the wider problem that Gold Fields would have to face before long. This was caused by the fact that the elderly Robinson Deep and Simmer and Jack mines would come to an end one day and there would be no new mines to replace them. The East Rand pay-shoots were not the only puzzle that Carleton Jones and Reinecke had been working on. They had also discussed the mystery of the West Rand, of what had happened to the Main Reef after Randfontein and they felt convinced that it would be picked up again somewhere in the west. They went through the old records of what Edward and David Pullinger had done in the area, until defeated by their flooded shafts. There was also the earlier work done by the Scottish geologist, Dr J T Carrick, who had succeeded J H Curle as Mining Editor of *The Star*. Carrick had worked with Dr F H Hatch, who had served under Hays Hammond at Gold Fields. Together they had mapped the area back in 1889.

Carrick was convinced that an important goldfield lay in the west and in 1909 he decided to go to Britain to raise money to float a company. He sailed from Durban in the SS *Waratah* and was never seen again; the disappearance of the *Waratah* without trace remains perhaps the greatest sea mystery of all times.

Carleton Jones, despite his many other preoccupations, constantly came back to the question of the lost reef. It was not only the professional problems of mining in Africa that intrigued him, but Africa itself, and from earliest time he felt he had been destined to play a role there, despite the fact that his own family had been making a contribution to the history of Canada for generations. His great grandfather, Guy Carleton Jones, had been named after General Sir Guy Carleton, who commanded the British forces at Quebec at the time of the American War of Independence. At the end of that war the Carleton Jones family, being loyalists, settled in Nova Scotia, where Carleton Jones's grandfather became Lieutenant Governor and he himself was born in 1888. The name Carleton meant much to him. In his early days in South Africa he hid it away, calling himself G C Jones, but as he went up in the world, he brought it out and wore it like a family signet ring. In the end he chose it for the name of the town

that would be the memorial to his work – Carletonville.

On the wall of his nursery in Nova Scotia hung a lithograph of a painting that Thomas Baines had made at the Victoria Falls in 1864. 'That picture,' he said many years later, 'caught my imagination and I was determined to come to Africa when I grew up.' He was also determined to become a mining engineer and, on growing up, he qualified at McGill University where his friend and fellow student was Stowe McLean, also destined to make his name on the mines of the Witwatersrand and even to be his colleague for a time at Sub Nigel. When he was ready to go to South Africa, he wrote to John Hays Hammond in the United States for advice about taking up a mining career there. The former consulting engineer to Gold Fields, however, thought he would do better to stay in Canada. It was not the advice Carleton Jones wanted and he set off for the Rand. His feelings about having an African destiny were reinforced in South Africa when he heard that the original of the Baines picture that had fascinated him in the nursery, was being offered for sale in London with thirty-nine other Baines pictures. When he offered to buy it, he was told he would have to take all forty pictures since the collection could not be divided. He then gambled every penny he had on the Stock Exchange and made enough money to buy ten. Finally he bought all forty. In due course they arrived and were stacked up in his room in Johannesburg, a somewhat unwieldy talisman for launching Carleton Jones upon his career as a mining engineer for Gold Fields in Southern Africa. He began humbly in the laboratories at Germiston, then went as a sampler to Knights Deep. The First World War intervened and Trooper G C Jones of the 5th South African Horse went off to serve under General Smuts in East Africa, until invalided back home.

Guy Carleton Jones (called Peter by his friends), a Canadian mining engineer of genius who played a major role at Gold Fields in South Africa over three decades. A lithograph of the picture by Thomas Baines, opposite, *painted on the Zambezi, hung in the Carleton Jones home in Nova Scotia. 'That picture caught my imagination as a youngster and I was determined to come to Africa when I grew up.' He arrived in 1913.*

After the war promotion at Gold Fields had come quickly and to have obtained at the age of thirty-three the plum job as manager at Sub Nigel was considered something of a triumph. His move in 1925 to Gold Fields' office in Johannesburg had a particular purpose; this time it was not gold but platinum that was to occupy his time. The previous year that great figure in South African mining, the German geologist Dr Hans Merensky, had discovered platinum in the Lydenburg district of the Bushveld. Gold Fields had wasted no time in obtaining interests there and Carleton Jones's job was to organize the company's platinum operations. Lydenburg Platinum Areas had been formed with Gold Fields in administrative control and Merensky himself retained as consulting geologist. Then came the formation of Waterval (Rustenburg) Platinum Mining Company. However, Carleton Jones had not been long in his job when the platinum market collapsed, the price of the metal dropping from some £12 to £4 an ounce. Almost as an act of mutual protection Gold Fields and JCI, the other main platinum operator, put their interests together to form a new operating company, Rustenburg Platinum Mines Limited. However, another decade would go by before platinum showed any sign of life or the company produce a dividend. Nevertheless, the foundation had been laid for many long years of collaboration between Gold Fields and JCI and Carleton Jones, assisting his resident director, Douglas Christopherson, had played a part in the making of their 'gentleman's agreement'.

124

That sense of destiny, of having a role to play, that seemed to determine the pattern of Carleton Jones's life was soon to be re-emphasized once more. In February 1930 W E Turvey, Gold Fields' consulting engineer in Johannesburg since 1923, died. Within six months B Orpen, who was Carleton Jones's other colleague and a former manager at Robinson Deep, had also died.

Carleton Jones, five years before he might have expected it, became consulting engineer in Johannesburg. As the top technical man, he was in the driving seat but would there be anything to drive? Would there be a future? It was the old question, old mines growing older and no new ones to take their place.

There was gloom and a sense of hopelessness everywhere. In London, Lord Brabourne was telling shareholders about the 'disastrous period of stagnation and depression which set in in practically all markets in the autumn of 1929 and of which the end is not in sight....' In South Africa, even the Government Mining Engineer, Dr Hans Pirow, believed the end of the gold mining industry was over the horizon. He had published figures which indicated that gold output in South Africa, estimated in 1930 to be worth £43 500 000 would by 1949 have fallen to a mere £10 000 000. 'This disquieting estimate,' said the Chamber of Mines, 'has been confirmed by a technical investigation carried out by the Gold Producers Committee.' The seriousness of the position for South Africa's economic future was underlined by the Chamber which reported that 'of the revenue of the State...for the financial year ended 31 March 1930, approximately one-half is derived directly or indirectly from the gold mining industry and that one-half of the population of the Union obtains its livelihood directly or indirectly from that industry'. If the mining industry had no real future, what kind of future had South Africa? The discovery of a new field was vital for the future of all South Africans. That it fell to Gold Fields to make this discovery has ensured it a permanent place in the history of South Africa. Its achievement in doing so is enhanced by the fact that it came when the country's fortunes, like those of most of the industrialized world, were at their lowest ebb.

Historic events often occur as the result of the right people being in the right place at the right time. Carleton Jones, the mining engineer and his geologist colleague, Reinecke, were ready to play their part. Both were intensely interested in the enigma of the lost reef, of what lay beyond Randfontein, beyond the major fault at the southern end of the mining area. Soon after Carleton Jones arrived in the Johannesburg office in 1925, Gold Fields made another effort to find out. They invited Professor R B Young of the University of the Witwatersrand for an opinion. He came back to say that he felt, but was not sure, that the conglomerates at Middelvlei, Rhodes's old property, and those exposed in the Pullinger boreholes, belonged to the Kimberley-Elsburg series and were of no special interest. Dr E T Mellor, a former Professor of Geology at Southampton University, had produced a similar opinion for the Corner House. In the end, it was by a totally new method of investigation, never before used in South Africa, 'the magnetic method of prospecting', that the truth was determined. And that brought in a complete newcomer, not only to Gold Fields, but to South Africa itself. His name was Dr Rudolf Krahmann and he was to play a crucial role in the discovery of the West Wits Line.

Krahmann, accompanied by his wife, had arrived in South Africa from Germany at the beginning of 1930. Like many other highly trained, highly educated men there was no work for him at home; Germany, like the rest of the Western world, had been brought to a standstill by the Depression. Krahmann was the son of Professor M Krahmann, head of the faculty of Economic Mining in the University of Berlin, and having qualified as a Doctor of Engineering and Mining Engineering, specializing in economic geology, he had worked for a while as his father's assistant in the university. Then he had spent six years with the Elbof Geophysical Prospecting Company of Kassel where his duties had taken him not only to many countries in Europe but also to the Antipodes and to Indonesia. His particular contribution to the company was to introduce to them the new science of geophysical prospecting by means of an instrument known as a magnetometer. This was the magnetic method of prospecting. By the end of 1929, however, Krahmann's activities had dried up. 'I spent a fortnight in Berlin completely in vain,' he wrote that December to a friend at Kassel. 'Wherever I called I found the position hopeless for us miners and geologists. We have therefore decided for better or for worse to emigrate and will leave Hamburg by the SS *Toledo*...for Cape Town on 8 February.... I feel relieved after the long months of enforced idleness and am very busy with preparations for the move.' Later,

Rudolf Krahmann at work with his magnetometer.

after he had reached South Africa, he wrote again to Kassel. 'It took some courage to sail away into the blue with my wife and fifteen trunks – we left our three children with our in-laws in Germany in the meantime. The depression is serious here, too, and if I had conducted a lengthy correspondence beforehand I would certainly have been dissuaded from coming.' Krahmann set himself up as a consultant in Johannesburg but in the first few months he earned only £75. 'It brought me to the brink of desperation,' he recorded. Then an extraordinary thing happened.

'We were invited to watch the mountain motor race on the slopes of Muldersdrift near Krugersdorp on Whitsunday,' he recorded on 11 June 1930. 'We accepted with pleasure.' They settled themselves comfortably and waited for the race to begin. Then the trained eye of the geologist picked up something. 'In the sharp glare of the sun my attention was drawn by the glitter of the surrounding shales. This together with the reddish colouring of the soil indicated a high iron content. If so, the glitter must originate from minute magnetic crystals. And so it proved to be; by moving about a barely pea-sized fragment of shale, I could turn the needle of my geologist's compass in any direction I liked. While playing around with this shale fragment, the idea struck me whether it would not be possible to use this ferruginous shale horizon of the Lower Witwatersrand System as a guide to locate the Main Reef of the Upper Witwatersrand System which disappears under young rocks south of Randfontein.'

Krahmann was tremendously excited by this sudden flash of inspiration and the motor race was almost forgotten. All he wanted to do was to get back home and start reading up everything that had ever been written about the Witwatersrand series. Ironically, it was in the writings of Dr Mellor, the Corner House geologist, that he found what he was looking for. Mellor reckoned that there were at least five major and several minor magnetite-bearing shale horizons all occurring below the Main Reef. Krahmann worked out that if he could detect with his magnetometer the position of the magnetic shales then in all likelihood the Main Reef would be found some 400 feet above it. It was a totally new approach. In the past, prospectors, concentrating on the gold they were after, had always made a direct approach, knocking on the front door as it were. Krahmann intended to go round to the back door. 'My idea – it was the egg of Columbus – was to ignore the direct approach to the gold-bearing reefs and to study the physical characteristics of the accompanying rocks. Of these the magnetic content of certain horizons was the most obvious and appeared the most promising. These iron-rich shales of the Lower Witwatersrand System, occurring at reasonably constant intervals below the Main Reef, could then be used, indirectly, as markers to trace the continuation of the gold-bearing horizons of the Upper Witwatersrand System.' What Krahmann believed he could do with his magnetometer was to show where the reef should be looked for – nothing more. Only boreholes could locate the reef and its gold content but if they were drilled at places indicated by his magnetometer, they would hit the target. He was right. When, in due course, the boreholes went down, they invariably scored a bullseye.

At first the whole thing seemed highly improbable. Krahmann knew he would have to convince someone in authority and gain his support. He chose one of the best known mining personalities, a fervent German, like himself. 'With this egg hatching in my pocket I went straight to Dr Hans Merensky and laid my cards on the table,' he recorded. 'He was immediately interested.' Merensky, with his platinum and diamond triumphs behind him, had become a rich man; he was prepared to help Krahmann, who on 9 August 1930 sent a cable to his father in Germany: 'Please order immediately magnet vertical field balance with reserve magnet system at Askaniawerke. Both to be tuned to Johannesburg with reserve quartz bearings and edges. Await cable reply on shortest delivery date.' Then he recorded: 'Behind the above cable is of course Merensky's purse. He decided to let me carry out the requisite preliminary experimental measurements.' The instrument arrived at the end of October and throughout November Krahmann was out in the field putting his theory to the test. He was very happy. 'The beautiful dream to carry out fieldwork in shorts, in company with Gertrud, has become a reality; we could really not wish it to be nicer...' Then on 7 December he recorded excitedly: 'What I hoped for and wanted to prove has been confirmed with absolute certainty; that careful measurements of the magnetic vertical intensity are capable of correctly locating the various horizons of the Lower Witwatersrand System even under a thick cover of younger formations. This result can be of great importance in the future search for the Upper Witwatersrand System which contains the extensive, gold-bearing reefs, as these are more or less conformable to and sub-outcrop parallel to the Lower Witwatersrand System. Where to the east and to the west of the present mining area, which has already attained a length of about 70 miles, the continuation of the Witwatersrand System is covered and still unknown, I can now with this method determine the position of the Lower Witwatersrand System. The gold-bearing conglomerates of the Upper Witwatersrand System should then be sought at a given parallel distance and explored by boreholes.'

Krahmann was convinced that he had tumbled on something of immense importance to South Africa's mining industry but he would require financial backing and a large organization to promote him. 'Dr Merensky would have the capital but appears to be too tired for such a big project and his interest is constantly deflected by his farm, government commissions, trips to Europe etc,' Krahmann tells his father, adding, 'It is not always easy, due to my highly sensitive make-up to get on with him as well as I would like to...' Merensky directed Krahmann to another geologist who, like himself, was the son of German missionaries. This was Leopold Reinecke, a gentle and sensitive man. Krahmann took to him at once. 'There is something in it,' Reinecke told him after listening to his theories. He also understood Krahmann's problem of how to exploit the idea and, said Krahmann later, 'suggested approaching the Gold Fields group with whom he himself co-operates on an independent, part-time basis'. Soon

Krahmann was writing home again: 'The very first door at which I knocked, that of the Gold Fields group, are taking the matter up and details of a three-month contract await only the sanction of their resident director who is expected back tonight....Reinecke told me that experience with all the big mining houses makes him prefer Gold Fields to any of the others. This very English company has advantages over all other houses...'

Douglas Christopherson together with Carleton Jones received Reinecke and Krahmann at Gold Fields on 19 December 1930. This was the historic date on which the fortunes of Gold Fields took a new direction. Carleton Jones and Reinecke had so often discussed the enigma of the Far West Rand. Was little Krahmann and his machine going to solve it for them? It was worth a try. Krahmann was hired but he was so hard-up he had to ask for an immediate advance of £100. Then, sworn to secrecy, he set off for Randfontein to begin, under Carleton Jones's instructions, a survey of the farms that lay to the south-west, following in the footsteps of the Pullinger brothers, and of those academic geologists who had returned from the Middelvlei area with their pessimistic reports that had never really convinced Carleton Jones.

It was from the Gold Fields property, Middelvlei, that Krahmann began to make his surveys. In due course these took him again and again, back and forth, over the fifty kilometres that lay between Randfontein and the banks of the Mooi River. It was a task that required tremendous stamina as he worked on throughout the mid-summer heat, traipsing over the veld, completing 143 traverses in due course. But it all worked out as he expected it to. The surveys showed clearly the presence of the Lower Witwatersrand beds and that might mean that the overlying Main Reef would be close by. The instrument had shown the presence of the magnetic shales where the old boreholes were, at Venterspost and Libanon. Round the area of Bank railway station, through which went the Rand-Cape railway line, there was no reading, indicating, perhaps, another major fault. But along the Wonderfontein valley below the Gatsrante the magnetic pull was there again, as strong as it had been at Randfontein. Krahmann spoke of the 'sleeping beauty fate' of these areas 'before we appeared on the scene'. While Krahmann worked with his magnetometer, Reinecke was backing up, carrying out geological observations of the formations in the area. A team of twenty black labourers was helping him, digging trenches, exposing the earth. Meanwhile, in Johannesburg as their reports came in, Carleton Jones was becoming convinced that Gold Fields was on to the biggest development that South African mining had ever seen. 'Great rejoicing at two subsequent Gold Fields conferences and of course with Reinecke,' Krahmann recorded.

Douglas Christopherson was as supportive and enthusiastic as any, although he had somewhat timidly informed London of what he was doing, adding 'I hope you will agree that it is worth expending £500 on a matter of this kind...' In March 1931 he was so bold as to ask London if its distinguished geologist, Dr Malcolm Maclaren, who was coming out to take a look at Sub Nigel, might be asked to give a view on the company's secret activities out beyond Randfontein.

As a result of Maclaren's visit, Sub Nigel got a new lease and Gold Fields a new lease of life, as a Gold Fields director put it many years later. Maclaren's report to London clinched the matter. Whatever doubts may have existed in London were dispelled when they read: 'In view of the tremendous prize at stake, which might well be another Rand, I have not hesitated to advise your Johannesburg office to proceed energetically with the magnetic survey.' Maclaren's voice carried enormous authority. Born in 1874 in the Thames district of Hauraki Peninsula, in New Zealand, where his father was the County Engineer, Maclaren had grown up in a gold mining environment and, following his profession as a geologist, had by the 1930s become a world authority in his chosen field.

With London having given the green light, things began to move fast. Krahmann got a year's contract and an assistant, H Wallisch. Boreholes would have to be drilled, but the only ground in the area that Gold Fields owned was Middelvlei, so mineral rights had to be sought over a number of farms stretching to the Mooi River. Option hunters were sent out to scour the area that Krahmann had been covering with his traverses. Here was a potential mining area of some 30 000 claims and in due course it would cost Gold Fields £233 000 to take up the options. In charge of the operation, as head of the Mining Rights and Estates Department, was none other than W S Smits, who had been dealing with mining rights and leases since the days when President Kruger had boxed his ears for joining Gold Fields in the 1890s. He knew his subject backwards and bit by bit he put together what came to be known as the West Wits Line. Into the bag of properties that Gold Fields was gathering between Randfontein and the Mooi River were the old Pullinger possessions of their pioneering Western Rand Estates, registered on 4 April 1902 'to prove the continuation of the Randfontein or Main Reef Series'. The Pullinger Shaft put down in 1911 had filled with water and in due course the company went into liquidation. In 1926 the Rand pioneer Colonel James Donaldson and his partner William Carlis paid £80 000 for the old Pullinger interests, taking them into their Western Areas company. Gold Fields now negotiated with Western Areas and obtained options on their farms in return for a one-third interest in any company that might be formed to exploit the mineral rights. Eventually Gold Fields, seeing how things were developing on their West Wits Line, bought the rights outright for £225 000 and Donaldson and Carlis, in those hard times, were pleased to have money in their pockets. The acquisition of the properties where one day the great mines of the West Wits Line emerged was tremendously complicated; Gold Fields' need to keep its activities secret made it more so. Smits had fourteen farms on his list and their owners had to be traced. One of the farms was entailed and there were twelve heirs who had to be consulted before papers could be signed. In their initial dealings with Donaldson and Carlis, Gold Fields had undertaken to drill a borehole within three months but this was delayed for the sake of secrecy. It was becoming more and more difficult to conceal Gold Fields' interest in the area. The Press had begun to report 'increased activity in the South West Rand' and 'extensive prospecting at Middelvlei'. Farmers had had to be put off the scent by being told that Krahmann was using his instrument to test the dew content of the grass! Some of the farmers thought that a search for diamonds was in progress and even that famous diamond discoverer, Sir Thomas Cullinan, was taken in to the extent of pegging valueless claims outside the Gold Fields area at Middelvlei. There was even talk of an oil search. Few suspected gold, since the old route of the Potchefstroom-Pretoria coach that wound through the valley had long since ceased to be considered a possible new gold field. It was also fortunate for Gold Fields that when it went out shopping for mineral rights and options, the economic hardship of the farmers was such that they were only too pleased to part with their land and rights for hard cash.

If Gold Fields gave the impression that it was playing Fairy Godmother to the farmers, distributing its riches among them, it was a false impression because the company in these hard times had little to spare. There was no dividend for the shareholders in 1931, its mines only managing an income of £100 000 that year. All this makes it all the more remarkable that the company, normally so conservative and cautious, should have gone ahead with what must have seemed like a revolutionary undertaking. That it did so says something about the courage of those who had to take the decisions. However, history repeatedly shows that the moment of greatest danger is often the moment of greatest opportunity.

It was rather like that for Gold Fields in 1931. The circumstances could not have been less auspicious. In the British capital where the decisions had to be made, there was already an atmosphere of crisis. Britain was facing economic collapse; a government of national emergency had been established with Labour and Conservatives serving together under Ramsay MacDonald. In September Britain went off the Gold Standard. At 49 Moorgate, John Agnew was increasingly having to take the place of his chairman, the ailing Lord Brabourne. Agnew, assisted by his fellow engineer Robert Annan, studied closely the reports coming from Carleton Jones in Johannesburg. He was asking for up to £90 000 so that they could drill eleven boreholes where they expected to locate the reef. Agnew also had Douglas Christopherson permanently at his side at this time, for after thirty-two years in South Africa, Christopherson had finally returned to London to join his brother on the Board. William Mackenzie and Dr W S McCann were joint managers in Johannesburg with Carleton Jones as consulting engineer. Christopherson, who knew exactly what was at stake and had been working closely with Carleton Jones, Reinecke and Krahmann from the beginning, proposed the formation of a South African company to take over the mineral rights and go on with the prospecting. If the boreholes showed the presence of gold, the existence of this holding company in South Africa would allow other mining houses there to come in and contribute the capital that would be needed. Gold Fields would of course have the major interest. Thus on 12 November 1932 was born West Witwatersrand Areas Limited, before long to be known to stock exchanges round the world as West Wits. It had an authorized capital of £500 000 in one million shares of ten shillings each and of which Gold Fields acquired 200 000 as vendor shares. The new company took over all the mineral rights that Gold Fields had been so painstakingly and secretly acquiring. These included in the western sector mineral rights over some 33 494 hectares as well as the freehold of 6 868 hectares, and in the eastern sector mineral rights over 17 452 hectares and freehold over some seventy-seven hectares which had been obtained from Western Areas Limited.

That Gold Fields was up to something on the Far West Rand could no longer be hidden. Nevertheless the company remained discreet and shareholders were given very little information as to what was going on behind the scenes. One of the advantages of creating a subsidiary is that it does precisely that. In any case, the boreholes had still to perform their task of proving Krahmann's theories. At the 1932 meeting John Agnew, deputizing for Lord Brabourne who was ill, spoke almost casually of a 'geological investigation of certain properties over which it holds options on the Far West Rand' and of the formation of a company called West Witwatersrand Areas, 'to which important financial interests in London and Johannesburg have subscribed'. When Agnew came to the part where he would have to refer to the money that Johannesburg wanted for the boreholes, he made it sound as unimportant as possible. 'The cost estimated at £70 000 to £90 000 is trifling expenditure in view of the magnitude of the possible prize to be won,' he said.

There was no time to waste and Johannesburg went ahead at once with the borehole programme. Carleton Jones gave instructions for the drilling of eleven boreholes at 3,6 kilometre intervals along a line of forty-three kilometres in length and to a depth varying from 972 metres to 1 533 metres. All the boreholes, moreover, were to be drilled at the same time so that there would be no risk of the scheme falling through if, for instance, the first or second borehole proved unfavourable. In the event the drilling programme was an unqualified success and in due course some twenty-one boreholes found payable reef. With that touch of historical continuity, of carrying on where the pioneers had left off, Carleton Jones ordered the cleaning out and deepening of borehole E4 on the farm Driefontein which thirty years earlier Goertz and Company (later Union Corporation) had abandoned at 789 metres. The drill now entered the Upper Witwatersrand System at a mere 114 metres deeper and at 1 100 metres struck the Main Reef. Here was the future West Driefontein mine which, long after the Canadian's day, would become the greatest mine in the world. There would be other excitements at the boreholes.

Agnew, in his report to shareholders, had referred to the support of 'important financial interests in London and Johannesburg' for the new company, West Wits. This, however, had not been easily acquired. Carleton Jones, who had prepared detailed reports for other mining houses in Johannesburg in the hope that they would participate, had found little warmth to match his own enthusiasm. The exception was Anglo American where the consulting engineer, Frank Unger and his geologist, Joe Bancroft, had been very impressed. On 16 October 1932 Unger wrote a glowing report for Sir Ernest Oppenheimer. 'The scheme as submitted to us has many attractions and it appeals to the imagination.

The possibilities are immense and if fortune favours the bold, the outlook for the Witwatersrand will undergo a complete change,' he wrote. Unger, who was also a manager, felt it necessary to tell his chairman, 'I must warn you, however, that the scheme submitted is a gamble, certainly a very attractive one and of a type in which a mining house is absolutely justified in risking even a considerable sum of money.' Oppenheimer, like Carleton Jones and Agnew, was also a man of courage. Anglo American came in with a £50 000 participation, its shareholders being told 'the venture has considerable speculative chances and given reasonable good fortune, should prove to be a most important enterprise'. For Anglo American, West Wits would turn out to be a signpost putting it on the road going further west to Klerksdorp and in due course this company was to have its own great mine on the West Wits Line, Western Deep Levels. Sir George Albu of General Mining and Sir Abe Bailey, always ready for an adventure, took a similar view to Unger and joined Gold Fields in its new initiative.

To Gold Fields' surprise and disappointment they were turned down by their oldest ally, the Corner House, which later realized it had made a mistake. With the goodwill of Gold Fields, it came in later by a side door and took charge, in due course, of one of the great West Wits mines, Blyvooruitzicht. Mackenzie at Gold Fields had hoped the Corner House would come in with a twenty percent participation at a cost of £100 000, and although John Martin, chairman of Rand Mines and of the Argus newspaper group, had recommended acceptance, his London board turned it down. There were a couple of stumbling blocks. One of these was their consulting geologist Dr Mellor who, having made his unfavourable report on the area in the 1920s 'finds no reason to alter the views expressed in his report', as the Corner House told London. The other difficulty was the inclusion in the scheme of the Western Areas properties, the former Pullinger interests. Not only the Pullingers in their day but Donaldson and Carlin in their turn had tried no less than four times to get the Corner House to buy them, and each time had been refused. It had become a kind of psychological block for the Corner House who told Gold Fields that these properties would have to be excluded before they could consider coming in. 'I learned from Gold Fields privately today that the whole thing has now been completed,' Martin informed London on 26 October 1932, 'but I have no information as to the final participants....although as I said by cable we favoured participation on the assumption that all the other groups were likely to accept, regarding the whole thing as a large-scale prospecting gamble, we readily accepted and acted upon your view that it was in all the circumstances advisable to leave it alone.'

Six or seven months later the whole situation had changed and the Corner House like everyone else was trying to get hold of West Wits shares; even Dr Mellor melted. 'The speculative nature of the enterprise and the possible magnitude of the rewards of success have undoubtedly appealed to a large section of the public,' he wrote, 'the enterprise certainly seems the most attractive of the many which have been started in its wake.' What had happened?

Gold Fields, not for the first time in its golden century, was lucky and at a crucial point in its affairs. The Greeks and Romans believed that fortune, under various guises, had her favourites and went into reverse only when the chosen ones became arrogant and boastful. Fortune favours the brave, said the Roman Terence, which is probably why she smiled on Gold Fields at the end of 1932. Six weeks after the flotation of West Witwatersrand Areas, South Africa went off the Gold Standard, on 28 December 1932, and in the New Year of 1933 the price of gold soared and a share boom started. Struggling mines and mining houses took on a new lease of life as their results were soon to show. Ore reserves doubled overnight in value in the old mines whose lives extended by twenty years. Rupert Gettliffe, who was about to join Gold Fields as an electrical engineer, had been working in the Springs area and had not heard the news. On going into the pub he saw a strange sight, miners standing round the bar, their glasses of beer at their side but still full, miners doing little sums with pencil and paper and queuing up for the telephone. They knew the new worth of their mine, that its shares would rise steeply and they were busily getting in on ground level.

The mining houses began to throw themselves into new prospecting programmes. Gold Fields, however, had already started and was six months ahead of everyone else, having had the courage to do so before the economic scene had changed. Once again, it was South Africa where the mines were and not London where the board sat, that was moulding the company's career.

Britain had gone off gold eighteen months earlier. South Africa, under General Hertzog's leadership, was in a mood of national independence and was not prepared to follow Britain automatically. Hertzog had gone to London in 1926 to make a major contribution to the Imperial Conference, which produced the Balfour Declaration, leading to the Statute of Westminster of 1931. By this act of the British Parliament, South Africa, like Australia, Canada and New Zealand, had become a sovereign independent nation and equal partner with Britain in the Commonwealth presided over by King George V. As London loosened its constitutional grip on South Africa, the Afrikaner dream of national independence was slowly becoming reality. Staying on the Gold Standard expressed this new spirit. In any case, it was argued, South Africa was a leading producer of gold and it did not behove her to reduce its international monetary significance. It was a fine display of patriotism but it made no economic sense, as South Africa discovered to its cost throughout 1932 when funds flowed out of the country. The Chamber of Mines produced evidence to show that the industry would collapse, and with it the South African economy, if the country stuck obstinately to the Gold Standard. The Minister of Finance, N C Havenga, was finally, though reluctantly, persuaded to act. South Africa abandoned the Gold Standard and thereby launched itself into a new golden era. In December 1932 the price of gold had been eighty-four shillings; in January it went to 120 shillings and the following year reached 140 shillings. In 1934 the United States changed its official gold price from twenty dollars to thirty-five dollars an ounce, a price that was destined to live for a generation and more. The burst of mining excitement revealed itself not only on the Johannesburg Stock Exchange where in five months the value of mining shares increased from £125 million to more than £350 million but in the appearance of some forty-two new mining companies. Some of these had no substance and, as it was said in Johannesburg at the time 'even the best mining proposition can be spoilt by premature shaft-sinking'. Gold Fields kept its head down and got on with the job, but with the satisfaction of seeing the ten shilling shares of West Witwatersrand Areas go up to £10. As the Stock Exchange was to say later of West Wits, it was 'the most spectacular share and the most outstanding flotation introduced in the sixty years since the discovery of gold on the Rand'.

Exactly a year after South Africa left the Gold Standard, Gold Fields came up with another surprise, not only for itself but for the whole mining world. It was Christmas 1933. Douglas Christopherson was visiting Johannesburg from Britain when it happened and on Boxing Day he informed Agnew in London: 'Kirkman, who is our Field Superintendent on West Wits, brought in on Saturday morning a piece of core which they had drawn up at 5 pm on Friday afternoon....here was a small piece of core showing what was believed to be visible gold with all the characteristics of the Randfontein Leader contact. Although Jones was inclined to agree with the others it was visible gold, he was not at all convinced about it and preferred not to be definite on the point until he had further opinions.' But how could one do this over Christmas? Reinecke was on the train somewhere between Johannesburg and the Cape, where he was going on holiday. Gold Fields managed to stop the train and get Reinecke off. The geologist then caught the next upward train and was in Johannesburg on Christmas morning.

'Before putting it under the microscope he was none too sure about it,' said Christopherson, 'and asked whether there was any objection to his having Merensky in. I quite agreed with Jones that this should be done especially as we felt Merensky was reliable and would keep it to himself. So Jones went off to search for Merensky and had the luck to find him doing a Christmas round of visits to his friends before going to Pretoria for lunch. By the time they arrived back at the office, Reinecke was all smiles, being then quite satisfied as to the visible gold and so was Merensky but until they have it assayed they are not prepared to say it is the Randfontein Leader. Tomorrow Jones is showing the core not only to the engineers of other houses associated with us in this business but also to others who have special knowledge of the Randfontein Leader....from tomorrow on....it will be impossible to keep it so secret as we have been able to do since Saturday....so far nothing has leaked out.' Christopherson ended his message by saying that he hoped the news 'helped to make Christmas all the brighter for you and the others'. Then, sportsman that he was, he announced: 'I am just off to the races. Yesterday (Christmas Day) was much spoilt by very violent rain and hailstorms.'

But not for Gold Fields; for them the sun had begun to shine permanently, for what they had just found in the old Goertz E4 borehole on what is now Driefontein was the Carbon Leader, a new reef below the Main Reef (or Randfontein Leader) and the richest formation ever found in South Africa.

Gold Fields began to make a habit of filling the Christmas stocking with good news. In December 1935 they did it again. In the eastern sector at borehole E4 they intercepted at 600 metres yet another hitherto unknown reef which was also extremely rich in gold and this they called the Ventersdorp Contact Reef – the VCR. Some seven months later, on 10 August 1936, on one and the same day they intercepted the Carbon Leader in two different boreholes, E5 on the present West Driefontein and E7 on what became Doornfontein. Each new strike excited fresh interest on the Johannesburg Stock Exchange. It was even said that punters kept a watch on the Gold Fields garage and whenever a car with Western Transvaal number plates drew in, up went West Wits shares.

The excitement provided by the discovery with a new method of prospecting of the path of the Main Reef beyond Randfontein and of the new reefs, the Carbon Leader and the Ventersdorp Contact Reef, which in due course were to prove more significant for the riches of the West Wits Line than the Main Reef, tended to overshadow in these opening years of the 1930s whatever else was happening in the South African life of the company. New personalities were appearing both in London and in Johannesburg to direct the company's affairs into the new era that was beginning, the golden age from 1933 until the outbreak of the Second World War in 1939. And, as if a new era required a new working environment, Gold Fields had acquired new homes both in London and in Johannesburg.

In 1929 shortly before the retirement of Lord Harris, Consolidated Gold Fields moved to a very imposing new address, 49 Moorgate, near the Bank of England in the heart of the City of London. They were to stay here until September 1985 when they transferred to St James's Square in London's West End. The Gold Fields move to 49 Moorgate was preceded by dramatic events that took place there late on the afternoon of Thursday, 12 May 1927. The building was surrounded and entered by a force of 150 policemen commanded by Sir Wyndham Childs, Assistant Commissioner of the Metropolitan Police. At this time 49 Moorgate bore the name Soviet House since it was the London headquarters of what purported to be an Anglo–Russian trading organization named Arcos. For some time British Military Intelligence, MI5, suspected that Arcos was a cover for Russian subversive activities in Britain and that they had had something to do with the General Strike which had paralysed Britain in 1926. However, it was only after the disappearance of a vital top secret document from the War Office, which was thought to have found its way to 49 Moorgate, that the British authorities decided to act. The raid on 12 May 1927 was meant to recover the lost document. The Russians, pleading diplomatic immunity, refused to allow the police into their vaults. That did not deter Sir Wyndham who ordered pneumatic drills to be brought in and before long the police had blasted their way into the vaults. They did not discover the document, but as the British Prime Minister told the House of Commons, they found evidence of a massive Russian spy

1933: Gold Fields went down the road to 75 Fox Street, and the old premises made way for the present SA Reserve Bank building.

138

organization. Twelve days later Britain and Russia broke off diplomatic relations. The 1 000 Russians who had packed into 49 Moorgate returned home, the building with its massive vaults was emptied and its long lease put up for sale. On 13 November 1928 Gold Fields bought it for £140 000 and the 200 members of the London staff quit 8 Old Jewry to occupy the seven floors and basement which had formerly accommodated 1 000. Thenceforth reports coming from Johannesburg on the progress of the West Wits Line or results at Sub Nigel were tucked up in the files which had formerly held the reports of Russian spies in Britain. Nothing as dramatic as this attended the acquisition of new offices in Johannesburg. The old offices with their classical facade on the corner of Fox and Simmonds Streets – now replaced by the South African Reserve Bank – had become too small to cope with the company's growing activities. In 1933, new offices next door in Fox Street closer to the old Stock Exchange became Gold Fields' headquarters on the Rand but soon even these were not adequate. The old Rand Water Board site in Commissioner Street which backed on to the Fox Street premises was obtained and provided a convenient overflow.

Lord Harris, born in 1851, two years before Cecil Rhodes, announced his retirement as chairman of Consolidated Gold Fields at the shareholders' meeting in December 1929. His last address was his 31st consecutive address as chairman and to depart after thirty-three years as a director was a sad moment not only for himself but for his shareholders. He died in March 1932 at the age of eighty-one just as his company was about to gain a new life in South Africa. Today he is remembered above all as a cricketer and the Harris Garden at Lords cricket ground is the memorial he would have valued most. Lord Brabourne, his successor, was already a sick man. He took a trip to South Africa to try to regain his health but died at sea on the return journey in 1933. Stanley Christopherson, as the senior director, would have been the natural successor but his time was being taken increasingly by the Midland Bank whose chairman he became. The way was clear for Gold Fields to have for the first time as chairman a mining engineer. John Agnew became head of the company at exactly the right moment in its development and his chairmanship coincided exactly with that golden era, 1933-39. There had been other changes on the board. Geoffrey Dawson had gone back to be Editor of *The Times* and in the 1930s he exerted enormous influence on Britain's national policies both at home and abroad. In 1931 a prominent Tory politician, Sir Philip Cunliffe-Lister, joined the board. He is better remembered as the Earl of Swinton, who as Britain's Minister for Commonwealth Affairs demonstrated the friendship and sympathy for South Africa that he had no doubt learned at Gold Fields. This was particularly valuable in the early 1950s when Dr Malan's National Party Government was feeling its way in international affairs. By a curious coincidence Swinton left Gold Fields to become President of the Board of Trade. Another British politician, Frederick Erroll, did the journey in the opposite direction. Having been President of the Board of Trade, he then in 1975, as Lord Erroll of Hale, became chairman of Consolidated

John Agnew (right) at Venterspost with (centre) Rudolf Krahmann and (left) Guy Carleton Jones, 1932.

Opposite, top, *Another Canadian, Robert Pelletier, who took over the geological department at Gold Fields following Reinecke's death in 1935, is seen here, the following year, in South West Africa, standing on the Hoba meteorite near Grootfontein. Fifty years later, after a long and distinguished career at Gold Fields, he was writing his memoirs in Johannesburg.*

Below, left, *Dr W P de Kock, a brilliant geologist and fervent Afrikaner, joined Gold Fields in the early 1930s at a time when it was still that 'very English company'. He almost immediately made his mark in mining history by identifying the Carbon Leader, a hitherto unknown reef and an outstanding feature of the West Wits Line.*

Below, right, *Albert Truter in the field, Venterspost area, circa 1932. Recruited from the University of Stellenbosch, he later became consulting geologist.*

141

Gold Fields. Serving under Agnew on the Gold Fields board in the early 1930s were men such as Prinsep and Porter who had joined the company in the early days, whom Lord Harris would probably have considered 'players' since they had started at the bottom and worked their way to the top.

In Johannesburg with the departure of Dr McCann, Carleton Jones became joint manager with William Mackenzie, at the same time continuing to be consulting engineer. Reinecke had become consulting geologist and was building up his department, having brought into the company another Canadian, Dr Robert Pelletier who had done distinguished work in the Rhodesias. Later the company's first South African geologist joined, in the person of Dr Willem de Kock, who had been working in South West Africa. At Gold Fields de Kock almost immediately made his mark when, with Pelletier, he studied the unusual cores that had been brought up from boreholes at Driefontein and Blyvooruit-zicht and come to the conclusion that they were not from the Main Reef. They were different because of their high carbon content, the visible gold, and they were always found below a marker formation known because of its colour as the Green Bar. There could be only one conclusion; it must be a different reef. De Kock and Pelletier called it the Carbon Leader.

The days were ending when South Africa had to import its mining technicians from abroad. Young South African geologists were being trained, for instance, at Stellenbosch University and from time to time the head of the faculty there would get in touch with Reinecke and ask him if he could help place his young men. The kind-hearted Reinecke did his best. Thus another young Afrikaner trained as a geologist found his way to Gold Fields. He was Albert Truter. Two of his fellow students at Stellenbosch who had preceded him to the Rand had had to make the journey from Stellenbosch on their bicycles since they had no money. Truter, a future consulting geologist, was not much better off. Reinecke really had no job for him and sent him into the veld to do some surveying. When he received his first month's pay of £10, he believed it came not from Gold Fields but out of Reinecke's own pocket. Reinecke would visit his young men in the field, taking them sacks of oranges and other comforts. A devout Christian, he insisted that they should go to church on Sundays. Reinecke himself was now ill and the Krahmanns took him in and found a nurse. In 1934, a brain tumour was diagnosed and he went to England for treatment but died and was buried at sea on the return journey. His death at the moment of his success was a particular tragedy. It was left to Robert Pelletier as consulting geologist to build up the department. In that department Krahmann had his own section, as geophysical investigations increased. Another magnetometer was bought and Krahmann's section had two teams in the field. He had recruited his men from Germany, where Adolf Hitler had just come to power.

All that had been done on the Far West Rand was by way of preparation for Gold Fields' bright future in South Africa; the first of the West Wits mines, Venterspost, would not begin to produce until 1939. Meanwhile, other areas had not been forgotten. Robinson Deep and Simmer and Jack were still demonstrating their seemingly inexhaustible worth, having been given a new lease of life when South Africa went off the Gold Standard. Robinson Deep, in particular, had been well placed to profit from the rise in the gold price, since in 1930 it had acquired, at the bargain price of £337 000, the whole of the mining rights and most of the equipment of the adjoining Village Deep, then at more than 8 500 feet the deepest mine in the world. Mining at Robinson Deep was then conducted at three shafts, No 1, the Chris shaft and Turf shaft and soon its miners, working more deeply than anyone had ever worked before, were feeling the heat. In 1936, for the first time, an effort was made to get an air cooling system going. Up till that time Robinson Deep methods had been 'Heath Robinson'; blocks of ice had been passed down the Turf shaft to try to keep the temperature down. Meanwhile, Robinson Deep remained a popular place to take important visitors. On one occasion a party of these knew all about heat; they had come from India and at a time when that country was represented in South Africa by an Agent-General. They were six Maharajahs and, since they were visiting a gold mine, they felt it appropriate to arrive wearing their Crown Jewels. When they went underground they left their jewellery in a locked room under guard.

On the East Rand, Sub Nigel had been rising to ever-increasing stardom. In 1936 it announced new records; some 632 700 tons of ore milled, £2 328 000 profits, dividends of £1 500 000 and working costs at 33/9d a ton the lowest since 1918. It had begun to create a little empire of its own. In 1932 it had increased its own area to more than 6 500 claims, having acquired further Grootfontein claims, and had improved its efficiency with its new Betty shaft, named after the daughter of W A Quince, the mine manager. Two new mines, Vlakfontein in 1934, followed by Spaarwater had come into existence to work claim areas adjoining the Sub Nigel property. The new mine, Vlakfontein, was being developed from Sub Nigel under a royalty agreement and when, in 1984, Vlakfontein celebrated its 50th anniversary, this initial help from Sub Nigel was not forgotten. Gold Fields had acquired Vlakfontein after negotiations with Lace Proprietary Mines; the property had originally been bought in 1902 by Dale Lace, a pioneer with great panache who wore foppish clothes and was considered to be the most handsome man in Johannesburg, whose society he dominated from his great Parktown house, Northwards. Vlakfontein had other distinctions. It was the first mine to profit from the change in the Gold Law in 1934, when the procedure whereby the Government granted mining leases was greatly simplified. Two years later it hit the headlines with a shaft-sinking record, 128 metres in No 1 shaft in a single month.

In 1933 another East Rand mine, Vogelstruisbult, came into existence as a joint initiative of Gold Fields and Rand Mines, where each company had about the same amount of ground and each wanted control. As they could not agree they went to arbitration and the decision was in Gold Fields' favour. Gold Fields had hoped to have Anglo American money in the venture but when Christopherson, while in Johannesburg in January 1934, approached Ernest Oppenheimer on the subject, he discovered there had been a misunderstanding about

West Wits. 'During my talk with Oppenheimer about the Vogelstruisbult pool he told me he felt very sore that the original participants in the West Wits venture were not given some opportunity for subscribing to the working capital of the subsidiary companies,' he informed Agnew. Christopherson was amazed that Oppenheimer should have been under this impression. 'I am sure the whole trouble is he never saw the agreement and his office did not read it sufficiently carefully to advise him of the contents. It is really his office which is to blame....the result, he sold if not the whole at any rate, all but a very small proportion of their shares, thinking he would come in again on the subsidiaries.' Christopherson had perhaps over-reacted to Oppenheimer's pique, for the Anglo American historian, Sir Theodore Gregory, was to write that 'relations with New Consolidated Gold Fields became closer in the east just at the moment when new developments were taking place in the west'. The incident was one of the first of the hiccups that occurred in the relations between the two companies; only occasionally did it deteriorate into indigestion but hard words were usually followed by renewed smiles and this kind of see-saw relationship goes on to the present day. Anglo did take an interest in Vogelstruisbult which was developed from their own Daggafontein and Springs mines, and they also acquired a substantial interest in Vlakfontein after the death of Sir Abe Bailey in 1940.

There was not much that Anglo did not have an interest in, for little escaped the probing financial genius of Sir Ernest Oppenheimer. And by 1935 Gold Fields became aware that Anglo American were buying heavily into West Wits. Sir Ernest was in London and suggested to the head of his office there, J S Wetzler, that he should go along to Gold Fields and buy a load of West Wits shares; it was the best place to find them, he said. Wetzler did not think it was quite the thing to do and was only persuaded to go to 49 Moorgate after Sir Ernest had threatened to go himself. He came back with some 20 000 shares. Anglo was not alone in seeking West Wits shares.

Rand Mines was now doing its best to make up for its lost opportunity. 'It certainly looks as if they are coming to the conclusion that they have missed the bus in not coming in which will call for some explanation, more especially in view of their having crabbed it so much,' said Christopherson. He was referring to the fact that the Corner House consulting engineer, R S G Stokes, had asked to see Carleton Jones urgently. Brigadier Stokes, CBE, DSO, MC, as he was to become, had with his soldier's eye detected a likely beachhead on the West Wits Line. Gold Fields, in getting options and mineral rights, had almost but not quite made a clean sweep of the area. They had failed to get a small piece of ground on Blyvooruitzicht, just 724 morgen owned by a company called New Witwatersrand Gold Exploration Company with whom Gold Fields had not been able to agree terms. This company had then gone to the Corner House hoping to do better. Stokes was on good terms with his fellow engineer, Carleton Jones, and with Mackenzie who had always wanted the Corner House to be in on the project. The upshot of their talks was that the Corner House, having acquired the 724 morgen in the midst of Gold Fields' 4 000 morgen, was generously given by Gold Fields the administration and control of the Blyvooruitzicht mining company and therefore of the mine that it developed. The mining company came into existence in 1937 with Stokes as chairman and in due course Blyvooruitzicht, working the Carbon Leader, became the first mine to show 100 percent payability from boundary to boundary. Blyvooruitzicht became a wonder mine a decade before West Driefontein appeared on the scene with even greater capability. Although Gold Fields derived great financial benefit from its stake in Blyvoor, it was perhaps a blow to its pride that it was not their flag but that of Rand Mines which flew from the masthead.

It was not pride, however, but water that was Carleton Jones's problem when Gold Fields set the West Wits Line to work with the first of its mines, Venterspost, in 1934. Water was the last big hurdle. They had found the reefs, the gold was there but Nature, as if to protect it from the intruder, had put the dolomite in the way. Through the dolomitic caverns filled with water the shafts would have to go to reach the reef and the gold. Cementation was Carleton Jones's answer to the problem. A Belgian named Albert Francois had shown that it was possible to inject cement – or grout as it was called – into any crack or hole below the water table and thus to seal the flow of water. In 1916 he had been invited to South Africa by the Corner House to help with water problems at their ERPM mine; the process had even been used to shore up the ancient masonry of St Paul's Cathedral near 49 Moorgate in London. In 1920, the Francois Cementation Company was formed in London to exploit the Francois patents and John Agnew had become a director. Agnew arranged for the company to form a subsidiary in South Africa under Gold Fields management, the forerunner of GF Cementation and other offshoots. For a dozen years, Dr G A Voskule was in charge of its operations and Carleton Jones brought him in as a consultant when the time came to sink the first shafts at Venterspost. He brought out from Britain a team led by a young mining engineer named John Crawhall who, having won an MC in the war, had joined the Cementation Company in Britain. Venterspost was the beginning of a long association with Gold Fields and a distinguished career in South Africa for this future chairman of the Rand Club. The two Venterspost shafts were sited 3,6 kilometres apart and as far as possible from the old Pullinger shaft – outside a radius of 1,5 kilometres. In August and September 1934 the drills were at work and the battle with the water began. At both shafts water came bursting through the fissures at 112 feet, again at 200 feet and yet again at 450 feet, but in the end, and a million sacks of cement later, the battle was won. The whole mining industry watched and held its breath.

Harald Krahmann remembered how tense his father had been during this crucial period, particularly when a burst plug was followed by an inrush of water at the rate of three million litres an hour and six pumps were submerged. Water, however, was to remain a problem for miners on the Far West Rand and later on for its farmers too, as a result of gold mining in the area. Some forty years after that first nerve-wracking experience at Venterspost, the mine was to say: 'Venterspost's problem of keeping its workings dry in the face of the waterlogged dolomite is common to all the mines in the area but somewhat more severe in its own case. The mine pumps between forty and forty-three million litres of water a day....'

Development at Venterspost took time, three and a half years to complete the two shafts which went down to 950 metres, no great depth by today's standards. In the beginning, Dick Soulsby, the mine secretary, recalled, those trying to get the mine started lived an isolated and frugal existence in the old Pullinger homestead. But there were excitements. In October 1936 a world record for shaft-sinking in dolomite was set – 265 feet in No 2 shaft that month. Sometimes there were signs of impatience. Carleton Jones was particularly riled by a report in the London *Sunday Express* in 1937 which was headed 'Water, water everywhere and not a spot of gold'. The paper said: 'Two weeks ago that was what disappointed speculators were saying about one of the new South African mining enterprises....' The report rankled for years and perhaps put Carleton Jones against the Press. He had persuaded his brother, Hervey Jones, to give up his editor's chair in Canada and come and work for Gold Fields in Johannesburg, where among other things he became in due time chairman of Luipaards Vlei.

In the event West Wits shareholders did show great patience for it was fourteen years before they received a dividend but that was because the outbreak of war in 1939 set the programme back. Early that year, as West Wits' first mining subsidiary, Venterspost, was about to produce the first gold on the West Wits Line, John Agnew became a little apprehensive. As he told Carleton Jones, who had sent him figures on ore reserves, grades and likely profit per ton, Venterspost 'is regarded as the bell wether of the West Witwatersrand flock and any disappointment that may be felt over the results there would be reflected in a disastrous degree over the whole line. Whether, rightly or wrongly, the public has formed a very high opinion of Venterspost....' In the event everything turned out all right for Venterspost and West Wits shareholders. No one had reason to doubt what Agnew had said about the West Wits Line in 1936: 'The prospects of this area grow brighter every year and I do not think we could have a finer endorsement of our confidence in the outcome than to point to the success which attended the recent offer of 100 000 shares of 10/- each to the original subscribers at £10 a share...every share offered was subscribed without hesitation and the majority of subscribers are prominent South African houses. In all £2 000 000 has been subscribed...and yet the nominal capital at the present time is only £650 000.'

During the 1930s when the preparatory work to launch the West Wits Line was going on, and while new mines were being developed round Sub Nigel, Carleton Jones wanted to gain control of other producing mines to 'balance our list' as he put it. In order to do this, he once again picked up the thread of historical continuity that is such a feature of the Gold Fields story. Having launched the West Wits Line from Rhodes' old property, Middelvlei, he now brought back to Gold Fields after a generation two more of Rhodes's old properties. In 1937 Luipaardsvlei, south of Krugersdorp, and Rietfontein, near the present site of Jan Smuts airport, were once more being controlled by Gold Fields. They came back in unusual circumstances.

In 1933, after the steep rise in the sterling price of gold following the departure from the Gold Standard, a new mining house was born, the company that is now known as Anglovaal. Its creators were A S 'Bob' Hersov and S G 'Slip' Menell. They realized that with the new prospects for gold mining, some of the older properties might be revived. One of these properties which eventually became part of the Anglovaal stable was the old Gold Fields property, Village Main, which had been put out of action in October 1921 when an earth tremor caused the collapse of 15 level. In 1934, under the initiative of J C Bitcon, it was brought to life again. Hersov and Menell were joined at Anglovaal by the son of Ludwig Erlich, the pioneer who had gone into business with Frederic Hamilton to form the HE Proprietary Company and to control Luipaards Vlei. The son, who had grown up in England and was a Cambridge graduate, had anglicized his name to Erleigh. Coming to Anglovaal, Norbert Erleigh brought with him the agency in South Africa for HE Proprietary.

Luipaards Vlei, after Gold Fields had parted with it in the last century, had been reconstituted and registered in London and, until 1912, Gold Fields had administered the mine for Hamilton and Erlich, who acquired a third partner in Eric Turk. After 1912 the partners had established their own presence in South Africa, with first of all the Transvaal Agency and then the South Africa HE Proprietary Company so Gold Fields backed out. These were the South African interests that Norbert Erleigh had brought to Anglovaal. However, Eric Turk thought that Gold Fields were better equipped, being an old established company, to operate Luipaards Vlei and urged Erleigh to talk to Carleton Jones. The result was that in 1936 Gold Fields was again running the old mine. Carleton Jones was, as he said, keen to protect the prestige of the new company Anglovaal since Luipaards Vlei was their only producing mine, so a place was found on the board for their Norbert Erleigh. 'While one may not enthuse over the prospect of having Mr Erleigh on the board there is nothing really against his record....' he told Agnew. The mine on the other hand was just what he wanted, 'having added another producer to our list, without buying an interest, while more or less reserving for ourselves the right to participate in the financing of any future programme of expansion'. Very soon, Carleton Jones, applying to the mine the Gold Fields policy of mining to a stope width comparatively smaller than with other mines, had notably improved the yield at the mine. Rietfontein, like Village Main, had also been brought out of mothballs, having been idle since 1915. Once again being run by Gold Fields, it had by the end of 1936 a milling rate of nearly 20 000 tons a month – 'a miniature Witwatersrand mine', Carleton Jones called it.

These new developments had brought Gold Fields in Johannesburg into a direct and close relationship with the HE Proprietary companies in London, with Eric Turk and Carleton Jones writing to each other regularly. Soon Gold Fields took over further duties as secretaries for the South African HE company

147

which combined all the Hamilton/Erlich interests outside Luipaards Vlei. The significance of this would become clearer twenty years later when, after a curious turn of events related to the rise and fall of Norbert Erleigh, Gold Fields of South Africa acquired all these interests.

HE Proprietary had brought Carleton Jones into direct contact with Eric Turk who spent most of his time in London. Spaarwater and West Vlakfontein, out on the East Rand, produced a business relationship with Herbert Latilla, who stayed permanently in England. He believed it was possible to do that and be chairman of two South African companies. This was in due course to produce a row in the South African Parliament, and to reveal for the first time the growing sensitivity in South Africa about control and interference from London. This was a left-over from colonial times and no longer tolerable in a country that had become almost obsessively aware of the independent status conferred upon it by the Statute of Westminster.

There was, after 1933, a new spirit abroad in South Africa and a new confidence in its national destiny. Lord Gladstone, the first Governor-General in his first public speech in 1910 had said: 'The bane of South Africa is politics' and he called on South Africans to call a halt. It was not until 1933 that his message got through. The economic crisis had brought together Hertzog's National Party and Smuts's South African Party to form a pact Government. Hertzog was Prime Minister and Smuts his deputy. Out of fusion came their United Party. Those of Hertzog's Nationalists who could not accept the new dispensation followed Dr D F Malan into the Opposition as the Hervormde Nasionale Party and bided their time.

South Africa, united at home in a country that was becoming increasingly prosperous on the back of its gold mining industry, was also growing in stature abroad. One of the country's foremost diplomats, Charles te Water, its High Commissioner in London, had gone to Geneva to become President of the League of Nations, forerunner of the United Nations. The country spoke for itself on major international issues and while enjoying a fruitful relationship with Britain and its equal partners in the Commonwealth, the name that had replaced the Empire, it was no longer prepared to accept the London view automatically. In 1937, its Minister of Mines, Patrick Duncan, gave up politics to become the first South African Governor-General of the Union of South Africa. This sense of independence, this new South African consciousness, was also growing among businessmen and shareholders but was not at first appreciated in London. Even John Agnew, who had visited South Africa in 1935 and was back in 1939, had been slow to detect the changes. In May 1937 he was writing to Carleton Jones: 'The procedure followed in this country is vastly different from that in South Africa. In Johannesburg it is only necessary to tell the shareholders what has been decided upon and they are perfectly satisfied that the right course is being followed – I speak now of those companies controlled by the Group. Here we have a great number of small shareholders who like to take advantage of every opportunity of cross-examining the chairman at a public meeting – the

148

only opportunity of talking to "the boss".' Agnew was mistaken and Carleton Jones told him so.

Decisions made in London were no longer so easily swallowed in South Africa. A new sophistication had emerged. Times had changed since the days when a Cape Town shareholder named Malan, who had 6 000 shares in Sub Nigel which he referred to as 'my company', had written to Christopherson, chairman of the company, asking him if he would send him a sample of the mine's gold-bearing reef. Christopherson replied: 'I am sending you by registered parcel post a sample of the reef from this property containing a value of 2 500 inch dwts. As from your letter you appear to be under the impression that we are mining a gold-bearing quartz instead of a conglomerate, I am also sending you in the parcel a small piece of gold-bearing quartz which was come across in the mine some two years ago.' This cosy little exchange between chairman and shareholder says as much for Christopherson's humanity as it does about the kind of relationship that existed at that time. But times were changing and the Spaarwater affair with Herbert Latilla in May 1939 highlighted the new mood in the country.

The Minister of Mines at the time was that legendary figure, Colonel Deneys Reitz, internationally known because of his book *Commando* about his experiences in the Boer War. He had just taken over the portfolio after the resignation of J H Hofmeyr from the Hertzog Government. He was almost immediately precipitated into the deep end by the Spaarwater affair, when J S Marwick, an Opposition member, stood up in the House of Assembly and asked: 'Will the Minister say whether the order for the closing down of this mine emanated from Mr Latilla in London who declared that the property should be closed down and the mine flooded?' West Spaarwater had got into financial difficulties and Reitz, in order to prevent it getting even further into difficulty, had waived the three months' notice to close required under the Gold Law. Marwick accused the Minister of having 'merely surrendered to the stampeding tactics of the company which had been dictated by cabled instructions from Mr Latilla in London', and he spoke of the 'irreparable injury to the investing public and to public confidence in the administration of the Mines Department'. A well known Labour MP, Walter Madeley, also attacked Reitz for having accepted the situation where someone in London had made a decision that deeply affected South African workers and shareholders. The position was grave, he said, because of the London decision to flood the mine. 'A share ramp is now in progress,' he claimed.

The row in Parliament and the publicity given to it in the Press had repercussions for Gold Fields in Johannesburg, because Latilla was also chairman of Spaarwater in addition to West Spaarwater and Gold Fields was managing Spaarwater. Carleton Jones informed Agnew: 'There is no doubt that the remarks which were made at the West Vlakfontein and Spaarwater meetings concerning Mr Latilla continuing to act as chairman of these companies whilst resident in England and the motion at the Spaarwater meeting expressing dissatisfaction at his remaining in that capacity were occasioned as a result of the West Spaarwater business.' South African shareholders were beginning to declare themselves; the outbreak of the Second World War put the whole question in cold storage but ten years after the row in Parliament, Gold Fields in Johannesburg was again writing to London: 'As we see it, it is not in the best interests of good management for the chairman of these two South African companies to be permanently non-resident. To my mind it does not reduce our responsibility as managers and technical advisers even if the chairman is overseas but I do appreciate your point of view that as a matter of policy it would not be wise to have the chairman's position filled by a member of our organization, particularly if we do so, it could be constructed that we had a voting control which of course is not the case.' By this time Gold Fields had as its resident director in Johannesburg, for the first time in half a century's activity in the country, a man who had been born and bred in South Africa and who could interpret the feelings of national sentiment and pride of the people among whom he worked.

Nothing in the Gold Fields world better reflects those halcyon South African days of the 1930s, with their political unity, rising prosperity and national confidence, than the life of the mining community of Sub Nigel. They left an indelible memory with those who lived there at the time. Many of these rose later to the highest positions in Gold Fields and other companies; these even included some who were born at Sub Nigel or who, as children, ran about its playing-fields. Carleton Jones always recalled Sub Nigel as the happiest period of his life. Donald McCall got his first job there as an underground official in 1930 and when, more than thirty years later, as chairman of Consolidated Gold Fields in London, he had reluctantly to cut the painter and cast Gold Fields of South Africa loose as an independent company, he felt that something of his own life at Sub Nigel was going with it. A A von Maltitz, who became a distinguished president of the Chamber of Mines, had sought advice from his uncle, Peter Maltitz Anderson, chairman of Union Corporation, about his career as a mining engineer but in the end he chose Sub Nigel because, he said, it was the richest mine in the world. And that was true. His colleagues at Sub Nigel took a sympathetic interest in young Attie von Maltitz because his father, who had been mayor of Dewetsdorp in the Free State, and two fellow town councillors, had been assassinated in sensational circumstances. Pieter von Maltitz, who had been a prisoner of the British in Ceylon during the Anglo-Boer War, was blown up in Dewetsdorp Town Hall on 8 April 1927 with two others, Viljoen and Ortlepp. The man who placed the bomb was the Town Clerk, H J de Leeuw, whose fraudulent conduct of the town's affairs was about to be investigated. He was tried and executed for murder.

Sub Nigel in its heyday was many things to many people; it also created its own legends. Being somewhat isolated from the city life of Johannesburg with its bright lights, it created its own self-sufficient community, organized its own life. Like all communities it had its 'characters', it is remembered for some of its eccentrics, men such as a mine captain called 'Wild Bill' Heuston, who treated the East Rand as if it were the Far West, and who rode to the mine each day dressed as a cowboy. He had formerly worked in a circus, exercising his talents as a crack shot with a pistol. He kept his six-shooter handy, and anyone so rash as to enter his office with a cigarette sticking out of his mouth ran the risk of having it shot out, in the manner of the circus act. C D Storrar, who became group surveyor and wrote a book on mine valuation, remembered Sub Nigel in the 'Thirties' as creating its own entertainments and gaining a reputation for its parties, with lively personalities, such as the red-bearded Alan Pole, who became in time manager of West Driefontein. And there was the Sub Nigel 'bucket shop' run by Reginald Courtney, 'a perfect English gentleman'. His strict sense of time was not confined to clocking in horses; when the hour struck that signalled the end of his working day, he would put his hat on his head and walk off, whatever the circumstances. On one occasion this happened in the office of the mine manager, who on Courtney's abrupt departure was left open-mouthed and in mid-sentence.

Stanley Hallett, an Oxford graduate, was another Gold Fields luminary who spent his early days at Sub Nigel; his engineer brother, Arthur,[1] also worked for Gold Fields and invented a skip-arresting device for the company. Their father, W E J Hallett, built the first plant for extracting oil from coal at Ballengeich in Natal. Stanley Hallett was a man in the Gold Fields tradition; he was a cricketer and had played county cricket for Gloucestershire, where one of England's greatest cricketers of all times was emerging, W R Hammond. At the same time, a young South African at Cambridge was playing for Somerset. His name was C S Barlow, known to his friends as 'Punch', not yet dreaming of the day when he would be the successor of Wernher and Beit and take over the Corner House, absorbing its historic companies into his Barlow Rand. Hallett recalled how Sub Nigel in the 1930s was reaping the rewards of mining according to the Carleton Jones formula, with small stopes, but he had mingled feelings about them. 'I remember in my early years at Sub Nigel being completely stuck when measuring a stope which was only eleven inches high,' he said. 'I had to be pulled out by a rope tied round my ankles.'

That might have been considered an amusing game by some of the children on the mine; the Gibbs family, for instance, Stan Gibbs, who became manager of West Driefontein and consulting engineer to the company in Johannesburg, his brother Tommy, the Government Mining Engineer, and three younger brothers who also worked on the mines. When Stan Gibbs's son, Len, joined Gold Fields the family had marked up three generations with the company. There was the equally remarkable Robinson family which also served the company through three generations. L R 'Bob' Robinson, who was Gold Fields' top technical man when he retired in 1985, had been born at Sub Nigel in 1926 and his grandfather, who was an engineer fitter, was still working there in his eighties, never having felt a need to retire.

Sub Nigel in the 1930s is, above all, the era of the Fleischer family. Spencer Fleischer, born in Johannesburg, educated at Michaelhouse, decorated for

Left: *Tommy Gibbs setting off the first sinking blast at Deelkraal, September 1975. The family Gibbs, with Tommy, his brother Stan and Stan's brother Len, is part of a Sub Nigel mining tradition.*

Right: *Sub Nigel Family Robinson. S A Robinson (left), his son L R and L R's son Bob, three generations of Gold Fields technical men.*

gallantry in the First World War in France, a reluctant striker in 1922, became mine manager at Sub Nigel in 1934 on £150 a month. He stayed there until the advent of the Second World War in 1939 turned him into a soldier again. During the 1930s his sons, Tony Fleischer, who became a prominent official in the Chamber of Mines and a writer, and his brother Derek, spent their holidays there from school. Their mother, Di Fleischer, who kept a chronicle of her Gold Fields days and made a niche in the annals of the company as the founder of the Gold Fields book clubs, wrote: 'Both the boys loved Sub Nigel. We had horses, lots of friends, an interesting life for young fellows.' She herself had been born on a mine, at Geldenhuis Deep in the year the Anglo-Boer War ended. Like her children she had grown up on a mine, New Modder, where her father, Tom Duff, was compound manager and where, as a schoolgirl, she met and fell in love with Spencer Fleischer who worked there. The influence of the mining environment on a growing boy is best described by George Nisbet, President of the Chamber of Mines in 1985. He, too, grew up on New Modder in the 1930s. 'I suppose I once or twice accompanied my father underground but generally I was contaminated from the beginning with the smell of the mines in my nostrils,' he said. 'There was no doubt that this boyhood environment and mixing

152

with mining people decided me on a mining career.'

By 1936 mining had been going on in South Africa for half a century and a mining tradition was becoming part of the social fabric of the country, where men and women, born on the mines, produced families that continued the process. The time was passing when mining engineers, geologists, managers had to be imported from Britain or Canada; they were evolving on the spot and carried the label 'Made in South Africa'. Early that year of 1936 a young South African from the Orange Free State who was about to complete the three years at Oxford that a Rhodes Scholarship had given him, thought it would be a good idea to obtain employment in Rhodes's old company. He got in touch with Agnew in London who asked Carleton Jones to make some enquiries about the young man and to offer him a place if he thought it fit. In due course he wrote to Agnew: 'I have had replies from the people in South Africa to whom I wrote regarding this young man and they all speak most highly of him, so highly that I have decided to make him a firm offer and shall be glad if you will get in touch with him....I said we would be prepared to offer him £50 a month but his qualifications impress me so much that we are now willing to offer him a commencing salary of £60 a month, believing that the higher rate would enable us to hold him,

Spencer and Di Fleischer, at Sub Nigel in the Thirties and later in Johannesburg, created a sense of community among Gold Fields people. The book clubs founded on the Reef by Mrs Fleischer became an institution.

153

*Rhodes and his scholar
eyeball to eyeball.
William Busschau
was the first Oxford
Rhodes Scholar to
reach the top of the
company co-founded
by his patron;
chairman of GFSA,
1960-1965.*

as I would not be surprised if he received offers from one of the other groups.' The young man certainly had unusual qualifications; he was a trained economist, a chartered accountant, and he had even been to the Soviet Union to study its five-year plan. Gold, however, was already his consuming passion. 'I decided in 1931,' he was to say later, 'that in twenty years I wanted to know more about gold than any other man in the world.' By the end of 1936 when his first book, *The Theory of Gold Supply*, appeared, he was at work at Gold Fields in Johannesburg. His name was Bill Busschau and in due course, if any man deserved the title 'Mr Gold', it would be Dr William Busschau. He became in time resident director of the company in South Africa but from the start he was regarded as the resident genius.

Busschau had arrived at Gold Fields in time for a celebration, for in 1937 the company decided to mark its golden jubilee with a series of dinner parties both in London and in Johannesburg. Plans were already in hand for the celebration when news was received of a near disaster at Simmer and Jack. 'When we learned of the fire on Friday morning we were filled with dismay at the thought of what

154

this might mean if the fire once got a hold on an old mine like Simmer,' Agnew wrote to Carleton Jones on 22 March. Simmer was saved but the strain and the effort broke the health of the Mine Manager, W C Coe, who resigned and asked to return to England.... 'his health and mental outlook have been considerably affected by recent happenings', Johannesburg told London. In view of Coe's excellent service in South Africa, a place was found for him at 49 Moorgate, where he once again flourished.

Within two years of Coe's departure, the new manager at Simmer and Jack, Archie Kennedy and his Mine Engineer, C R 'Mick' Anderson, were having to cope with another drama. Anderson was in Kennedy's office when the telephone rang. An agitated woman on the line was saying that a locomotive had appeared in her back garden. It was no hallucination; the heavy rains had caused a slimes dam to burst and in the rush of mud and water a 200 ton loco had been carried away towards a group of mine cottages that narrowly escaped the same fate. The loco had come to rest in one of the gardens; the driver was saved but his fireman had been lost in the accident.

Gold Fields' golden jubilee in 1937 was preceded by that of the City of Johannesburg the previous year, when its Empire Exhibition brought people from all over the world to see what fifty years had done for Colonel Ferreira's camp. John Agnew told shareholders at the time: 'There may be some in this hall today who will live to see Johannesburg's centenary and I venture to express my profound

In February 1939 the slimes dam at Simmer and Jack burst after heavy rains, and railway vehicles were swept away towards mine dwellings. 'There's a loco in my garden,' said a woman anxiously on the telephone to the mine manager.

155

belief that, when the time comes, there will be found such a number of gold mining companies still existing as to make the Witwatersrand still a factor in the world production of gold.' In 1935 the Union of South Africa produced 10,7 million ounces of gold worth some £74 million; fifty years later the Republic of South Africa was producing 22 million ounces with a value of more than R15 billion.

At a dinner at the Savoy Hotel in London, after Sir Frederic Hamilton had proposed a toast to the company and recalled, as one of the last survivors of the Reform Committee, the early days of Rhodes and Rudd, John Agnew got up to remind the company how Rudd had been ridiculed when he had prophesied that the Rand would turn out £1 000 million worth of gold. That figure had been reached about twelve years before the dinner, said Agnew and 'it would be a bold man today who would assert that his figure of £1 000 million will not ultimately be doubled'. A reinforcement of such optimism was given by Lord McGowan, chairman of ICI, Britain's biggest company, who on his return from Johannesburg was talking of the millions of tons of low-grade ore that would be worked profitably and he spoke of 'vast new areas being explored'.

In Johannesburg, Gold Fields celebrated with a dinner where the London board was represented by H C Porter, who was soon to celebrate his own half century with the company, which he had joined as a clerk in 1889. John Martin, chairman of Rand Mines, spoke warmly of the company whose career had been so intimately linked with that of his own. Shareholders were given more than just fine words to celebrate the occasion. A special Jubilee dividend of two shillings and sixpence to make thirty-two-and-a-half percent for the year, was paid. They were also reminded that through good years and bad the company had managed an average dividend of just over seventeen percent, which Lord Harris and the Gold Fields cricketers might have regarded as a respectable average in fifty innings. In July that year shareholders in West Wits were given the opportunity to acquire new shares when the third of its offspring, the Blyvooruitzicht Gold Mining Company, was floated, following in the footsteps of Venterspost and Libanon but with the difference that Rand Mines would control the resulting mine.

Everything looked set fair in 1937 not only for Gold Fields in South Africa but for the country as a whole, where under the impetus given by the mining industry, new industries such as the iron and steel of Iscor and the power stations of the supply commission, Escom, and the biggest explosives factory in the world, African Explosives and Chemical Industries, with its link to Lord McGowan's ICI, were the visible signs of an expanding industrial economy. Plans were being laid which would come to fruition in the 1940s. All this, however, was not to be. Not for the first time events in Europe were threatening South Africa's future. Another World War was on its way.

A year after Gold Fields celebrated its golden jubilee, Nazi Germany under Adolf Hitler, having re-occupied the Rhineland and marched into Austria, was threatening Czechoslovakia. His fellow dictator, the Italian Mussolini, had launched himself into creating a new Roman empire in Africa and had invaded Abyssinia, chasing out its Emperor, Haile Selassie. Hitler's activities, while increasingly alarming Europe, were rousing Germans to heights of patriotic fervour. Not all of his ardent supporters were in Germany, some were in South Africa and one in particular was in Gold Fields. Dr Rudolf Krahmann, one of the heroes of the discovery of the West Wits Line, had never disguised his Nazi sympathies nor his admiration for Hitler. Rhodes in his day may have regarded his work at Gold Fields as being for the greater glory of the British Empire; Rudolf Krahmann wanted his efforts at Gold Fields to be a contribution to the greater glory of the Third Reich. 'It will be difficult – if not impossible,' he recorded 'to exploit the potential of my idea for the benefit of Germans. German capital (mainly the Dresdner Bank and the Goertz group) participated to the extent of forty percent in certain gold mines but were pushed out after the First World War... Dr Merensky would have the capital but appears to be too tired...' Hans Merensky, who had been interned in South Africa during the First World War as an enemy alien and a reserve officer in the German Army, appeared to share Krahmann's enthusiasm for Hitler to the extent of making him a gift of platinum. Krahmann in a letter to his father had recorded his satisfaction that Gold Fields was the only mining house not under Jewish direction and when, in due course, a Jewish refugee from Nazi Germany, Oscar Weiss, appeared on the South African mining scene and came into the Gold Fields orbit, Krahmann took an immediate dislike to him. Krahmann's decision to promote the Nazi movement in South Africa seems to have been reinforced by a visit to Germany in 1936 when he took his family to watch the Olympic Games in Berlin. It was at these same games that one of the South African team, the boxer Robey Leibrandt, was won over to the Nazi cause and began the activities that led to his conviction for high treason. While he was in Germany, Krahmann received a letter from Gold Fields advising him that the company was making him a bonus of £3 000 for his outstanding work. Carleton Jones was saying how fortunate Gold Fields had been in 'persuading him to place his services at our disposal in 1932' and John Agnew wrote of 'the enormous value of Dr Krahmann's worth to us'. Krahmann received a further £2 000 in lieu of a participation – some 4 000 shares – in West Wits which he refused on ethical grounds. When Krahmann returned to South Africa he left his elder son in Germany, where he later went into the *Wehrmacht* and did not survive the war.

By February 1937, Krahmann, back at Gold Fields in Johannesburg, was working on his 'Proposals for making use of the mineral wealth of Portuguese East Africa for the German four-year plan', which he had discussed the previous year in Lourenço Marques with a man he referred to as Comrade Schroder, like himself an ardent Nazi. German activity to get hold of this wealth would have to be suitably cloaked. 'I would prefer that as in the case of Abyssinia a big German-Portuguese company were formed in Lisbon or Berlin so that the whole affair could then get the right background and colour, especially politically from Lisbon...well, Berlin is sure to know, also from the Italo–Abyssinia case (the

Germans sailed from Naples yesterday) how such a matter is managed.' Krahmann records that he had sent a copy of his proposals to Dr Merensky.

By January the following year the activities of the Nazi movement in South Africa had become so widespread that *The Star* in Johannesburg decided to publish on successive days two articles on 'Nazis in the Union'. The paper said: 'The *Stuetzpunkt* at Tzaneen is most active and owes its existence to German settlers on and around the Westphalia Estates belonging to Dr Hans Merensky. It spoke of festivities on the farm of Herr Krauss "where the Union Flag and the Swastika were hoisted" and mentioned "among prominent Germans on the Rand who are identified with the movement are Dr R Krahmann, the well-known geologist…".'

In September 1938 when Neville Chamberlain, the British Prime Minister, flew to see Hitler in Germany to try to prevent the outbreak of war over Czechoslovakia, Douglas Christopherson wrote a personal letter in his own hand to Carleton Jones. 'Everyone was astounded not to say equally delighted when it came through the wireless last night that the Prime Minister was going to fly over to see Hitler. Incidentally it is the first time he has been off the ground….P M Anderson was dining with us when the news came through. When talking after, he was telling me about Merensky's activities on behalf of Hitler in South Africa, with whom he mentioned Krahmann was thought to be working. I asked the chairman whether Mackenzie had mentioned anything of this to him and he replied in the negative but added he had entirely forgotten to mention that you had spoken to him about Krahmann's possible activities and that you had spoken very sharply to him about it. I believe Hitler tried the same sort of thing in America but it was quickly squashed. It would be a good thing if the Union Government could do the same.'

Dr Robert Pelletier, as consulting geologist, was responsible for the department where Krahmann had his own section and where his colleagues were fervent Germans such as himself. It was not, however, until war broke out in September 1939 that the company took action. Krahmann was locked out of his office and told to stay away from the Gold Fields premises. Within a few days he had been arrested by the Union authorities, among the first four people to be detained. He was interned first at Leeukop and later at Baviaanspoort. Since he could not work for Gold Fields, the company considered his contract had lapsed. But, as will be seen, this was by no means the end of the Krahmann story.

During the 1930s Gold Fields in Johannesburg had other preoccupations not directly connected with drilling boreholes, locating reefs or floating new companies; these were on the periphery of their mining activities. Crime, for instance. In 1936, Agnew, whose son, R J Agnew, held a senior position with the company in Australia, sent an SOS to Johannesburg asking if they could help in tackling a problem that had arisen on one of their Australian mines, where gold was disappearing. Johannesburg responded at once, since the security team at Gold Fields was the envy of other houses. The head of it had the appropriate name of Trigger though few would have been rash enough to ask Colonel A E

Hans Merensky, who bought Rudolf Krahmann his first magnetometer, and on Christmas Day, 1933, at Gold Fields' request examined a core containing visible gold which had been brought up on the West Wits Line. A new reef, the Carbon Leader, had been tapped. More than fifty years later Gold Fields was preparing to mine for platinum on the Merensky Reef in the Transvaal. Here Merensky explains his platinum discoveries of the 1920s.

In 1936 Gold Fields in Johannesburg, in response to an SOS, sent a crack detective from its security service to the aid of R J ('Dolf') Agnew of Consolidated Gold Fields in Australia to help solve the mystery of gold thefts at Kalgoorlie. Dolf Agnew was the son of John Agnew, chairman of Consolidated Gold Fields in the 1930s, and the father of Rudolph Agnew, chairman of that company in the 1980s.

Trigger if he were happy! 'We have just the man for your purposes,' Carleton Jones informed Agnew. This was a detective named Raymond Emms 'of our Mines Police Staff' who had made a reputation as a catcher of gold thieves on the Rand. He was now expected to do the same in Australia. He left an account of his experience written in a style much favoured by policemen.

'Acting on instructions, I proceeded from Johannesburg to London, arriving in London on 1 June where I reported to Mr J Agnew and was informed that large quantities of gold were disappearing from various mines in Western Australia and that he suspected it was being bought by a number of gold buyers on behalf of a principal and being sent to him by aeroplane and that I was to find out their methods of dealing and to determine who the principal was. I was given a letter of introduction to Mr R J Agnew of Kalgoorlie who.... would arrange for me to be employed on one of the mines with the object of getting in touch with the men who were involved in illicit gold dealings.'

From London Emms went overland to Marseilles to pick up a boat for Australia, where he arrived at Fremantle on 30 June, going on to Kalgoorlie by rail. Within half-an-hour he had seen Agnew who then got in touch with Mr Thorne who was the manager of Lake View and Star Gold Mine. 'I again interviewed Mr R J Agnew at 3h30 pm and he informed me that Mr Thorne and himself had agreed that it would be in the best interests to spend three weeks having a look round the town and to get acquainted with the place in general. He then collected my luggage at the station and drove me to the Kalgoorlie Hotel and advised me to stay at same. After having registered at the hotel I took a walk around the town.... after dinner I decided to have another walk round the town and as I stepped out of the hotel I was approached by a stranger who said that he wanted a few words with me. The following are the actual words that were spoken: "We know who you are and you cannot get away with anything here and you had better clear out as soon as you can, otherwise you are going to get it in the neck!" I was surprised to receive this very abrupt warning and before I could reply to the stranger he had walked away. I attempted to follow the man and was immediately stopped by two men who demanded a match to light their cigarettes. They detained me long enough to allow the stranger to get out of sight; this was obviously planned beforehand in the event of any attempt being made to follow the man who warned me to get out of Kalgoorlie. I made a report to Mr Agnew the following morning at 9 am. He immediately took me in his car and left me a few miles outside the town, and then went back and picked up Mr Thorne and brought him to the spot where he had left me. I then related my experience of the previous evening to him. Mr Thorne and Mr Agnew agreed that it was not safe for me to stay in the town and under the circumstances they decided to cable London office. A reply was received the following day instructing me to proceed to South Africa immediately. I left Kalgoorlie on 3 July at 5 pm. A few minutes before the train left Kalgoorlie I saw a man on the station platform who resembled a man by the name of Wham who...was involved in illicit gold dealing in Johannesburg. I arrived at Perth on the following day and made a report to Mr

160

Thorne at the Imperial Hotel regarding Wham. I was instructed by Mr Thorne to stay at the Imperial Hotel until 28 July on which day I sailed for South Africa, arriving in Johannesburg on 12 August 1936.'

It was a long way to have gone in order to have recognized a Johannesburg crook on the Kalgoorlie railway station but it was an encounter that may have been vital if that was the reason why the thefts on the Gold Fields mines in Australia ceased. It was a busy time for Colonel Trigger. Another Gold Fields company, this time in West Africa, was having trouble with theft and illicit dealings. The consulting engineer of the Ashanti Gold Fields Company came down to Johannesburg and Trigger gave him advice about placing agents from various tribes among the work force as the best means of dealing with the problem.

John Agnew's visit to South Africa at the beginning of 1939 was a great success and had confirmed in his mind that all was going well with Gold Fields in South Africa. The shareholders at their meeting in December just before Agnew's departure had been told that a new subsidiary of West Witwatersrand Areas was being formed; this was West Driefontein which would have 4 769 claims on the eastern portion of Blyvooruitzicht and on Driefontein. Gold Fields had made a profit in 1938 of £1 180 394 and for the first time since 1912 the reserves had topped £2 million. The company now had seventy percent of its investments in gold, and Agnew as he looked at the situation on the spot was happy that that should be so. He had been impressed, particularly by the way the various mining houses worked together, exchanging information freely. He himself had impressed the black miners whom he had made a point of meeting; they saluted him as the *Mkulu Baas*. Addressing a gathering of some 400 Gold Fields people he said it was his sincere desire to see Gold Fields as the greatest mining house of all. He decided that he would have to come to South Africa more frequently. 'It is not easy to arrange what one would like to do on account of our interests in other parts of the world,' he wrote to Carleton Jones from the Mount Nelson Hotel in Cape Town before taking a ship for England in February 1939, 'but if I can possibly help it, I do not intend to let as long an interval pass before my next visit as has been the case on the present occasion.' It was not, alas, to be. He never came back.

War was coming closer though few wished to believe it, including Carleton Jones who recorded that March having lunched at the Cape with Abe Bailey to meet Lord Rothermere, the newspaper baron, proprietor of the London *Daily Mail*. 'In his views of the international situation, he struck us all as unnecessarily pessimistic.'

Sir Abe Bailey, one of Gold Fields' oldest associates and one of the first directors of West Wits, was in Britain in May and sent a message to Agnew, asking him when he was leaving for Canada. 'If you are doing any business there please give me a small interest.' Agnew had already informed Carleton Jones that he was 'to leave for the Yukon on 14 June, returning to London in the middle of August...' After visiting Canada, Agnew went south to California where in July he became desperately ill with pneumonia. He died, aged sixty-seven, on

2 August 1939. His death, just a month before the outbreak of war, would be deeply felt. 'From the South African point of view,' Carleton Jones said, 'it is sad indeed that Mr Agnew did not live to see Venterspost come to production. We both know that his was the guiding spirit from the very beginning of West Wits and now only a month before the first mine actually starts upon its producing career, he passes on.'

Carleton Jones had been looking forward to an even closer relationship with Agnew as he had just been appointed resident director, following the retirement, due to failing health, of William Mackenzie. Mackenzie, a reticent and modest man who disliked publicity, had played a valuable part in the company's affairs during the surge forward in the 1930s, and indeed in the industry as a whole, having been President of the Chamber of Mines in 1935, and in that capacity involved in important trade union negotiations. Returning to his birthplace in Scotland, he was appointed a non-executive director in London. He died in 1947.

In London, Consolidated Gold Fields entered the difficult period of the Second World War in September 1939, with two old men in the top positions. Herbert Porter, the new chairman, was seventy-four, his deputy, Douglas Christopherson, seventy. Porter had completed fifty years with the company and to mark the occasion his colleagues in Johannesburg had sent him a fine inkstand to sit upon the chairman's desk. He had only recently lost some of his companions from the early days, Prinsep in 1937 after forty-two years service, and in 1938 Edward Birkenruth at the age of eighty-three. Gold Fields had lost a fine engineer in London with the death of Agnew but Porter had in Robert Annan, his consulting engineer, someone who would prove a tower of strength in the days ahead and indeed, when Porter died in 1944, Robert Annan became chairman, and Gold Fields once more had a mining engineer directing its affairs.

From Johannesburg Carleton Jones, who was no longer consulting engineer, having handed these duties over to J V Muller, sent Porter a brief account of how the Gold Fields picture in South Africa had been transformed between 1932 and 1939.

'In the month of October 1932 our three producing mines treated 217 000 tons and produced 84 300 ounces of gold, the working costs amounting to £241 500 and the working profits to £115 500 while the development footage advanced amounted to 15 404 feet.' At this time, Carleton Jones went on, Gold Fields was employing 21 349 workers of whom 1 962 were whites and 19 387 blacks. Seven years later, in October 1939, 'our seven producing mines treated 510 000 tons and produced 137 000 ounces of gold and working costs amounted to £617 500 and working profit £411 100, after allowing for the working loss of £25 500 in Venterspost's first month of production, while the aggregate development footage advanced in respect of the seven producing mines and the four developing mines amounted to 40 780 feet'. At the outbreak of war in 1939 Gold Fields was employing 5 891 whites and its share of the black labour force on the mines was 41 877 out of 316 000.

When Porter passed on to shareholders at the annual meeting in December

162

1939 the good news that Carleton Jones had sent him on the progress made during the decade in South Africa, he was, in reality, giving them the balance sheet of a golden era that had already ended. During this time Gold Fields had been advancing step by step along the West Wits Line; four new mining subsidiaries had been created by West Witwatersrand Areas to develop four new mines and the first of these was producing. The company had been in step with the country itself, for South Africa too had been advancing steadily, little by little, away from the divisions of the past towards a united future, whose well-being would be guaranteed by an ever-expanding gold mining industry. Overnight the dream vanished.

The outbreak of war found the Union Parliament assembled in special session in Cape Town to prolong the life of the Senate for a few weeks. Parliament was now faced with a crisis, for the Cabinet was divided on the war issue. General Hertzog and some of his colleagues wished South Africa to remain neutral while his deputy, General Smuts, and some of his colleagues were in favour of entering the war alongside Britain. Each put his case to Parliament which voted eighty votes against sixty-seven in favour of war. Hertzog asked the Governor-General

Luipaardsvlei, 1939. Mineworkers line up for a ration of mieliemeal.

163

to dissolve Parliament and call a general election. Patrick Duncan, however, took the view that Parliament had expressed itself by taking a vote and he asked Smuts to form a government. The war which was to have such far-reaching effects on the whole world in the decades that followed, had opened up old South African wounds, disrupting the healing process that had been going on during the 1930s within the white communities, English-speakers and Afrikaners. When, after six long years of war, peace eventually returned, it would be to a different world and a different South Africa. The re-opening of the old divisions in 1939 would lead to the creation of a new social and political environment in South Africa with far-reaching consequences for the future career of Gold Fields in that country.

[1] Arthur had been at Cambridge. He died suddenly in 1966 after a heart attack following an Oxford and Cambridge luncheon in Johannesburg. He had only just retired from Gold Fields.

CHAPTER SIX

War and Aftermath
1939 – 1949

At first Carleton Jones, the resident director in Johannesburg, had not expected that the war in Europe would unduly upset his plans in South Africa. As he told Porter in November 1939, 'we do not anticipate much difficulty in obtaining items of plant and equipment required for the present programme of expansion at the various mines. Should manufacturers in England be unable to effect deliveries it will be possible in most cases to obtain the necessary machinery in South Africa....' By the middle of 1940, however, such optimism had evaporated with the dramatic decline of Allied fortunes in the war. By mid-June France and most of Western Europe had fallen, overcome by the power of the German blitzkrieg. Britain, where Winston Churchill had become Prime Minister at a moment of crisis, and the Commonwealth stood alone against Hitler. Mussolini, determined to be in at the kill, had entered the war alongside Germany just as France was about to surrender. South Africa, with its all-volunteer forces, was preparing to send its first contingent 'up north' to meet the Italian threat to East Africa. Carleton Jones, like everyone else in the mining industry, realized that all the plans so carefully scheduled to come to fruition in the 1940s, would have to be shelved until the world crisis was over.

On the Far West Rand, Venterspost was already at work late in 1939 and in 1940 it paid its first dividend. Libanon would have been the next but in 1942 development work on the mine was stopped for the duration of the war. The third mine under Gold Fields control, West Driefontein, had been designed in 1938 and a mining lease applied for from the Government. By mid-1940, however, it was clear that nothing more could be done about West Driefontein while the war was in progress and the Minister of Mines agreed to cancel the lease. Some thought had already been given to a fourth mine, Doornfontein, but that, too, would have to wait for better times. However, in 1942 Blyvooruitzicht, as yet with only one shaft, followed in the footsteps of Venterspost and also began to produce its first gold, the first mine to tap the rich Carbon Leader. Stokes of the Corner House, who was the chairman of Blyvoor, had been called back to the British Army and in 1940 had taken part in the abortive British expedition to Narvik in Norway in an attempt to stop the German advance. Gold Fields had a very large stake in Blyvoor and Carleton Jones made frequent visits to the mine. On his instruction the Gold Fields geologist, Willem de Kock, conducted some important investigations in the mine into the nature of the Carbon Leader. It was clear that this reef was much richer than had at first been realized from an examination of the first borehole results. In due course values as high as sixty-nine dwts were obtained, ten times greater than the first boreholes had revealed. De Kock's tests showed that where the drills had cut the reef, this ore band, so heavily impregnated with carbon, was so friable that some of the gold in the borehole cores had been lost as the drill cut through the reef. Blyvooruitzicht was a vastly richer mine than had at first been expected – 'the unforeseen success of that property', as Annan was to say. The results confirmed this; some 600 000 ounces of gold were obtained from the first 900 000 tons of ore milled. Meanwhile, the tests carried out in the mine by the Gold Fields geologist were the subject of a learned paper that Dr De Kock prepared and it proved of great value to the industry as a whole, in particular in the Free State when the Basal Reef was intercepted.

On the East Rand, too, Gold Fields had had to make adjustments to its development programmes. At Spaarwater development work stopped in August 1940 and would not be resumed until the war was over. In the meantime, the mine provided accommodation and a training base for non-white elements of the Union Defence Force. Vlakfontein, on the other hand, began milling in 1942 under the direction of Algy Cundill, who had been at Spaarwater and who was to become a legend among Gold Fields mine managers, a man of great physical and moral courage. He was destined to spend twenty years at Vlakfontein, and, with his unyielding devotion to mine safety, he set an example for the whole group. Vlakfontein had required very careful planning due to the complexity of the ore body, which is a single conglomerate band of the Main Reef, only thirty-three centimetres wide and in exploiting it, particular attention had to be given to the ventilation of the mine.

The war made tremendous demands on the South African gold industry; as in the First World War, gold was essential to pay for the Allied effort to defeat the Axis, and despite the dangers of enemy action at sea, gold was shipped from South Africa to its traditional destination overseas, sometimes even being carried in warships of the Allied navies. As usual the mines were carrying a heavy burden of taxation; at the beginning the Union Government took everything that gold earned above 150 shillings an ounce. Some forty-five mining workshops were turned over to the making of munitions and Carleton Jones sent Porter an account of Gold Fields' contribution to the making of war supplies. Men went from the mining houses to assist other industries, such as shipbuilding. Dr Busschau put his intellect at the disposal of General Smuts's Government to whom he became an economic adviser. At the Prime Minister's request, Spencer Fleischer was called away from Sub Nigel to form and command as a Colonel the Mines Engineering Brigade as a part of the South African Engineers. John Crawhall, whose Cementation team had won the battle at Venterspost, became one of his majors and Stanley Hallett a Second Lieutenant. Gold Fields released two of its mechanical engineers, L T Campbell Pitt and F G Zep-

Algy Cundill, a mine manager for the book. Vlakfontein, 1942-1962.

penfeld, who went off to the Middle East, where Fleischer's brigade distinguished itself by, among other things, blasting tunnels to enable the railway line to get through from what was then Palestine and is now Israel, to Syria. Rupert Gettliffe, being the only electrical engineer, could not be spared but fought his battles on the home front, seeing that Gold Fields mines got their fair share of whatever supplies were available. He did his job so conscientiously that the Chamber of Mines once complained that he had had more than his proper share of copper cable. The South African gold mines were carrying on, despite all the difficulties that war had brought them and their output actually increased. From some 12 800 000 ounces in 1939, it went the following year to more than 14 000 000 ounces, maintaining that figure for another year, after which it declined again to the pre-war level. With so much of its manpower on active service or engaged in making munitions, the industry's achievement was altogether remarkable. It had seen 6 000 of its men go to the war; 1 000 men from all the Gold Fields companies served in the war and of these seventy never returned.

Carleton Jones was carrying a greater burden at Gold Fields than any of his predecessors; in addition to his duties for the company, he also shouldered those of the Chamber of Mines, becoming its president in 1942, and again soon after the war and at other times he was a vice president. In 1942, he retrieved Colonel Fleischer from the army and brought him to Fox Street as joint manager with

167

A G Petyt who, in 1944, retired after forty-two years with the company. The Gold Fields connection was then continued through his daughter, married to Deryck Gettliffe, who had joined the company in 1938 and in due course became a director. He and his brother Rupert were two of seven brothers. When Petyt retired, Percy Hammond, who had arrived in South Africa during the 1922 troubles and had been working his way up in the Gold Fields service, was appointed joint manager with Fleischer. Since Hammond's tall, soldierly bearing reflected his early training at the Royal Military Academy of Sandhurst in England, the top echelons of Gold Fields in wartime had a pronounced military aspect. Carleton Jones was able to pass some of his burdens to his brother Hervey Jones, who in 1941 assumed control of Luipaards Vlei. At this time Gold Fields acquired the services of an interesting Afrikaner who was an expert on mining titles and had been working for years for the company's legal advisers Webber Wentzel. This was 'Sandy' Sandenbergh who was a worthy successor to his fellow Afrikaner, W S Smits, who died in 1935. As a boy he had gone off with his father in the Boer commandos during the Anglo-Boer War and he had had little formal education. He had learned everything he knew about mining titles from working as a clerk in legal offices.

Throughout the war Carleton Jones kept up his regular reporting to his chairman in Britain and maintained also direct contact with Eric Turk of HE Proprietary, for whose interests in South Africa Gold Fields was responsible. Carleton Jones was no longer directing his correspondence to 49 Moorgate, since Consolidated Gold Fields had wisely decided to move out of the City of London before it became a target for the German blitz during the Battle of Britain in 1940. They had taken refuge in a country mansion, Motcombe House, near Shaftesbury in Dorset. Here old age and ill health, rather than the war, were carrying off the senior men; in 1943 Douglas Christopherson, then seventy-five, retired after forty-three years service. He died on 15 April 1944. Exactly a week later Herbert Porter, who was seventy-eight, also died. He had spent fifty-five years with the company. He had not been well enough to chair the 1943 meeting of shareholders and Robert Annan stood in for him. Annan now became chairman of the company and for the second time a mining engineer had assumed the top position.

In South Africa Carleton Jones had lost his own consulting engineer. J V Muller, whose lungs had been ruined by underground service, retired in 1942 through ill health. His successor, Huntley Smith, died a few months after taking over. New names appeared among the engineers, such as Buller Smart and Gerald Batty, who came to play an important role in the post-war era. The juxtaposition of their names was sometimes too much of a temptation for their colleagues. Some would ask if Batty were really smart; others suggested that Smart was actually batty!

Colonel Fleischer's return to Gold Fields from the army was followed by that of Captain Stanley Hallett, who was about to make his own unique contribution – and a highly secret one – to the Allied effort. Marian Hallett, his wife, remem-

Percy Hammond, who succeeded a distinguished soldier, Colonel Fleischer, as resident director in Johannesburg in 1954, was himself trained as a professional soldier (Sandhurst and the Dragoons), like one of his predecessors Colonel Frank Rhodes. He arrived in South Africa in the midst of the 1922 flare-up on the Rand but thereafter pursued a peaceful career at Gold Fields.

bered how he came and went from their home in Johannesburg day after day and she never dared ask him what he was doing nor for that matter did he give a hint, except to say it was secret. Even after the war, he remained reticent. But night after night the light in Hallett's room at Gold Fields was burning as he worked on behind a locked door. Uranium, as we now know, was the name of the game.

A few months before the United States entered the war following the Japanese bombing of Pearl Harbour on 7 December 1941, President Roosevelt had been in touch with Winston Churchill to compare notes on the progress being made in both countries towards the production of atomic weapons. He suggested that in view of the enormous expenditure involved in research, Britain and America should pool their efforts. As a result, a number of British scientists went to America to work on what was called the 'Manhattan Project', where one of their American colleagues was Professor G W Bain. His special function was to advise on sources and availability of uranium, the metal whose special qualities were necessary for the creation of nuclear energy and hence atomic weapons. He had been to South Africa and still had samples of gold ore from the Rand. When he put these to the test in the laboratory, they were found to be radio-active. General Smuts was informed of what was going on and that his country might play a valuable part in the provision of uranium, a rare metal of which the Manhattan Project had only enough for research purposes. Smuts spoke to Stowe McLean, then President of the Chamber of Mines, and in due course two Americans acting under their President's instructions, and a British scientist sent by Churchill, arrived in South Africa to carry out further investigations. They found that South Africa was probably the biggest source of low-grade uranium in the world. Moreover, there would be no necessity to mine for it since it could be obtained as a by-product of gold mining. It came to the surface in the gold-bearing rock and was dumped with the slimes left after the ore had been crushed and passed through the cyanide process. Pressed by Britain and America, who were conscious of the fact that Nazi Germany was also busy with similar projects, South Africa pushed ahead as quickly as possible with research into how the uranium was to be removed from the slimes after the gold itself had been taken from the ore. From these early efforts, under the pressure of war, the South African uranium industry emerged. But in 1944 only a few, specially selected men in the mining industry were involved and they lived with their secret. Stanley Hallett was one of these and when he died in Natal in 1968 the *Rand Daily Mail* carried the headline: 'Uranium Man Dies with War Secrets.' *The Times* of London referred to him as one 'who secretly organized a supply of South African uranium for the Allied war effort'. So no one will ever know what precisely went on in Hallett's room at Gold Fields where, night after night, the lights were burning late.

While Hallett and others were assisting in the birth of the atomic age, mining men who belonged to the early, heroic era that had seen the beginning of mining on the Rand, were disappearing one by one. In 1941 Sir William Dalrymple died. A prominent figure in Johannesburg since the 1890s, he was a member of the

Stanley Hallett, who kept the secret of his wartime work at Gold Fields – on uranium – until the end of his days.

Robinson Deep board and for nearly half a century had been chairman of Apex mines, serving with Chaplin and Birkenruth in the early days. Sir Abe Bailey had died a year earlier and his widespread interests, notably South African Townships, were up for sale. It was open to Consolidated Gold Fields in London to take them over; it might well have given Bailey pleasure if he had known that his old friend, Gold Fields, would inherit his interests, since in his lifetime the Corner House, to whom he had offered them, had found his price too high. John Martin was a particular friend of his and Bailey had appointed him as one of the executors of his estate.

It was wartime and Martin found it hard to dispose of the Bailey companies. Gold Fields thought about the interests in Rhodesia. 'Even before Bailey died,' Carleton Jones told Porter in 1942, 'I had given some thought to his interests in Southern Rhodesia,' and he went on to say, 'It would appear that if the Trustees wish to make fresh arrangements regarding the control of the Bailey interests in Southern Rhodesia, Gold Fields, as the only large Group now actively engaged in mining in that territory, would be the obvious party for them to approach'. There were, however, a number of complications attaching to the Bailey interests in Rhodesia and Carleton Jones pointed out that a purchase of Bailey shares 'would involve Gold Fields in the responsibility for carrying out the duties of London secretaries to Lonrho....a responsibility which I do not think you would welcome more particularly under existing conditions'. The matter was dropped. The Bailey interests in South Africa went eventually to Sir Ernest Oppenheimer, who said later, 'anyone could have had control of Townships from the Trustees for the asking and for a very small outlay'.

The Bailey interests provided Anglo American with new opportunities, particularly in the Orange Free State with Western Holdings, which had been established by SA Townships. Shortly before Bailey's death it had struck the Basal Reef with a borehole, and became the first company to find payable ore in the Free State. In the light of future events, Gold Fields might be thought to have lost an opportunity in not going for the Bailey interests but their attitude was understandable, for in 1942 the company was already committed to an expensive development programme on the West Wits Line. This, too, was the consideration that prevented them from having a part in another development which followed their pioneer work on the Far West Rand – the opening up of the Klerksdorp field. That, too, would be dominated by Anglo American with Western Reefs though Gold Fields had a participation. In acquiring the Bailey interests, Anglo American were also brought closer to Gold Fields in that they took over the considerable Bailey interest in Vlakfontein, SA Townships having been secretaries for Lace Proprietary Mines, the original vendor of Vlakfontein.

During the war, while Harry Oppenheimer was serving with distinction in the South African forces in the Western Desert of North Africa, his father on the home front was vigorously expanding the interests of the company that he would inherit in due time. But in a manner that began to worry Gold Fields.

In wartime Johannesburg the mining houses formed a close-knit community and there was frequent communication between their top men who tended to sit on each other's boards. Anglo had a director on the board of West Wits, whose chairman was Carleton Jones. Between Carleton Jones and Oppenheimer there was a measure of mutual confidence and trust as was exemplified by a curious incident which took place in 1942, and which ended by Gold Fields having to dismiss one of their employees, whose family was a friend of the Oppenheimers. The young man was employed in the diamond drilling research department. In due course that department informed Muller, the consulting engineer, of their suspicions that the young man 'was distributing certain information regarding the research work to outside parties' and this despite the undertaking given on his engagement to respect the confidential nature of his work. In September 1942 he asked for permission to go to Kimberley to meet his father who was arriving from the Belgian Congo. Before he left he wrote a report on the research work in progress and took a copy with him. This he showed to various people in Kimberley. Later, when questioned by Gold Fields, he admitted that, although he had given an undertaking not to disclose information, he had decided to do so anyway. For this 'flagrant breach of trust' he was dismissed. A little later Sir Ernest Oppenheimer wrote to Carleton Jones to enquire into the circumstances which had led to the dismissal of his friend's son. After hearing from Gold Fields' resident director, Oppenheimer wrote again to say: 'I fully agree that in the circumstances no step other than to dismiss him could have been taken.'

Sir Ernest Oppenheimer, according to one of his biographers, Edward Jessup, 'was as sharp in business and had as many points as there are quills in a porcupine'. He was, maintains Jessup 'relentless in waging financial war'. By mid-1944 Carleton Jones began to fear that he himself, or at any rate Gold Fields, might be impaled on the sharp end of one of those quills. He cabled his fears about Oppenheimer to Annan, who on 15 September wrote to Johannesburg: 'Until we get full details of the new situation with Anglo American it is too early to make much comment but I understand you feel that they are trying to get control of West Wits and that you suggest that we should now attempt to secure control ourselves by purchase of shares in the market – presumably in competition with them – and that we should realize large blocks of Libanons, Venters and Blyvoors. I may say at once that we shall never adopt such a course...I cannot put it too emphatically that competitive buying to secure control has been at the root of all the financial crashes in living memory and if anyone comes along, no matter who it is, who is prepared to push the price of West Wits beyond what they are worth we are not going to be led into unsound finance for any reasons of temporary prestige.'

At the time Carleton Jones was reworking his plans for West Driefontein; it was September 1944 and the war situation had completely changed and was moving strongly in the favour of the Allies. The previous June they had landed on the beaches of Normandy and little by little were moving along the road that would take them in the European Spring of the following year to the Rhine and ultimate victory against Germany. Preparing for the return of peace, Carleton

Jones was getting ready to launch West Driefontein. 'We are now finalizing the application to the Mining Leases Board on the basis of the original lease...' he told Annan, 'we intend to keep in constant touch with you in all matters pertaining to the lease and to the flotation of West Driefontein to ensure that we are working in keeping with your ideas.' In these circumstances it was disquieting to have Sir Ernest Oppenheimer hovering about in the background. 'The attitude of the Anglo American....has caused us a lot of worry...' he confessed to Annan in the same letter. Oppenheimer, financial wizard and Member of Parliament, had advantages over Carleton Jones. 'Where the cash liquidity of other mining houses may have been affected by exchange control between Britain and South Africa and local decisions were possibly inhibited by a controlling directorate 6 000 miles away in England, Oppenheimer was his own master. Anglo American was a South African registered corporation operating in South Africa. Its public image was South African and he had the ear of the Government in Parliament. Not for him lengthy board decisions, copious letters and explanatory letters to London. He exercised his own control on the spot and like any sound general was quick to seize opportunity when it was presented.' Thus wrote Edward Jessup. This was a situation that as time went by would become increasingly marked and, indeed, hasten the day when Gold Fields of South Africa, like Anglo American, would become a South African company and operate on equal terms. But in 1944 the particular problem prompting Gold Fields in Johannesburg to communicate its anxiety to London was Oppenheimer's determination to get his own wedge in the West Wits Line; the Anglo 'niche' would one day become Western Deep Levels, one of the biggest, deepest, most expensive mines ever created. In 1943 Anglo had formed the Western Ultra Deep Levels company to explore ground to the south of Blyvooruitzicht and West Driefontein and Gold Fields had participated. The name of the company was accurately chosen since the two reefs, the Carbon Leader and the Ventersdorp Contact Reef, passed under the southern boundaries of the properties at depths of 7 000 feet and 5 000 feet respectively. Any mine that was developed south of Blyvooruitzicht and Driefontein would have to sink shafts to depths of 10 000 feet and more. The costs would be enormous. However, the values that had been shown at Blyvooruitzicht, and later at West Driefontein, as the reefs were followed down were an indication of the riches that might eventually be obtained by anyone with the courage – and the capital – to undertake such an ambitious project. Oppenheimer was to show that he had both and Western Deep Levels is today the justification of his faith. During the last two years of the war, he was busily engaged in buying land, mineral rights and options all round the Gold Fields properties or at least those it controlled through its dominant stake in West Wits. To have gained control of West Wits would have greatly facilitated his task which was, in any case, a very complicated one. There would be other occasions in the future when Gold Fields felt Oppenheimer was breathing down its neck and it had to take prompt avoiding action to prevent Anglo getting a grip on West Wits.

As always, there would be good days and bad in the relationship between the

174

two houses; each was accustomed to take a part in the flotations of the other and for this reason each hoped to remain in the confidence of the other. Soon after the war ended Annan wrote to Carleton Jones: 'Sir Ernest Oppenheimer made a brief farewell call yesterday – he made no further reference to their demands on West Witwatersrand Areas Limited and I saw no reason to reopen the subject…it remains to be seen what further action they will take as I do not imagine for a moment that they will let the matter rest. The disclosure of the communication made by Anglo American to the Minister of Mines at the time when they floated Western Ultra Deep Levels when, at the same time they were large shareholders in West Wits and were represented on its board, is enough to indicate that they are not likely to stop at anything.'

Robert Annan, chairman of Consolidated Gold Fields, was a professional mining engineer rather than a financier; he was also a Scot with a clearcut view as to what was done and what was not done when doing business. Such views were probably not the same as those of Oppenheimer who might have been more attracted to the philosophy of Gold Fields' co-founder, Cecil Rhodes, whose maxim was 'If you can't buy them out, go in with them'. There was also a view held by some mining engineers that after other companies had done the spadework of discovery and development, Anglo American with its financial skills would move in and gain control. On the other hand, the development of Western Deep Levels by Anglo American is but one proof of the degree of prejudice in that view. Robert Annan was no doubt pleased to hear in due course from Johannesburg in a letter from Percy Hammond: 'Sir Ernest ended by saying again that he would like to make offers of participation to our company to cement further the happy relations which now existed between his Group and our own and asked that I mention the matter when next I was writing to you.' The sun had come out again.

The war was ending at last. All the mining houses were busy with their development plans, not least Gold Fields which was the first in the field by floating West Driefontein in 1945, the year the war ended. Annan thought it was essential that he and Carleton Jones should get together but civilian transport to England was still a problem. Carleton Jones was able to speak to Smuts and, in due course, he flew to London. The Prime Minister had in fact called Carleton Jones and other mining leaders, including Oppenheimer and John Martin, to Pretoria to discuss the needs and problems of an industry that was vital to the South African economy. Gold Fields' particular problem was its proposed new issues needed to finance the development programme on West Wits. British Treasury permission would have to be obtained since most of the money would have to come from overseas and Smuts promised 'to endorse applications which are considered desirable in the national interest', Carleton Jones reported, 'and we therefore are satisfied that consideration will be forthcoming in the case of issues contemplated by us'. West Wits increased its capital to £900 000 by splitting its shares into units of 2/6d and by creating 2 000 000 new shares in November 1945. In February 1946 there was a new issue of 520 000 shares at £3 each which raised more than £1 500 000. In the first two years of peace some £35 million was raised for the development of mining leases on the Rand and the OFS.

However, in the immediate post-war period the mining industry was facing all kinds of problems and not least the high rise in costs. Carleton Jones told Annan, 'our Gold Fields problems are multiplying rapidly. Doornfontein will be with us shortly....while Spaarwater, West Vlak, Libanon and West Driefontein require careful guiding. Added to this our Free State hunt remains unceasing though mostly unproductive to date.' Carleton Jones had taken on the presidency of the Chamber of Mines once more and told Annan he could not get away to London again. Annan decided that he would come to South Africa to see things for himself. He felt out of touch; questions were being put to him in London that he could not always answer. As a result of an enquiry, he wrote to Johannesburg to ask who or what was Thomas Barlow. The resident director replied: 'Messrs Thomas Barlow and Sons (Ltd) are a firm of well established electrical and mechanical engineers with branches in the chief cities of the Union.' It was a perfectly accurate description though, in retrospect, a somewhat quaint picture of the company that under Thomas's grandson, the Somerset cricketer 'Punch' Barlow, would take over the Corner House, absorbing Central Mining and Rand Mines into the modern giant, Barlow Rand. Annan's visit in 1947 was the first by the company's chairman since Agnew was there in 1939; Johannesburg told him that his itinerary was being arranged so that it did not clash with that of other important visitors coming from Britain at that time; these were members of the Royal Family, King George VI and Queen Elizabeth, their daughters, the future Queen Elizabeth II and Princess Margaret.

Meanwhile, for the man whose work had made West Driefontein possible, Dr Rudolf Krahmann, the war had taken on a new turn. In July 1944 he had been moved from his internment camp and taken to Port Elizabeth. Here he had been joined by his wife, son and daughter and been put aboard a Swedish ship bound for Portugal. The International Red Cross had arranged for an exchange of civilian prisoners and Krahmann was going home to Germany which was releasing a British prisoner. By the end of the year he was back in Berlin in time to see his aged and ailing father before the old Professor died. When the Russians reached Berlin they raided the building where the Krahmanns were and arrested Axmann, a Nazi youth leader, who also lived there. They decided to take Krahmann too, and once more he was behind barbed wire, this time a Russian camp in East Germany. When several years later he was released, he was one of few survivors. In order to keep his morale up and that of his fellow prisoners, he had narrated to them, night after night, and in ever increasing detail, the story of how he had discovered and helped to develop the West Wits Line. West Wits had saved their lives.

Carleton Jones, like his chairman Robert Annan, felt very strongly about the business integrity of Gold Fields and on one occasion he had written to his chairman to say that 'only by consistently being scrupulous and fair-minded in our dealing with the public, such as Gold Fields has always tried to be...can we hope that eventually honesty of purpose will be apparent to investors'. Soon after the war ended, he expressed this philosophy in a practical way. A South African Major-General had returned from the battlefields of Europe where he had been twice decorated to find that, due to his absence at the war and inability to attend to his private affairs, valuable West Wits rights had not been taken up by his wife. Carleton Jones in December 1945 wrote to London: 'We suggest for your consideration that our company might make a donation of 300 West Drie shares.' About this time, too, Carleton Jones arranged for his staff in Johannesburg to send food parcels to their less fortunate colleagues working at 49 Moorgate in conditions of extreme austerity.

The Royal visit to South Africa happened to coincide with an important Gold Fields date, the company's diamond jubilee. The company had been founded during the golden jubilee of the King's great-grandmother, Queen Victoria, and it was appropriate that he should be in South Africa where the company's activities had begun sixty years earlier. He did not come to the celebratory dinner in Johannesburg but he did receive in audience the Gold Fields manager Colonel Fleischer, when he presented him with the insignia of the CBE, awarded to him for his work in forming the Mines Engineering Brigade. In 1919 Fleischer had stood before the King's father, George V, in Buckingham Palace when he received the DSO and MC. During the King's visit, bonfires were lit on mines along the golden arc; the Chamber of Mines asked Gold Fields to produce a map which the King and his family, standing on the top of Johannesburg's highest building, Escom House, could use to identify the different mines where the bonfires were burning. The task was given to Arthur Stead, an exquisite draughtsman, whose map so impressed the King he asked if he might keep it for the map collection at Buckingham Palace. In due course it was parcelled up and sent to the King's ship, HMS *Vanguard*. Stead, on the other hand, kept the table on which the map had been placed and it is known to this day as the King's Table.

The anniversary dinner in 1947, attended by Robert Annan, was marred by the fact that the Witwatersrand mines were in the third week of a serious strike, 'the second greatest industrial upheaval we have had on the gold mines', as Carleton Jones told guests. It was a strike which reduced working profits of South Africa's gold mines by some £4 million that year.

Carleton Jones remained hopeful, however, that 'our company will be a powerful going concern when it has reached its hundredth year. I like to look ahead another forty years at least'. But he sounded a warning. 'We cannot visualize the next forty years without a great deal of difficulty. We are now expanding, we are hoping for a successful future but I ask you all to keep in mind the problems that confront us. Keep in front of you the problem of the colour bar. It is going to become a very important matter. Don't turn it to one side....we must search ourselves; make sure that we are doing enough, make sure that we are moving with modern progress.'

The word apartheid had not yet been heard; Smuts was still Prime Minister but already articles had been appearing in the British Press, notably the *Observer* and the *Manchester Guardian*, criticizing the treatment of black workers on the mines. Annan had thought it all very strange and had written to Carleton Jones: 'As questions relating to Rand labour are of limited interest in this country and of no concern to the Government here, it is rather remarkable that such prominence has been given to some of those articles...it is clear that the appearance of these articles is not accidental...'

Annan reminded the dinner guests in Johannesburg that February of 1947 that it was only 120 years since British capital had first been invested in mining and that in 1947 the history of Gold Fields covered half the history of modern mining; he described some of the company's activities in other parts of the world – a new office in Kenya would come under Johannesburg's supervision – and he maintained 'the interests of this company have always been predominantly in South Africa. This has been our main centre of activity'.

For Carleton Jones the jubilee dinner of 1947 was, alas, his swan-song. A few weeks later he had a heart attack which forced him to retire and Spencer Fleischer took over as resident director. It was a bitter blow for Carleton Jones to have to go just as West Driefontein was in the making and the next mine, Doornfontein, was getting ready to sink its Annan Shaft the following year. In thirty-three years he had had only three days sick leave. He had never spared himself, particularly during the war years, when short-staffed at Gold Fields he had also been President of the Chamber; he had even found time to devote himself to war charities, particularly the Navy League, the authorities turning a blind eye to the spinning roulette table at his Dunkeld home, where he and his wife raised thousands of pounds for charity. Those who worked with him said he knew how to relax, that he could 'turn himself off'. He would be seen at the Rand Club in the evenings playing billiards with another mining man, Bailey Southwell and John Cleary, one of the club 'characters'. Gordon Richdale, whom John Martin had brought to the Corner House from the Bank of England, remembered Carleton Jones as having 'a fiery red countenance crowned in his later years with a thatch of snow white hair and he always wore large amethyst cufflinks which seemed somehow to be oddly out of character'. Carleton Jones, as he recovered his health slowly, wanted to maintain his connection with the company on a part-time basis. He was still chairman of West Wits and at the shareholders' meeting in November 1948, with his usual courage and determination, he made a good speech. A newcomer to Gold Fields at this time, J C Williams, who had arrived from Britain after a distinguished war career, with a quick understanding of the ordeal that Carleton Jones was going to put himself through, exchanged the water jug on the table for a coloured jug. He then laced the water heavily with whisky. Carleton Jones spoke for an hour and twenty minutes; afterwards he expressed his gratitude to Williams. A fortnight later he died in his sleep. He already knew what Gold Fields thought of him for on his retirement the previous year Annan had told shareholders about Carleton Jones's work. 'It is, I feel, the greatest single contribution to the prosperity of South Africa's gold mining industry since the introduction of the cyanide process in 1890, and deserves to be

178

recognized as such.' It was so recognized. Lesser men had shafts in mines named after them, but Carleton Jones, before he died, had the satisfaction of knowing that his life's work was going to be commemorated with a memorial of a different kind; plans for the building of the town Carletonville, near West Driefontein, were in preparation.

As Annan was about to catch the boat to England from Cape Town in April 1947, he sent a letter of encouragement to his new resident director in Johannesburg, Spencer Fleischer. 'I am leaving with the impression that the producing mines are facing a difficult period and that you will have your hands very full with the task of bringing the new mines into production but I am confident that you have in the group and organization men with the ability and the spirit to see it through to a successful conclusion.' These men included Fleischer's immediate lieutenants as managers, Percy Hammond, Stanley Hallett and Carleton Jones's brother, Hervey Jones. Bill Busschau, described as 'a burly man who likes big figures' was once more putting his substantial intellectual shoulder to the Gold Fields wheel. Campbell Pitt, back from war service in Italy, was consulting mechanical engineer, while Buller Smart and K G McWilliam shared responsibility as consulting engineers.

After another war – World War II – more visitors to Robinson Deep. Marshal of the RAF Lord Tedder, deputy Allied Commander in Europe, and his wife seen underground in the mine, in the clean boiler-suits. Also present were Guy Carleton Jones and Spencer Fleischer, both standing behind Tedder. Behind Lady Tedder is Harry Player of Robinson Deep, father of Ian and Gary Player, and on the right Reg Cousens.

179

Robert Pelletier who, at London's request, had gone on a mission to India during the war to help save a copper mine near Madras, was back in charge of prospecting, together with Willem de Kock and 'Gavel' Truter.

A new team in a new post-war era was pushing ahead with new mines; but the old mines were not forgotten. In August 1947 the sixtieth anniversary of Simmer and Jack was celebrated and the old mine turned in a working profit of £120 000. In its sixty years it had earned more than £61 000 000 in gross revenue and overcome numerous crises including the fire of 1937. In 1949 its old stablemate, Robinson Deep, also went through an ordeal by fire when for ten days the life of the mine lay in the balance. The fire had started more than 7 000 feet below the surface of the Chris sub-incline shaft and proved extremely tenacious. It was days before its manager, F C Steinhobel and his men, assisted by teams from other mines, could get on top of it. At one stage a Proto team was attempting to work in a temperature of 183 degrees. As a result of the fire the mine only managed a profit of £6 000 in 1949. On 10 November 1948 Sub Nigel held its 50th annual general meeting, and Fleischer, its manager in the Thirties, returned nostalgically to address shareholders, who heard how the mine once more had come up trumps with profits of £2 million. There seemed to be something almost indestructible about these old mines.

Robert Annan, having wished good luck to the Gold Fields Colonel in Johannesburg, arrived back in London to confer with the Gold Fields Brigadier who had also been out in South Africa during 1947. Brigadier Sir George Harvie-Watt, MP, a man of many talents and accomplishments, had joined Gold Fields as an outside director in 1944 and in due course he would succeed Annan as chairman of the company. Like Annan he was a Scot. Having been an engineering apprentice, he then took up law and rose to become a Queen's Counsel. In the 1930s he had been elected a member of the House of Commons. He was also a keen soldier in the Territorial Army, the British equivalent of the Active Citizen Force and by the outbreak of war had risen to senior rank. His only experience of mining before coming to Gold Fields had been in Southern Rhodesia where he was a director of the Globe and Phoenix mine. In fact he was on his way to Rhodesia when war broke out in 1939 and had to hurry back immediately to Britain to join his regiment. By 1941 he had become a brigadier, commanding the 6th Anti-Aircraft Brigade. He was, however, still a member of Parliament and soon after the Prime Minister, Winston Churchill, had visited his brigade, he received a summons to 10 Downing Street. Churchill had decided to appoint him his own Parliamentary Private Secretary. The PPS to a minister in the British system performs a valuable job since he is the minister's link with Parliament, keeping him informed of what Parliament and his own supporters in the House of Commons feel about his policies. He has to protect his minister's position. As Churchill said to him: 'When the flies get at the meat, the meat goes bad. I am the meat. You have got to keep the flies off me.' Regretfully Harvie-Watt gave up his military post, abandoning his Ack-ack gun for a metaphorical fly-swatter and returned to Westminster. At the end of the war Churchill recom-

180

Left, *Brigadier Sir George Harvie-Watt Bt called the tune and paid the piper at Gold Fields for most of the 1950s and 1960s. Under his chairmanship the changes were made that led eventually to an independent Gold Fields of South Africa. On the road to Potchefstroom he left many a Scottish echo.*

mended him for a title; like the Randlords of old, he was made a baronet. The man whom Harvie-Watt had replaced as Churchill's PPS was Brendan Bracken, who had become a minister. By a curious coincidence Lord Bracken, as he became, was also the head of a mining house. After the war he was appointed chairman of Union Corporation and the Bracken mine is named after him. In 1947 Sir George Harvie-Watt and Robert Annan met several times over dinner. Annan wanted him to come fulltime to Gold Fields but he hesitated. 'I was attracted by the idea but I was not sure that office hours were what I wanted,' he was to write in his memoirs. But, as he said, 'I was being drawn closer to Gold Fields itself. It was not, however, until about 1950 that I felt that that was where my future lay.' Annan was anxious to build up the strength of the board for the important period of expansion that lay ahead. In 1949 the last of the old guard had died at the age of eighty-seven, Stanley Christopherson, whom Lord Harris had brought on the Board in 1900 during the Anglo-Boer War. Harvie-Watt, once he had decided to give all his time to Gold Fields, rose rapidly in authority,

181

first to being managing director, then chief executive and deputy-chairman. His forceful personality would leave a heavy imprint on the company which in due course he completely restructured, both in Britain and in South Africa. These changes, as will be seen, enabled Gold Fields in South Africa to take its first step along the road to independence and with many new properties that, thanks to Harvie-Watt, were gathered into its basket. Among these were companies and responsibilities that a decade earlier had been part of Norbert Erleigh's short-lived empire.

Within a few months of the end of the war Gold Fields had handed back to Erleigh control of the HE Proprietary Company's interests in South Africa. Erleigh was no longer associated with Anglovaal; on his father's death he had inherited valuable interests in the HE companies. In 1945 his father's old partner, Sir Frederic Hamilton, was over eighty and wanted to retire, so did Eric Turk, the other partner. Norbert Erleigh then took them over and brought them into his New Union Goldfields which had been developing interests in the Free State. On 17 December 1945 the *Rand Daily Mail* announced the Erleigh take-over and Johannesburg informed London that it was about to pass on to him its previous responsibilities for the South African HE Proprietary Company. There seemed to be some relief in Fox Street that there would be no more dealings with Erleigh, whose efforts to ingratiate himself with Gold Fields had been singularly un-successful. Johannesburg had informed London: 'It seems quite clear that he is anxious to have much closer relationships with us than hitherto but the feeling of all of us here is that while we are compelled in certain circumstances to do busi-ness with him....we certainly should not have any closer association with him than can be avoided in the ordinary course of business.'

Fleischer's first couple of years as resident director was a period of considerable difficulty. The return of peace in 1945 had created an extraordinary euphoria in the Treasury where J H Hofmeyr, the former Minister of Mines, was in charge. South Africa seemed to be awash in money and in his give-away budget of 1946 Hofmeyr remitted £15 million in taxation; even his bill to his main taxpayer, the mining industry, was not as steep as usual. Britain, exhausted by its effort in the war, was on its financial knees and South Africa made a gold loan of £80 million to help it up. South Africa's post-war euphoria did not last, however. It had been created by a buoyant economy, by a flow of imports, immigrants and capital escaping from a socialist Britain. Mr Attlee's Labour Government had taken over from Churchill's wartime administration and was trying to bring in the socialist millennium with widespread nationalization. All this was worrying Robert Annan in London but in Johannesburg Fleischer was concerned about rising inflation.

Working costs on the mines had gone up steeply and there was a shortage of black labour. 'The real solution,' Fleischer told Annan, 'is the abolition of the colour bar,' but he quickly adds, this would be 'political dynamite'. It was now May 1948 and South Africa was about to have a general election; the word apart-heid was being bandied about, being part of the National Party's election pro-

182

gramme. This party, led by Dr Malan, had a narrow victory at the polls; General Smuts not only lost his election, he also lost his own seat at Standerton. This victory for the National Party, which was to have far-reaching consequences for South Africa, slowed up the flow of funds to South Africa. Fleischer thought it would be only temporary. He also told Annan that, whereas he was no supporter of the National Party, 'I think it is only right that I should record as far as our Group is concerned that the new Government has been just as helpful if not more helpful than the previous one.'

In September 1949 Dr Malan's Government might well for reasons of national independence have repeated the mistake made by General Hertzog in 1931; the Minister of Finance was the same man, N C Havenga, but this time, September 1949, when Britain devalued the pound sterling, South Africa did so simultaneously. Once again, the South African gold mining industry had been saved by devaluation. The price of gold went up from £8.12.6 to its highest ever recorded price, £12.8.3. The low-grade producers that had been threatened not for the first time with extinction, received a new lease of life. Once more gold shares boomed on the stock markets and Gold Fields found its own prospects, like its assets, completely transformed. In the first year of the higher gold price, following the sterling devaluation, Gold Fields' producing mines in South Africa doubled their profits. The rich mines of the Far West Rand would become even richer; already the contribution being made by Venterspost and Blyvooruitzicht had enabled Consolidated Gold Fields to turn in an annual profit of £1 million in each of the post-war years; from the middle of the war they had maintained a dividend of twelve-and a-half percent.

The past was repeating itself. South Africa had gone off gold in 1932 just as Gold Fields was about to set off along the West Wits Line; now once again, with the 1949 devaluation, its luck was in. Here was grout for the Gold Fields future and the company departed for the new decade, the 1950s, in a mood to break all kinds of records, when West Driefontein would produce more gold than all the mines of the United States put together and proclaim itself as the richest mine the world had ever seen, while in Fox Street, Gold Fields would celebrate the making of £1 million profit in a single month.

CHAPTER SEVEN

The Flowering Fifties
1949-1959

The 1950s was a decisive decade not only for the company but also for the country where it had its major activity. The destiny of Gold Fields in South Africa and of South Africa itself moved inexorably closer in the new political and economic climate of the post-war world. By the end of the decade South Africa was about to celebrate the 50th anniversary of Union but it was to be a farewell party, because, soon after, the country set off upon an independent future as the Republic of South Africa. At the same time Consolidated Gold Fields at 49 Moorgate in London was putting together all its interests in Southern Africa, assembling them under one roof in Johannesburg in a house which would have the name Gold Fields of South Africa, a name which had not been used since the days of the old South African Republic. In that way Gold Fields of South Africa also took its first step towards following South Africa into an independent future.

This was a decade of tremendous prosperity for Gold Fields as the mines on the West Wits Line, held back by the war, got into their stride and produced results that astonished the world. In the mid-1950s Gold Fields in Johannesburg gave a dinner for its personnel to celebrate the fact that their efforts had produced a profit of £1 000 000 in a single month. Rand Mines had already achieved that figure; their Crown Mines was still the reigning champion but West Driefontein was now moving up strongly and in due course would eclipse Crown Mines. Indeed, within four years of that celebratory dinner, the mine by itself had marked up a monthly profit of £1 000 000. The 1950s was essentially the era of West Driefontein when its unfolding riches prompted one commentator to call it the eighth wonder of the world. Stan Gibbs, who as a child had run about another wonder mine, Sub Nigel, was manager at West Driefontein in 1952 when production started; almost twenty years had gone by since that memorable Christmas when Dr Reinecke had had to abandon his train journey to the Cape because they had intercepted the Carbon Leader at borehole E4. In 1952, Robert Annan was there to pour the first gold; he had been in South Africa three years earlier to press the button to start the Libanon plant. The chairman's presence during these symbolic occasions was an indication of how important the West Wits Line had become to the fortunes of the company, whose worldwide activities he directed from London.

Annan had already told shareholders that the South African company, West Witwatersrand Areas, which played mother to the family of subsidiary mining companies, was Gold Fields' biggest dividend earner. In 1951 he said: 'West Wits Areas is now in the 20th year of its development. Up to now the gross amount of capital raised for it and for the five mining companies it has formed is £42 405 462 and the output of gold from the three companies which have reached production has already exceeded £70 000 000 in value.' And that was before West Driefontein had started! Max Walker of Gold Fields in Johannesburg, in an article in the *South African Journal of Economics*, had given an idea of the amount of work that had been going on on the Far West Rand, when he disclosed that, with the eighty boreholes they had put down, they had covered a distance which was the equivalent of eighty-five miles.

Then came West Drie. Within a year of the first gold pour, Annan told shareholders that the mine had made a profit of £2 million; this went up steadily year after year and by 1957 had reached £7 million. In the thirty years that followed the first gold pour – and Annan survived twenty-nine of these – West Driefontein produced 1 700 tons of gold, amply proving the truth of Annan's early prophecy that the mine would become the biggest profit-earner in the Group. This giant mine tended to overshadow its brilliant neighbour, Blyvooruitzicht, which had been on the scene ten years earlier and had previously recorded the highest profits ever made by a gold mine, with consequent benefit to the Gold Fields coffers. And Doornfontein, where Marian and Stanley Hallett had made the first gold pour in 1954, was also proving a conscientious performer with £780 000 profits in its first year. Venterspost, Libanon, Blyvooruitzicht, West Driefontein and Doornfontein, the five mines that made up the stable of West Witwatersrand Areas, provided the wealth for Consolidated Gold Fields in London, where it could boast a dividend income of £1 000 000 a year. By 1958 eighty percent of Consolidated Gold Fields' revenue was coming from South Africa, more than £3 500 000. The calculated gamble it had taken in 1932 had paid off a quarter of a century later in a most spectacular manner. The company, whose very survival was in doubt, had by its activities in South Africa ensured its future security and its further progress and expansion. The time was soon coming when it would use its South African money to develop new interests in other parts of the world.

In Johannesburg, Fleischer saw the danger of the company giving its entire attention to the Far West Rand and he told Annan: 'The major portion of the West Wits Line has now been dealt with and it is incumbent upon this office to look further afield.' The company had missed out on Klerksdorp, where Anglo American with Western Reefs would have a dominant position. Then there was the Orange Free State. It was not that Gold Fields had not been making an effort there. During the war it had created New Consolidated Free State Exploration for that precise purpose and had spent £500 000. But as Annan said: 'Fortune has not been kind to us in the Free State.' Dr Willem de Kock, renowned for his work on the Carbon Leader, found that his efforts in the Free State, though promising at first, disappointed in the end. 'It is galling to us all here,' Fleischer told London in 1950, 'to have watched properties controlled by the other groups being proved to be underlain by payable reefs while our no less energetic and scientifically sound prospecting has failed so far to prove a mining area in the Free State for our administration.' It was to be another five years before Gold Fields got its own mine, Free State Saaiplaas, in the Ventersburg district where in 1949 boreholes had intersected the Basal Reef.

Had Gold Fields bought the Bailey interests in the Free State, they would have had Western Holdings but that had become another feather in the Oppenheimer cap. Then there was Harmony. Here it was moral principle, that good streak of Scottish Calvinism running through 49 Moorgate, that prevented Gold Fields from having what became a major prize in the Free State. The circumstances surrounding Harmony's beginnings were anything but harmonious. Anglovaal had been drilling near the Sand River in the area around Virginia and had found payable gold; the best result had come in 1948 on the farm Harmonie, just north of their option area where high values had been obtained at 4 000 feet. Harmonie was owned by a company called New Union Free State Coal and Gold Mines under the direction of Norbert Erleigh and Joseph Milne. Erleigh had once been a director of Anglovaal but was no longer on good terms with his former colleagues and did not see why they should have what he already possessed. Perhaps another mining house might be interested? Gold Fields was not the only company that was trying to find something in the Free State. Central Mining/ Rand Mines were also looking hard. Brigadier Stokes was sitting in his office in the Corner House when his colleague Gordon Richdale walked in and said: 'Does the board really want a Free State mine? There's a man in my office who wants to sell us one.' Over at Gold Fields Attie von Maltitz had already had the same experience – 'a man in my office who wants to sell us Harmonie'. Gold Fields already had rights over the adjoining property, La Riviera. London, however, was not prepared to sanction anything connected with Erleigh and Milne who were facing prosecution in the courts for infringements of the Companies Act. If that admirable Scot, John Martin, had been alive and in charge at Rand Mines, he might have taken up a similar attitude. Gordon Richdale, however, had no such scruples and, as he described in his memoirs, persuaded his chairman in London, Lord Baillieu, to buy Harmonie for £1 650 000, although negotiations with Erleigh and Milne, in their position, were complicated. The company was eventually to spend £25 000 000 before Harmony was brought to full production but it turned out to be a great mine. And that was fortunate for Gold Fields for once their old friend, Rand Mines, were in charge, they were happy to do business. As a result of the cession of a portion of La Riviera, they acquired a substantial holding in Harmony.

Rand Mines, in a different way, paid a high price for Harmony in having dealings with Erleigh and Milne. Milne also held rights on the farm Erfdeel, north of Saaiplaas and put down a series of boreholes. In June 1949, a couple of months after completing arrangements for Harmony, Rand Mines was asked by Milne's company to assay the Erfdeel cores. Milne was hoping to get Rand Mines to buy Erfdeel as well. Various other assays were done. In due course the Rand Mines laboratories issued a staggering assay certificate showing a result of 56 000 inch-dwt in one of the Erfdeel boreholes. The writer and journalist Piet Meiring, then working for *Die Transvaler,* recorded how he was awakened in the night by a telephone call from Milne who said: 'I just want to tell you that we have struck the biggest gold find of all times on Erfdeel.' Meiring called his office with the news, then went back to sleep. The following day he drove to Odendaalsrus to find out what was going on. Later, he spoke to the Government Mining Engineer, Dawie Malherbe, who assured him that 'it is just impossible that such values could be obtained in the Erfdeel core'. The Stock Exchange had meanwhile become very excited but this was to be short-lived; it was too good to be true and soon the police were carrying out investigations. Milne, meanwhile, with consummate cheek, had refused an offer for Erfdeel from Richdale of two and a half million shares in Central Mining Free State Areas, saying it was not enough! In due course a Rand Mines assayer, R C Stevenson and Joseph Milne were brought to trial on a charge of having added gold to the core in the laboratory. Stevenson was sentenced but Milne got off. However, before long he and Erleigh were before the courts on other charges and this time, they stuck. In April 1950 they were sent to prison; Erleigh, a prominent and popular figure in the social and sporting life of Johannesburg, went out of circulation for seven years. His mining interests were bought by a London financier named Harley Drayton and by the end of the decade he had brought these – and himself – to Gold Fields.

In 1955 Gold Fields acquired Free State Saaiplaas adjoining the old Erleigh properties, Harmony and Erfdeel. The company was floated with a nominal capital of £6 500 000. However, before that stage could be reached, negotiations had gone on with the owner of the farm Dirksburg in order to obtain mining rights over the area required for the mine. Dirksburg with 1 176 claims out of the 4 920 claims of the lease area was to provide the biggest individual lot of claims for Saaiplaas mine. The owner of these claims was Ida Robinson, the daughter of J B Robinson who, having married the Italian Minister to the Union of South Africa, had become the Princess Labia. Princess Labia had inherited the Free State farms on her father's death; he had been hoping to find diamonds. The long defunct Kaalvallei diamond mine, in fact, had been worked on ground immediately west of Saaiplaas. The Labia lease area at Saaiplaas was 793 000 morgen and since Dirksburg had provided so much land for the mine, the Princess, not unnaturally, hoped that the mine would bear her own name, Labia. Gold Fields, however, decided to stay with the original name Saaiplaas but the Princess' son, Natale Labia, became a director of the company. After having served for a while in the South African diplomatic service, he was by mid 1955 studying law in London. With J B Robinson's grandson sitting on the board of a Gold Fields company, it looked as if the hatchet had finally been buried, that the old Rhodes–Robinson feud had finally ended. But had it? Saaiplaas, in the end,

Count Natale Labia when he became a director of Saaiplaas in 1955 had a remarkable resemblance to his grandfather, J B Robinson, seen here (right) as a young man a century earlier.

never brought any joy to Gold Fields and proved as troublesome as the old buccaneer in his day. Willem de Kock's boreholes promised great rewards; it was estimated that the mine would produce some 240 000 ozs in its first year of production. His chief, Robert Pelletier, stated: 'A borehole core represents an ideal sample and must give the most accurate result possible at that particular point.' But at Saaiplaas it did not work out.

Pelletier a few years earlier had been impressed by the results of cores taken from boreholes near the village of Odendaalsrus on properties owned by African and European Investment, directed by Lewis and Marks. On Pelletier's advice, Gold Fields tried to go in with African and European but Lewis and Marks were not looking for partners and turned Gold Fields down. In due course they were successfully courted by Ernest Oppenheimer and from the boreholes that had impressed the Gold Fields geologist emerged President Brand, President Steyn and Welkom. The OFS looked increasingly like a no-go area for Gold Fields and in 1958 its exploration company was absorbed by West Witwatersrand Areas. Saaiplaas, nevertheless, had its moments. One of these was in September 1957 when the company made world headlines with a shaft-sinking record. A R O Williams from the board in London, and himself an engineer, was present at Saaiplaas when Stanley Hallett presented prizes to the shaft-sinkers. News of their exploit reached Russia which was also claiming a world record of 860 feet in one month. The deputy-editor of *Shachtace Stroitelstvo* wrote asking for more details and a paper read by Merricks of Saaiplaas to the Mine Managers Association was dispatched to the Soviet Union for publication. Merricks had been a member of the team that back in 1953 had brought Vlakfontein into the news; with his Saaiplaas colleague Hannes Jordan, with Algy Cundill, L R Robinson and, from Head Office, Marsh Thompson, they had developed the famous cactus grab, an air-operated device that is still used in shaft-sinking today for the loading of newly-broken rock. And they had pioneered the triple-deck stage – the platform used for protecting shaft-sinking crews in the shaft bottoms and from which shaft linings are constructed. They had sunk No 2 shaft at Vlakfontein at a speed faster than any other shaft had ever been sunk before. Doornfontein had followed with a world tunnelling record through hard rock, an advance of 1 903 feet in twenty-six days in a 9ft 8in haulage. Gold Fields technology was ahead in other ways, pioneering the use of igniter cord for blasting in the narrow gold mine stopes, making faster face advance possible.

A great impetus had been given to the use of new techniques in mining in South Africa by study trips overseas. Fleischer had been one of those who saw the necessity after the war, when communications had been difficult, to send technical men to Europe and the United States to see what new methods had been developed there. From Gold Fields went Attie von Maltitz, now manager of Robinson Deep, Zeppenfeld and Campbell Pitt, to see what was happening in North America. Other houses, at the instigation of the Chamber of Mines, sent men to Britain and the Continent. New information acquired was shared and as a result great technological progress was seen during the 1950s. The Gold Fields offices in Commissioner Street adjoined those of Anglovaal in Exploration Building and from time to time Von Maltitz, who became consulting engineer in 1952, provided them with technical advice for their gold mines in the OFS. At one of these mines, Virginia, was a young Afrikaner who had had some of his training as a mining engineer abroad and was applying there the new phenomenon of the circular concrete shaft. His name was Tommy Muller. In due course, Dr T F Muller, like his brother, Hilgard Muller, who became Foreign Minister, was to play an important role in South African affairs and, indeed, as a director of Gold Fields of South Africa, in this company's activities. Von Maltitz, on the other hand, in 1954 transferred his allegiance to Anglovaal which appointed him technical director. Gold Fields tried hard to keep him. 'They offered to double my salary but the Anglovaal conditions were too good to pass over,' he said. He went on to become President of the Chamber of Mines. By this time Gold Fields had got a new resident director in Johannesburg. In 1954, after seven years in the top post, Spencer Fleischer decided it was time to go. 'He had not been very well and decided to retire, much to everyone's surprise,' Di Fleischer wrote to one of their grandchildren, 'The London Office was most distressed and Mr Annan really wept.' Percy Hammond took over. He was to be the last of the many who since 1887 had come from Britain to run the company's affairs in South Africa.

In many ways Fleischer, aided by his wife, had transformed the atmosphere of Gold Fields. They had conferred on the company much of the humanity that they themselves possessed so abundantly. They had made a family out of Gold Fields, given it an *esprit de corps*, so that those who worked for Gold Fields felt that they belonged to a community; it was the old spirit of Sub Nigel in the thirties. From their home in Valley Road, Westcliff, Di Fleischer had launched the book clubs that continue to be a feature of the social life of the Gold Fields community. Long after, she was to write: 'It is quite gratifying in my old age to see how well all the book clubs I started on the Reef are doing. That is something that will carry on long after I have gone.' And about that she was also right.

Annan had noticed during a visit to South Africa what the Fleischers had achieved and he wrote of the 'fine spirit of co-operation which is so noticeable throughout the Group. It has been a particular pleasure to see the friendly, harmonious spirit that exists wherever I have been ...' Fleischer had stepped into Carleton Jones's shoes at a crucial period in the company's affairs and in the difficult conditions that followed the war. Under Dr Malan's National Party Government a new kind of South Africa was emerging and company affairs had to be conducted in a different social and political atmosphere. He took on the additional burden of the presidency of the Chamber of Mines in 1951. 'I found it very strenuous and almost broke down in health, the most trying part of the job was the social side, dinners and speeches. Speeches at various associations of mining people. I was not a good speaker and had to swot hard for each speech. Many times I was required to speak on the same platform as ministers who spoke nearly always the important part in Afrikaans but did say a few words in English. I cannot speak Afrikaans and found myself embarrassed on these occasions by my ineptitude.' But he had other advantages, having been a miner and a reluctant striker in 1922. 'My previous mining career, particularly as a miner, was very useful in dealing with the various trade unions – I knew something of their point of view and they knew I knew.'

Spencer Fleischer demonstrated his own human qualities when once more Rudolf Krahmann appeared on the Gold Fields scene. He had arrived back in South Africa in 1950 and had asked for an appointment to see the resident director. In Berlin, his family had not expected to see him again but one evening there was a knock on the door. They found a bearded, bedraggled figure standing there. It was Rudolf Krahmann, whom the Russians had finally released. He was suffering from tuberculosis and was one of very few who had survived the camp. The family nursed him back to health but their troubles were not yet over. Ilse Krahmann, the daughter, who was working for the Allied

Powers in Berlin, was kidnapped by the Russians who accused her of being a spy. She was condemned to twenty-five years in Siberia but after two years she was released and with the rest of the family returned to South Africa. Gold Fields did not re-employ Krahmann; the work of the magnetometer appeared to have been completed but it was recalled that before the war Agnew had wished Krahmann to have a further bonus. A further £2 000 was paid to him and the company also paid him for the magnetometer. Later on there was further un-official help. The Krahmanns went to live in Pretoria, where Krahmann worked as a geologist for the Tomlinson Commission, whose report set the parameters for the policy of Separate Development. Later he worked for Iscor and the Africa Institute. He died in 1971 at the age of seventy-five. In 1984, his son Harald was among the guests invited to the 50th anniversary of Venterspost, the first mine on the West Wits Line detected by his father's magnetometer.

In the early 1950s the resident director in Johannesburg also had responsibil-ities far north of the Union; Fleischer's duties took him to the Rhodesias and to East Africa. The company acted as technical consultants to the Geita mine in far off Tanganyika and when the Governor of this British colony, which would become Tanzania, Sir Edward Twining, visited South Africa, Percy Hammond and Buller Smart discussed with him how Gold Fields could further assist the development of his territory. Then H E Nelems, who had been manager at Venterspost, went north to become general manager of the fabulous diamond mine that the Canadian Dr John Williamson had discovered in Tanganyika. The move, however, was not a success and before long he was on his way back to South Africa. 'Nelems's main difficulty,' Johannesburg told London, 'seems to have been the impossibility of working with Williamson ... he is very seldom properly sober and is indeed unbalanced. Rumours have for some time been pre-valent of his peculiar personal characteristics ...' Williamson died in 1958, leaving the biggest diamond mine in the world to his brother Percy. Then Harry Oppenheimer bought it for £4 million.

By the mid-1950s South Africa was moving ever further along the road of racial separatism while away in the north the British colonies were preparing to become independent under black governments. In these circumstances it would have been increasingly difficult for Gold Fields in Johannesburg to play a part in Black Africa and in due course Annan wrote to Percy Hammond: 'The decision that our interests in East Africa should be administered from here was arrived at after mature consideration of the many factors to which you draw attention. There is no question of reflection on anyone and the change results purely and simply from the fact that we consider that contact with other parties concerned is easier made in London than from Johannesburg.' The wind of change that the British Prime Minister, Harold Macmillan, would be talking about at the end of the 1950s when he visited West Driefontein, was rising.

The new arrangements did not, however, apply to Rhodesia. Great hopes were being pinned on the Central African Federation, which brought Southern Rhodesia, Northern Rhodesia and Nyasaland into a single unit. But that, too, would be blown away in time, leaving three separate black-ruled countries, Zimbabwe, Zambia and Malawi. It had always been Rhodes's belief that Rhodesia – 'my country' – would do great things for Gold Fields, but it never played more than a minor role in the company's fortunes. The Gold Fields Rhodesian Development Company, founded in 1911, soldiered on through the years. From 1909 until his retirement through ill health in 1950 Major Ewan Tulloch, who like Fleischer had won a DSO and MC in the First World War, had played a prominent part. Mines came and went. Shamva of the early days had been closed down on the advice of Dr Malcolm Maclaren in 1937 and been superseded by the Wanderer, which had a big low-grade body and produced for a number of years until it too closed down in 1951. During the 1950s the company persevered with the Motapa mine north of Bulawayo and the Sebakwe mines. Motapa had unusual characteristics, the gold being located in arsenical needles and these had to be roasted to get rid of the arsenic. The fumes spread around the mine and contaminated the grass, killing the cattle that the mine manager, Alan Gilmore, ran at the mine. At the Sebakwe mines a mystery about a difference in the quantity of gold going in and coming out was finally solved when it was discovered that the black mineworkers were doing some primitive smelting of their own.

Dr Pelletier, the consulting geologist at that time, who had spent many years in the Rhodesias and on his retirement was given a sundial mounted on granite from Motapa, considered that the black tribesmen were very mineral-minded. In a report to Buller Smart in 1958, he said: 'The whole of the sub-continent is heavily populated with indigenous races who live in the bush and are familiar with every feature of it. These natives are most "mineral-minded" and have for generations now reported unusual rocks or minerals to their Native Commissioner or to other Europeans in the hope of receiving a reward. Many more mineral deposits have been discovered by this means than by all the European prospectors put together.' However true that may have been, the Gold Fields exploration company in Central Africa was having to use other, more expensive methods. As a memo from London in 1958 said, 'finance companies cannot avoid entirely the initial risks of prospecting which include aerial surveys of large and almost completely unknown areas'. What this sometimes involved for the geologist on the spot is illustrated by an experience of Dr Max Mehliss, who became resident geologist in Rhodesia in 1948 and spent a quarter of a century there in the service of the company. In 1955, in a joint venture with Rhodesian Selection Trust – RST – he was looking for uranium, carrying out an extensive radiometric survey over a large area of what is now northern Zambia and centred on Solwezi, west of Ndola. Mehliss, the geologist, had first of all to construct an airstrip on a dambo or natural clearing in the bush. This meant, to begin with, moving innumerable termite nests that are a marked feature of the terrain. After that he had to return to base to meet the pilot. Then, sitting at his side as his navigator, he had to guide the plane so that it could make a landing in the clearing. Mehliss felt that nothing in his geological training had equipped him for this kind of work. Such, however, were the hard facts of life for those who promoted the interests of Gold Fields in far-away places and who sometimes felt that their efforts were not always truly understood by those who directed the company's affairs in London. A meeting between Harvie-Watt and some of his men in Rhodesia, whose suggestions about the Dawn Mine acquired in 1958 had been turned down by London, had ended with one of the Rhodesians grumbling about 'pheasant-eating old Scotsmen'. A note to London from Johannesburg after a search for a new base metal mine stated: 'It may well be that this and other ventures which we explore will turn out to be valueless but the prizes when we achieve success easily outbalance the failures which of course is the history of our successful Gold Fields company … I am quite certain that if we don't continue to look for new business Gold Fields will ultimately suffer.'

Gold Fields' exploration work north of the Limpopo during the 1950s was often carried out in co-operation with other companies, not only with RST but also with Anglo American and the BSA Company, whose President until his death in 1955, Sir Dougal Malcolm, was also a director of Gold Fields. It was in the company of Anglo and of the BSA Company that Gold Fields in 1957 made a substantial entry into South West Africa.

During the period of German control of South West Africa, which ended with General Botha's victory there in 1915, the South West Africa Company (SWACo) had been established. As early as 1892 it had mineral rights over a vast area of unexplored country and freehold rights over 5 000 square miles of territory. From its various mines came concentrates of base metals – zinc, lead, tin and tungsten. This was the company that in 1957 became part of Gold Fields which had the major stake in it; at first it was administered directly from London but from the start Gold Fields in Johannesburg provided South Africans to run it. One of these was an outstanding mining engineer from the Eastern Cape, an Afrikaner named Andries Taute, popularly known as André, to whom was entrusted the task of launching Gold Fields activities in the territory. His fellow Afrikaner, the geologist Willem de Kock, who had been Inspector of Mines in South West Africa before joining Gold Fields, had provided a report for Percy Hammond in 1955 in which he had suggested that the best way for Gold Fields to go into South West Africa would be in association with SWACo.

The most significant and lasting importance of this company was that it provided Gold Fields with a backdoor into the Tsumeb Corporation. SWACo had, at various times, transferred some of its vast territories to the Tsumeb and Otavi copper mines and in so doing had acquired a holding in Tsumeb. At the beginning of the century it had actually helped Tsumeb to get started, putting down two small shafts which proved the continuity of ore to sixty feet. For many years the Germans controlled Tsumeb until, during the Second World War, the Custodian of Enemy Property took it over. In 1946 the South African Government put it up for sale as a result of which some important American interests, notably Newmont, came on the scene. The newly formed Tsumeb Corporation continued to produce zinc, lead, tin and tungsten.

André Taute, a mining engineer whose innovative skills in the design of mine shafts and underground layouts were employed at Kloof and elsewhere. In the late 1950s he played a leading role in the development of the company's interests in South West Africa, and twenty years later had become technical director on the GFSA board.

André Taute at Grootfontein, in charge of SWACo, reported to A R O Williams, the consulting engineer in London who was also chairman of that company. After a while he felt they were pulling in different directions, that what London really wanted him to do was to find them another Tsumeb and to set off round South West Africa drilling boreholes. Taute, on the other hand, wanted to go ahead developing existing properties, Berg Aukas, producing lead and vanadium concentrates, for instance, and the lead-zinc-vanadium mine, Abenab West; also the tin-wolfram mine in the Brandberg. At one point Williams flew out from England to Windhoek to confront Taute, but in the end a *modus vivendi* was worked out and Taute was to say in due course: 'The time I enjoyed most in my mining career was the two years in South West Africa as general manager of SWACo at Grootfontein. It was a job where I had to be jack-of-all-trades, where I did not have a wealth of people to do things for me. I had to be my own personnel officer and my own technical designer.' In the beginning, public relations had priority because SWACo was very unpopular among the local inhabitants. Farmers, for instance, had found their water supplies cut off because of the plugging on company lands of water boreholes. Taute had them unplugged and released a torrent of goodwill for Gold Fields. He arranged parties so as to get to know all the local people and soon he became a popular

194

figure in the community where the company operated. He even created beautiful gardens with elephant manure and all would have been well if the bottom had not dropped out of the base metal market, upsetting his new operations. At Brandberg these were started, stopped, then restarted. Over the years the pioneering efforts of Taute in the increasingly disputed territory of South West Africa/Namibia bore fruit. Gold Fields operations there were frequently to be restructured, particularly after Johannesburg assumed responsibility; and if Taute never found another Tsumeb, the company in the end got the major slice of the original.

Although it was a disappointment to Gold Fields to see a drastic fall in base metal prices just as it had acquired new interests in this field in South West Africa, the glitter of gold was so bright as to make it of little consequence. In June 1957 Gold Fields announced that for the first time South Africa's mines had produced gold worth more than £200 million. In December that year Annan told the shareholders: 'Since 1953 our total dividend income has risen seventy-four percent while in the same period that part of the dividends from South Africa has more than doubled.' Gold was not the only source of income. That year the directors reported the production of 1 119 000 lbs of uranium oxide. And, as if to underline this fact, it was announced that Gold Fields' uranium pioneer of the war years, Stanley Hallett, was joining the board in London to make his talents available to the company in other parts of the world.

For the gold mining industry uranium was a temporary bonanza. Its production for strategic purposes had provided the impetus of the early and mid-1950s. The United States and Britain, setting up the Combined Agency, signed undertakings with South Africa to buy all its uranium over a long-term period. At the zenith of the uranium boom in the late 1950s, as a by-product of gold mining, it added some £50 million to the working profits of the industry, with a peak production in 1959 of 6 500 tons of uranium oxide. After that time the Agency reduced its off-take to 6 200 tons a year for the remaining period of the contracts between producers and the Agency, due to expire about 1966. Gold Fields played its part in uranium but it was never more than a minor role. Of the twenty-three gold mines producing uranium only four were in the Gold Fields Group. Doornfontein was producing in 1956 just two years after the mine started and it shared the extraction plant located at West Driefontein, the main producer. Vogelstruisbult on the East Rand was another producer and that ancient performer, Luipaardsvlei, was given a new lease of life when, in 1955, its Bird Reef, commemorating the Potchefstroom physician who had first sent Dr Sauer to the Rand in 1886, was worked for uranium, or at least that part of it known as the Monarch Reef. These operations continued until 1964. West Driefontein remained a producer long after the demand for uranium had fallen away and by 1983 had produced more than 3 000 tons of uranium oxide. Luipaardsvlei was not subject to the 'stretch out' agreement whereby South African producers arranged to stretch out the unexpired portions of their contracts, deferring their deliveries of uranium to cover a longer period of years.

Harmony proved to be a good uranium producer; Saaiplaas would have been but came on the scene too late to profit from the boom.

Platinum, a Gold Fields interest since the mid–1920s, had been going in and out of favour since the war years. It became a notoriously volatile market but as Annan told Johannesburg, 'I still take an optimistic view of the future of platinum'. Between 1948 and 1956 production at Rustenburg had increased fourfold to meet demands coming from the oil industry which wanted platinum as a catalyst. Gold Fields, as has been seen, had combined its interests with JCI back in 1931 when the platinum industry had gone through a slack period. They had formed the operating company Rustenburg Platinum, which had brought together Waterval from the Gold Fields side and Potgietersrust Platinum from the JCI camp; JCI was in charge of the administration of Rustenburg under a kind of gentleman's agreement. In 1949, Gold Fields had been responsible for bringing another company into the Rustenburg basket, Union Platinum whose property some sixty miles north of Rustenburg had not been producing for some time. Rustenburg Platinum's shares were now held by three constituent companies. When the question arose at Gold Fields of their Waterval company possibly absorbing their Union company, a move which would have given them voting control of Rustenburg, Annan in London was concerned about upsetting JCI, whose Kenneth Richardson was chairman of Rustenburg. 'We feel that he might be upset if any such deal were carried out without the knowledge and participation of his group,' the chairman told Johannesburg. 'No doubt you have this well in mind but we did not want to run the risk that it might have been overlooked.' Such was the Gold Fields concern for a gentleman's agreement. However, some three years later, in 1955, Annan was writing again: 'There is little doubt that through its various holdings Gold Fields is the largest individual shareholder in the platinum business in spite of which we have only one representative on the board of Rustenburg as against two from JCI.' Nothing very much changed, however, and JCI remained in day-to-day control of what during the 1950s became the most important source of platinum in the world. Gentleman's agreements, as Gold Fields was to discover on more than one occasion, are not the best basis for doing business; the gentlemen who make the original agreement go in time, and are replaced by other gentlemen who are replaced by others who are not always gentlemen. Along the way the spirit of the agreement, if not the agreement, disappears. Gold Fields never acquired the commanding position in platinum that it ought to have had and in time London, with other things in view, let Gold Fields' interests in South African platinum slip out of its hands altogether. Later the South African company, Gold Fields of South Africa, decided to make its own, independent re-entry into the platinum world.

There were times during the 1950s when Gold Fields almost became the victim of its own success, when the publication of its increasingly impressive results merely advertised the fact that Consolidated Gold Fields was a very desirable property in itself. There were many people who wanted Gold Fields shares; there were also some who wanted Gold Fields, in order to put their hands on the source of its prosperity, that is to say, its gold mines in South Africa. The predators were South African. Ever since the creation of the West Witwatersrand Areas, Gold Fields, its major shareholder, while sitting in the driving seat had had to look regularly in the driver's mirror to see if anyone was coming up from behind. From time to time the ubiquitous figure of Sir Ernest Oppenheimer could be made out, and avoiding action had to be taken. Just as Doornfontein was about to become the fourth mine on the West Wits Line, Johannesburg was telling London: 'It would ... seem desirable that we should not bring about a situation which could easily lead to the Anglo American increasing its share of the equity of Doornfontein or West Wits, particularly the latter.' At one point Oppenheimer thought he had control of West Wits and was surprised to learn in Fox Street that this was not the case. Busschau and Hallett had got wind of Anglo activity and had persuaded London to increase its holding in West Wits. Oppenheimer was impressed and Hallett was invited to join Anglo but declined the offer. Gold Fields, concentrating its attention on Sir Ernest Oppenheimer, was unaware of another predator. This was not surprising since the new threat came from a totally unexpected quarter, but it was significant in that it was a reflection of how South Africa under its National Party Government had been changing.

Afrikaner nationalism was in the ascendant; the National Party throughout the 1950s increased its power at every general election and with each change of Prime Minister. Dr Malan had been succeeded by J G Strijdom who died in 1958 and was followed by Dr H F Verwoerd. In May that year one of the pioneering figures of Afrikaner business, Dr M S 'Tienie' Louw, in a challenging speech in Cape Town referred to South African mines being controlled from London. 'Sixty percent of mining is in the hands of foreigners,' he claimed and asked challengingly, 'To whom does South Africa belong?' But, as Louw well knew at the time, plans were afoot in Afrikaner circles to change this situation. At the *volkskongres* in Bloemfontein back in 1940, Afrikaner nationalists had decided that it was not enough for Afrikanerdom to strive for political control in South Africa; it must go after economic power, too. Afrikaner business organizations began to emerge – Federale Volksbeleggings, Bonuskor, Sanlam. The heart of economic power in South Africa was the gold mining industry, however. In 1949 a Free Stater named Willem Coetzer, who had started his business life in Barclays Bank at Aliwal North but had since become Federale Volksbeleggings' one and only man in Johannesburg, wrote to Cape Town urging the formation of an Afrikaner mining house. In 1953 he saw his wish come true with the formation of Federale Mynbou. At the time the great majority of white miners, who numbered 47 000, were Afrikaners and it seemed only logical that Afrikaners should have a part in the ownership and direction of gold mining in South Africa. To them the unilingual Chamber of Mines still looked like the outpost of the British Empire that it had once been. But how were they to make an entry?

Federale Mynbou made a start with coal interests. During the war two brothers, Jacques and Wennie du Plessis, using oxen and donkeys had been

197

getting coal out of the Acme mine on the farm Honingkrans in the Witbank district. Wennie du Plessis was not a miner but a diplomat by profession and served abroad in South Africa's legations. He had resigned from the Department of External Affairs when Smuts was in control, and in the 1948 general election he stood against Smuts and defeated him at Standerton. He stayed a short time in Parliament, then went back to diplomacy and became Ambassador in the United States. The Du Plessis brothers had been helped by Federale Volksbeleggings and their interests, which had expanded in scope and profitability, were finally taken over by Federale Mynbou. In due course Coetzer got to know a British financier who became interested in the coal business in South Africa. This was Harley Drayton, the man who took over the Erleigh companies during the 1950s. Coetzer wanted to get into the gold mining industry since that was the only way that he could make something significant out of South Africa's first Afrikaner mining house. 'I began to make a study of existing mining houses with a view to co-operation, merging or a take-over,' he was to say. Having looked at all the mining houses, Coetzer decided that Gold Fields was the one to go for. There appeared to be no large single shareholder who would be in a position to block a take-over. There was a considerable number of bearer shares that might be picked up in France; in fact a later investigation by Gold Fields in London revealed that some eighty percent of its bearer shares were held abroad. Coetzer decided to ask Harley Drayton to help him make an attempt on Gold Fields. He was going to London with M S Louw and had decided to go and see Drayton in his office in Old Broad Street. However, as Coetzer was to say, Louw's personality was full of contradictions and his attitude to mining was ambivalent. He supported the buying of shares in the Strathmore group of Klerksdorp mines but in the end he was against taking over a mining house. In London he had second thoughts about a Gold Fields take-over and Coetzer was unable to proceed.

Coetzer, however, was soon to be joined by another Afrikaner who shared his views that Federale Mynbou ought to have a foothold in gold mining. He was a man with an established reputation as a mining engineer. This was Tommy Muller who, after his successes as Mine Manager at Virginia, had joined von Maltitz at Anglovaal in Johannesburg. In 1957 he left to join Coetzer at Federale Mynbou and together they built up what became a considerable mining house.

Gold Fields, meanwhile, had become aware that covetous eyes were on them and they began to look to their defences. Their vulnerability to a take-over, they discovered, lay in the fact that their 3 000 000 preference shares had voting rights and if a determined predator could get hold of these, he would be in a position to get control. The board in London decided to remove these voting rights and a special meeting of shareholders gave it authority to do so; the preference share-holders were compensated with an extra one percent on their shares. Gold Fields had pulled up the drawbridge and thought it was safe. This, however, could not be the end of the story. What Consolidated Gold Fields had in South Africa was so valuable, it could not but attract the attention of others in South Africa who wanted to harness these riches to their own. And as long as these were controlled from London, it would be there that any future raid would be made.

Gold Fields, however, was not the only historic mining house that was vulnerable. Central Mining, which in the old days had been called Wernher, Beit, and its South African arm, Rand Mines, was a company like Gold Fields whose shares were widely held. It also had very large liquid assets. In August 1956 an announcement was made in London and Johannesburg which said: 'The Consolidated Gold Fields of South Africa and the Central Mining and Investment Corporation announce that they have entered into conversations with a view to a merger of the two companies.' It was an exciting prospect that seemed to give practical expression to what sixty or so years earlier had been the informal ad hoc business partnerships of Rhodes and Beit. Gold Fields was already, indirectly, connected with the situation whereby in mid-1956 Central Mining found itself sitting with more than £8 000 000 of liquid assets. The money had come from oil. Central Mining had just parted with its Trinidad Leaseholds to the Texas Company of America on terms which had been so favourable it could not but recommend the sale to the Americans. Trinidad Leaseholds was meant to be a Gold Fields company for when it all started back in 1910 with the discovery of oil on the island, the landowners there had sent a deputation to see Lord Harris, who had been born in Trinidad during the time his father was Governor there. In 1911 Gold Fields announced that they had taken up options in 'oil-bearing' lands in Trinidad. Then followed long negotiations with the British Colonial Office. Lord Harris, never the most patient or tactful of men, appears to have been irritated by the long delays and finally he broke off the negotiations. In 1912, shareholders were told that the oil deal was not on. The following year there was further news. This was that Central Mining had acquired the oil interests and that Gold Fields had a substantial share. And that was why in 1956 Robert Annan told Gold Fields shareholders that when the Americans bought the company, Gold Fields had made 'substantial profits from the transaction'.

Circumstances for the merger of Gold Fields and Central Mining – the companies that controlled West Driefontein and Crown Mines – looked most propitious. Gold Fields could use extra cash for development and Central Mining had £8,25 million waiting to be invested. For five months the talks went on between the two companies, whose offices were only 300 yards apart in the City of London but in February 1957 they had to announce that no merger had been arranged. Both companies, however, were 'determined to strengthen in every possible way their traditional co-operation in the field of overseas mining'. The Central Mining chairman, Lord Baillieu, an Australian, said 'one of the most important lessons we have learned is the difficulty in merging two companies with almost identical interests. It is, in my experience, easier to arrange an amalgamation between companies whose activities are, rather, complementary'. Later Sir George Harvie-Watt, by then chief executive and deputy-chairman of Consolidated Gold Fields, commented: 'In my view it was a natural but we failed to reach agreement. Not long afterwards Sir Archibald Forbes became chairman of Central Mining. We were old friends and we often mourned the fact that the merger had not taken place. If he had been in the chair at the time of the merger talks, I'm certain it would have been a *fait accompli* with real advantages to both companies.' The pooling of the resources of the two companies would have created an entity of enormous power in South Africa. The fact that it did not happen enabled the Anglo American Corporation in 1957 to become the leading mining house in the country. It was the year in which Sir Ernest Oppenheimer died, not long after he had inaugurated Western Deep Levels on the West Wits Line. It would be his son, and the new chairman, Harry Oppenheimer who, in due course, would take Federale Mynbou by the hand and lead it to the bigger future that Coetzer had originally sought by way of Gold Fields. And when that happened M S Louw showed his disapproval by resigning.

In 1957 Central Mining, without the protection that a merger with Gold Fields would have provided, was out in the open. The raid when it came was mounted in Johannesburg by two brothers named Glazer who had considerable property interests. A rescue operation was mounted by John Martin's old protégé, Gordon Richdale, who was now working for the American mining magnate Charles Engelhard. Richdale, with the help of Engelhard and others, set up a syndicate which bought Central Mining shares in sufficient quantity to forestall the Glazer brothers. Charles Engelhard from then on came to play a big part on the South African mining scene, taking over the chairmanship of Rand Mines in Johannesburg in 1958.

Down the street from Central Mining's London headquarters, Annan and Harvie-Watt had watched the defence of Gold Fields' old ally with close interest and drew obvious lessons for themselves. The Brigadier looked to his own defences. Gold Fields had already had to repel would-be boarders from South Africa and Harvie-Watt now began to work out what he regarded as a master plan for the future of the company. The failure of the merger talks with Central Mining seemed to act like a catalyst, for during 1958 and 1959 he put through a whole series of changes which had the most far-reaching effects on the company. In fact, they laid the base, indeed created a launching pad, for Gold Fields of South Africa to become an independent South African company.

The name of Harvie-Watt's fortress was Diversification. 'In my view,' he was to write, 'we had come to a crossroads. We had too many eggs in one basket.' He also felt that 'in order to secure Gold Fields from the predator, it was necessary that we should enlarge our interests by friendly take-overs where possible'. All his plans would need considerable capital but he had chosen a good moment to set off. In 1957 Gold Fields had record working profits and record dividends; this was the year in which gold produced in South Africa exceeded £200 million for the first time. Consolidated Gold Fields needed more money to meet its commitments in South Africa, at Saaiplaas, for instance, the Free State mine whose first shafts were going down. There was, also, a commitment to provide £3,25 million for a participation in Western Deep Levels, the Anglo American mine bordering on West Driefontein. In June 1957 the authorized capital of the company was increased to £8 million with the creation of 3 000 000 ordinary

200

shares of £1 each and was pushed up even further by the creation of a convertible unsecured loan stock. In 1959 it was increased again when another 3 000 000 ordinary shares increased the ordinary share capital to £11 million. That year the company turned in record profits of some £5$^{1}/_{2}$ million. Harvie-Watt had plenty of money in his purse as he went out shopping for Gold Fields. 'The more I pondered its problems the more I considered changes in its interests and in the countries of its operations,' he said. The QC was taking a brief out of the past from Lord Harris but Harvie-Watt was living in a different age. Gold was providing some 80 percent of the company's income but as Harris had once said: 'Gold Fields habitually invested in properties with terminable lives.' Harvie-Watt, like Harris, wanted Gold Fields to be a company whose life was not terminable. This would mean, as in the past, new investments which had nothing to do with mining. The new policy had a *déjà vu* look about it. 'The largest interests of the company were in Africa,' he was to write. 'In fact at one time we had over 90 percent of our interests in Africa while the rest – in America, Australia and the United Kingdom – were to a certain extent minor interests.' One of the first things that Harvie-Watt did with his new broom was to sweep away the company's interests in what was now being referred to as Black Africa where, through the action of the British Parliament, of which he was a member, the colonies of the old empire were becoming independent members of the Commonwealth under black governments. The old Gold Coast of Robert Fricker's day had now become the Ghana of Kwame Nkrumah; Nigeria was about to become independent. By 1960 the white members of the Commonwealth would be outnumbered by the black and brown members. All this boded ill for the Union of South Africa whose official policy was to separate whites and blacks within its own borders. South Africa and the multi-racial Commonwealth were on different roads.

London, seeing the writing on the wall, had already taken away from Johannesburg control of Gold Fields' interests in East Africa. Now Harvie-Watt decided that the time had come 'to unload our investments in the less safe areas of Africa … we therefore got rid of our interests in Kenya, Tanganyika and even Rhodesia. In their place I wanted to open up in Australia … there were also New Zealand and Canada and we had an American office but our interests were small … above all I wanted to develop in the United Kingdom. I was trying to build up in what I considered to be the safest areas in the world'.

So what about South Africa? Harvie-Watt felt that it 'had a longer life than the northern states. That was my thinking in 1954'. The observation was significant since it appeared to classify the country in terms of its gold mines – that it had a terminable life. South Africans who were responsible for directing the company's affairs in their own country might well have taken a different view. In any case they were confident that the golden egg which had made the fortune of the company in London, would continue to be laid in South Africa. Harvie-Watt was taking steps to see that it had the best possible chance of doing so. He completely restructured the company. There were now to be two separate baskets, one labelled 'Africa' and the other 'Rest of the World'. This meant that all the Gold Fields subsidiary companies and shareholdings in Africa – in practical terms, Southern Africa – were to be brought together and administered by one subsidiary in Johannesburg. All the rest of the company's interests round the world would be placed in another subsidiary company and administered by London. In South Africa an existing company had to be chosen to serve as a vehicle for bringing together all the other companies and interests, to act as mother, as it were, to this new South African family. The honour went to African Land and Investment Company, the property company which had been registered at the beginning of the century and been responsible for the Johannesburg suburbs of Illovo and Dunkeld among other things. Gold Fields had some eighty-eight percent of the ordinary shares and thirty-six percent of the preference shares. At the beginning of 1959 it acquired the entire shareholding. It was now ready to be parent to all the other companies in Southern Africa. All it needed was a new name. Dr Busschau, whose combination of gifts included a strong sense of history, suggested that this new totally South African company should be called Gold Fields of South Africa, the name that Rhodes and Rudd had chosen in 1887 and which had not been used since 1892 when the company in London had taken the name Consolidated Gold Fields of South Africa, later changed in 1919 to New Consolidated Gold Fields Limited. Since the legal circumstances of 1919, which had necessitated the last change, no longer applied, Annan and Harvie-Watt in London reverted to the 1892 name. In due course when the separation between London and Johannesburg became even more pronounced, the name of the company at 49 Moorgate became simply Consolidated Gold Fields, the name South Africa disappearing from the company's title. The game of name-changing was very much part of the process of decolonization and it happened in the commercial field, too. As the company in London said: 'It had become apparent in past years that there were disadvantages in a system whereby administrative and technical services for a number of important South African companies were provided by a British company having its Head Office 6 000 miles away.' Gold Fields of South Africa would remain for a decade a wholly-owned subsidiary of the London company which would in the beginning continue to provide it with financial services. For this reason three of the GFSA directors were from the board in London, though one of these, Stanley Hallett, was still at heart a Fox Street man.

Gold Fields of South Africa had appeared, fully-fledged, like Venus from the sea; it had a ready-made family of subsidiary companies and among these were some newcomers, for Harvie-Watt in the course of his shopping had acquired important new interests for Gold Fields in South Africa. He had bought the historic Anglo-French Exploration Company which, in the 1890s, had been associated with the names of the pioneers, Sir George Farrar and Sir William Dalrymple. Through Anglo-French, Rooiberg (tin) and Apex (coal) became part of Gold Fields of South Africa. With Apex it was the renewal of an old acquaintance since in the 1890s Gold Fields had provided directors for the company. Buying Anglo-French had been a straightforward transaction, Gold Fields offering 500 000 of its own shares and £125 000 in cash making an overall cost of £1 981 000. Its chairman, Roland Cottell, joined the board of Consolidated Gold Fields.

The next group of companies that Harvie-Watt bought for Gold Fields of South Africa had also had an in-and-out relationship with 75 Fox Street over the years, as has already been shown. These were the old interests of Sir Frederic Hamilton, Ludwig Erlich and Eric Turk, the HE Proprietary Company with its Luipaardsvlei connections; the same interests that had passed into the hands of Norbert Erleigh of New Union Goldfields. After Erleigh's demise, they had become part of the empire of Harley Drayton. New Union Goldfields had interests in Britain as well as South Africa and to Harvie-Watt it seemed to fit in very well with his plans for expansion. 'These Drayton interests were well studied and in due course I got in touch with Harley Drayton,' Harvie-Watt recorded. 'He at once asked me to dine with him at his house in Millionaire's Row.' Later Harvie-Watt was to say that it was the simplest takeover he had ever had. Drayton, the man whom Willem Coetzer had hoped might have helped him to get a foot in the Gold Fields door, was apparently delighted that Gold Fields should take over his wide interests in South Africa. He even seemed to be in a hurry and before long sent through to 49 Moorgate minutes of his directors' meetings – 'a little irregular as you have not yet acquired the company'.

Harvie-Watt insisted that Drayton should join the board of Consolidated Gold Fields and he in his turn brought in Martin Rich, who had been working in South Africa getting New Union Goldfields back into shape after its somewhat checkered career. Harry Mackay and Sidney Segal were others who came across into the service of Consolidated Gold Fields with Drayton. The importance to Gold Fields of South Africa of all these deliberations in London was that it acquired a variety of new interests and thereby increased the scope of its activities. From Anglo-French it had obtained Rooiberg Tin; now it had Union Tin as well. In the Free State it acquired the Star Diamond mine with a production of 50 000 carats a year and it even obtained a place in the Klerksdorp field with Dominion Reefs, a company whose records had been destroyed during the German blitz on London. 'It is our intention,' London told Johannesburg, 'that New Union should come under the direct control of Gold Fields of South Africa.'

Harvie-Watt obviously admired Harley Drayton as a self-made man who had left school at 15 but Drayton always remained something of a mystery man. When he died in 1966 at the age of 64, *The Times* in London said: 'For a great many years he remained an enigma even to many of his close friends' and it went on to say: 'He was criticised for the support he brought, moral and financial, to small and little known undertakings in need of capital for expansion.' He did help Coetzer and Federale Mynbou by selling them his coal interests, Natal Navigation which, together with their Transvaal mines, became Trans-Natal, and that in turn led to bigger and more important developments for the Afrikaner

Donald McCall, who started his career at the bottom of a Sub Nigel mine shaft in 1930, climbed up to become chairman of Consolidated Gold Fields in London in 1969. Seen here in Johannesburg with a friend after his contribution from Gold Fields had brought The Star Teach Fund *up to the million Rand mark.*

mining house. Drayton was an unusual acquisition for the board of Consolidated Gold Fields but he would seem to have had a feeling for its history. When the private papers of Rhodes's friend, Rudyard Kipling, came up for auction at Christie's, he went in and bought them against tough American competition.

Harvie-Watt, having put through the fundamental changes in the structure of the company during 1959, on the eve of his becoming its chairman, looked around for new men who would help him to operate the company in the changed world that had emerged with the disappearance of the old colonial empires. One such man was an astute and able accountant who had proved the strength of his will and determination as a wartime pilot in the Royal Air Force when he had won the DFC. His name was G G Potier and he soon acquired considerable influence in the company, becoming in due course its deputy-chairman. Another

204

new director at this time was Donald McCall who, having started at Sub Nigel in 1930, had later worked for the company in West Africa. After military service during the war, he had gone to 49 Moorgate and been working his way up the managerial ladder. Another South African trained man who was coming to the fore in London at this time was Gerald Mortimer, who was to project Harvie-Watt's ambitions in Australia and in due course become chief executive of the company. Mortimer had obtained his degree at the Royal School of Mines before military service in the Royal Engineers. He was the first British officer to enter Berlin at the end of World War II and was awarded the OBE. Soon after the war he joined Gold Fields and was sent out to work on Vogelstruisbult.

For those who worked at 75 Fox Street, Johannesburg, 1959 had been an important milestone in the history of the company's activities in South Africa. The office stationery now bore the name Gold Fields of South Africa, the name chosen so long ago by Rhodes and Rudd. They had their own chairman and board of directors, nearly all of whom had been born and bred in South Africa. To underline the continuity in the South African story one of these directors was H P Rudd, son of the co-founder. Harvie-Watt had given them a great start. He had bought for their administration companies which, like their own, had been growing with South Africa since the 19th Century, and their own colourful history had now become part of the heritage of Gold Fields of South Africa, and at a time when it was proclaiming its true South African identity. The greatly expanded activities of the company in Johannesburg required additional premises and, appropriately, Gold Fields acquired for this purpose an historic landmark of Johannesburg. This was Exploration Building close by in Commissioner Street, one of the early stone buildings erected in 1896 by Sir Herbert Baker who had had his own architect's offices there. Gold Fields paid Anglovaal £40 000 for the building. They had already extended the Fox Street premises through to Commissioner Street after acquiring in 1952 the Rand Water Board building, which was then demolished to make way for new offices. The Gold Fields offices now occupied a sizeable chunk of the western end of Fox Street and Commissioner Street; in 1956 it had been valued by Curries at £500 000. In 1959 Gold Fields of South Africa was providing managers, secretaries, transfer secretaries, buyers and, where appropriate, technical advisers to fourteen gold mining companies, five financial companies, including West Wits, four property companies, four engineering companies and three other companies of varying interests, including company laboratories.

William Busschau had taken over as resident director on the retirement of Percy Hammond in time to become the first chairman of Gold Fields of South Africa and with the determination to run the company in the best interests of his country; between company and country, gold was the binding link and by promoting gold he believed he would serve both. By 1959 he had become one of the world's leading authorities on gold; his vigorous advocacy of gold as the essential element in the world's monetary system had brought him an international reputation. Ever since 1950, when he had accompanied that other great

1962: Gold Fields opened a new building in Commissioner Street on two stands previously occupied by the Rand Water Board and Exploration Building which had been linked to the Fox Street premises in the 1950s. (The latest home of Gold Fields is illustrated in the colour section.)

South African gold expert, Dr J E Holloway, then Secretary for Finance, to the Bretton Woods conference of the International Monetary Fund, he had tirelessly kept up his advocacy of gold. His books, such as 'The Measure of Gold' had won him high acclaim, particularly in academic circles. Although he had a successful career as a business leader, he was at heart an academic, on whom Christ Church College, Oxford, had left a lasting influence; he was to be appropriately honoured by becoming Chancellor of Rhodes University. It was noticeable that under his influence the company, once dominated by aristocrats, cricketers and engineers, came strongly under the influence of university graduates, some of whom like himself had been Rhodes Scholars at Oxford. He even admitted one or two who had been at what he – and Rhodes – might have called 'the other place' – Cambridge University.

Busschau, as if to underline the importance of the changes in company structure which had brought into being Gold Fields of South Africa, took over the Presidency of the Chamber of Mines and became a governor of the South African Reserve Bank. He became an establishment figure in the country; as the Press said, he was one of those on whom South Africa relied to calculate the national income. High finance, however, could not occupy all his time. There came a moment in May 1958 when he had to deal with low cunning. This was the sensational and skilful theft of gold from Vlakfontein. The discovery that the gold was missing was made on 13 May 1958; some 5 000 ounces of fine gold belonging to Vlakfontein was missing, as well as some 116 ounces belonging to Spaarwater which shared smelting facilities with Vlakfontein. The value of the stolen gold was £65 000. The Police were called in at once and it was soon clear that it could only have been what they called 'an inside job'. The theft was a great shock to that great mine manager Algy Cundill, particularly when it was discovered that some of the 'insiders' were men who had worked with him at Vlakfontein since 1942 and had enjoyed the prestige that the mine had won for its achievements in mining techniques. On 17 May Busschau cabled Harvie-Watt that the Police had taken various people into custody. Hammond followed up with a letter listing the names of eight men, one of whom was an Indian and the other an African. The latter, who was referred to as Appelkoos, was apparently employed by one of the white burglars in the time-honoured South African manner, to carry his tools! The Indian, who hid the gold in the Benoni Location, was making arrangements to sell it for £24 000 but his plans were upset after the arrest of one of the whites who worked in the Reduction Works at Vlakfontein and who told the full story to the Police.

High finance, low cunning – that was not all. Busschau and others were having to cope with the General Nuisance. This was a man who had appointed himself as chairman of shareholders' rights and who disrupted meetings of Gold Fields subsidiary companies when, in the words of one who was present, he 'took over each meeting and waffled on, removing his glasses and replacing them with irritating regularity until his diatribe was forcibly cut short'. His war against Gold Fields' directors produced various counter measures. Busschau, as

207

a change from working out the national income, came up with a scheme whereby the lift taking up the difficult shareholder to the meeting might be stopped between the floors and held there until the meeting was over. Sterner measures, however, were found to be necessary. The climax came at the Vogelstruisbult meeting of 27 May 1955 when in the shareholder's own words, as expressed in a memorandum sent to Gold Fields and copied to other mining houses, he was 'set upon by Gettliffe, secretary, Gold Fields Group, two porters and other employees, assaulted, frogmarched out of the meeting, thrown into the street (Commissioner) on the orders of the chairman, J M Ewing'. In due course investigations into the background of the tiresome shareholder revealed that he had entered South Africa under false pretences; he was invited by the Union immigration authorities to return to his native Southampton in England. Thereafter, comparative peace returned to the meetings of Gold Fields' companies in Johannesburg.

During the 1950s Bill Busschau was accustomed to go to lunch once a week at the Johannesburg Country Club; here he would be joined by the representatives of five other mining houses, all of whom were members of the Gold Producers Committee of the Chamber of Mines. There was a ritual whereby, once in the bar, they would spin a coin to see who was going to pay for the lunch and drive the group to the club for the lunch the following week. When Busschau became a member of the group and was introduced to the ritual, he was astounded, records John Lang of the Chamber of Mines. These gold men were spinning a silver coin. He procured for them six United States Double Eagles which contained about one ounce of gold, worth at issue before 1934 the coin's face value of US 20 dollars. The next time the drinks were called around the bar, six ounces of gold went spinning, scintillating in the air, says Lang. Here were South African gold men, meeting at lunch to talk about gold and, since Busschau's arrival, were spinning gold coins to decide who should pay for it all. But they were spinning American gold coins. Why not a South African gold coin? In 1955, Busschau became chairman of a special sub-committee on the disposal of gold; one of its main objects was to work for an international agreement on revaluation of gold in terms of world currencies. Gold was more important than paper money, they wished to tell the world. From this committee, almost as a passing thought, came the idea of issuing a South African gold medallion of one ounce that would commemorate the 50th anniversary of Union in 1960. Little by little, from spinning American gold coins in the bar of the Country Club to striking a commemorative medallion for Union, developed the idea of the Krugerrand, South Africa's own gold coin. Bill Busschau's pioneering role in the 1950s would be built upon by his successors at Gold Fields when, after the establishment of the International Gold Corporation, the Krugerrand would be marketed around the world.

The momentous changes that took place in the structure of the company during 1959 leading to the creation of Gold Fields of South Africa were a prelude to momentous changes in South Africa itself. Once more the company and

208

Britain's Prime Minister in 1960, Harold Macmillan – later the Earl of Stockton – seen stocktaking at West Driefontein in the company of consulting engineer Stan Gibbs, born at Sub Nigel, and GFSA chairman William Busschau, President of the Chamber of Mines in the year that saw the first visit to South Africa of a British premier.

country seemed to be in step. In December that year Queen Elizabeth II received at Buckingham Palace South Africa's new Governor-General, Charles Robbertz Swart who had been appointed on the death of Dr Ernst Jansen, and was destined to be the last Governor-General. In London, Harvie-Watt's leader in the British House of Commons, Harold Macmillan, was packing his bags for his historic visit to the African Continent, when he became the first British Prime Minister to visit South Africa. More than half a century earlier another British minister, Joseph Chamberlain, had been taken to Robinson Deep by Gold Fields' Drummond Chaplin. Now Gold Fields' William Busschau was getting ready to take the visiting Prime Minister to West Driefontein. Macmillan was going to Cape Town to tell the South African Parliament that a wind of change was blowing down Africa; Harvie-Watt had already given that news to Gold Fields and had got rid of the company's interests in areas where the wind was rising. In so doing, he had employed his political instincts to the company's advantage. South Africa, he felt, 'had a longer life than the northern States'.

However, even that optimistic statement would sometimes be doubted, both in South Africa and elsewhere in the world, in the first dark year or so of the new decade, the 1960s, as Sir George settled in in the chairman's room at 49 Moorgate, London, while in Johannesburg, Dr William Busschau began to steer Gold Fields of South Africa through its first years as a South African company.

CHAPTER EIGHT

New Wine in an Old Bottle 1959-1971

Gold Fields of South Africa had been reborn in 1959 as a South African company which was entirely owned by a British company, Consolidated Gold Fields. A dozen years later it ceased to be a British subsidiary and assumed the status that it has enjoyed ever since, of being an independent South African company. The years between – the 1960s – were, in a way, apprenticeship years preceding its assumption of full responsibility. They turned out to be dramatic years, not only for Gold Fields but also for South Africa, since the 1960s was also the opening decade of an independent South African Republic. Gold Fields saluted the tenth anniversary of the Republic by announcing its own independence as a South African company.

The year 1960, the 50th anniversary of Union, was one of the most difficult in the country's history, a year of drama and disaster. The British Prime Minister, Harold Macmillan after his historic visit to South Africa – and to West Driefontein – had returned to London. In January the South African Prime Minister, Dr Verwoerd, had announced that a referendum would be held the following October to determine whether the white electorate wished the country to become a republic. Meanwhile, among the black population there was mounting civil disobedience and disaffection, culminating in the tragic shooting at Sharpeville. In April, while visiting the Rand Easter Show, Dr Verwoerd was severely wounded in the head in an assassination attempt by a white farmer. As a result he was unable to attend the Commonwealth Conference that year, when the South African Foreign Minister, Eric Louw, sought to obtain an assurance that if South Africa, as a result of the referendum, became a republic, it might nevertheless continue to be a member of the Commonwealth. He did not get this assurance and the following March, at a further meeting of Commonwealth Prime Ministers in London, Dr Verwoerd announced that South Africa would leave the Commonwealth. On 31 May 1961 South Africa became a republic and henceforth would have to fend for itself in a world that was changing rapidly. The old empires had been dissolved and were being replaced by new associations of states, such as the European Economic Community and the Organization of African Unity. There was a danger that South Africa, no longer in the Commonwealth, might find itself isolated in this reassembling world, and for the next eighteen months there was a crisis of confidence in the country's future. The disturbances during 1960, leading to a declaration of a state of emergency, followed by the withdrawal from the Commonwealth the following year, had alarmed investors round the world. The country's economic lifeblood – its foreign reserves – was draining away. From a level of R250 million in March 1960, it fell to an all-time low of R175 million in May the following year. The Government was forced to introduce both exchange and import controls.

Following the Sharpeville crisis, Dr Busschau had led a delegation of South African industrialists to Pretoria to see the Prime Minister to express their disquiet over the political situation and to ask for a new deal for Black South Africa. Colin Anderson, President of the Chamber of Mines, also spoke out. 'In the conditions of economic stress that have accompanied South Africa's withdrawal from the Commonwealth the prime duty of the authorities must be to restore faith in the country's ability to solve its problems in a rational and peaceable way.' He went on to declare his faith that South Africans would succeed in solving their dilemma in their own way. 'The capacities of South Africans are greater than their failings,' he maintained, 'and they have the incentive of the great opportunities that lie beyond the settlement of their difficulties.' These sentiments were echoed by Sir George Harvie-Watt in London. He told shareholders in 1961: 'We are proud of our long association with the South Africans and have confidence in their ability to work out a just, realistic and lasting solution to their problems and to develop for the benefit of all sections of the community the vast natural resources of their country.' It was very much a 'We and They' speech, though this was no doubt not intended. Nevertheless, it was clear that Gold Fields of South Africa would have increasingly to paddle its own canoe through waters that would certainly be choppy, since storm signals were flying both in South Africa and London. South Africa was going its own way, however difficult that might be. And Gold Fields of South Africa could not but be part of its destiny. However, in 1961, Harvie-Watt was insisting that 'the expansion of our business into new fields does not entail any diminution of our interests in the Republic of South Africa'. And the following year, when he came to South Africa for the 75th anniversary of the founding of the company, he was to make this clear once again. This time there were two South African Cabinet Ministers present to hear him say it.

It was a very grand occasion that was held in Johannesburg on 9 February 1962. It was almost a year since South Africa had introduced its own currency and in giving it the name Rand, it had in a way raised its hat to the mining industry, whose oldest mining house was having a birthday party. The dinner had been arranged appropriately on the old Gold Fields property of Illovo, at the Wanderers Club in fact, which also appropriately was the cricketing heart of South Africa. Dr Dönges, Minister of Finance, and Dr Diederichs, Minister of Mines, heard Dr Busschau say that they were celebrating the founding of a British group of companies whose activities were world-wide 'but whose South African assets remain their most important and in these assets South African shareholders now hold a substantial share'. Busschau probably had in mind the

Coalbrook Colliery, 20km from Sasolburg and near the Taaibos and Highveld power stations, belonged to the Clydesdale Company which, founded early in the century, became Gold Fields Coal in 1986

Top: *The guest cottages at West Driefontein where the wives and families of African miners come and stay for a month at a time*

Left: *Sonny Nkomo, a computer instructor at the Gold Fields training centre at Kloof, seen here teaching Alison Green*

Right: *Setting the pace: Peter Ngobeni, breaker of South African sprint records in the mid 1980s, keeps alive the sporting tradition of Gold Fields at West Driefontein*

A snake in the hand is worth two in the bush! Scene at the Gold Fields Resource Centre in the Pilanesberg National Park

Pella Church, built by Catholic fathers while Rhodes and Rudd were still at Kimberley, was restored by The Gold Fields Foundation in 1985, and serves the Black Mountain community

*Robinson Deep Mine,
1935-6: watercolour
by Walter Battiss*

*Chris Shaft, 1936:
graphite on paper by
W H Coetzer*

*'Simmer & Jack
Saterdag Middag
1919': watercolour by
J H Pierneef*

*Sub Nigel locomotive:
painting by David
Shepherd*

After a century in Johannesburg, Gold Fields is firmly planted 'downtown'. Rising on the old site bordering Fox, Sauer and Commissioner Streets, a modern and massive new building was being completed in time for the company's centenary. Exterior and part of interior

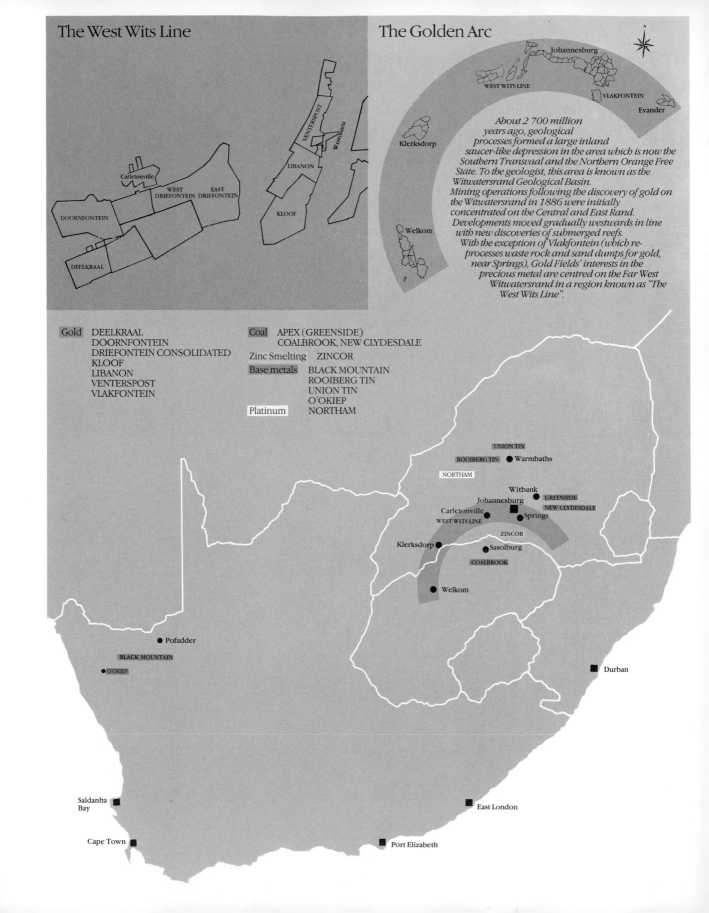

The West Wits Line

Carletonville

VENTERSPOST
Westdriefontein
LIBANON
WEST DRIEFONTEIN
EAST DRIEFONTEIN
DOORNFONTEIN
KLOOF
DEELKRAAL

The Golden Arc

Johannesburg
WEST WITS LINE
VLAKFONTEIN
Evander
Klerksdorp
Welkom

About 2 700 million years ago, geological processes formed a large inland saucer-like depression in the area which is now the Southern Transvaal and the Northern Orange Free State. To the geologist, this area is known as the Witwatersrand Geological Basin.

Mining operations following the discovery of gold on the Witwatersrand in 1886 were initially concentrated on the Central and East Rand. Developments moved gradually westwards in line with new discoveries of submerged reefs. With the exception of Vlakfontein (which re-processes waste rock and sand dumps for gold, near Springs), Gold Fields' interests in the precious metal are centred on the Far West Witwatersrand in a region known as "The West Wits Line".

Gold	DEELKRAAL
	DOORNFONTEIN
	DRIEFONTEIN CONSOLIDATED
	KLOOF
	LIBANON
	VENTERSPOST
	VLAKFONTEIN
Coal	APEX (GREENSIDE)
	COALBROOK, NEW CLYDESDALE
Zinc Smelting	ZINCOR
Base metals	BLACK MOUNTAIN
	ROOIBERG TIN
	UNION TIN
	O'OKIEP
Platinum	NORTHAM

UNION TIN
ROOIBERG TIN • Warmbaths
NORTHAM
Witbank
Johannesburg GREENSIDE
NEW CLYDESDALE
Carletonville Springs
WEST WITS LINE
ZINCOR
Klerksdorp • Sasolburg
COALBROOK
• Welkom

• Pofadder
BLACK MOUNTAIN
• O'OKIEP

■ Durban

Saldanha Bay ■

East London ■

Cape Town ■

Port Elizabeth ■

fact that the South African Mutual had taken up some 250 000 Gold Fields shares. At a time of grave difficulty in South Africa, Gold Fields of South Africa was making a major contribution to the country for in that year of 1961 it broke records in everything – tonnage, profits, dividends. Total working profit that year of R46 million was no less than fifty percent up on the 1959 figure. And that, as Dönges could well appreciate, meant record tax payments to his Treasury. That year he scooped up R73 million from the gold mining industry. Diederichs took a particular pride in the Gold Fields performance since a good part of the West Wits Line was in his own constituency of Losberg. These mines by 1962 were accounting for almost one-fifth of the gold output of South Africa, and GFSA was handing over to Dönges seventeen percent of its revenue. 'Production from your companies has been adding millions of Rand to the national income' said Diederichs, 'and the beneficial effects of this wealth is of almost incalculable importance to our country.' The Government understood only too well how important to the economic health of South Africa was a mine like West Driefontein; if disaster were to strike there, as it did during the 1960s, Pretoria would view it as no less than a national emergency.

The accident, unprecedented in South African mining history, occurred only a few months after that dinner at the Wanderers. Early on the morning of 12

The sinkhole which swallowed a seven-storey building at West Driefontein on 12 December 1962, when 29 lives were lost.

December 1962 the earth opened and a seven-storey building at West Driefontein, housing the screening, sorting and crushing plant at No 2 shaft, collapsed into an enormous sinkhole which swallowed all 85 feet of it. Into that great hole with almost vertical sides, 150 feet in diameter and 100 feet deep, went the men who had been working in the building at the time. Desperate efforts to rescue them were made but as Reg Cousens,[1] the Gold Fields consulting engineer, said later, 'despite heroic deeds beyond the normal demands of duty by those who conducted impromptu rescue operations, 29 Africans lost their lives. Men on surface threw air hoses and ropes over the side of the sinkhole and rescued many men by hauling them up the sides of the crater … rescue work continued until there was no further sign of life in the flooded hole'. The flood had added to the tragedy, for a 3 feet-wide pipe carrying water pumped from No 2 shaft had been severed at the edge of the hole by the crash and water poured in at the rate of four

Reg Cousens, the consulting engineer who had to cope with both West Driefontein disasters of the 1960s, seen here at the opening of Doornfontein in November 1953. Next to him is Marion Hallett, who, with her husband Stanley Hallett, poured the mine's first gold.

214

million litres an hour. There was no hope of retrieving the bodies of the lost men since it was unsafe for their fellow miners to go in search of them. The situation was explained to the relatives of the victims and on 15 December a religious service was held at the mine and the bodies remained buried there.

The precarious nature of mining in the Wonderfontein valley with its miles of dolomitic caverns had been signalled in a spectacular and tragic fashion. Gold Fields had at once to set in train a whole series of investigations of the dolomitic area to establish where there might be a danger of subsidence. What had happened at West Driefontein that morning was that an enormous underground cavity had collapsed and subsidence had taken place just where the mine plant was located. Hundreds of boreholes were sunk. A gravimetric survey was started. Telescopic benchmarkers were installed to record movement in the ground and eventually the entire dolomitic area of the valley was covered in an effort to prevent a further tragedy. It was a combined effort by the State, the mining companies, and the South African Railways. The Council of Scientific and Industrial Research (C S I R) in Pretoria made cameras available that could be lowered in boreholes to detect suspected cavities. By 1965 the number of exploratory boreholes had grown to 10 000.

At the time of the accident West Driefontein was milling 187 000 tons a month and, with a working profit of nearly R3 million, was getting the highest return ever achieved by a gold mine. The need to get the mine going again was obviously urgent. Since the ground was unsafe, the entire reduction plant had to be moved and rebuilt on a new site covering an area of sixteen hectares; the cost was put at R9 million. That all this was achieved in just under one year constitutes one of the outstanding episodes in mining history. Design work had begun in January 1963 and excavation on the site at the beginning of March. For the first time a computer controlled programme kept construction and installation of plant on schedule with a clockwork precision and in December the new plant was operating. Meanwhile, production at the mine had continued, thanks to the help given by other members of the West Wits family who rallied round, Venterspost, Libanon and Doornfontein to which the ore from West Drie went by rail or road. Some 200 million tons were moved over eleven months at a cost of R1 million. By working their plants non-stop, even on Sundays, the sister mines managed to cope. This co-operation between the mines of the group says much for that sense of community and purpose that has always characterized those who have served the company in a difficult and often dangerous occupation. Only fifteen days of production were lost as a result of the 1962 disaster and soon the mine was crushing at a rate of 200 000 tons a month as it went gamely in pursuit of new records. Only a year later, Stanley Hallett was able to tell an audience in New York that West Drie was producing more gold than all the American mines put together, that it had a working profit of 40 million US dollars a year and that since it started milling in 1952, it had produced over 10 million ounces of gold.

When the crisis was over, *The Star* in Johannesburg commented on the frank and honest way that Gold Fields had kept the world informed about what was going on. This had something to do with the character of Gold Fields but also of the man most closely involved in the restoration of the mine. The recovery was due to the combined effort of many people forming a team, but for one man in particular it presented a special challenge. It was not the first he had had to face nor would it be his last at West Driefontein. His name was Adriaan Louw, one of the most remarkable men ever to work for Gold Fields. At the end of November 1962, he had given up the managership of West Drie to become a consulting engineer at 75 Fox Street but had barely settled in when the news came through of the disaster. His successor at the mine was away on holiday. Louw immediately went back to the mine and during the next three weeks seldom left it. Under his guidance the great work of restoration was organized.

Ian Louw's rise to eminence at Gold Fields is usually – and accurately – described as meteoric; indeed, within three years of the West Driefontein disaster he would succeed Busschau as chairman of GFSA and at the age of forty-five would be the youngest man ever to take charge of a mining house in South Africa. The Louw family had been in South Africa since 1658; his grandfather was a predikant of the Dutch Reformed Church, Moderator of the Church in the Transvaal and Chancellor of Pretoria University; his father, having fought in the Anglo-Boer War at the age of sixteen, qualified as a medical doctor at Edinburgh University and married an English-speaking bride. Ian Louw was educated in the English medium at King Edward VII School in Johannesburg and qualified as a mining engineer at Witwatersrand University in 1947. However, he had made a start in mining back in 1938 when, at the age of 18, he had worked as a learner at Robinson Deep. In 1939 he went to University. Then the war came and he left to become a pilot in the SAAF; he was shot down over the Mediterranean coast of North Africa but managed to swim some five kilometres to the shore. Here he was picked up by the Italians from whom he escaped. Later, captured by the Germans he remained their prisoner for the rest of the war. After the war, having graduated at Wits, he returned to Robinson Deep; in 1953 he transferred to West Driefontein, where within eight years he had become general manager.

In 1963, with West Driefontein back on form, Louw became consulting engineer in Johannesburg and the following year was appointed a manager of Gold Fields. In 1965, on Busschau's retirement, he reached the top as chairman and chief executive. All his talents as a mining engineer, indeed all his qualities as a man, would have to bear on the very special problems, both technical and social, that were emerging in the Wonderfontein valley as a result of mining the West Wits Line, and of which the 1962 accident at West Driefontein had given notice in a dramatic way.

There is an old adage among miners that the richer the ore, the more difficult it is to mine. The gold-bearing reefs of the West Rand were proving wonderfully rich and were producing great profits for the mining companies. At the same time they were proving exceptionally difficult to mine because of the dolomitic

216

Ian Louw, predikant's grandson, wartime pilot, mining engineer, was at 45 the youngest man ever to take charge of a South African mining house. He was chairman of GFSA when it became an independent South African company in 1971.

217

caverns, full of water, through which the shafts had to go. As West Drie had shown, the danger of subsidence was always there; the spectre of the sinkhole was to haunt the mining communities of the valley for a decade. Several horrifying episodes took place before a relative sense of security could be restored in what had once been the peaceful Wonderfontein valley below the Gatsrante, whose very name – the hill of holes – indicated the precarious nature of the terrain.

This was a period when, for the first time, Gold Fields had to cope with the social and environmental consequences of their mining operations. Other houses, such as Rand Mines and Anglo-American, were mining on the West Wits Line but the area was overwhelmingly a Gold Fields responsibility since they had got there first and were the biggest operators in that particular field. The new mining fields had thrown up new communities living in new towns near the mines. In the Free State, Welkom had grown into one of the biggest towns in the province. On the Far West Rand, Carletonville, adjoining West Driefontein and Blyvooruitzicht, and Westonaria, near Venterspost and Libanon, had become modern flourishing towns by the 1960s. In these towns the mining companies owned attractive houses where their employees and their families lived but all kinds of other activities, stimulated by but not directly concerned with mining, were developing. Great care had gone into the designing of the town named after Carleton Jones. One of the outstanding South African – and world – architects of his generation was William Holford. Having qualified at Cape Town University, he later made a career in Britain where in later life he was honoured with a peerage and became Lord Holford. Soon after the end of the Second World War, Gold Fields asked Holford to work on plans for Carletonville. By 1960 it had shops, a garage, a cinema, local government offices, a modern recreation centre with a swimming pool and tennis courts, while out in the folds of the Gatsrante an 18-hole golf course had been laid out. Gold Fields, in helping to provide all this, was playing a creative social role in the life of the country. Where these modern towns had arisen was once an impoverished valley whose small communities had clustered round the railway line at places like Bank and their only excitement was the Blue Train on its way to or from the Cape. The gold mines had transformed everything and their wealth had created new communities. But these communities were vulnerable, both in the towns and on the farms, because of the instability of the ground beneath them. The problems for them, as for the miners, was the dolomite.

Dolomite is a rich water-bearing rock formation and its chemical composition is such that it is readily soluble in slightly acidic water, such as rain water, so that solution cavities are common. Through the dolomitic areas run what are known as dykes – dolerite and syenite dykes – which in a north/south direction divide the dolomite up into six main compartments. These underground reservoirs have names such as Venterspost Compartment, Oberholzer Compartment and Bank Compartment. The effect is rather like one of those compartmentalized trays for making ice cubes in a refrigerator. The water table in any compartment is usually level, but this level differs appreciably from that in adjoining compartments. At the lowest point of each dyke outcrop there is an 'eye' or spring and the water flows over the barrier from the higher to the lower compartments. When mines, located in these compartments, begin to pump water, they disturb the level of the water in the compartments. In fact, they disturb the natural order.

Soon after the West Wits disaster of 1962, a Government expert, Dr F C Truter of the Department of Mines, explained in a SABC broadcast the nature of the problem. He said that 'the formation of sinkholes which constitute the real menace to the community is principally caused by the activities of man himself, and are confined to dolomitic areas that are subject to human activities that characterize modern civilization'. The highest incidence was in the most densely populated areas where the greatest activity took place, such as the erection of heavy buildings, laying of railway lines, water mains, sewage pipes, building macadamized roads. Recognition of the cause of the problem gave a clue, he said, as to how to combat it.

Even before the West Drie disaster it had been noticed that buidings in Carletonville and Westonaria, situated in the Oberholzer and Venterspost Compartments, had developed cracks. Investigations showed that groundwater levels in the two compartments were gradually being lowered and this lowering was due to the pumping of water by the mines from their underground workings; the water was not being returned to the dolomitic compartments from which it was being pumped. These investigations were to lead to a decision in 1963 by the State and the mining industry to dewater these compartments. During the next

Sinkhole at Venterspost disrupts the railway line, April 1963.

219

five years all the accidents caused by sinkholes took place in the area of these two compartments. In January 1966 the Minister of Mines, Jan Haak, gave a sombre account of the toll of lives and property. Sinkholes and subsidence on the Far West Rand had killed thirty-four people and caused damage and losses totalling more than R14 million, he said. At Carletonville 113 mine houses and five private houses had had to be demolished and another twenty-seven evacuated. At Blyvooruitzicht mine five houses had been demolished and 250 evacuated. Houses had also been evacuated at Westonaria where, on 22 October 1964, a sinkhole had threatened the whole of Briggs Street. The Blyvooruitzicht disaster on 3 August 1964 had been particularly ghastly; in the early hours of the morning the earth opened up and the Oosthuizen family of five, who had returned from a holiday only the previous evening, disappeared when their house was engulfed. On Christmas morning 1966 the family of Douglas Bird at Carletonville had a narrow escape when a 50 foot sinkhole opened up on the front lawn of their house. Earlier that year *The Star* reported that some 900 families had fled in the four years since the West Drie disaster. Only a fortnight after Haak's statement in Parliament, a sinkhole, 30 feet wide and 28 feet deep, appeared a bare 100 yards from the Rand-Cape railway line. Trains were instructed to proceed at 5 mph. A special branch line was constructed via Houtkop and Fochville so that passenger trains could avoid the sinkhole area. In the open veld near Westonaria a hole bigger than the West Driefontein one had appeared and it took three days to fill it up again. Rumours of disaster, and even malicious hoaxes, were rife. In February 1965 the Editor of *Die Vaderland*, A M van Schoor, was called away from a civic lunch in the City Hall as a result of a report of a new disaster at West Driefontein. A plane had been chartered to fly him to the area and was about to take off when he was informed that the report was false.

Passenger train hanging over a sinkhole.

Today at Venterspost there is a memorial plaque which is a poignant reminder of those years of anxiety and tragedy that provided the dark side of the glittering success of the West Wits Line. It commemorates Karl Nortjc, a fifty-eight year-old miner who in October 1970 was watching the tennis from the club house on the mine when it suddenly collapsed into a sinkhole. It was not the first incident at Venterspost. On 22 April 1965, a large sinkhole disrupted a rock crusher in the middle of the reduction plant.

Each of these human tragedies underlined the dilemma confronting the State and the mining houses as a result of mining on the Far West Rand. These rich gold mines were vitally important for the economic well-being of the country because of the revenues they provided for the Treasury in the form of taxation; if they were forced to close down, the nation as a whole would suffer. The problem could only be eased if there were a combined effort by all those involved to ensure that mining was carried on in safety, not only for the miners working at great depth underground, but also for those who had their homes and families living in towns or on farms above the mining area. Gold Fields, the mining house most closely involved in mining the West Wits Line, faced up to the responsibility presented by this national dilemma and played a leading role in trying to resolve it. Lyle Campbell Pitt was entrusted with finding a solution to this watery problem. As a result of discussions between representatives of the mining companies and Tommy Gibbs, the Government Mining Engineer, there came into existence in July 1964 the Far West Rand Dolomitic Water Association. Its members were the mining companies operating on the Far West Rand and its task was to handle the problems resulting from dewatering. A joint committee had concluded that gold production outweighed in economic importance agricultural production in the area and recommended that dewatering would be in the national interest. It would make the lives of thousands of miners more secure since the flooding of the mines had been recognized as a real hazard. However, removing the water hazard for the miners meant at the same time depriving the farmers of an essential ingredient in their own activity. This being the case, the mines would have to compensate for damage done by dewatering. It was agreed, therefore, that where necessary the Association might buy out the farmers, taking over the lands that had lost their water. Over the years this was done to a considerable extent and as a result the Association became a major landowner, acquiring some 30 000 hectares of farming land and more than 2 000 township stands. There were many traumatic events in the early years ably handled by the chairman of the Association, B T 'Tank' Tindall, who was legal adviser to the Chamber of Mines. In the first twenty years of its existence it handled 2 897 applications for compensation. The Association has over the years become very much part of the local scene on the Far West Rand and took the initiative in establishing the West Wits Regional Planning Committee, whose task it is to consider the long-term future, when mining will eventually come to an end. Since 1972 Gold Fields has provided chairmen for the Association.

Dewatering created problems for the farmers but it also caused the worries about sinkholes and subsidence and once again the Association, with its emergency fund, would be required to compensate those whose property might have been damaged in this way. At the same time the Association worked with another body, the State Co-ordinating Technical Committee on Sinkholes, whose duty was to examine potentially dangerous areas to determine if they were safe for development. One of the most difficult decisions, in human terms, that the Association had to make concerned the little hamlet of Bank which, once the dewatering of the Bank Compartment had begun, ceased to be safe. Some forty white families and 200 Indians had to move away; today Bank presents a picture of a ghost town of crumbling buildings and overgrown streets. 'Ghost Town by Order' was the disturbing title in a popular magazine describing the sad dissolution of a community. In 1963 Gold Fields had to face up to a similar situation after the Dominion Reefs mine in the Klerksdorp field, inherited in the 1959 acquisitions by Harvie-Watt, closed down. 'Mine gone, must town die too' was the Press headline over a report stating that 100 houses were for sale in a place that looked neglected and abandoned. Dominion Reefs had never been more than a modest gold producer – R13 million since 1935. In 1955 the demand for uranium had given it a further lease of life but in 1961 underground working stopped, although the uranium plant went on treating the slimes for a further year. 'At the village of Dominion Reefs is every facility an industry could need,' the *Rand Daily Mail* reported, and in due time industry did come in to save it from the fate that had overtaken Bank.

Gold Fields, despite the social and human problems that had accompanied the

222

technical and commercial success of gold mining on the West Wits Line, was pushing ahead with plans for two new mines in the area. These were Kloof, south of Libanon, and East Driefontein, lying adjacent to West Driefontein. The flotation of the Kloof company in 1964 with an authorized capital of R17^1/$_2$ million had followed highly promising results from drilling into the Ventersdorp Contact Reef from the Libanon mine; and it was from Libanon that the new mine with its 7 367 claims was developed. Kloof came to production in 1968. The previous year East Driefontein was floated and it followed the same pattern, being developed, like Kloof, from an existing mine, in this case West Driefontein. It too would work the VCR, whose value really came to be properly appreciated in the 1960s. Up till that time it had been mined almost as a side issue. Using the shafts of an existing mine to develop a new mine became very much the pattern of Gold Fields' operations on the West Wits Line; it made economic sense since it not only reduced the costs of the new development by using existing infrastructure but enabled the new mines to come to production several years sooner – and in the world of finance – 'time is money'.

Sir George Harvie-Watt took a particular interest in the new Kloof mine; in 1964 he had been at his wife's side when she had cut the first turf for shaft-sinking; she had already done the same at Libanon for the Harvie-Watt shaft, which would be used for the development of Kloof. He took particular pride in the fact that the residential area serving the mines would be called Glenharvie. Earlier that year of 1964 he had organized a great gathering of the Gold Fields clan at Gleneagles in Scotland. Bill Busschau, Ian Louw and others from GFSA were present to read papers on various aspects of their work. Back in South Africa in 1968 for the opening of Kloof, he once more introduced a Scottish flavour to the proceedings, though somewhat unexpectedly. The Minister of Mines, Dr Carel de Wet, who had been Ambassador in London, was present to do the honours; as is customary in South Africa, he spoke partly in Afrikaans. Harvie-Watt realized, of course, that the Minister was speaking his own native language though he himself was at a loss to know what was going on. When it was his turn to reply, he took a leaf out of the Minister's book and he too spoke in his native language. This was perplexing for Carel de Wet and everyone else at Kloof that day, for Harvie-Watt was speaking Gaelic, a Scottish language that may still be heard in the Outer Hebrides but had not yet caught on in Glenharvie, Western Transvaal. The sound of the tit-for-tat was clearly audible on the high-veld air; thereafter English provided the medium for Scotsmen and Afrikaners to talk to each other about Kloof.

Kloof, working the VCR, was to become one of the most distinguished mines, not only on the West Wits Line but in the industry as a whole, since in terms of the gold content of its ore, it stands at the top of the list. At about thirteen grams a ton in 1986, it is about two grams a ton higher than East Drie, for instance. Kloof is also interesting from a technical point of view since new concepts and exciting innovations in mine design were put into practice by the Gold Fields engineers. André Taute, back from Grootfontein and Saaiplaas, worked on the shaft systems and underground layouts, his particular speciality and the subject of his doctoral thesis, which he submitted as a mature student. The design provided for the sinking of both the main hoisting shaft and the adjoining ventilation shaft to a depth of about 2 000 metres below surface, from which elevation mining would be extended to further depths via a pair of sub-vertical shafts. In order to expedite the opening of the mine at depth, the ventilation shaft would be extended to serve as the first of the two sub-vertical shafts; in other words, a sub-vertical shaft sunk from the surface by simply deepening the ventilation shaft. To Taute's immense disappointment, however, things did not work out as planned; money, not technology, was lacking. Water problems delayed the sinking of the main shaft, putting the programme back. That in turn delayed production and, in any case, to bring the mine to production was going to cost R43 million. Economies were necessary. As a limited amount of development had taken place from Libanon, it was decided to discontinue sinking the sub-vertical shaft from surface and to use the ventilation shaft as a temporary reef-hoisting shaft. Money had been saved but at the cost of a highly interesting technical innovation. Despite Taute's disappointment in not being able to get his ventilation shaft to the designed depth, Kloof nevertheless marked up some impressive features, including an enormous shaft of $31^1/_2$ feet in diameter and the biggest winders in the world. Rupert Gettliffe, who had succeeded Zeppenfeld as consulting mechanical engineer in 1963, worked on these with his up-and-coming colleague, Bob Robinson. But it was the pioneering of computer techniques at Kloof that made it the most modern mine in the world at that time, and had a profound effect on the industry as a whole. Everyone[2] wanted to see its central control centre in the reduction plant, where it was possible to keep an eye on everything that was going on. Kloof paid particular attention to the welfare of its personnel; many mine families were accommodated comfortably at Glenharvie. The mine was not only big on winders; it was also generous with its kitchens, the biggest in Africa, providing 13 000 men with three meals a day right round the clock. Thought had also been given to the comfort of mineworkers waiting to go underground. Kloof, partly on a hillside, is very cold in winter. Consequently, an underground approach to the mine, rather like a pen, was built so that miners going to their work might be protected from the biting winds.

In 1967, the year before Kloof began to produce, came news of another mine, East Driefontein, the new mining company having taken cession of a lease from West Witwatersrand Areas to develop a mine alongside West Driefontein, from whose No 4 shaft, in fact, the upper levels of East Driefontein would be opened up to expose and prepare for stoping the VCR and the Main Reef. This would make it possible to start the hoisting of rock soon after completing the East Drie shaft system. The close relationship that existed between East Drie and West Drie had led Gold Fields in September 1967 to apply to the Government Mining authorities not for a separate lease for East Drie but rather an extension of the West Drie lease over the whole area to be mined. Such a move, if it had succeeded, would have made the operation less costly since payment of taxes might have been deferred while development of a larger West Driefontein took place. The Government decided, however, that East Drie would have to be treated as a separate entity. The mining authorities believed they were already making valuable tax concessions to viable new propositions. In May 1968, therefore, East Drie obtained its own lease over some 4 137 hectares. A rights issue raised R30 million and was well supported; two years later the same sum was raised again. Two years after that a further R20 million had to be raised largely because of the traumatic experience that the embryo mine had just gone through.

As with Kloof, so with East Driefontein, the design of the mine had revealed great innovative skills, indeed originality. At 75 Fox Street another engineer, Peter van Rensburg in the Valuation Department, and his colleague, A A Truter from the Geological Department, had been putting their heads together. Truter had come a long way since the early 1930s, when Leopold Reinecke had sent him out surveying, and was now the company's top geologist. Like Truter, Van Rensburg had had an unusual introduction to mining. As a small schoolboy at St Andrews, Grahamstown in 1936, he had been a member of a school party that had visited Johannesburg at the time of the Empire Exhibition, marking the golden jubilee of Johannesburg. The master in charge of the boys was a keen cricketer; his name was Charles Fortune, who obtained permission for some of the older boys to go down a mine. Van Rensburg, pretending to be older than he was, succeeded in joining the party and, once underground, decided that mining was to be his career when he grew up. Let others join the fire brigade or drive trains; he would be a mining engineer. He graduated at Wits and after war service was ready to go. His baptism of fire – literally – was at Robinson Deep where he experienced the great fire of 1949; after a period as an underground manager at Venterspost, he came to Head Office. He was to play a long and important role as chairman of the Far West Rand Dolomitic Water Association; he also became deputy-chairman of Gold Fields of South Africa.

While working on the East Driefontein design, Van Rensburg and Truter made an unusual suggestion concerning their North Shaft to the consulting engineer, 'Pat' Savile Davis. Instead of sinking this 5,75 metre diameter shaft through the dolomite, they put it down through the impervious 'Bank' dyke, separating the Bank and Oberholzer dolomitic water compartments, some 1 300 metres on the West Driefontein side of the common boundary. This was to serve as a ventilation shaft and man/material shaft for the northern part of the mine. In the event, as a result of changes that had to be made, it was to be used only for pumping and ventilation.

Shaft-sinking at the North Shaft began in September 1968, by which time a considerable amount of development had been taking place from the No 4 shaft of West Driefontein. A month later, on 26 October 1968, the blow fell. And it fell, as in 1962, at West Driefontein. The new mine, East Driefontein, being developed from the existing mine, could not but be part of the catastrophe.

'The near disaster that descended upon the West Driefontein gold mine out of

The West Driefontein flood disaster in October 1968 when for three weeks the life of the mine was in jeopardy.

a clear sky on a sunny Saturday morning in October 1968 bears some resemblance to that moment of horror at sea when, on a calm day, a liner strikes an unchartered reef.' Thus wrote A P Cartwright, himself a distinguished naval officer, in his account entitled, 'West Driefontein; Ordeal by Water'. 'Here was a great gold mine,' he continued, 'carrying out its normal Saturday routine. The morning shift had gone underground at 7 o'clock. Hoists, ventilation fans and such pumps as were on duty, lifting water from the bottom of the mine, were working smoothly. Everything seemed in apple pie order.'

At 10 am Gold Fields issued a statement to the effect that there had been an inrush in a stope at the mine's No 4 shaft – between 4 and 6 level – and that water was pouring into the shaft from huge caverns in the overlying dolomites. Pumps were working in vain to stem the flow of 228 million litres a day. 'If the inflow cannot be stemmed,' the GFSA statement said ominously, 'the mine will have to cease production.' The richest gold mine in the world would be drowned unless the water could be stopped.

226

The battle to save West Driefontein continued for the next three weeks. When it was finally won and details were known of what the struggle had involved, it emerged as an epic of courage, skill and endurance. Men faced death every minute of the protracted struggle as they worked, often waist deep in water, moving materials through the fast flowing flood to where they were needed. Time and again their barricades were washed away by the rising water but eventually they were able to divert the water long enough to build concrete plugs to seal off the flooded drives of the mine.

Throughout the crisis Ian Louw, chairman of GFSA, whose own career had been so intimately connected with this mine and indeed its previous disaster in 1962, kept South Africa and the world frankly informed of what was going on. At one stage he confessed: 'Any one of a number of things can go wrong and the mine could be lost. If the battle for survival fails, the mine at best has only eighty-three days to live before its full storage capacity of 400 million litres is flooded.' That was on 1 November. West Drie's pumping facilities had been boosted to a

Two heroes of the West Driefontein flood drama of 1968, shaft timberman W C Theron and Vasco Masingwe from Mozambique, who together saved the lives of fellow miners. Vasco received the gold helmet for bravery and both men the 'miner's V C', the Chamber of Mines bronze medal.

227

point where they were moving seventy-two million litres of water a day. But it was not enough, the water level had risen sixty-four metres in twenty-four hours. On 4 November *The Star* carried a frontpage headline: 'West Drie may die in 13 days.' The water was now approaching the critical 14 level; if it reached it, the mine would have to be abandoned. Reg Cousens, the consulting engineer, had assembled all the expertise that Gold Fields could summon up in order to support the mine manager, Ray Buley, at this desperate time. W S Garrett, head of the Cementation Company, and a world expert on plugs, had bravely gone into the mine alone to see what had to be done. A survey of 10 level was carried out by Bob Robinson and Willie Malan. In due course some 20 000 cubic metres of concrete were poured into two massive plugs. It was fortunate that some years earlier Garrett and Campbell Pitt had carried out careful scientific research on test plugs, which made it possible to quickly design these very intricate install-ations to withstand great pressure and stop the torrent that was drowning the vital No 4 shaft. By 9 November the plugs were complete but not yet ready to take the full pressure of the flood. Two days later, however, there was a leak in a water door on the 5A sub-vertical shaft and the flooding of that shaft was threatening four emergency pumps that had been brought in. The crucial days were 12 and 13 November when the fate of the mine lay in the balance. On 18 November the valves on drainage pipes through the plugs were closed; the plugs held. Tom Harvey, the consulting electrical engineer, redistributed the power so that all the pumps could work together. There was an anxious moment when news came of a power failure which had blacked out the Far West Rand from Randfontein to Libanon for an hour. West Driefontein, for whom five minutes without power would have meant disaster, was spared. The pumps were getting on top at last. On 18 November Ian Louw was able to announce: 'Production at West Driefontein will be back to normal in six months if the present rate of progress continues.'

There was a great sigh of relief around the world and not least in Pretoria where the Government viewed the event as a national crisis. The Prime Minister, John Vorster, had instructed Carel de Wet, the Minister of Mines, to miss the next Cabinet meeting and fly out to the mine by helicopter. Dr De Wet remained constantly in touch, giving encouragement to those struggling in the mine to stop the water. It was said there were anxious men in the Treasury in Pretoria who were calculating what the loss of West Driefontein would mean for the national revenue. There had also been considerable anxiety in the stock exchanges of the world; West Drie, after all, had been producing on its own more gold than Canada, the free world's second largest gold producer. On Monday, 28 October, the share price fell from 1 450 cents to 900 cents. Throughout the crisis the price went up and down like the temperature of a sick patient. The price touched a bottom of 730 cents then started up again. The in-vesting world refused to believe that the Gold Fields doctors would not save the ailing mine in the end. Their faith was justified.

By the end of June the following year Gold Fields reported: 'The western section of the mine has now been completely dewatered and the restoration of some 85 percent of the former rate of underground production has been achieved ... draining of the eastern section has also commenced and will entail a major dewatering operation.' Large quantities of mechanical and electrical equipment had been brought to surface, cleaned, dried, renovated and reinstalled in record time. In spite of this major setback, West Drie was able to produce in the year to June 1969 1,9 million ounces of gold and, with a working profit of R29 million, paid out dividends of R10,5 million, only slightly less than the previous year. Having survived two disasters in eight years, West Driefontein was still a wonder mine. In November 1969 Ray Buley, the mine manager, on behalf of all those who had saved the mine, received the National Award of the Associated Scientific and Technical Societies who declared that 'the fight to save the mine gripped the imagination of people all over the world'. *Die Suid-Afrikaanse Akademie vir Wetenskap en Kuns* awarded its medal of honour for achievement in the natural sciences to Bill Garrett, an award that in the previous year had gone to Professor Christiaan Barnard and his heart-transplant team. In August 1972 the Prime Minister, John Vorster, went underground at West Drie and its new manager, Gerald Hinds, described to him how the mine had been rehabilitated.

Laurels were showered on West Driefontein but it was the still-to-be-born East Driefontein which had been the real sufferer; its development area had been flooded by the inrush of water. The dewatering and rehabilitation of the western portion of West Drie was completed in eight months. While this was going on plans were being made for dewatering No 4 shaft from which East Drie was being developed. This, it soon became clear, would be a longer process since the future security of the mine depended on dewatering the Bank Compartment. Up till that inrush of water the previous October, only the Oberholzer and Venterspost Compartments had received attention. It was the dewatering of the Bank Compartment that led to the evacuation of Bank itself. It was February 1971 before the Mines Department gave permission to work in the flooded No 4 shaft. This provided a new experience in gold mining. Water flowed under gravity through large boreholes into East Driefontein's pump chambers excavated from its newly completed North Shaft. It was indeed fortunate that this shaft had been sited on the Bank Dyke and was sunk quickly. Sinking of No 3 shaft at West Drie, plagued by intersection of water-bearing fissures had taken seven years! With both East and West Driefontein pump chambers operating at full bore, the mine was finally dewatered in September 1971, just three years after the disaster. The intervening years had not been wasted. Shaft-sinking at No 1 and No 2 shafts had been proceeding apace. However, the flooding meant that East Driefontein would have to increase its financial resources to cope with the costs of its difficult birth. 'For nearly three years this company's future has been clouded by the spectre of water,' its shareholders were told. 'The controlling of this water has removed a major unknown factor and brings closer the day when the mine will be able to get down to the business of producing gold and making profits for its shareholders.' And this it assuredly did, just as the international prospects for gold were transformed by the emergence of new political and economic factors in the world. Gold Fields was still in luck.

After the traumatic opening years of the 1960s, the Republic of South Africa had begun to flourish; the economy was booming and expansion was taking place at a rate to make even a Japanese smile; in one remarkable year it was as high as eight percent. By 1965 the gross national product had risen by nearly thirty percent. The world had been regaining confidence in the South African economy and foreign money had returned to take its share in South African investment. The period was marked by tremendous diversification into industry and the economy was moving away from its heavy reliance on gold mining. This did not mean any slackening in gold production. On the contrary the gold mining index went up by a third. The value of gold output in the first year of the Republic had been R576 million. In 1965 it was R775 million, pushing up the country's contribution to the free world's gold by ten percent, to some seventy-three percent. But manufacturing's index was matching this performance and by the end of 1965 had put on more than forty percent. Gold Fields of South Africa was following the fashion and extending its interests into manufacturing industry. This fitted in with Harvie-Watt's philosophy in London and was actively encouraged by his lieutenant, Gillie Potier. In 1964 Gold Fields took a fifty percent interest in Hunslet Taylor – increased the following year to ninety percent. This was a company that specialized in various kinds of mining equipment, including hoists and locomotives and had proudly proclaimed in its advertisements: 'Still more evidence of South Africa's approaching industrial self-sufficiency and irresistibly expanding economy is the delivery of Hunslet's first 500 hp shunting locomotive, Johannesburg–built and specially designed for the exacting conditions at Fisons' Sasolburg fertiliser factory ...' Hunslet Taylor then acquired a further interest in the Durban engineering company, Chalmers. Gold Fields' shareholders were told that in January 1964 the company had completed its 1 000th loco in ten years. In May that year Gold Fields acquired a fifty-five percent interest in Eimco (South Africa) which had been a subsidiary of an American parent, acting as its agents for selling mining and earthmoving equipment. 'I am confident,' said Harvie-Watt, 'that with the buoyancy in the South African economy, these new acquisitions in the industrial field will do well.'

These industrial ventures might have excited Harvie-Watt and Potier but they did not do a great deal for Bill Busschau, resident director in Johannesburg of Consolidated Gold Fields and chairman of Gold Fields of South Africa, who had but one abiding interest and that was gold. 'Diversification,' he was to say later, 'is a fashionable cry today, as it has been in other periods of inflation, but "diversification" can be intelligent or not. At its worst it can mean, as someone has said, that one neglects a business one knows something about and goes into business one knows nothing about.' He went on to say: 'The most obvious avenue of diversification for a mining house heavily interested in gold mining, and having difficulty in finding new gold mines, would seem to be in a search for new mines of other types ... I must admit that I am surprised and puzzled that much more money has not been spent on such prospecting.' At the time he was speaking – 1968 – he had retired from the chairmanship of GFSA and was Chancellor of Rhodes University. There was little doubt that he clung to the view that Gold Fields was a mining company with gold its main interest. However, in 1965 when he decided to retire from Gold Fields, handing over to Ian Louw, the prospects for gold, despite his own personal propaganda efforts round the world, did not look too good. The price of an expanding economy in South Africa had been inflation and the cost of gold mining was rising alarmingly but the price of gold stuck obstinately at thirty-five dollars an ounce. Between 1960 and 1965 the industry had had to abandon ore containing over R1 billion of gold because it was not economic to mine. As De Kiewiet, the South African historian, once said: 'The problem of mining ... has not been to find the rich ore but to make the poor ore pay.' Busschau, on his frequent trips overseas, had called again and again for an increase in the price of gold. His case was clear and logical. Measured in terms of the ratio of gold to the obligations of central banks, and by other yardsticks, the dollar price of gold should have doubled. The IMF, he thought, had failed in its duty, which was to oil the wheels of international trade by ensuring the liquidity of funds. Without a rise in the price of gold the South African mining industry, which in the mid-1960s was providing the Treasury with R563 million in taxation and still accounting for forty percent of the country's export earnings, would not survive, despite production and other records.

Ironically, after Busschau's departure from Gold Fields, the picture began to change; by 1968 there were clear signs that the shackles on the gold price were loosening. Back in 1958 the external convertibility of the leading world currencies had been restored. This was regarded as a first step towards currency adjustments along a road that would lead eventually to the end of a fixed price for gold. After that the South African Reserve Bank made arrangements for the sale of gold to private buyers and sometimes, usually during moments of world political crisis, the price moved up as far as forty dollars an ounce. In the United States President Kennedy was determined to stick to the old official price. Large-scale sales by the Russians in 1963 and the operation of an international gold pool, set up in 1961 by the central banks to sell at the official price, tended to keep the price pegged down. Then in France, General de Gaulle, in a typical act of independence, stepped out of line and announced that France was converting a large part of its dollar holdings into gold. Pressures on both the American dollar and the British pound had already caused a rush into gold. The Americans were determined, they said, to defend the fixed price 'to the last ingot'. In March 1968 American military aircraft were airlifting 1 000 tons of gold to London in a single week in pursuit of this policy. But it was the end of the gold pool; it collapsed at the same time as the floor of the weighing room at the Bank of England, where all the American gold had been stacked. The British Government, at the request of the Americans, closed the gold market until a new system, the two-tier system, had been devised. There was now to be an official price at which gold would be sold to the central banks and a free market in which gold would find a price according to the normal rules of supply and demand. The official side of the two-tier did not last long. In March 1969 the watershed was reached, for the new system separated gold into monetary gold and non-monetary gold. South Africa's gold production was now available for the free market. At this point the three biggest Swiss banks formed their own gold pool and persuaded South Africa that Zurich, not London, would be the best place for selling its gold. This was just one more break with the past that had bound South Africa to Britain.

Gold was now free to make its own way in the world markets and find its own level. At first the price moved slowly upwards but it would not be until the next decade, the 1970s, that it really got up steam and moved rapidly upwards, carrying the fortunes of Gold Fields of South Africa with it. Nevertheless, 1968 was a year to remember. Kloof began to produce just as gold was given its freedom; the Driefonteins faced disaster but lived to mine another day. And, in London, Consolidated Gold Fields had been doing some research whose results were important for the gold producers of the world. They showed that total industrial demand for gold was virtually equal to the Western world's annual gold production of that time, 1 245 tons. *Gold 1969*, compiled by David Lloyd Jacob of CGF in London, set out the facts of the investigation; it became the first of an annual authoritative digest of what was going on in the world of gold. For those in South Africa who were going down ever deeper into the earth to get at the gold, it was an encouraging thought that there were better uses for their product than to decorate the vaults of central banks or be used like chips in a currency game.

Apart from the price of gold and the international monetary system, there were, after 1964, other matters demanding the attention of the chairman and directors of GFSA in Johannesburg. Political and economic factors, both in Britain and in South Africa, affecting the relationship between the two countries, had appeared and could not be ignored by a company like Consolidated Gold Fields, which dropped 'South Africa' from its title that year, and its totally owned subsidiary, Gold Fields of South Africa. After thirteen years of Tory rule, Britain once more had a Labour Government, under Harold Wilson. Ever since Sharpeville, he and his party had become increasingly hostile towards South Africa and the relationship between the two countries was bound to deteriorate. The problem became more complex the following year when the Rhodesia of Ian Smith made its Unilateral Declaration of Independence, leading to the imposition of sanctions against that country. Consolidated Gold Fields, a British company, had to take cognizance of the fact of sanctions. However, it was Gold Fields of South Africa that had responsibility for the company's interests in Rhodesia. GFSA was part of South Africa and the Republic was to play a major role in helping Ian Smith to defy sanctions. Political considerations were, willy nilly, beginning to put Consolidated Gold Fields and Gold Fields of South Africa upon different roads.

In 1967 Harold Wilson again went to the polls and was returned with a comfortable majority. The British Government began to put teeth into its hostility towards the South African Government by abandoning the Simonstown Agreement whereby it co-operated with South Africa in naval matters; it also refused to supply the Republic with combat aircraft. Mr Wilson, however, was in no position to throw his weight about. He was soon in economic difficulties and had to devalue the pound sterling. There was an acute problem with the British balance of payments and British companies were asked to follow a policy of voluntary restraint with overseas investment. This was of some concern for Consolidated Gold Fields because this was the time when East Driefontein was about to be launched by GFSA, who would need financial support from its British parent. Here, then, was a project of great importance for South Africa which might be jeopardized because of the situation in a foreign country. British Treasury regulations regarding portfolio investment abroad were vague. It appeared that if a British company like CGF wished to take up rights in South Africa in order to come into East Driefontein, it would need to pay for these by selling other interests already held abroad. In this way, no fresh funds would flow out of Britain. At 49 Moorgate they debated how to proceed. An internal memorandum at that time reflects the difficulties that the company was beginning to experience as a result of the South African connection. 'The alternative would be to by-pass the Civil Service machinery and make an approach direct to the Chancellor (of the Exchequer). Here we would be exposing ourselves to the really unpredictable political risks attendant upon the current state of relations between the UK and South Africa. The question of the supply of "heavy arms" to South Africa is now blowing up into a major political dispute, the Rhodesian problem is becoming more intractable and South Africa's co-operation in maintaining the orderly conduct of the international gold market is being openly questioned. A top-level request for an official blessing of the East Driefontein investment could, therefore, easily be caught up in wider events and refused in a game of diplomatic tit-for-tat.' The memorandum went on to recommend 'that there is everything to be lost and little to be gained by seeking official guidance and consent to the East Driefontein investment. The only real risk is that before the 2nd tranche is raised formal exchange control may be imposed. This, however, is a risk related primarily to the health of sterling and one we would face even if we had the formal consent of the Prime Minister himself to making the East Driefontein investment'. It was finally decided to proceed with the West Wits and East Driefontein issues without taking the matter up officially with the British authorities.

Several meetings were arranged and held in Johannesburg between representatives from CGF and GFSA to discuss the question of the financing of East Driefontein. The view had been expressed from London that the money required should be raised as soon as possible in case 'some unforeseen event might render it difficult or impossible for West Wits to raise a substantial sum late in 1969 ... such an event could include civil disturbances, not necessarily in South Africa itself but, say, in Rhodesia, which might seriously undermine investment confidence, or a continued deterioration in the British balance of payments might result in the imposition of more stringent and mandatory restrictions on overseas investment by UK companies. Under such circumstances West Wits might be unable to raise funds from the general public or Gold Fields itself could be prevented from following its rights in a West Wits issue with the result that the Group position in East Driefontein would be seriously reduced'. Such were the considerations, which had nothing to do with mining, that were exercising the minds of the two companies, Consolidated Gold Fields in London and Gold Fields of South Africa in Johannesburg. In the end the British company did its very utmost to help GFSA in the launching of East Driefontein. In turn the South African company did what it could to make matters easier for the British company. As Louw told Potier in September 1967: 'GFSA and Group companies will continue to make judicious efforts towards covering their own entitlement and if opportunities exist for sales to cover some part of CGF's entitlement these will be referred to you before proceeding.' GFSA, meanwhile, had had talks with Anglo American, who were playing their part in launching East Driefontein, and GFSA may well have been envious of a fellow mining house whose affairs were untrammelled by the economic and political problems of a country ten thousand kilometres away. This was the background to the application in September 1967 to the Government Mining Engineer when it was hoped that East Driefontein could be developed as part of a greater West Driefontein, which would have meant a cash outlay of half that required for a separate mine. The approach did not succeed and, as a result of the flooding of West Driefontein the following year, the cost of launching the mine would be a good deal higher still.

The difficulties that Consolidated Gold Fields was experiencing, through no fault of its own, in pursuing its interests in South Africa would soon be aggravated by the mere fact of being a British company operating in South Africa. A British Press campaign began about this time which was strongly critical of the wages and conditions of work of black labour in South Africa and of the record of British companies in this regard. British companies were urged to improve these conditions and to get rid of any kind of racial discrimination in their South African subsidiaries. The British Government gave its support to this campaign and a Parliamentary Committee at Westminster was empowered to take evidence from British parent companies on how their South African subsidiaries behaved. This meant that Gold Fields of South Africa, an important company in the Republic of South Africa, would have to justify itself to the members of a foreign Parliament. In 1969, the year in which Donald McCall succeeded Sir George Harvie-Watt as chairman of Consolidated Gold Fields, the chairman had something to say to shareholders about these new developments. 'We have been associated with the mining industry in South Africa for over 80 years, an industry whose growth has been vital to that country's economic progress and one which has brought benefits to all sections of its community. Whilst fully realizing the difficulties facing South Africa in shaping the future destiny of its

234

people, I am convinced that progress towards peaceful change will be best achieved, not by political isolation or contrived economic pressures from outside, but by maintaining industrial, commercial and social ties with the free world. The two-way trade between South Africa and the United Kingdom is presently running at around £600 million per annum and I believe that this is good for South Africa and all its peoples and that it is good for Britain.' It was a statement worthy of the Sub Nigel miner that Donald McCall had once been. Nevertheless, there was something incongruous about his having to speak up on behalf of his company's South African offspring since GFSA was itself the very stalwart parent of its own growing and flourishing family of subsidiaries.

During the 1960s Gold Fields of South Africa had been pushing ahead vigorously developing and expanding the old-established interests in tin mining and coal mining that had come to it with the acquisition of properties that had belonged to Anglo-French or New Union Goldfields. Rooiberg Minerals, renamed Rooiberg Tin in 1979, had been registered in 1908 and two years later Anglo-French took it over to run, in due course, four small underground mines some sixty-four kilometres west of Warmbaths in the Transvaal. However, mining operations had been going on at Rooiberg some 500 years before Anglo-French came on the scene. The 'ancients', whoever they were, are reckoned to have extracted some 2 000 tons of tin from 30 000 tons of ore. One romantic view suggests that they may have been Phoenicians. They would have fitted in well since the Phoenicians were pioneers in the metal markets. Before the invention of coinage they settled international debts by weighing out metals on the basis of bargains struck in the market. Various ancient artifacts, including a slave chain, had been discovered in the area of the ancient workings. It was the rediscovery of these workings in 1905 that led to a resumption of mining at Rooiberg; in fact the ore deposits which have been mined in modern times were often an extension in depth of the old diggings. In the early days miners from a number of countries worked at Rooiberg but they were predominantly Cornishmen who have a long tradition of tin mining. Rooiberg sometimes became the scene of dramatic events in South African history. In 1914 a battle was fought between the forces of the Union Government and the Boer Rebellion; men from the mines at Rooiberg joined the battle and helped to rout the rebels; one of the miners was killed. Later Rooiberg established a link with the most important tin area in the world, Malaya. It entered into a business relationship with the Straits Trading Company of Singapore who smelted Rooiberg's tin and then arranged shipping direct to the markets of Europe.

Union Tin, which came to Goldfields from New Union Goldfields, also had a colourful background. In 1908 a Johannesburg company named South African Tin Mines obtained mineral rights on the farm Doornhoek in the Potgietersrus district of the Waterberg. Some three years earlier, however, the prospector Dolf Erasmus had claimed discoverer's rights after being shown tin in rocks by a black man named Izak. Soon he was joined by several other prospectors. One of these became a famous writer and he recorded: 'An old acquaintance, Dolf Erasmus,

235

Eugene Marais (left), Afrikaans writer and intermediary in 1895 with the Reformers, wrote My Friends the Baboons *after working as a mine 'doctor' at Doornhoek – now Union Tin – in 1908. Here he is seen in Pretoria with the prospector who discovered the tin mine, his friend Dolf Erasmus, and Dolf's young son.*

met me in Nylstroom with a cart and four horses and for the first time in my life I was to enter the Waterberg, the mystery region of my boyhood.' The writer was Eugene Marais, the same man who, ten years earlier, had been led blindfold into the Gold Fields Building by Abe Bailey to meet the Reform Committee at the time of the Jameson Raid. When South African Tin took over Doornhoek, the first manager, Fred Thomas, offered Marais a job as mine doctor, which Marais accepted though he was not a qualified physician. This did not worry Thomas and his Welshmen who were working the mine and on several occasions, as a result of accidents, the 'doctor' had to give medical aid. He himself narrowly escaped death in dynamite explosions on two occasions. The writer seems to have been something of a jack-of-all-trades at the mine, not only helping in its administration – he had had a legal training – but he also built a road down the ridge to the mine. His main interest, however, was not Welsh miners but Transvaal baboons, some 300 of which had moved into a kloof near the mine. He observed them over a long period and in time moved freely and happily among them. They form the subject of his famous book, *My Friends the Baboons* and its sequel, *The Soul of the Ape*. All those who came to work at Union Tin in later years would have recognized the description of the natural world that surrounds the mine. 'I was caught by a sense of vastness which held me breathless for a moment,' he wrote. 'It seemed as if we stood on some mighty projection thrust out into the heavens, that below us the rim of the sky dipped all round … immediately overhead was Canopus, the star for some mysterious reason best known to us dwellers of the veld, observed by the Voortrekkers and their descendants who fix their knowledge of the heavens by its conjunction with other stars or constellations.'

This was the world that Gold Fields had inherited when it came, in the 1960s, to reorganize the tin interests of Rooiberg and Union Tin. Rooiberg, which in due course had four operating areas – Rooiberg, Leeuwpoort, Nieuwpoort and Vellefontein, the last named acquired in 1970 – had together with Union Tin pushed up production by sixteen percent in 1964. The company was fortunate in that the price of tin began to go up just as it had appeared on the scene. A working profit of R200 000 in 1961 had within a year gone up to R370 000 and dividends increased by fifty percent. 'The exploration is steadily improving the longer-term outlook,' shareholders were reassured. However, the company's tin interests were very much at the mercy of a notoriously volatile tin price; in one five-year period the price fluctuated between R5 000 and R13 000 a ton. Apart from the Transvaal tin mines, Gold Fields also had another source in South West Africa, at Brandberg West, where it came as a by-product, being combined with wolfram in concentrates marketed by the South West Africa Company. They also had an eye on the Kamativi tin mine in Rhodesia, but this eluded them.

As with Rooiberg and Union Tin, so with the Apex coal interests, Gold Fields added some colourful history to its own. In the 1890s, in the days of Birkenruth and later of Chaplin, Gold Fields had had a part in its early development. Sir William Dalrymple was beginning his half-century in the chair on behalf of Anglo-French. Over the years the company declined with the rest of the Anglo-French interests; it was said of Anglo-French that they never made a mistake because they said no to every suggestion. Sir George Farrar had been the driving force in the early days. He had expected Apex, which was near the New Klein-fontein mine, to produce gold as well as coal but as the company's report was to say in 1915, after Farrar's death on active service, 'In 1895 this company had exhausted its funds in prospecting for gold and Sir George brought forward a scheme for reconstruction which re-established its position and from that time its coal deposits were profitably developed.' In 1914 the gold section of Apex was sold to New Kleinfontein while the coal section went on mining on the original farm Rietfontein until May 1947. By this time it had sold over nine million tons of coal and distributed £1 000 000 in dividends. In 1944, the company took over control of the old Middelburg steam colliery in the Witbank district. But this, like the Apex mine, closed down in 1947, owing to the spreading of underground fires.

All Apex Mines now had was its new Greenside Colliery, established on the farm Groenfontein in the Witbank district, which had been acquired during the war. It turned out to be a wonderful deposit, with wide and continuous seams of good quality coal. Life was very tough at Greenside in 1944. The first manager lived in the Witbank Hotel; two workmen put up in an old farmhouse on the property which was quite devoid of trees. Others lived in tents and got their drinking water from a spring. But gradually the mine got under way. Nevertheless, when Gold Fields arrived on the scene and the mine manager was given a company car, the acquisition of such riches convinced him that Gold Fields of South Africa was presided over by Father Christmas. That Apex Mines, and in due course Gold Fields, had acquired Greenside Colliery was due to the Mackenzie family, to George and John, brothers of William Mackenzie, a Gold Fields director in the 1930s. The two Mackenzies had become directors of Apex Mines because of their connection with New Kleinfontein, whose chairman George had been since 1931. Believing that the gold reef might possibly extend under the coal of the Apex Mines, they bought shares in the company and eventually their holding was greater than that of Anglo-French. As directors of Apex they were concerned about what would happen to the coal interests if no new colliery was found to replace the original. It was on their initiative that Groenfontein was acquired and that Greenside Colliery came into existence. Under Gold Fields' administration it was to develop into one of the most successful collieries in the country, after having to overcome early safety problems when, at one point, it was declared 'fiery'. Although control of Apex could have been acquired by the Mackenzies for their Northern African group, they were happy that their brother's old company, Gold Fields, should become responsible for it. Gold Fields in its turn recognized the family contribution to the prosperity of Apex Mines and a Mackenzie has always been a member of the board. In due course George's son, Ian Mackenzie, for many years chairman of the Standard Bank of South Africa, became an Apex director. George Mackenzie, who died in 1963, was chairman of another company, William Bain & Co (South Africa) that also came into the Gold Fields sphere when it became a wholly-owned subsidiary of another Gold Fields associate, the Cementation Company (Africa).

By coming into coal at the beginning of the 1960s, Gold Fields demonstrated once again its ability to be in the right place at the right time. Coal was about to become very important to South Africa's economy and its future expansion. The

Transvaal and northern Orange Free State, with more than ninety percent of the country's vast coal reserves, was at the heart of a nation-wide power grid. Transvaal coal, of lower quality than the coking coal of Natal, was also cheap to produce, in the mid-1960s coming out at about R1,50 a ton compared with a price in Britain, for instance, of R8,15. At this time production had risen to 53,4 million tons. Without this coal there could have been no Sasolburg, the industrial complex which had provided a base for the country's first oil-from-coal plant and a steadily diversifying chemical industry. Here were born grandiose ambitions for the future oil needs of the country.

Now that Greenside was part of a great mining house, it could call on a whole group of specialists to promote its development. Before long it was announcing a record output of 111 000 tons a month. As a member of the Transvaal Coal Owners Association, Apex sales were made through the Association on a quota system which gave the company a percentage of total sales made by the Association. In 1968 Apex was able to increase its quota by buying the Bellevue Colliery at Ermelo. In that same year Greenside, opening up No 5 seam with another type of coal – a blend of coking coal – obtained a valuable thirty-year contract. This was with Highveld Steel and Vanadium, who helped to finance the operation by taking up one-seventh of the new shares issued to raise the R2,8 million required. Highveld Steel then said they needed the coal in a hurry and, as a result of a tremendous effort at the mine, the first deliveries were made four months earlier than the first agreed date of July 1968. The following year, thanks to the Highveld Steel contract, which was not part of the quota, Apex Mines had a working profit of some R942 000.

The chairman of both Rooiberg Minerals and Apex Mines at the time they were taken over by Gold Fields was A W Stewart, who had held the posts since 1948. The day after the announcement of the take-over, he had a heart attack and died. During his chairmanship of Apex he had had to consult the company's lawyers about an extraordinary event that had taken place on the mine. In the files of Webber Wentzel it is known as 'The case of the disappearing ice-cream factory'. John Wentzel recorded what took place. The legal point, according to Michael Barry, the young lawyer handling the case, was an intriguing one because the building had originally been erected as a church on grounds which, according to all available information, was not undermined. In any case the mining operations had been conducted many years before by a predecessor in title of Apex Mines and which had gone into liquidation. Where the incident occurred in the Transvaal the coal seams lie only about twenty metres below the surface. The early miners were accustomed to taking as much coal as possible out of the seam but left substantial pillars of coal to support the hanging wall. This method of mining led to obvious hazards. The old mine workings filled with water which became acidic and later polluted the surroundings; the pillars of coal sometimes ignited by spontaneous combustion so that underground fires were a constant menace; the destruction of the pillars caused the hanging wall to collapse. A third hazard was the custom of unauthorized people entering the mine workings and robbing the pillars of their coal. Once the seams had been worked out, the community moved away from the old mine workings and their church was sold to an Italian, who converted it into an ice-cream factory. For this he needed water and sank a borehole beside the building. All went well for the first twenty metres then, in the words of the Italian, the drill 'slipped'. He tried to recover it and approached the hole down which it had disappeared. He was a simple man and was not altogether happy about turning a holy place, a church, into an ice-cream factory. He had further misgivings when at the hole he could hear voices coming from below. By this time he was convinced that he had drilled into Hell and had got Lucifer on the line. In panic, he fled. His wife, a stronger character, came back to the hole and shouted down 'Who is there?'. A voice replied: 'It doesn't matter who we are. Take your bloody drill out of our mine!'

The Italians realized that their building was not on solid ground and, sure enough, a couple of days later there was an ominous rumbling sound, caused no doubt because coal had been removed from the pillars. The building and surrounding ground began to sink. As the Italian and his wife scrambled to safety, they looked round to see their ice-cream factory disappearing into the pit caused by the mine's collapse.

Since all this had happened on Apex property, Stewart decided to consult Webber Wentzel for an opinion. He accepted their view that Apex had no liability but he felt it would be in the interests of the company nevertheless to settle the claim rather than to attempt to explain to the Italian that he was without remedy. Stewart signed a deed of settlement, without any admission of liability. As he did so, he said, 'I would have given a lot to have been there when our friend heard those satanic voices!'

Stewart's death the day after Gold Fields took over Apex Mines with its colourful history cast a shadow over the event since the chairman of Apex and of Rooiberg was a man admired as much for his straight dealing as he was for his sense of humour, which never deserted him although he was crippled with arthritis.

On 31 March 1966 *The Star* in Johannesburg carried in its news columns what amounted to an obituary. It was not for the chairman of a mining company but for a mine itself. The paper reported: 'One of the great and historic mines of the Central Rand, pivotal sector of the Reef, died this month. It was the Robinson Deep, which for more than 70 years has been an integral part of the life and story of Johannesburg and its amazing gold mines.' Robinson Deep was not the only one among the old mines that had given the Government the three months' notice to close required by the Gold Law. Simmer and Jack, the splendid old stablemate of Robinson Deep, had already done so. The Government Mining Engineer was reported to be considering the consequences of several mines on the Central Rand closing at about the same time. City Deep and Crown Mines were also closing. In their final operations these two had each had a tribute agreement with Robinson Deep to mine areas of the latter on a royalty basis which

240

gave the Gold Fields mine one-third of the profit. Johannesburg had informed London in November 1965 that all development at Robinson Deep had ended that September and as much ore as possible would be got out by March 1966. As *The Star* reported: 'The last "shots" of dynamite were fired in the bowels of the old mine on 15 March and the equipment and other assets of the property are now up for sale.' The surface rights of the company had considerable value and all the company's shares were eventually acquired by the Schlesinger organization. This might not have been to the liking of William Mackenzie, though he had been dead twenty years. In the 1930s, asked by London for a view of the Schlesinger activities, he had replied: 'There is not one of the concerns under Schlesinger's wing in which I would like to be interested.' I W Schlesinger also was no longer about and Mandy Moross was in charge of the organization that bought Robinson Deep.

Mining executives come and go and, since they are mortal, they eventually go for good. Old mines, on the other hand, though they are dead, have a disinclination to lie down. 'Old mines are reputed to die hard and The Sub Nigel Limited is no exception.' Thus said the chairman back in 1962 when Sub Nigel was in its 54th year of production. Mark Twain's celebrated remark that reports of his death had been exaggerated could well have been applied to an old mine like Sub Nigel, for which notice was regularly given that it was about to give up. It may even have got the idea from Mark Twain himself since the American humorist visited South Africa in 1896 and went to see one of the founding fathers of Sub Nigel, his old friend, John Hays Hammond. At the time the consulting engineer was in Pretoria Gaol awaiting trial; he asked Mark Twain how he had managed to get into the gaol. Twain said that getting into a gaol was easy; the problem was how to get out.

It was not until 1971 when Sub Nigel gave itself another six months, that anyone really took seriously the mine's decision to shut up shop; before that the old mines that belonged to the heroic age of gold mining in South Africa had been giving up one by one. On 4 February 1967 Rietfontein worked its last underground shift and what had been Rhodes's old Du Preez property had completed its task. In the thirty years that had gone by since it had re-opened in 1935 under Carleton Jones's supervision, it had produced forty-five million grams of gold worth R35 million. It had the further distinction of being the first mine to complete a million shifts without a fatal accident. Luipaardsvlei also ceased operations in 1970 by which time it had paid out R23 million in dividends. Its later years had been notable for its entry into the nuclear age when it developed hitherto unpayable reefs, to provide 3 700 tons of uranium oxide.

Simmer and Jack was another story. Anyone reading the stock exchange prices in the Press in the mid-1980s and seeing that famous name in the list, might well wonder if in fact it had ever died. The mine ceased operations in April 1964 after a working life of seventy-six years, during which time it had milled 64,4 million tons of ore, producing 14,5 million ounces of gold and given its shareholders R24,9 million in dividends and capital repayments. The company's assets were offered for sale at R1,5 million. However a new consortium made an equivalent offer for all the shares of the company. This was accepted by Gold Fields and most of the shareholders. Then Gold Fields itself paid R400 000 for five of its mine hoists, some of which had been the largest in the world when installed at the South Deep shaft. There were various historic items, including a stamp battery that had been in use from 1886 till 1946. Company records had been handed over in 1965 to Stewart Scott, the new owners, but ten years later Gold Fields was still receiving enquiries about some ancient mining rights in the area it still possessed. If it were to exercise these, it might well disturb the modern world of Johannesburg. The company apparently had the right to place a slimes dam on the race course at Germiston, which of course would have been inconvenient for the punters. Germiston Sporting Club had freehold rights but not mineral rights; hence surface activities could be disrupted if Gold Fields decided to dig up the turf. In this quite hypothetical situation the Administrator of the Transvaal said the race course must remain, and Douglas Christopherson[3], if he had still been around, would surely have said 'hear, hear'. Back in November 1952 the Town Clerk of Johannesburg had written to enquire what part of the Rand Airport would be required by Simmer and Jack for mining purposes. The following February Gold Fields replied that they did not know, but that in three or four years' time they would be in a better position to give an answer.

Such were the mining ghosts of the Simmer and Jack past but, as was said when Gold Fields parted with the mine in 1965, it bore 'its scars of old age with quiet dignity befitting a mine that blossomed in the Queen Victoria–Paul Kruger era. While so many of its comtemporaries have slipped into oblivion, Simmer and Jack still exists in the Atomic Age ...' Even the Space Age, for in 1978, well after prospecting astronauts had returned from the moon with samples of lunar ore, Simmer and Jack produced gold and silver worth R629 000. By that time the price of gold had reached Space Age heights, and it was worthwhile putting the old cement paths through the mill to pick up the tailings left behind by the pioneers of John Jack's day.

In 1967, another Gold Fields mine was approaching retirement after a mere thirty years of work. This was Vogelstruisbult near Springs on the East Rand. When it finally closed down its gold operations in 1968, it had produced 7 million ozs. from 29,8 million tons of Main Reef and Kimberley Reef ore. This, together with its uranium earnings between 1955 and 1964, had enabled it to reward its shareholders with R18 million in dividends and another R4,9 million in capital repayments. This, however, was not the end of Vogelstruisbult, more a change of occupation since an exciting new future had been devised for it, and this had nothing to do with gold. The mine itself seemed to show a reluctance to accept the change; the headgear at No 3 shaft proved very obstinate and refused to come down. After one day they managed to get it to lean over and for a time, out on the Springs–Nigel road, it stuck out like the Tower of Pisa. After three days it finally gave up the struggle and fell with a thunderous roar of protest.

On 28th March 1967 an announcement from 75 Fox Street, couched in un-

The 'Leaning Tower of Vogelstruisbult'. In August 1969 the headgear at the mine stubbornly defied for several days attempts to pull it down.

dramatic language, proclaimed what in effect was to be a major contribution by Gold Fields to the industrial development of South Africa. The statement said that GFSA in co-operation with the State iron and steel corporation, Iscor and with Vogelstruisbult, was forming a new company, the Zinc Corporation of South Africa (Zincor), to construct and operate an electrolytic zinc plant which would have a productive capacity of 36 500 tons a year. Zincor would be managed by GFSA which would act as technical advisers and secretaries to the company. The plant would be sited at the old uranium plant at Vogelstruisbult where it had been maintained in good condition since ceasing operations in 1964. Vogelstruisbult parted with some of its assets, including 310 morgen of freehold to Zincor for R1 million.

On the same day another announcement informed the mining world that GFSA, with Anglo American, JCI and Vogelstruisbult had formed a company called Kiln Products in South West Africa. It would build and operate a kiln near Grootfontein at the Berg Aukas mine belonging to the South West Africa Company. Kiln Products would be managed by Gold Fields. The connection between the two announcements was that the high-grade zinc oxide concentrates produced at Berg Aukas would be sold to Zincor down at Vogelstruisbult for the production of electrolytic zinc. In turn Zincor would provide Iscor with its entire zinc requirements on a fifteen-year contract. Iscor also had thirty-five percent of the Zincor equity, two percent more than GFSA; Vogels and Kiln Products had the rest. Zincor was to raise R10 million for its capital needs, half in equity capital, half in loans. GFSA's co-operation with a South African State organization, Iscor, was also extended to South West Africa. The refinery, whose primary task was to produce ingot zinc, was designed also to produce sulphuric acid for Iscor, whose Rosh Pinah mine in South West Africa would provide the zinc sulphide feed.

The Zincor refinery experienced the usual teething troubles of a new industry but these were soon overcome. Over the years the initial capacity of 36 500 tons was expanded. At the end of the first fifteen-year contract with Iscor, the plant was producing 84 000 tons a year, working a twenty-four hour day with three shifts. Iscor was still the biggest customer. In giving South Africa its first electrolytic zinc refinery, Gold Fields, with the mining and metallurgical expertise that it commanded at 75 Fox Street, had taken the known technology related to the mining of metals by means of electrolytic process and adapted it to its own needs. Gold Fields, in these apprenticeship years of 'responsible government' leading eventually to full independence, had become a highly sophisticated, dynamic company, and although at this time still a British-owned company, it was becoming ever more deeply involved in South Africa's development. With Zincor it had performed a national service. Whereas before South Africa had had to import its zinc, now it had become self-sufficient in zinc.

Zinc was a success. Glenover Phosphate in the Northern Transvaal was another worthwhile operation. Fluorspar, on the other hand, was not. Zwartkloof Fluorspar had been registered in October 1968 and at the end of June 1970 pro-

244

duction was on schedule at the plant near Warmbaths. The first shipments were being made from Lourenço Marques. The company was expecting to provide some 50 000 tons a year of material. Demand was increasing due to a bigger use of electric furnaces for steel manufacture. (South Africa on the other hand was never more than a minor producer.) Zwartkloof, however, was only able to make a contribution until 1973 when the supply of economic ore ran out and the plant had to be closed.

By the end of the decade Gold Fields had collected such a wide range of new interests, other than gold, that it was constantly having to reorganize these to facilitate their efficient administration. All the metal and mineral interests were brought together into a single 'hold-all', Vogelstruisbult Metal Holdings. Then there was G F Industrial Holdings for dealing with the companies manufacturing such items as locos, rock handling equipment and aluminium electrical conductors. And New Durban Gold and Industrial was its principal property holding company. Industrial and property holdings and small mining finance companies had to be consolidated into fewer but larger units to make for more efficient administration.

Platinum, like everything else in South Africa, had been swinging with the Sixties and in 1970 Consolidated Gold Fields was prompted to say: 'Our interest in platinum through the Rustenburg Company is a very important factor in our group earnings and one we are glad to have.' Platinum was one of the investments in South Africa that had remained in the hands of the London company, and although 75 Fox Street provided directors for the platinum companies administered by JCI, they were there to look after London's interests. In 1964 an expansion programme had been launched to increase production of the platinum mines by forty percent over two years.

Rustenburg Platinum Mines then embarked on a further scheme to increase capacity to 750 000 ounces a year. This was later pushed to 850 000 ounces but it never seemed to be enough to meet demand. One expansion programme had hardly been completed when another had to be started. In 1970 Rustenburg was producing a million ounces a year, and although the price weakened a little at that time, there was no lack of confidence in the future of the industry. There was talk of using platinum to combat air pollution and this, CGF shareholders were told, 'could open up new markets of some significance'. JCI, which administered the mines in which CGF had its big shareholding, had already announced that Rustenburg was the largest producer in the Western world and the only major mining undertaking in the West whose main purpose was the recovery of platinum. This was being done from two mines, Rustenburg, situated a few kilometres to the east of the town of Rustenburg and at the Union section which operated at Zwartklip some 90 kilometres north of Rustenburg and which had been brought into the company by Gold Fields.

Meanwhile, in the Orange Free State there was still no joy for Gold Fields. Considerable sums of money had been spent on Saaiplaas which continued to disappoint. Methods of financing not previously favoured by Gold Fields had been used, including loans, but by 1964 the financial situation was sombre; the loan could not be serviced and Gold Fields had to take special measures. In 1965 they gave up the struggle and parted with the mine to Anglo American which was able to run it with their President Brand mine. Even parting with Saaiplaas proved problematical, when some of the shareholders expressed their dissatisfaction with the arrangements by actually taking proceedings in court.

Saaiplaas may have refused to give up its gold. Star Diamond Mine forty kilometres to the south, at Theron, near Theunissen, however, was more accommodating and managed to produce up to 50 000 carats a year. In 1969 came problems of a different sort. The chairman of Star Diamond Mine at the time was Deryck Gettliffe who, as a result of continuing thefts at the mine, ended up by dismissing the entire black labour force of 500. A new team of Mozambicans, generally regarded as among the most reliable of mine workers, was signed on in their place.

During South Africa's boom years in the 1960s, Gold Fields of South Africa had been booming, too. Despite the setbacks of the West Driefontein accidents, the company through its substantial stake in West Witwatersrand Areas had been reaping a tremendous harvest in the Wonderfontein valley. At the same time it had been building out the base of its activities with expansion into the base metals and minerals field, into industry and property. Although it was still totally owned by a British company, it had become with the passing years ever more South African, its chairman and directors well-known personalities in the country's business establishment. All this had been taking place against a political background that was changing both at home and abroad. The hostility of the outside world towards the political policies of the South African Government had not only increased the sensitivity of Afrikaner nationalism from which that Government came but had also made it aware of external dangers. There was talk of sanctions and boycotts and the Government would have to take steps to protect the country's vital interests. There was the question of strategic minerals, of the development of nuclear power and the mining industry was involved. In any case, the mining industry was the heart of the South African economy and the source of its power. The Government would not take kindly to any attempt at interference from abroad. All this would have a bearing on a gold mining house in Johannesburg that was still controlled ultimately from London and where already the parent company was being called to account by a British Parliamentary committee; this was as unpalatable in 75 Fox Street as it was in the Union Buildings.

In September 1970, on the occasion of the 80th anniversary of the Chamber of Mines, the State President, Jim Fouche, said: 'The mining industry today is a South African industry owned and operated by South Africans for the benefit of South Africans and provides an example of the co-operation of all races for the common good. These men have put South Africa among the top mining countries of the world and undisputed leaders in the winning of minerals at depth. The mining industry draws its strength from the soil and the people of

South Africa and the future of South Africa and its people is closely linked in turn with the economic strength and the fortunes of mining.' The patriotic trumpet note was loud and clear in that opening year of the 1970s, but Gold Fields of South Africa, the oldest member of the orchestra, seemed just slightly out of tune, since the owner of the company was not a South African.

There had been a time when Afrikaner nationalists, notably Dr Albert Hertzog, felt that the Government should nationalize the gold mining industry. The industry itself saw that the best way to defuse the situation would be for Afrikanerdom to have a good stake in it; in that way they might discover that the Chamber of Mines was not a Trojan Horse. In the 1950s Willem Coetzer's Federale Mynbou had had its eye on Gold Fields; in 1965 it gained control of another historic mining house, General Mining, the old Albu company. Sir George Albu had died in 1963 and been succeeded as chairman by Stowe Mc-Lean; Anglo American acquired an important interest and was in a position to give Federale Mynbou a helping hand. Harry Oppenheimer, as schooled in politics as he is skilled in business, played the role of honest broker. This was ironic for he was the man of whom the Prime Minister, Dr Verwoerd, had said: 'He can secretly cause a good many things to happen. In other words he can pull strings. With all that monetary power and with this powerful machine which is spread over the whole of the country, he can if he chooses exercise an enormous influence against the Government and the State.' When Willem Coetzer entered into negotiations with Oppenheimer, he forfeited the support of some of his colleagues at Federale Mynbou. 'Many Afrikaners,' he said, 'were against it and even some of our directors resigned. According to them the ideal of an Afrikaner mining house was being buried in a 22-carat coffin in Hollard Street. But they were proved wrong. I had absolute trust in Mr Oppenheimer and in our own case.' Oppenheimer himself was to say: 'I think it is a very good thing for the gold mining industry that there should be a large house which is Afrikaner-orientated.' The upshot of the deal was that Willem Coetzer and Tommy Muller saw the assets of Federale Mynbou leap from R70 million to R300 million. They were now ready to go places and they did. Somewhere along the way there would be a confrontation with GFSA; later still, Oppenheimer himself would feel the necessity to slow up progress with a spanner in the *disselboom*. Two years after the General Mining take-over, Tommy Muller, speaking at Stellenbosch, took a look into the future and said: 'As a first prospect it seems reasonable to expect that the control and management of the mining industry will be vested to an increasing extent in this country and that it will be spread wider among all sections of the population, probably linked with an ever-increasing participation by the Afrikaner.' In due course Tommy Muller set a personal course of his own. He left Willem Coetzer to become chairman of Iscor and when Iscor went into business with Gold Fields over Zincor it was not long before he became familiar with 75 Fox Street. A director of West Witwatersrand Areas, he became in 1971 a director of Gold Fields. And that, in a way, was to come home, for he had spent much of his childhood on Leeuwpoort, the family farm of the Dreyers, of whom his mother was one. And Leeuwpoort had become part of the mining area of the West Wits Line.

A year after the impressive Afrikaner take-over of General Mining by way of Harry Oppenheimer, the Prime Minister Dr Verwoerd was assassinated in Parliament and was succeeded as Prime Minister by John Vorster. Carel de Wet was recalled from London to become Minister of Mines in time to perform the opening ceremony at Kloof.

At Gold Fields, too, there had been changes in the cabinet as new men joined the board in a period of rapid expansion. Bill Busschau had given up the chairmanship of GFSA in 1965 but he remained a director of Consolidated Gold Fields in London. He had been away in the United States when the announcement was made and Ian Louw was named as his successor. There was a certain amount of comment in the South African Press at the way the announcement had been made. Ian Louw, who was described as a man who ran upstairs two at a time, had clearly applied this athletic philosophy to his career, since at forty-five he was the youngest man ever to take charge of a South African mining house. The Afrikaans Press, already *in hul skik* over the take-over of General Mining, were even more so when they were able to announce, as they did, that a *boereseun* had become head of Rhodes's old company. That seemed like the ultimate achievement. The company was even being called *Goudvelde van Suid-Afrika*, even in the company's own handouts in Afrikaans, though that name has never been registered. As far as Louw was concerned, mining not lineage was what mattered. He had proved himself as a mining engineer and that was all he had ever wished to be, but events, particularly the accidents at West Driefontein, had shown him to be an outstanding leader and this he fully confirmed in the fifteen years of his chairmanship.

Ian Louw was strongly supported by consulting mining engineers who were playing a leading role in the industry at a time of great technological development. Reg Cousens, who had had to cope with the two disasters at West Drie, joined the board as technical director in 1969. David Jamieson[4], who had been closely associated with many of the developments on the East Rand, had also held important posts on the Far West Rand and, as he was to say, the change from one end of the Reef to the other had required some sharp adjustments since the conditions of mining the West Wits Line were very different from those he understood at Sub Nigel or Vogels.

Jack Bocock and Stan Gibbs, who had succeeded Cousens at West Drie before it started to mill, were also consulting engineers during the expanding 1960s. Younger men were on their way up, some of whom had gone to the United States to widen their experience and their training. Andries Taute, a graduate of Wits to which he had returned after military service, had won a bursary to Columbia. Peter van Rensburg, too, had been in America on a Chamber of Mines scholarship and Bob Robinson in 1968 had been at the Harvard Business School. William Wouter Malan, who had been with Robinson during the West Drie flooding, and like Robinson was the son of a mining man, had become

248

manager of Doornfontein at thirty-eight after a spell at Libanon. Well liked and respected, he nevertheless had a reputation for being 'fiery', an expression usually used to describe dangerous coal mines. Malan in due course followed in the footsteps of Attie von Maltitz and went to Anglovaal, becoming a director of that company and in 1981 President of the Chamber of Mines.

Although he had chosen a mining engineer to take his place at Gold Fields, Bill Busschau, economist, accountant, academic, might well have thought that gold mining was too serious a business to be left to mining engineers. Certainly, during his time at Gold Fields he had expedited the age of the university graduate which superseded the hegemony of aristocrats, cricketers and engineers. Mining engineers, of course, were graduates of the universities, notably in the case of Gold Fields, of Witwatersrand University, where they had received their specialized training for their chosen profession. Busschau's graduates, however, were men such as himself whose university education had not specifically trained them for a career in mining. They came to Gold Fields from a variety of university disciplines and contributed to the company the intellectual skills that were required in the management and direction of a modern business organization that came to employ 94 000 people.

Robin Hope, like Busschau, had been a Rhodes Scholar at Oxford, going up to Corpus Christi College immediately after the war when he had served in the South African forces Up North. At school at St John's College in Johannesburg, he was already a graduate of Rhodes University, Grahamstown, before taking up his Rhodes Scholarship. Among his contemporaries at Oxford were others who later, like himself, made a name in mining on the Rand, Gavin Relly and Graham Boustred of Anglo American, Syd Newman of Lonrho, for instance. A man very much in the Busschau mould with a brilliantly incisive mind, Hope made rapid progress at Gold Fields, becoming a manager in the 1950s and also chairman of some of the subsidiary companies later on. He was already a director of GFSA, both under Busschau's chairmanship and that of Ian Louw, when he was invited to join the board of Consolidated Gold Fields in London, which still totally owned GFSA. In 1969 he was appointed a deputy-chairman of that company. It was the first time in the eighty-two years that Consolidated Gold Fields had been operating in South Africa that a born-and-bred South African had been appointed to such a position. Busschau and Louw were also members of that board but they were permanently resident in South Africa, which was the exclusive scene of their interests. With Robin Hope going to London, it looked as if the colonial process was going into reverse. One even began to visualize the day of a South African chairman at 49 Moorgate in the City of London.

In 1957, Bill Busschau persuaded Gold Fields to make one of its most successful investments. There was not a lot of money involved, in fact, just enough to cover a fare from England to South Africa to bring home a twenty-two year old South African who had just completed his three years at Oxford that a Rhodes Scholarship had given him. What Carleton Jones had done for Busschau twenty years earlier, Busschau was now doing for Robin Allan Plumbridge, for

Robin Hope, a South African Rhodes Scholar at Oxford in 1946, had the unique distinction of being, at different times, deputy chairman of Consolidated Gold Fields in London and of Gold Fields of South Africa in Johannesburg.

250

that was the name of the young Rhodes Scholar in question. 'I had tempting offers from elsewhere in the world but I decided to come home – I suppose I was too much of a South African to consider anywhere else,' he was to say later. At the age of forty-five, when he succeeded Ian Louw as chairman of Gold Fields of South Africa, he had amply proved Busschau's ability to pick an investment with growth prospects. When Plumbridge became chairman in December 1980, his deputy-chairman was Peter van Rensburg. Both had been educated at St Andrews, Grahamstown, though Van Rensburg was of a much earlier vintage than his youthful chairman. But once more the historical continuity had shown itself in the Gold Fields outcrop; Ronald Currey, St Andrews' famous headmaster, was none other than the son of Harry Currey, whom Rhodes had sent to run the Gold Fields office in Johannesburg back in 1889 and whose highly articulate but rather rude letters to London had drawn a rebuke from Thomas Rudd. It would have appealed to his sense of humour to know that his own son had taken charge of an educational establishment that was providing the company with its future directors.

At Oxford Robin Plumbridge had done something rare for a South African; he had read mathematics and this against the advice of the Oxford authorities who believed that mathematical training in South Africa was not up to British standards. Plumbridge proved them to be resoundingly wrong. But he also did what many Rhodes Scholars from South Africa have done; he won a Rugby Blue. At the same time, no doubt with Lord Harris's company in his sights, he thought it might be as well to play cricket for the university. However, it was maths rather than cricket that would be of use to him when he reached Gold Fields for he had arrived just as the computer dawn was coming up in Fox Street; in the early 1960s he led the team that introduced computerization into the Group. During this decade he was also very much involved with the development of the base metals and minerals activities of the company. He was the first chairman of Zincor and in 1971 set an interesting precedent by organizing an 'open day' so that the business community at Springs and Benoni could come and see what Gold Fields were doing with their new initiative. In the end, however, like Busschau, he was to find that gold dominated his life at Gold Fields, after he had taken charge of the East Driefontein project. During the 1950s, while he had been at Oxford, his patron, Bill Busschau, had been spinning gold coins at the Johannesburg Country Club and getting ideas for the Krugerrand. It would be Plumbridge's role in due course to pick up Busschau's baton and take the gold message – and Krugerrands – to all parts of the world.

In the meantime, Plumbridge, like Louw his chairman and others at Gold Fields of South Africa, were beginning to take stock of the changed situation in South Africa and the world at large as the 1960s began to close. They were looking in particular at the relationship between their own company and the company that owned it, Consolidated Gold Fields of 49 Moorgate, London. There, too, new men were in charge.

Sir George Harvie-Watt had given up the chairmanship in 1969 to become president of the company. The new chairman was Donald McCall, who had started his company climb back in 1930 at the bottom of a Sub Nigel mine shaft. That climb might have ended prematurely in 1956 when he narrowly missed being involved in the Comet air disaster that year; as it was, his arrival back in London from a visit to South Africa was delayed. Harvie-Watt had expected Gillie Potier to be his successor. Potier, however, like Reinecke in the 1930s, had become seriously ill in 1968 with a brain tumour. He died early the following year. A man of strong will, he had exercised considerable influence in the company; he had believed that financial control and ultimate power in the Group should be concentrated in London. Busschau and others in South Africa, however, did not see it that way. It would be some time before London grasped that 'by having local finance, local talent and local management, national loyalties are realized to the advantage of the operation', in the words of a later chairman of Consolidated Gold Fields.

Harvie-Watt's departure from the Gold Fields scene was in some ways a watershed. He had carried out the most far-reaching changes, not only in the structure of the company, which had led to the formation in 1959 of Gold Fields of South Africa; he had also widened enormously the range of activities not only of his own Consolidated Gold Fields around the world but, as a director of GFSA, had strongly advised the South African company to widen its own operational base. At a farewell dinner for him in Johannesburg, Ian Louw paid handsome tribute to what he had achieved for Gold Fields from 1954 until 1968. During that time, said Louw, the assets of Consolidated Gold Fields had increased from the equivalent of R68 million to nearly R400 million. Profits rose from R2,6 million in 1954 to R12,4 million in 1967. Louw also paid tribute to his far-sightedness as chief executive in pulling out of projects, though proved, in Central Africa in order to concentrate on investment in South Africa, South West Africa, the United States, Canada and Australia. An even more glowing appreciation of these achievements was expressed by Harvie-Watt himself who, in the course of his memoirs wrote: 'Well known though this company was when I first joined the Board after the war, it was really well down the league table of Britain's largest companies. In December 1951 the issued capital (ordinary) was £4 200 000, share price 49/4½d, and market capitalization £10,4 million. That was the year I became Managing Director. In 1969 when I retired from the Chair of Gold Fields it was the 25th largest company in Britain at £280 million. The Board was not at all keen for me to retire.

'The year 1968 was a wonderful year for Gold Fields and for me,' Sir George recorded. 'One City financial writer emphasized the wonder of it for Harvie-Watt who reported profits for the year of £16 348 000 before tax, against £11 231 000 in the previous year. In October 1969 the *Investors Chronicle* ran a headline "Sir George departs in a Blaze of Glory".' And so he did. Like his predecessor, Robert Annan, he had been elevated to president of Consolidated Gold Fields and, like Charles Rudd, he retired to a home in Scotland. There, in his 84th year, he was contemplating in 1986 the approaching centenary of the company which he had served so conspicuously. The Harvie-Watt shaft at Libanon and the town of Glenharvie on the Far West Rand will keep his memory alive in South Africa.

Perhaps the most significant feature of the Harvie-Watt era was the way that Consolidated Gold Fields in London and Gold Fields of South Africa began each to establish new identities, the one very different from the other. This happened partly as a result of Harvie-Watt and Potier's policy, and partly because of a change in the political and social climate in the world as a whole. This was a time when Consolidated Gold Fields, though based in London, became increasingly international in character; at the same time Gold Fields of South Africa was becoming increasingly aware of its own national character. Whereas the identity of the London company was becoming fudged and unclear and even the true nature of its business uncertain, that of the Johannesburg company, by contrast, became ever more distinct. Since the great mines that it controlled through West Witwatersrand Areas, such as West Driefontein and Kloof, were household words around the world, there was absolutely no doubt as to what its business was. Whatever else it might have acquired during the 1960s, often with prompting from London, there was no doubt at all that gold mining was its real business.

By the time the 1970s arrived, it was clear that the company in London which still owned the company in South Africa, had moved many of its preoccupations and ambitions elsewhere, despite the fact that forty-one percent of its income was still coming from the Republic. Nevertheless, CGF in order to finance its diversification around the world had been selling from its South African portfolio of investments, including in due course its Libanon holdings, for instance. Moreover, members of the board in London had differing views about South Africa and its place in the company's affairs. Looking to the future, which some suspected might be sombre in South Africa, there were those who felt it would be wiser to be in a country like Australia. What would happen if they got out of South Africa altogether? The unlikely thought did cross the minds of some at 75 Fox Street.

The fact that Consolidated Gold Fields had a South African connection had already turned it into a political target in London. At the same time in South Africa the fact that Gold Fields of South Africa was not South African-owned, as was the case with the other big mining houses in Johannesburg, was also becoming more conspicuous. The possibility of GFSA being floated off as an independent South African company was already beginning to interest the Press. In April 1968, in the course of an interview with the *Rand Daily Mail*, Ian Louw, in response to a question as to whether the East Driefontein rights issue meant that Consolidated Gold Fields did not intend to float off its South African operating company, stated: 'The rights issue has no relationship whatsoever to any future decision which may be taken in connection with floating off Gold Fields of South Africa as a public company.'

It was not, however, until 7 June 1971 that a statement was issued from 75 Fox Street which informed the world and South Africa in particular that steps were about to be taken 'to create a South African-based mining house, not subsidiary to any foreign-controlled company'.

Peter van Rensburg completed a long and distinguished career at GFSA in 1983 when he was deputy chairman. A mining engineer, he joined the company after military service in World War II. As chairman for many years of the Far West Rand Dolomitic Water Association, he had to cope with the social problems connected with mining on the West Wits Line, such as dewatering and sinkholes.

[1] R R M Cousens was the son of a Gold Fields man. His father, W R G Cousens, had been underground manager at the Jupiter mine early in the century.

[2] Including a prominent British Government Minister. Sir Geoffrey Howe, in 1986 Britain's Foreign Secretary, visited Kloof in February 1976 when he was conducted over the mine by its manager, Bertie Oberholzer.

[3] He is suitably commemorated by Christopherson Park near the Turffontein race course.

[4] Jamieson had been a South African champion long-distance runner. In 1927, during the diamond rushes in the Western Transvaal, he made his athletic prowess available to his friends who were staking claims. He ran for them and out-distanced their competitors.

CHAPTER NINE

1971 and All That

Everything, it seemed, was happening in 1971, that *annus mirabilis* in the life of Gold Fields. And, as so often in the past, it was all happening at exactly the right time. Fortune had smiled on West Witwatersrand Areas when it had come into existence in 1932 six weeks before the gold price began to soar, after the Gold Standard was abandoned. Now, nearly forty years later, it was happening all over again. This time West Wits was exchanging clothes with GFSA; thereafter, it not only looked like GFSA, it was GFSA. No one would deny that West Wits deserved to wear the antique mantle of Gold Fields of South Africa. It had, after all, mothered all the West Wits mining companies and produced outsize off-spring, such as West Driefontein, thereby assuring the fortunes of Gold Fields and amply deserving its historic name.

Anyone attempting to write the history of Gold Fields of South Africa is sometimes tempted to call out down the long corridor of the past: 'Will the real Gold Fields of South Africa please stand up.' There have been several. There was the Gold Fields of South Africa that operated out of an office in the old Johannes-burg suburb of Doornfontein until 1892, when Consolidated Gold Fields came into existence. There was the Gold Fields of South Africa that was really African Land and Investment until 1959 and there is Gold Fields of South Africa that is really West Witwatersrand Areas. There is a famous equestrian statue in Paris; it stands on the Pont Neuf looking down on the Seine below. The statue looks like King Henry IV – the great Henry of Navarre who protected the Huguenots with his Edict of Nantes. Underneath, however, it is really Napoleon. When the Emperor went out of favour, they melted him down and turned him into Henry IV. It was not that West Wits had gone out of favour and had to be melted down. On the contrary, this company, which had been born a South African in 1932, was the favourite at the Gold Fields court and was the obvious choice for the Gold Fields crown when it was decided 'to create a South African mining house not subsidiary to any foreign-controlled company', in the words of the announcement of 7 June 1971, which heralded the negotiations to merge West Wits and GFSA.

Gold Fields had, as usual, taken its cue with impeccable timing, for 1971 marked the centenary of the first gold discovered in the Transvaal, on the farm *Eersteling* – 300 kilometres north of Johannesburg, between Potgietersrus and

Pietersburg. South Africa saluted the occasion by announcing that for the first time in history its gold mines had produced 1 000 tons of gold in that year, a peak that has not been scaled since. Gold Fields' mines alone that year had been responsible for a record 195 tons of gold; there had been an exceptional yield of 19,1 grams a ton[1] and working profits of R75,5 million. In London, Donald McCall told his shareholders that Consolidated Gold Fields was getting 41 percent of its profits from South Africa. And, in Johannesburg, GFSA was confident that gold production on the West Wits Line 'will continue to increase for several years as increased production from the newer mines exceeds reduced output from the older mines'.

Great mining, industrial or commercial organizations do not re-organize themselves simply because it makes for a tidy history or even to suit the prevailing economic or political climate. This may have a background influence, paint in the decor for negotiations, but in the end changes are made because they are in the best interests of business. And that, finally, persuaded Consolidated Gold Fields in London to make the difficult, even painful decision, to cut the painter and let its totally owned subsidiary in South Africa float off as an independent South African mining house in its own right. It made economic sense.

Discussions had taken place over two or three years and various schemes had been considered of how best to effect the change. In the end it was a well-thought out plan that was announced since it seemed to confer benefits on all three companies involved, Consolidated Gold Fields, Gold Fields of South Africa and West Witwatersrand Areas. McCall, in his Chairman's Report in 1970, had spoken of constant changes that had been going on in South Africa. 'Administratively, there were many changes in our South African organization. The re-grouping of the base metals and minerals interests continued and steps were taken to re-organize the smaller mining finance companies and also our industrial and property interests. The consolidation of these holdings into fewer but larger units should make the running of the companies more efficient.'

On 29 September 1971 Gold Fields put out a Press statement in Johannesburg to say that six days earlier they and West Wits had signed an agreement whereby West Wits, through its wholly-owned subsidiary, West Wits Investments, would acquire the undertaking of GFSA, other than the shares it held in West Wits itself. These assets were valued at R45,4 million. In return West Wits was to issue GFSA 3 350 000 shares of twenty-five cents each credited as fully paid. In order to do this West Wits would raise additional funds of R20 million by means of a rights issue to its shareholders before the end of June 1972. Everything, however, was subject to West Wits changing its name to Gold Fields of South Africa. Meanwhile, to ensure that the enlarged West Wits company under its new name should not be a subsidiary of Consolidated Gold Fields, the British company would arrange for sufficient of the rights to which it and its subsidiaries were entitled on existing holdings, to be placed with South African institutions. In that way, it would end up with less than fifty percent in the new GFSA. It would be a minority shareholder.

The emergence in 1971 of Gold Fields of South Africa as an independent South African company inspired Len Lindeque's cartoon in the Financial Gazette *on 8 October 1971.*

The assets of the new South African mining house, Gold Fields of South Africa, would be some R225 million. A special meeting of West Wits shareholders on 21 October 1971 accepted the scheme without modification. The circular they had received beforehand was most convincing. It pointed out the tremendous advantages to their almost exclusively gold mining company would be the base metals and minerals interests that GFSA had been developing. In effect, they would be acquiring a ready-made family of subsidiary companies. In June 1971 the companies in the GFSA group had an estimated value of R750 million. These included eight gold mining companies, seven other mines producing coal, diamonds, fluorspar, lead, phosphates, tin, vanadium, wolfram and zinc, a company operating an electrolytic zinc refinery, a group of property companies and a cluster of engineering firms. The list reflected the activity that had been going on during the 1960s at 75 Fox Street. It was quite clear to West Wits shareholders that GFSA was bringing a handsome dowry to the merger. They did not know whether to shout hurrah or *uhuru!*

The new and powerful South African mining house, Gold Fields of South Africa, that emerged in the latter half of 1971 as a result of this merger, aroused considerable interest in the country. The *Financial Gazette* in Johannesburg published a cartoon to illustrate the new South African image of the company. In Cape Town, *Die Burger*, major mouthpiece of Afrikanerdom, after describing the background to the changes, commented: 'Another aim is to create a South African controlled mining house ... the fact that the new Gold Fields will be South African controlled has many advantages for the group. In the first place its

257

borrowing powers will be expanded. Secondly, the group will now be able to expand to Rhodesia, something that Gold Fields as a British company could not do. Thirdly, there is the limitation placed on foreign companies' participation in prescribed mineral ventures, such as uranium. The theoretical merger is in fact a take-over of Gold Fields by West Witwatersrand Areas but because the two companies are in the same group, it is in actual fact a merger.'

A leading South African financial journalist, Harold Fridjhon, commented: 'By detaching the Gold Fields operation in this country from its British parent, it opens the way for this powerful South African company to stride independently forward. GFSA will no longer be dependent on external finance. Financing can be local – particularly loan capital. And as South African institutions, among them SA Mutual, will have a reasonably large stake in GFSA the financing of interesting long-term projects should not prove difficult.' The *Sunday Express* in Johannesburg saw it quite simply as 'the group is now proceeding with the merger largely for fund-raising purposes'. Borrowing powers in the past may have been restricted but now GFSA had become a mining house in its own right, a name on the Stock Exchange. It had freed itself from the economic conditions of another country, Britain, which controlled the operations of its former custodian, Consolidated Gold Fields. That company's rights above forty-nine percent in the new GFSA had been parcelled out among several South African institutions, including SA Mutual and Syfrets. When that happened, new blood was introduced to the board at Gold Fields. Jan Pijper came in from the Old Mutual and Len Abrahamse from Syfrets.

For the board of Consolidated Gold Fields in London it had been a difficult decision to take. As the initial Press statement of 7 June 1971 had pointed out to the South African public, it was this company, Consolidated Gold Fields, that 'was largely responsible for the finding of the bulk of the capital required during the Thirties and immediately after World War II to finance the development of the West Wits Line'. In the deteriorating relationship between Britain and South Africa during the 1980s, it has often been forgotten that it was British capital and the faith of the British investor that made possible the spectacular achievements in so many fields in South Africa and not least on the West Wits Line. For Donald McCall, chairman of CGF in 1971, it was a painful duty to let GFSA go. 'I was against it,' he was to say some fifteen years later, though he acknowledged that subsequent events had proved that the decision was right. Consolidated Gold Fields' participation in the old West Wits company had been pushed up to forty-nine percent of the new GFSA and the British company, with the increased rights that this conferred on it, stood to gain even more than it had done in the past from its interests in South Africa. And this would be an important factor when it had to find money to finance its developments in other parts of the world.

While, under the new arrangements, CGF increased its participation, Anglo-American which had had three directors on the board of West Wits, saw its own participation reduced to fourteen percent by the merger. The old fear, so often expressed in the past at 75 Fox Street, that Anglo was after the West Wits Line, had finally receded. Or so it seemed. For the first time Gold Fields of South Africa had an Anglo American director on its board. So perhaps the old cat and mouse game would merely take a different form. As *Finance Week* was to say in 1984: 'There is something timeless about Anglo's moves on GFSA and its high quality gold mines on the West Wits Line.'

The change that took place in 1971 in the relationship between the company in London and the company in Johannesburg was part of a process that had been going on generally since the end of the Second World War, whereby the dominance of international mining houses, whether in Britain or the United States, was being challenged by the rise of domestically-controlled or national mining companies in the major producing countries. The result, as seen in South Africa in 1971, was a switch in the balance of power to the host countries, from the 'we' in London to the 'they' in South Africa. The day had passed when, as a London memorandum could say: 'Johannesburg has been instructed to remit £500 000 of their surplus funds ... it is recommended that Johannesburg be instructed to make a further round sum remittance of £1,5 million as soon as they are in a position to do so.' A British financial writer commented: 'No longer could the South African board be instructed to do anything; it could only be persuaded by its largest shareholder, subject of course to South African laws and conditions. The South African company quickly and determinedly stood at arm's length from London and the once voluminous correspondence dwindled to a trickle.' J C Williams, a director of the old GFSA and until his retirement in 1975 of the new GFSA, remembered that when he first came to 75 Fox Street after the Second World War, reporting to London was on an extensive scale; in fact it was the ambition of his colleague, W M Barclay, to get the regular report up to fifty pages. Richard Kitzinger, who was at 49 Moorgate at the time of the changeover in 1971, recalled that considerable care was taken to respect the new status of GFSA and not to give offence by a lack of tact. Neither company, however, was prepared to surrender to the other the colloquial name 'Gold Fields'; the London company continued to refer to itself as such and stamped its envelopes accordingly. Gold Fields of South Africa did likewise and believed it had a better claim to it since it was geographically located in the gold fields and the London company, obviously, was not.

Fortune, which had taken an unwavering interest in Gold Fields, had apparently been watching the merger with approval for this had barely become effective when it intervened once again on the side of the company. In December 1971 the price of gold on the free market began to take off sharply and started the process of turning Gold Fields into a very rich company. Ever since 1968, when the two-tier system came in, the international monetary authorities had been fighting a series of rearguard actions to preserve the status quo to keep the official price of gold pegged down. For South Africa the battle for a higher gold price was crucial. Men like Busschau, Holloway and Diederichs had been keeping up their offensive. In December 1969 South Africa had been able to make an agreement with the IMF in Washington whereby it supplied substantial quantities of newly-mined gold to replenish national reserves. This, South Africa felt, acknowledged the continuing importance of gold to the monetary system. The need for a higher gold price was becoming urgent for South Africa because inflation was sending up costs steeply, making it uneconomic to mine low-grade ore. Between 1935 and 1968 the fixed selling price of gold had kept the industry in a straitjacket, a fact which nevertheless had had a salutary influence on successive South African governments since it forced them to make a strenuous effort to combat inflation. During the 1960s the gold mining industry had restrained unit cost increases to an annual rate which was on average in line with the inflation rate of the country as a whole. But in the 1970s these costs began to gallop away, in some years to almost double the inflation rate.

In December 1971, as the new GFSA was spreading its wings, the international gold price peggers were once more in flight. John Shilling, the Anglo American director who joined the GFSA board, was President of the Chamber of Mines at the time, and commented: 'The international monetary system agreed at Bretton Woods in 1944 and spelt out in the Articles of Agreement of the IMF finally broke down on August 15, 1971.' The American President, Richard Nixon, had announced the suspension of the convertibility of the US dollar into gold. This was intended to stimulate employment and to adjust the balance of foreign trade in the United States' favour. In December that year came the Smithsonian Agreement, named after the Smithsonian Institute in Washington where it was signed; this came after long negotiations between major trading countries and resulted in a small reduction in the gold parity of the inconvertible dollar. The mighty dollar was clearly no longer 'as good as gold', as the anti-gold lobby had claimed. Other countries adjusted their currencies in relation to the dollar. Shilling put his finger on the significance of this when he said: 'The devaluation of the dollar resulting in an increase in the official dollar price of gold from thirty-five to thirty-eight US dollars an ounce was the first such rise since 1934 and was a step of potential importance because, despite the nominal amount of the adjustment, it emphasized the basic role of gold and that the dollar price was not in fact immutable.' The practical effect of the change in the official price of gold was minimal as far as the gold producers were concerned but it was important psychologically and would lead in due time to the end of the official price. The practical effect on the gold producers was seen on the free market, for just as the dollar was devalued in relation to gold, so on 21 December 1971 did South Africa devalue the Rand by 12,25 percent in relation to other currencies. The gold producers, selling their product abroad, now stood to have many more Rand in their pockets as a result. Ian Louw commented: 'Shareholders would have expectations of rising dividends. Established mines with no expansion costs would pass on profits and it would make a marked difference to struggling mines. Devaluation has removed the uncertainty for foreign investors about the position of the Rand and has improved the investment climate.'

Coming to Johannesburg to address a financial conference, David Lloyd Jacob of Consolidated Gold Fields in London made the startling forecast that gold might reach eighty dollars by 1980! The free market price had already set off in hot pursuit of that distant target. By June 1972 it reached sixty-six dollars and on the first anniversary of the Smithsonian Agreement was only ten dollars short of Lloyd Jacob's figure. Later it fell back to sixty-five dollars. Lloyd Jacob's investigations had already brought additional comfort for the gold producers since these revealed that the non-monetary market for gold had suddenly become extremely important. In 1968, for instance, of 1 300 tons of gold produced in the free world, some 1 270 was required for jewellery and industry. In 1970, despite a recession in the United States, demand for gold as a commodity rose to 1 418 tons, and in 1971 the non-monetary consumption of gold actually exceeded the aggregate of the free world's production and Soviet sales. The shortfall had to be made up from official and private dishoarding. All this was good news for the newly independent Gold Fields of South Africa, whose investment in gold mining companies in 1971 made up eighty-one percent of its assets and the same percentage of its income. It was particularly well positioned to profit from the dramatic rise in the gold price, which in July 1973 briefly topped 130 dollars. Then in November that year came the climactic event of the year when the two-tier system was finally abandoned. The psychological war was over. The attempt to demonetize gold and recast it solely as a commodity had failed. The two-tier system, which had followed the failure of the gold pool in 1968, was designed to allow buying and selling of newly mined gold in the open market while placing severe restrictions on trading in monetary gold. 'Gold,' said Robin Plumbridge, 'from being threatened, experienced a renaissance. It withstood the attempts to remove it entirely from the monetary scene and remained an important part of the reserve assets of central banks. Attempts to contain its price similarly failed and, once agreed, the price rose nearly six-fold in a two-and-a-half year period.' That was very nice for Gold Fields and very nice for Plumbridge, who in 1972 had taken over the 'gold portfolio' in the cabinet of the new GFSA.

'A rising gold price has brought long delayed benefits to investors in gold mining companies and to the country,' said John Shilling in his presidential address to the Chamber. 'It may also prepare the way for further advances in the mining of other minerals and in the economy in general. It would seem vital that the opportunity be grasped and not wasted by lack of reasonable capacity for innovation and adaptation to changing times.' It was a time of fresh opportunity for South Africa, he said. This was particularly true for Gold Fields of South Africa, whose new-found independence as a South African company had been achieved at exactly the right moment to profit from the transformation in the prospects of its main product, gold. By a curious turn of events, the six months in which the changes were being put through to bring the new GFSA into existence, were the same six months in which the international negotiations were going on and which established the market conditions for gold mining in the 1970s. Gold Fields of South Africa more than matched the performance of South Africa itself, when between 1972 and 1974 the Republic showed a growth rate that was the envy of the world. Each year Ian Louw had a better story to tell his shareholders. In 1974, GFSA profits had gone up by 145 percent on those of the previous year and had reached R35,6 million; this was largely due to the increase of seventy-eight percent in the average price of the gold coming from its mines, going up from R1 588 a kilogram in 1973 to R2 820 a kilogram; this compared with a price four years earlier of R860. In 1974, it was up to R3 300. Group mines, that year of 1974, had increased working profits by 107 percent, from R164 million to R340 million. Shareholders, having received R56 million in 1973, got more than twice that amount the following year, R120 million. The company, which in the past had had to rely on handouts from London to finance its development and expansion, appeared to be awash in money. In London, too, Donald McCall was smiling all the way to the bank. His company's forty-nine percent interest in GFSA was providing in 1973 some forty-two percent of the revenue of the British company. Two years later he was telling his shareholders what he had been doing with the money. 'During the past five years we have spent over £50 million in the United Kingdom on the plant and equipment of our operations in this country and have done so partly from the income from our investments overseas. Our interests abroad have thus been of direct help to investment and employment in Britain.' It was no doubt a comforting thought for those at 75 Fox Street to know that the fruits of their labours in the South African vineyard were promoting the economic development of Britain. However, the increasingly vociferous anti-South Africa lobby in Britain could hardly be expected to see it in this way. In fact, that year, 1975, the Christian Concern for Southern Africa organization brought out a report in which Gold Fields of South Africa was singled out for special criticism. And the Church of England sold its 70 000 shares in Consolidated Gold Fields.

There was much else happening in that memorable year of 1971 to emphasize that the old Gold Fields chapter had ended and that a new, totally different one had begun. Sub Nigel, for instance, acknowledged the fact and, at the end of the year, closed down the mining operations that for so long, in good times and bad, had sustained the company. However, since changing names and functions seemed to be all the fashion, with West Wits becoming GFSA, Sub Nigel, having hung up its helmet, decided to go into the property business. It joined another old faithful, Luipaards Vlei and the existing property company, New Durban, to form the Gold Fields Property Company. An echo from the distant past was the necessity for Gold Fields to seek from the courts in England permission for Luipaards Vlei to take on its new role, since England was where it had been registered during Queen Victoria's reign. Sub Nigel clung on to its mining title until 1984, but it was more than a souvenir and fetched R1,2 million. It had, meanwhile, got rid of some of its old props; one of its little locos became a feature at the Mining Museum at Crown Mines; another went to Australia where it was run as a private venture on sixty-four kilometres of track.

Sub Nigel was a piece of South African history; in 1971 it lost its name but had found a new role. That was also the fate that year of Gold Fields' oldest ally among the mining houses, Rand Mines. It had been created in the last century to be the South African arm of Wernher, Beit, later Central Mining, the companies with which Gold Fields might have merged, had the negotiations of 1956 not failed. That other historical house, General Mining, had already gone to Federale Mynbou with the help of Harry Oppenheimer. Now Rand Mines, again with some prompting from Harry Oppenheimer, had been taken over by Punch Barlow on very favourable terms and joined his industrial empire under the name Barlow Rand. When that happened, many felt that that would be the end of the historic mining company, but they were wrong, for the mining division of Barlow Rand developed once more into one of the giants of the mining industry. And Robert Annan, who had once enquired who or what was Thomas Barlow, was still alive to see it happen.

The old order was changing, however. In 1971 some of the old mines, like Sub Nigel, were signing off. So, too, were some of those who had been part of the history of the company in earlier times. Rudolf Krahmann, the man who had traced the West Wits Line in 1931, using his magnetometer as if it were a compass setting a course for Gold Fields' golden future, died that year at the age of seventy-five. Two of Gold Fields' directors retired that year. Deryck Gettliffe, after thirty-four years with the company, followed his brother Rupert into retirement and went to live in the Natal Midlands. Max Walker, too, decided to go. He had been chairman of Rooiberg during an important period of expansion in the company's tin interests.

As a result of the reorganization that had taken place during 1971 with the emergence of an independent GFSA, Louw had been putting together his new team. Robin Hope had decided to give up his London post as deputy-chairman of Consolidated Gold Fields and returned to Johannesburg to rejoin the GFSA board. In 1974 he became joint deputy-chairman, together with Robin Plumbridge, thereby gaining the unique distinction of having been deputy-chairman, first of the London company, then of the Johannesburg company. Back on the Rand, he took on the challenging task of directing the company's drive into the field of base metals and minerals. Among other things, he became Chairman of Rooiberg Minerals and Apex Mines. The other Robin and fellow Rhodes Scholar took over responsibility for the gold division where he was assisted by Peter van Rensburg, the mining engineer. Oxford, however, did not have it all its own way. Cambridge, in the person of Dru Gnodde, was also there. Among the variety of his duties was responsibility for the company's industrial interests. André Taute was the board's technical director. J C Williams, who had built up a reputation as a skilful negotiator, was in charge of the property interests, where he was being assisted by Bernard van Rooyen who, like Robin Hope, had returned home from CGF in London. Bruce Forsyth, like Gnodde a product of St John's College and Cambridge, had also returned to Fox Street after a spell with the British company, and was working with Hope in the base metals section.

The euphoria created by a rising gold price just as Gold Fields was setting off along independence road, did not make the company any less conscious of the problems that it was facing on the West Wits Line. Here its ambitious plans for East Driefontein had had to be revised because of the setback of the West Driefontein flooding in 1968. Until the long drawn-out dewatering of the Bank Compartment had been completed, it could not start milling. The battle that the two Driefonteins had waged against the water with so much skill and determination had aroused the sympathy and admiration of mining men everywhere. As the *SA Mining and Engineering Journal* commented at the end of 1971: 'Apart from what this has meant for the two mines involved, the knowledge acquired cannot but contribute substantially to the solution of underground water problems on mines throughout the world.'

East Drie's misfortunes were due to what had happened at West Drie; now West Drie, to make up for this, was helping East Drie to get moving, an act of co-operation that was perhaps the curtain-raiser for the merging of the two mines later on. A tributing agreement between the two mining companies gave East Drie a chance to start mining the VCR in part of West Drie's No 4 shaft. By the end of 1971 the dewatering had been completed and soon East Drie was carrying out trial milling. By the end of June 1972, there were working profits of some R71 000. East Drie at last was on its way but it had a long way to go to make up for what had been lost in 1968. The mine had already absorbed R54 million in capital and in May 1972 it had to raise another R20,6 million with a rights issue. But it fully justified all the effort that had been put into it and has become one of the world's great mines. By 1980 that R100 million that had gone into its development looked somewhat less alarming than it had done in the early 1970s; by 1980 East Drie was producing revenue of R50 million a month! And it had an expected life of half a century.

Water was not the only worry that Gold Fields had during the first year of its operating as an independent company, although even on the East Rand water had caused complications; at Vlakfontein abnormally heavy rains had caused flooding in the mine and a temporary suspension of mining. Fire had been another hazard. At West Driefontein at the beginning of 1972 and at Kloof the previous year, serious outbreaks of underground fires had curtailed operations and would have reduced earnings of the mine had not the lower production been bought at the higher gold price, thus reducing the financial damage.

Neither fire nor water, however, would deter Gold Fields during the 1970s from pressing on further with new exploitation of the West Wits Line. With their seven producing mines, one of which, West Driefontein, was the largest single producer in the world, Gold Fields was providing 15 percent of the gold of the non-Communist world. Now there was talk of an eighth mine to exploit the VCR south of Doornfontein. At the top of the drawing boards at 75 Fox Street the name Deelkraal had appeared, the name of one of the oldest farms in the Transvaal. In 1971 Donald McCall had told his shareholders: 'At Deelkraal, drilling for gold has now finished and an evaluation of the area is being made.' The next year he spoke of the feasibility of establishing a mine in the Deelkraal area, and yet again a year later he said that drilling around Deelkraal 'has confirmed our conclusion reached last year that the reef would support the establishment of a new gold mine'. Gold Fields of South Africa had already gone to work, acquiring further mineral rights and applying for a lease to cover an area of 2 366 hectares. In 1974 appeared the Deelkraal company.

It was not only Gold Fields who was busy in the area. Anglo American had been looking westward towards Deelkraal from their Western Deep Levels. Between the two of them lay Elandsrand and less than a year after Deelkraal was floated, Elandsrand joined the West Wits Line mining family. The two mines adjoin each other and when, in 1976, Harry Oppenheimer set off the first shaft-sinking blast, he could see the Gold Fields property over the fence. Perhaps with his father in mind and the past history of rivalry between the companies, he spoke about the benefit friendly rivalry could have upon the achievement of excellence. Gold Fields had its own reasons for hoping Anglo would achieve excellence at Elandsrand; it had a valuable financial interest in it which had come about in unusual circumstances. One of the Gold Fields subsidiaries was Witwatersrand Deep Limited which had an interest in portions of the Elandsrand and Buffelsdoorn farms on which the Anglo American mine was to be established. This gave it a nine-and-a-half percent interest in the equity of the new gold mining company.

In the list of Wit Deep directors appeared the name A E Short which, to the uninitiated might seem strange since Bert Short was the Town Treasurer of Paarl in the Cape and had held the post for thirty years. His interest in gold mining had been aroused in 1957 by an advertisement in a newspaper relating to shares in Wit Deep, which came to Gold Fields with the acquisition of New Union Goldfields. The farm Leeuwpoort, where Tommy Muller had run around as a child, was part of Wit Deep's interests and Short, having bought shares in the company, developed an obsession about Leeuwpoort which he believed would produce great riches. Eventually he built up a hoard of 300 000 Wit Deep shares and when, in the 1960s, West Wits Areas set about acquiring all of Wit Deep with its Leeuwpoort interests, Short did his best to prevent it. He won what the Press called a David and Goliath contest and was invited to join the Wit Deep board. 'It was a nice gesture to invite me,' he was to say, 'they were not obliged to do so.' He had the satisfaction also of seeing his faith in Leeuwpoort rewarded. Portion of that farm was incorporated in the East Drie lease area.

In launching Western Deep Levels back in the 1950s, Sir Ernest Oppenheimer had shown great courage, since in terms of the money values of that time, a vast capital sum was required. In making a start with Deelkraal in 1974, Gold Fields also showed courage for the gold reefs lay at considerable depth and in the intervening six years before the mine was due to produce, anything might happen. During the previous four years costs had gone up by forty-three percent while throughout the 1970s the gold price went up and down like a yo-yo. It was becoming increasingly difficult to make financial plans for the elephantine pregnancy of a modern gold mine. In 1974, Gold Fields reckoned on R85 million to take Deelkraal through to production. Later this sum was adjusted to R100 million; in February 1977 it reached R125 million and in the end there was a bill for R140 million. This sum would have been even higher had not management acted with intelligent foresight. They bought equipment before it was needed and stored it. The reduction plant was up a full year before it could be used. Housing was ready before there was anyone to live there. Gold Fields had stolen a march on inflation.

If Gold Fields had shown courage in developing Deelkraal with all the attendant economic risks, it was at the same time acting within the spirit and legends of Deelkraal. The place was part of South African mythology. It is probably the oldest farm name in the Transvaal and describes an historic event that took place on the property in 1837. Here the wagons of the Voortrekkers had gone into laager; here conferred the great Trek leaders, Hendrik Potgieter, founder of Potchefstroom, Gert Maritz, Pretorius and Uys. After the battle of Vegkop that year, the Matabele had got away with 55 000 head of Boer cattle. Two punitive raids by the Trekkers brought them back to where the Boers were in laager in the Gatsrante. The cattle were then divided up – hence the name Deelkraal. The affair also divided the Boers, causing them to quarrel. Potgieter and Maritz parted and went their separate ways into South African history. Later the Geldenhuys family developed a farm there.

From Deelkraal the Voortrekkers had blazed new trails across Southern Africa; at Deelkraal in another century GFSA mining engineers pioneered new methods and took new initiatives which advanced the technology of mining at depth. Unlike the two mines that preceded Deelkraal, Kloof and East Driefontein, each of which had been developed from an adjoining mine, Deelkraal was on its own. Two vertical shafts had to be sunk simultaneously and as quickly as possible to allow access to the reef. Some brilliantly conceived innovations were seen. For instance, the No 1 sub-vertical shaft was positioned vertically below No 2 shaft and was sunk as a continuation of the barrel of No 2 shaft. When the time came for No 2 shaft and No 1 sub-vertical shaft to be equipped, No 1 shaft had already been commissioned. It was therefore possible for the sub-vertical shaft hoist chambers to be excavated and equipped concurrently with the equipping of the other two shafts. Time – and therefore money – was saved. By this time South African mine-shaft sinkers had become world famous for their exploits. One was beginning to see some surprising developments in new mines such as Deelkraal and East Drie. 'The idea of a lumbering earthmoving machine and 10 ton dumper trucks moving along underground, below sea level, on the Witwatersrand is difficult to imagine,' wrote the *Mining Survey*. This was what was happening in 1975 when the so-called 'Big End' at East Driefontein was being created with a cross-sectional area of twenty-seven square metres to provide ventilation for all the lower working areas between No 1 and No 2 shafts.

Deelkraal was to share with the two Driefonteins the distinction of having the most powerful fans ever installed on the mines to blow cool air down the shafts; they move 31 000 tons of air through the mine every twenty-four hours. Deelkraal marked up another record with the most powerful hoists needed to move men and materials in elevators up and down the shafts. The mine hoists at No 1 shaft at Deelkraal has a motor capacity of 8 250 kilowatt which is about the equivalent of the power generated by 1 200 small cars pulling together. The hoists can pull as much as twenty-three tons of rock and conveyance up two and a half kilometres of shaft. As Gold Fields went from Kloof to East Driefontein to Deelkraal, its progress along the West Wits Line was marked by massiveness in all its aspects, not only in the size of the mines but in everything else, shafts, winders, equipment, capital costs, production figures, profits. In 1979 West Driefontein proved its own particular massiveness by finally overtaking the Crown Mines record to become the world's largest gold producer. With 1 500 tons of gold, it had been responsible for two percent of all the gold ever found.

Deelkraal was never expected to become another Driefontein but it came to justify all the effort and money that had been invested in it. Indirectly, Deelkraal provided the occasion for Consolidated Gold Fields in London to dispose of its platinum interests in South Africa which it had held since 1924. Platinum had not been among the interests that Harvie-Watt had handed over to Gold Fields of South Africa in 1959. At this stage CGF had a substantial interest in Rustenburg Platinum mines. From time to time during the 1970s, whenever there was a large-scale buying of platinum shares, the Johannesburg Press would suggest that Gold Fields was trying to wrest control of the platinum industry from JCI; they even suggested that the old gentleman's agreement between CGF and JCI had been forgotten. JCI's position had grown stronger as a result of a compli-cated scheme implemented in 1972 with the approval of Consolidated Gold Fields. Through this scheme the rights of a Rand Mines-Anglo American-General Mining consortium were acquired for Rustenburg by the issuing of a large block of Union Platinum shares. As a result of this deal, JCI obtained control of Union which, with Waterval, had been a Consolidated Gold Fields company. As has been seen, these two companies together with JCI's P P Rust were the corporate shareholders in the operating company, Rustenburg Platinum. In due course, following a further rationalization, Union Platinum acquired all the shares in Rustenburg Platinum and changed its name to Rusten-burg Platinum Holdings. Consolidated Gold Fields ended up with a 15 percent interest compared with JCI's 21,1 percent. In August 1976 Consolidated Gold Fields, in advising its shareholders that they were about to move out of platinum, said: 'A substantial investment in a company which is effectively controlled by others is not always in the Company's best interests in the long term.' CGF had been inhibited in the past from selling its platinum interests because of the revenue it was bringing in. This revenue had now begun to decline. In 1975 Deelkraal, appearing in the stock exchanges, increased its capital to R50 million. Britain was once more in economic difficulties and overseas investment was not being encouraged since it meant an outflow of funds from Britain. A British in-stitution wishing to take up shares would have had to go through the dollar pool, paying the dollar premium and thereby adding to its costs. CGF decided to take up its participation in Deelkraal by using the proceeds of its sale of platinum interests in South Africa. It seemed to offer better prospects as an investment.

After Consolidated Gold Fields had given up its platinum interests in South Africa, Gold Fields of South Africa felt it was free to take its own independent look at platinum. In due course it began its own exploration in the Bushveld Igneous Complex, as it was called, where Merensky back in the 1920s had made his discoveries and given his name to the Merensky Reef. JCI, though very big in platinum after the departure of Consolidated Gold Fields, was not alone in the field. Union Corporation, for instance, had in its Impala mine in what became Bophuthatswana a very valuable property. When, as happened at this time, GFSA was casting an eye on the whole of Union Corporation, Impala added, in its view, to the attractions of the company that Adolf Goertz had founded in the last century.

The attempt by Gold Fields of South Africa to gain control of Union Corporation, and the battle that followed, involving other mining houses, enlivened the Johannesburg mining scene from late 1974 into the early part of the following year. The battle went this way and that. At times it seemed that Gold Fields was going to win, then new cohorts were moved in and the battle was rejoined with increasing bitterness.

In the scuffle, as might be expected, Gold Fields perhaps lost something of its dignified image. It had all been gentlemanly enough to begin with, in fact long before the events of 1974/75. In Busschau's time, J C Williams recalled, they had put up a suggestion that a take-over of Union Corporation might be a worthwhile exercise but how to proceed? Perhaps a chat with Colin Anderson, the Union Corporation chairman for a start? Williams thought that that would lead nowhere. In January 1974 Gold Fields made a detailed study of what a merger of these two historic mining houses might do for Gold Fields. As Louw was to say later, the greatly strengthened mining house that would result 'will be able to tackle mining ventures on a scale which would be beyond the capability of either company on its own'. Still nothing happened. Pre-emptive strikes, dawn raids had never been part of Gold Fields' tactics. However, by failing to take the initiative and deciding to act only after someone else had done so, Gold Fields entered the arena with the sun in its eyes and the wind in its face. It was Barlow Rand that had made the move. Having acquired Rand Mines cheaply, they thought they might repeat the performance with Union Corporation. Union Corporation, though German in origin, had been registered as a British company and had remained so until T P Stratton, as chairman, had transferred its domicile to South Africa. Its chairman in 1974 was Edward Pavitt, who was keen to link up with Barlows. He had realized that Union Corporation needed stronger backing, that it was vulnerable to a take-over. Looking round the mining houses, he had decided that Barlow Rand would suit him best. The mild nature of the Barlow Rand bid made it look like a defensive get-together. Once the news was out that Barlow Rand was bidding for Union Corporation, Gold Fields realized that it was now or never. They quickly pulled their dormant plans out of the files and in August 1974 made a better bid than that of Barlows, at the same time interfering with Pavitt's plans.

Ted Pavitt, a distinguished mining engineer, had joined Union Corporation in 1946 after military service with the South African Engineers, when he had carried out a dangerous rescue mission in a minefield and been awarded the Military Cross. When the Unicorp battle began, he may well have imagined himself back in the minefield.

Gold Fields had made an offer for the entire capital of Union Corporation. For every 100 Unicorp shares it offered six new ordinary shares and seven convertible redeemable preference shares of its own. The interest on the preference shares was to be a cumulative seven and a half percent per annum. Barlow Rand decided to withdraw but this did not mean that it was all over. The Afrikaner mining house, General Mining, since 1971 under the dynamic direction of Wim de Villiers, decided that it, too, would make an attempt on Union Corporation. Mining finance houses did not come on the market every day and even though it was not a particularly convenient time for Genmin, it decided to act all the same. De Villiers obtained the support of Sanlam, his major shareholder, and he believed he had the support of Harry Oppenheimer, who had a minority holding in Genmin and, through Charter Consolidated in London, ten percent of Union Corporation. General Mining, aware that it must not endanger Sanlam's own share of Genmin, put up a partial bid for Union Corporation. It already owned four percent of Unicorp shares. It was now trying to get forty-eight percent and expected to pay for these with a mixture of Genmin and Sentrust shares, together with cash. It was a better bid than Gold Fields' even though it was for only part of the capital. At that point there was an unexpected intervention in what looked like a purely South African affair, from London. The London Take-over Panel, pointing out that all the companies involved in the affair were quoted on the London Stock Exchange, said it could not accept a partial bid from General Mining when GFSA had already made a bid for all the capital. It was now October and it looked as if General Mining would also have to withdraw. Gold Fields, meanwhile, rather half-heartedly, increased its bid, raising the rate on the preference shares from seven and a half to eight and a half percent. This did not seem to impress anyone so for the third time it improved the offer, this time by adding R120 in cash for each 100 Unicorp shares. This now looked as if it might tip the scales. This time the Union Corporation board, which had rejected the earlier offers, not only of Gold Fields but also of General Mining, recommended its shareholders to accept the GFSA bid. 'Throughout the battle,' the *Rand Daily Mail* was to comment, 'Mr Pavitt acted on what he felt was right and in the best interests of staff and shareholders.' It was now December and Unicorp shareholders were given until mid-January to make up their minds. GFSA decided that they would need 50 percent acceptances to proceed. Soon after New Year 1975, readers of the South African Press began to see large advertisements in their newspapers which had been placed by General Mining. They had big headlines in black type, such as 'Reject the Offer by Gold Fields of South Africa' and again 'Ignore the Take-over Bid by GFSA', Unicorp shareholders were being advised – 'Take no action now.' This was fighting talk and General Mining was assembling its forces for a counter-attack. As Tom de Beer of General Mining was to say later: 'We accepted the Panel's ruling but that did not mean we gave up our plans for making a partial bid. In any case we weren't sure what we needed for control. But we reckoned that with 30 percent ourselves and 10 percent through Charter we would be alright.' General Mining had arranged bridging finance of some eighty-five million dollars and was buying shares through the market with the help of London brokers. General Mining with Sentrust had raised its stake to ten percent, satisfying the London Take-over Panel's rules. By the end of November it claimed to have twenty percent of the Union Corporation equity. Later announcements put this at 29,9 percent which, with Charter's ten percent, would have given it a commanding position. At this point, however, Union Corporation advised acceptance of the Gold Fields offer and Wim de Villiers learned that Oppenheimer had decided to throw in the ten percent Charter interest into the GFSA camp. This looked promising for Gold Fields but was bad news for General Mining, which risked being locked into an expensive minority stake in a Union Corporation controlled by Gold Fields. It looked as if the old Boer-Brit rivalry might rear its ugly head once more, for other Afrikaner-dominated institutions now came to General Mining's support. Fortunately for General Mining, Anton Rupert's Rembrandt organization operating world-wide, happened to have funds in London waiting to be employed. It was therefore possible to arrange off-shore facilities for General Mining to do some large-scale buying of Union Corporation shares abroad. Volkskas, too, was throwing in its weight to procure shares. The race was on to get a further twenty percent of them before 25 January, and with the knowledge that GFSA had probably already secured forty-three percent of the equity. It must have been a difficult time of divided loyalties for Tommy Muller, the man who had done so much to build up General Mining but who was now a director of Gold Fields. In the final ten days Gold Fields was pulling out all the stops in its effort to give General Mining the *coup de grâce*. It had everything to offer, since the profits revealed in the December quarterlies were a record. Seven gold mines, after tax, had returned R147 million, an increase of R32 million on the September figures. On 10 January 1975 the *Financial Gazette* in Johannesburg reported: 'As part of its Union Corporation take-over strategy GFSA made an unprecedented move in releasing their December quarterlies a week earlier, thus shattering the traditional Chamber of Mines agreement on publication.' In bending the rules a little at the height of battle, Gold Fields was only following the advice that Lord Harris used to give in the old days. 'Rules are made to be broken, laws are made to be kept.'

However, it did not change anything. Gold Fields did not get its 50 percent and the battle was over. General Mining gained control of Union Corporation and in a couple of years made a bid for the remaining shares. The modern Gencor was born, and after the departure of Wim de Villiers, Ted Pavitt became its chairman. Five years after the battle, in 1979, the *Financial Mail*, looking back, commented: 'Had GFSA won the battle for Unicorp, its earnings and assets growth picture might have been a lot different. And that perhaps underlies the thesis that to be top dog, management has to be bold. Genmin's attitude was that mining houses come up for sale only once in a blue moon. On that basis, climb in and buy control at whatever price and worry about how it is to be paid for afterwards.'

Gold Fields had perhaps learned a lesson but at considerable cost. If its third and final bid had been made at the beginning, there might never have been a battle at all. The bid attempt had cost R2 million but this was not the real cost. Looking back with hindsight, one can see that the acquisition of Union Corporation would have quite transformed GFSA and enormously increased its strength in South Africa, not only in relation to Anglo American, whose giant shadow was never far from Fox Street, but in safeguarding its independence. The figures of those December quarterlies are instructive; Gold Fields' record profits were twenty-five percent of the total profits of the industry; Anglo American had thirty-six percent of them and Union Corporation nine and a half percent. If the bid had succeeded, Gold Fields would have taken on something of the girth of Anglo American. There would have been another interesting development for, if the bid had succeeded, Consolidated Gold Fields' share in GFSA would have been reduced from 49 percent to 29,8 percent. In that study that GFSA had prepared six months before the battle began, it was stated: 'A reduction in CGF interest in an enlarged GFSA to less than forty percent should therefore discourage potential predators and relieve CGF from political pressure to promote social change in South Africa.' As it was, GFSA continued to be vulnerable because it had one big minority shareholder, Consolidated Gold Fields, based in another country, and a would-be predator could still break into 75 Fox Street by climbing through a window at 49 Moorgate. The political predators would also continue to gather there. An enlarged GFSA might also have produced an interesting change in the relationship between the British company and the South African company, whereby the child might become father of the man. GFSA might have been in a position to take over CGF. Even without the acquisition of Union Corporation, GFSA was beginning to outstrip the company from which it had sprung. In mid-1974 Richard Kitzinger was playing a round of golf with his colleague Rudolph Agnew who, in due course, would become chairman of Consolidated Gold Fields as his grandfather, John Agnew, had been. Agnew was about to drive off when Kitzinger remarked to him that the market value of Consolidated Gold Fields was less than the market value of the shareholding in GFSA, so GFSA could buy CGF and get all its other assets for next to nothing. That stopped Agnew for a moment. 'I hope Ian Louw doesn't find out,' he said, then drove off calmly to the next hole.

In the story of a great company the Union Corporation episode belongs to the category, 'All that we shall never be.' It was, of course, a disappointment but in those middle years of the 1970s Gold Fields was fulfilling itself in other ways, busying itself with the multifarious activities which by the end of the decade brought it to the top. In 1980 Gold Fields of South Africa was No 1 in the list of *The Sunday Times* 'Top 100 Companies'. Back in 1972, Ian Louw himself had been listed as one of the Five Businessmen of the Year, after completing the first year of GFSA's operations as an independent company. *The Sunday Times* had said of him: 'Adriaan Louw floated a new mining house on the Stock Exchange, opened a new gold mine, and became one of the first mining house heads to make a definite forecast.'

Ian Louw had confided the gold division on his board to Robin Plumbridge, who soon began to play a prominent role not only for Gold Fields but for South Africa in the new gold game that the country was playing internationally. Inter-gold – the International Gold Corporation – was in a sense a twin of the new GFSA since it had been born in July 1971, the year when everything happened. It was formally registered as a company on the initiative of the Chamber of Mines. Its function was to exploit the market for gold as an industrial and commercial commodity; the existence of demand had already been proved not only by David Lloyd Jacob's researches on behalf of Consolidated Gold Fields but also by those carried out by the Chamber itself. It had sent its research adviser Dr W S Rapson to Europe and North America. He had reported back that the gold producers ought to be preparing themselves to supply a market that would be increasingly industrial in character. Bill Rapson saw a particular opportunity in promoting the use of gold for jewellery. Intergold had opened up a totally new field. The moment had been well chosen for in the early 1970s the gold price had begun to soar and the product that Intergold was promoting round the world from the offices it opened abroad, had increased substantially in value. In 1973 Intergold got a further responsibility, the task of promoting the sale of South Africa's own gold coin, the Krugerrand, that Bill Busschau had done so much to encourage. To Busschau's protégé, Robin Plumbridge, fell the task of building up Intergold and selling the Krugerrand idea and in this way he was to give practical expression to the gold message preached by his predecessor at Gold Fields.

At the age of thirty-four, Plumbridge had become a member of the Gold Producers Committee of the Chamber, and in 1972 was in charge of its gold portfolio, as he was by this time at Gold Fields itself. Two years later he was President of the Chamber of Mines, a post he would fill for the second time before the 1970s were out. The manager of Intergold was a young man named Don Mackay-Coghill, a familiar figure on the Wanderers Ground, since he was one of Transvaal's fast bowlers. He had had no difficulty in transferring his speed off the wicket into his deliveries to the gold markets. 'He received vital guidance and support from another young man who had climbed fast, Robin Plumbridge,' wrote John Lang in his story of the Krugerrand, *Everyman's Gold*. Plumbridge, said Lang, had the special responsibility for launching Intergold. 'He guided the new organization through its formative years, learned as he went, the to him unfamiliar fields of advertising promotion and Press relations while furnishing the company with the firm base of his knowledge of gold's role in the world and of his financial flair. His colleagues on the committee knew him as conservative and sound as well as a brilliant analyst of the factors of profit and loss. When Plumbridge gave the nod to Mackay-Coghill's plans, his older colleagues offered only token resistance to soaring budgets, fed in from the Intergold regional machine.' However, as Lang went on, 'Intergold's arrival on the scene coincided with the beginnings of a new gold rush and an astonishing bonanza … as the new era for gold quickened and flourished, the gold producers' dream of placing a piece of gold in the hands of the man-in-the-street everywhere was soon to be realized to an astonishing degree.' In 1971, Intergold and the new GFSA were making their debut together and as they moved further into the flourishing 1970s, they had in Robin Plumbridge a man with a foot in each of them. When he took over the Presidency of the Chamber, he was the first Gold Fields man to do so since Busschau. Once more he was following in the same footsteps. In due course, these would take him, with Mackay-Coghill or Tom Main of the Chamber of Mines, all over the United States, as they promoted South Africa's gold coin with increasing success. In 1978 an incredible six million ounces of gold had been put into world circulation as Krugerrands. Plumbridge, with the others, was becoming a supersalesman and was growing accustomed to the way things were done in the United States, where public relations was an art of its own. At the New York annual jewellery show in 1976, 600 Krugerrands glittered in a fish tank guarded by a voracious Piranha fish imported from the Amazon for the purpose. Visitors were invited to guess the value of the coins and win a Krugerrand. In Houston a mannequin was presented, wearing a jacket literally studded with Krugerrands. The Krugerrand became a familiar part of American life and over a decade there was an average sale of 3 million coins a year. In 1985 sales had reached 50 million coins in the four sizes that are minted. But that was also the year when, for political reasons, the Krugerrand became a prohibited immigrant in much of the Western world, including the United States and Britain.

During the 1970s, which saw the gold price go from thirty-six dollars in 1970 to 613 dollars in 1979, with numerous gyrations in between, neither Gold Fields nor South Africa itself allowed its head to be turned by the wealth that the gold mines earned. In that single decade GFSA saw its earnings increase elevenfold, its dividends more than eightfold and its assets more than fivefold. But the gold story of this decade had not been without accident. If the price of gold, shorn of its old shackles, was free to rise, it was also free to fall. And this it sometimes did disconcertingly. In December 1974 it was touching 180 dollars and began to nudge the 200 dollar mark, the level chosen, somewhat prematurely, by Diederichs as the basis of calculations for future plans. In mid-1976 it had dropped to 103; in the opening month of 1980 it hit 850 dollars but later dropped 250 dollars in two days. Such yo-yo movements reflected the rise and fall of confidence in world currencies and doubts about the world economy, suddenly hit by steep rises in the price of oil. There was anxiety about future supplies of energy.

The international monetary system was still trying to make sense of itself. In November 1973 the ill-conceived two-tier system for marketing gold was abandoned. Cynics pointed out that any agreement signed in an anthropological museum, such as the Smithsonian Institute, was a dead duck from the start. The Americans declared that the end of the two-tier system would open the way for central banks to sell gold on the free market and that, they believed, would drive the price down. All this was unsettling for gold producers and they watched the several IMF gold auctions with some nervousness. These began in June 1976. The market had no difficulty in absorbing sales from the first two auctions. Then the price dropped to 103 dollars in August 1976, as it became clear that during a seasonal weakness the market would not be able to take in further offerings from the Fund at realistic prices. In due course, however, gold got its head up once more. The decision of IMF members, including South Africa, to revalue their gold reserves at a market related price was encouraging, particularly in South Africa where the producers could then get the market price on delivering the goods to the Reserve Bank. By the end of 1979 the gold price was getting into the stratosphere.

There was, however, another kind of gold that the world, hit by the oil crisis, was talking about – black gold. This was the new, fancy name for old-fashioned, common-or-garden coal. Coal, as a source of power in a world that feared an energy famine, had suddenly become very important. South Africa had vast reserves. Its coalfields, stretching from the southern Transvaal into Natal and covering an area of some 800 square kilometres is one of the four great mineralized areas of the country. Gold Fields was already on the scene when attention was suddenly focused on coal. Its Apex Mines had in the Greenside Colliery one of the largest underground coal mines in the Witbank area. It was already playing a valuable part in providing coal for Highveld Steel and for other sections of the domestic market. Both Escom and Sasol had an expanding appetite for coal. Now, in the mid-1970s there were exciting prospects for important export markets for coal. At the beginning of the 1960s such a market barely existed, but by the end of the Sixties Japan had appeared on the scene to demand a blend of South African coal for its steel mills. Apex joined in with others to meet this demand, undertaking to provide 412 000 tons of low-ash coal annually for a period of eleven years. These new opportunities meant some swift modernization for which R5,5 million in new capital had to be raised. In the early 1960s the coal industry in South Africa was still very much a shovel and muscle industry; the next decade transformed its technology, largely by adapting and improving techniques and machines imported from Europe and America. Mechanization problems at Apex Mines sometimes slowed up progress but from a fairly small mine, producing 1,6 million tons in 1975, developed in due course a very large mine which six years later was producing 2,7 million tons. When Gold Fields took over Apex Mines in 1959, working profits were around R440 000; in 1976, even before the full benefit of the export contracts had been felt, they had reached R6 million. Gold Fields, very aware of the new importance of coal, had stepped up its exploration programmes. Boreholes put down in the Breyten area of the Eastern Transvaal in 1975 had indicated substantial reserves, prompting the *Sunday Express* in Johannesburg to wonder if coal might one day replace gold in the title of the company! In any case, within two years coal had become second to gold as an earner of foreign currency for the country. By the end of the decade production had hit the 100 million tons a year mark, and Gold Fields had started to look around for another colliery. That path would lead to Clydesdale.

The physical signs of South Africa's growth were becoming ever more noticeable. On the Indian Ocean coast at Richards Bay and on the Atlantic at Saldanha Bay, two great new ports were taking shape. Richards Bay was to be South Africa's first deep-water port, about eight times the size of Durban harbour, and would have the world's most advanced coal-loading terminal. Work, financed by the coal mining companies, began at the same time on the construction of a new railway line to link the port, with its harbour facilities, with the coalfields of the Transvaal. The formation of the OPEC oil cartel in 1973 and the steep rise in the price of oil had alarmed the industrialized countries of Western Europe and they saw coal as one of the ways out of their energy problems. This gave a country like South Africa a new opportunity and before long, in addition to supplying Japan, South Africa had become the main external supplier of coal to the European Community until overtaken later by the United States. At Saldanha Bay on the other side of the country, dredgers were preparing the harbour to receive ships of 250 000 tons, coming to fetch the iron ore being railed from Sishen, a very rich iron and manganese field, which had been mined since 1953.

From Saldanha would be exported also some of the fifty or so important minerals that the country possessed and for some of these South Africa had the biggest reserves in the free world. There was a tremendous incentive for Gold Fields, backed by the wealth provided by its gold mines, to participate fully in these developments and to go out and exploit determinedly the base metals and minerals interests which it had inherited or acquired.

Gold Fields had already performed a national service by starting Zincor which had made the country self-sufficient in zinc. Now it took a look at tin in this light. Its interests were concentrated at Rooiberg and Union Tin. Here, too, it took a do-it-yourself decision. The concentrates from these producers which in the old days had been shipped to Malaya, had been treated at the Williams Harvey smelter in England until 1973 when it closed; after that they went to the Dutch company, Phillip AG. Gold Fields had a feasibility study made into the possibility of having its own smelter at Rooiberg and as a result decided to go ahead. In October 1979 this R2 million smelter came into existence. Rooiberg Minerals became Rooiberg Tin and South Africa became self-sufficient in tin. First with zinc, then with tin, Gold Fields was playing a role in the national interest. In a world that was threatening South Africa with boycotts and sanctions, self-sufficiency meant self-preservation.

One of those countries that had introduced a boycott of South Africa was Malaysia, one of the leading tin producers. In due course the little island of Singapore detached itself from Malaya and became an independent republic within the Commonwealth. By this time, the early 1960s, Rooiberg was no longer having its tin smelted by the Straits Trading Company in Singapore. Some years earlier the two families associated with the company, the Bagnalls and the Fergussons, who were related to each other by marriage, had invested heavily in Rooiberg. In 1954, at a time when Rooiberg and the price of tin were beginning to look seedy, an anxious Sir John Bagnall, a director of Rooiberg, had a heart attack and died in the Anglo-French offices in Johannesburg, setting a sad precedent for the chairman of Rooiberg, A W Stewart, who did the same five years later, when Gold Fields took over the company. Sir John Bagnall and Sir Ewen Fergusson had each been chairman of the Singapore company, but Sir John was not succeeded immediately on the Rooiberg board by Sir Ewen.

Hervey Jones, who had retired from Gold Fields in 1951, some four years after the death of his brother 'Peter' Carleton Jones, came in as a director at Rooiberg until 1958, when his place was taken by Sir Ewen Fergusson, who remained a director until his death in 1974. His son, D S B Fergusson, a Singaporean by birth and nationality, took his place. In the official list of directors of this South African company in 1986 his name appears with Singaporean in brackets next to it. His brother, Ewen Fergusson, a career diplomat in the British Foreign Service, was the British Ambassador in Pretoria in the early 1980s.

The Bagnalls and the Straits Trading Company parted with their holdings in Rooiberg but the Fergussons remained to provide a link with the distant past. Some South African companies have British or American directors on their boards but Rooiberg is unique in having a Singaporean. But, then, Rooiberg has always been somewhat different. In addition to its antique past and its links with the outside world, it has always had a very special mining community and has been served by outstanding personalities, men such as G St J 'Sig' Oxley Oxland, who was manager for nearly twenty years and E K 'Ted' McDermott, consulting engineer for seventeen years and chairman for a year following Stewart's death. In later years men such as Brian Moore, who became senior consulting engineer at Gold Fields in 1985, also made their mark at Rooiberg.

In 1983, at the time of the 75th anniversary of Rooiberg, a skilfully researched and highly sympathetic account of the life of this community was produced by Gail Nattrass, herself the wife of a Gold Fields executive. 'In 1970,' she recounted, 'the Government indicated that they might tar the road between Leeuwpoort and Rooiberg if there were enough traffic on it. The people got to hear when the inspectors were coming along to watch and they made hasty arrangements to ride along the road. Dr Baskind was particularly obliging. He made something like fifteen trips that day, using various cars. They got their road.'

Rooiberg's people were resourceful. Many of them were unusual, and two in particular were so unusual that they found a place in the Guinness Book of

Records. Hyla Basson of Vellefontein, who won prizes for her delicate needle-work, was so physically strong she could carry a sack of mielies with one hand or hoist her father and brother on to her shoulders at the same time. Mary Anne Coetzer, who weighed a normal four kilos at birth, grew so fast that, at the age of two, she weighed thirty-five kilos. Between 1977 and the end of the decade, Rooiberg looked as if it were trying to compete with its young inhabitant; it recorded remarkable growth in tonnage, grades and the price of tin. Vellefontein had been re-opened in 1975 and was playing a useful part in contributing to overall output at Rooiberg. In 1980 – in a single year – the before-tax profit at Rooiberg exceeded the total profit-before-tax of the first sixty-three years of its life, from 1908 till 1971.

Union Tin, whose imminent demise had been regularly announced with the annual report over the years, obstinately refused to give up. In 1975 Gold Fields reported that 'its remaining life will probably not exceed two years'. The following year its earnings were the best in its history, for the high price of tin had enabled the mine to treat the waste material from old operations. A commentator in the Press said it looked as if Union Tin was determined to go out 'with a bang, not a whimper'. But not yet. Nearly ten years later its chairman, Michael Fuller-Good, was reporting, 'it is likely that underground mining will, under present circumstances, become unprofitable within the next 18 months. Thereafter the mine will have to be closed and the assets disposed of'. As the mine's 'doctor', Eugene Marais, observed all those decades ago, there is something eternal about the world of the Waterberg.

Gold's glamour, and in the 1970s its increasing glister as a result of a bulging price, tended to overshadow the dramatic growth that took place in the non-gold sector of mining. Certainly, the money earned by gold enabled many of the non-gold projects to get off the ground. South Africa was making itself significant in the whole field of mining, not just in gold and diamonds. And mining was making it possible for the country to develop more rapidly in the non-mining sector. South Africa's economic development was becoming more rounded, more varied and more widely based. Gold Fields, the oldest of the mining houses though the latest to gain its national independence, was in the van of these developments. 'The discovery and acquisition of new ore bodies and of extensions to existing ore bodies is a vital aspect of GFSA's continuing search for new projects,' Ian Louw was to say. 'New Business' had become an important responsibility on the board. If some of the old business, meanwhile, was less than satisfactory, Gold Fields had no scruples about closing it down. In 1975 Star Diamond mine had run at a loss and the following year it was closed down. Fluorspar, too, had gone the same way. There was disenchantment with some of the industrial undertakings that belonged to the diversification fashion of the 1960s. In 1975, Hunslet Taylor was sold for R2 400 000 to Abercom, a company that had been built up with flair by David Lurie and Murray McLean, son of Carleton Jones's Canadian friend, Stowe McLean. Making a success of industrial companies, Gold Fields had discovered, required different entrepreneurial skills from those that made for successful mine management. Gold Fields was turning away from the big conglomerate ambition being pursued by Consolidated Gold Fields in London, and by some of the mining houses in Johannesburg.

In 1975, however, GFSA had been tempted to take a leaf out of CGF's book and become an international company. 'The exploration programme has been expanded in the search for new gold, uranium, base metals and mineral projects and is now being extended,' GFSA reported, 'into Brazil.' This somewhat unusual foray into the international field which was really Consolidated Gold Fields' territory, was done perhaps more in the national interest of South Africa than out of a new-found enthusiasm for foreign fields. South Africa, struggling diplomatically in a largely hostile world, was trying to make friends in South America whose varied countries commanded votes at the United Nations. Gold Fields and other mining companies were prepared to make capital and mining expertise available for the development of mining in South America. Anglo American was another that became active in Peru, Chile and Brazil. Gencor, the Afrikaner mining house, also took an interest though this had nothing to do with the 'Afrikaners' of South America, the descendants of the Boers who had settled there after the Anglo-Boer War.

Among the names of the subsidiaries of Gold Fields of South Africa appeared a new investment company – Gold Fields do Brasil Participacoes. Later, to establish an operating presence, a thirty percent interest was obtained in a company named Minas Del Rey Dom Pedro, which sounded as if it might produce a good sherry but in fact turned out to be a disappointing iron ore producer, and Gold Fields eventually had to write it off as a loss. A Gold Fields consulting geologist, Max Mehliss, whose usual stamping ground was north of the Limpopo, went to Brazil to have a look round but was not greatly enthusiastic about its prospects. Mehliss, throughout his Gold Fields career as a geologist, would sometimes let off steam by writing verse. 'I recall one such occasion after a particularly uncomfortable night in a small Brazilian hostelry in the town of Jacobina whose facilities left much to be desired,' he said, and he concluded:

> 'No, Oppenheimer's welcome here,
> His geologists from far and near,
> May well bemoan their wretched fate
> As they hunt the pennyweight.
>
> GFSA, wiser, far,
> Spend their time in Rio bar,
> Picking brains of better men,
> With some Group Training now and then.'

It was a pity about the Brazilian adventure; it was no more successful commercially than South Africa's diplomatic foray into the area. The Brazilian

Government grew increasingly shy about being seen in South Africa's company; having at first provided a winning post for the annual, much publicized, Cape-to-Rio yacht race, they even withdrew that and the yachts had to make land elsewhere. If going into business with Brazilians on their own ground turned out to be a disappointment, other forms of international co-operation that Gold Fields tried, this time on home ground, were far more promising. In 1977 they decided to join hands with a United States company and the result was one of the most exciting developments in the company's more recent history.

First of all, however, Gold Fields had been reorganizing its interests in the increasingly disputed territory of South West Africa/Namibia, where it had already had contact with the Americans. The capital of the long established South West Africa Company which had come to Gold Fields in 1957, was acquired by Kiln Products which then controlled the zinc, lead, vanadium production at Berg Aukas and the tin/wolfram output from Brandberg West. Kiln Products was responsible for processing the zinc-bearing material produced by these subsidiaries, and for supplying Zincor, whose Springs plant had trebled capacity from 30 000 to 90 000 tons a year during its first ten years of operations.

Meanwhile, Gold Fields had been extending its exploration programmes in Namibia with the energy question in mind; that question meant not only coal but also uranium if nuclear power were to be the answer to the oil problem. In 1977, for the first time in five years, uranium production had increased. Gold Fields was hoping that its Trekkopje prospect near the important Rössing uranium development of the British company, Rio Tinto Zinc (RTZ), might prove worthwhile. It had also been looking at coal prospects in Zimbabwe/Rhodesia. In the late 1970s these territories were in political trouble, as was Angola to the north of Namibia, where the departure of the Portuguese had not brought peace and even South African troops had been involved. The United Nations maintained that South Africa was in illegal possession of Namibia. British companies, such as Consolidated Gold Fields and RTZ, who were involved in the mineral development of Namibia, became caught up in the political struggle. Political activists, such as the Catholic priest Monsignor Bruce Kent, who later became a leading figure in the anti-nuclear campaign, had begun to sharpen their teeth at shareholders' meetings in London, as Ian Louw witnessed when, as a director of CGF, he too was present.

GFSA, in going into partnership in 1977 with the Americans, had the satisfaction at least of knowing that it was doing so in the territory of the Republic of South Africa, albeit only a matter of thirty kilometres south of the Namibian border. This was the North West Cape, the last and possibly one of the most prosperous of the mineralized areas of the country. Black Mountain was the name of the project and Phelps Dodge was the American company that partnered Gold Fields. Here at Black Mountain appeared to be a treasure-house of riches: silver, lead, zinc and copper. There were those who suggested that Aladdin had been a local lad from Aggeneys. No one went so far as to say that it was another Palabora though it had aspects in common with that storehouse of riches on the fringes of the Kruger National Park.

Phelps Dodge and Gold Fields were not strangers to each other. Nearly forty years earlier the New York office of Consolidated Gold Fields had maintained contact with it. In November 1949 Spencer Fleischer in Johannesburg had written to Robert Annan in London: 'We would of course welcome association with some of the American groups ... notably Mr Gates's Phelps Dodge Corporation or the Newmont Mining Corporation ... Mr Gates was impressed with West Wits but a little apprehensive about the Free State and this coincides with the views so often expressed to me by American engineers who cannot bring themselves to rely on borehole results to the extent that we do.' In May 1977 Phelps Dodge announced that an agreement in principle had been made with GFSA whereby Gold Fields would take a fifty-one percent interest at a subscription price of R15 million in the Black Mountain Mineral Development Company and would also administer the company. In addition to the total equity of R30 million, it was estimated that R155 million in loan funds would be needed to bring Black Mountain to the point where it could support itself. Gold Fields said it would provide R35 million of these loans, raised both in South Africa and abroad. This was a tremendous financial undertaking for a company that only six years earlier had assumed responsibility for financing its own affairs. But the prizes, as evaluated by the company's experts, promised to be glittering.

In addition to a proven economic reserve of thirty-eight million tons of ore deposit, diamond drilling on Black Mountain's extensive property had indicated geological reserves of lead, zinc and copper of the order of 200 million tons. The project was planned on 187 000 tons of concentrates a year, obtained from ore being mined underground and worth R50 million. When the time came for commissioning Black Mountain, the *Financial Mail* described it as 'one of the most exciting developments on South Africa's base metals horizon', and it added, 'for this will represent the first flowering of an area long known to be fabulously rich in minerals'. However, by this time, late 1979, Gold Fields was having to keep its fingers crossed. Prices of many base metals, particularly copper, had slumped but the company was hopeful. Lead, by contrast, had performed well and it was expected that the value of lead production would exceed that of any other base metal produced within the Group.

Black Mountain was coming to production just as Deelkraal on the West Wits Line was preparing to do the same. Some R220 million had gone into these two projects by June 1979. As Louw said at the time: 'Over the past few years GFSA financial resources and its technical and administrative skills have to a large extent been committed to the development of its two new mines.' They would launch the company into the 1980s as it came in sight of its century.

Once again, Gold Fields seemed to have got itself in step with the march of South African history. With its American partner, it was about to bring into the modern world of mining an area that had been penetrated as long ago as 1685 when Governor Simon van der Stel had taken his prospectors to put down their primitive shafts at O'okiep near Springbok west of Aggeneys, having earlier been impressed by the copper ornaments worn by Hottentots on a visit to the castle at Cape Town. This was the first deliberate mineral expedition mounted in modern times in South Africa, and Commander Van der Stel did posterity a favour by keeping a diary at this time. On Thursday, 1 November 1685, for instance, he recorded: 'The miners had progressed to a depth of twice a man's length at one place and not quite so deep at another, and found that the mineral improved more and more.' It was not, however, until the middle of the 19th Century that any serious attempt was made to mine copper at O'okiep. The African Copper Mining Company at Cape Town played a prominent part. Its secretary was Edward Chiappini of the well-known Cape family into which Charles Rudd married, when Fanny Chiappini, Edward's daughter, became his wife in 1868. It seems in every way appropriate that O'okiep should have become a Gold Fields company.

In 1970 Phelps Dodge had begun a drilling programme in the region around Aggeneys and had identified three ore bodies, one of which was Black Mountain. In 1976 they acquired an area of 23 000 hectares at Aggeneys, some sixty-five kilometres from Pofadder on the road to Springbok. The man who had been doing the work for them and proved the Aggeneys deposits was not an American. He was really a Gold Fields man, for Pat Ryan, the exploration manager for Phelps Dodge, had not only been born on Venterspost, where his father was a civil engineer in 1937, but he had worked as a learner on the West Wits Line before going to Witwatersrand University to qualify as a geologist. After working for Gold Fields for a while, he had departed for Rhodesia. However, in discovering and proving the Black Mountain lead, silver, copper and zinc mine which Gold Fields was to develop, the Ryan family relationship with the company had gone full circle. Ryan had carried out some 90 000 metres of diamond drilling, bulk sampling, metallurgical testing and feasibility studies and by 1978 at the age of forty-one he became general manager of Phelps Dodge in South Africa. Ryan was not the first to have taken a look at Black Mountain. Back in 1929 a German prospector named Horneman had sunk a prospecting shaft and between 1932 and 1963 geologists from various mining houses had come to take a look but missed the potential that the owner of the property, Willem Burger, insisted was there. The Burger family's faith was justified in the end when they picked up One and-a-half million Rand for having held on to it.

Phelps Dodge's activities had been attracting other foreign companies. 'A feature of the Northern Cape prospecting rush is the large-scale entry of foreign companies indicating their belief that the investment future is safe in South Africa,' wrote the *SA Mining and Engineering Journal* at the end of 1974. 'They see this area as one with possibilities of more large payable deposits such as those found by Phelps Dodge and by O'okiep copper mining in the Gamsberg area west of Pofadder.' One of these companies was Newmont Mining, an American company already well known to Gold Fields in Namibia through their joint interest in Tsumeb. From Newmont in due course Gold Fields acquired its interest in O'okiep.

The man who really had had faith in the North West Cape and backed it by buying large tracts of land there, had unfortunately died before he could see his faith vindicated. This was David Graaff, bachelor brother of Sir De Villiers Graaff, long time Leader of the Opposition in the South African Parliament. Among much else he had mineral rights at Aggeneys and it was with Graaff Investments that Phelps Dodge had had to deal when they came to prove the vast deposits of Black Mountain. The Graaff Trust, which after Graaff's death continued to operate his interests, became an extremely rich charitable organization as a result of the mining activities in the North West Cape. Phelps Dodge had handed over R1,7 million for the mineral rights.

If the opening up of the North West Cape came late in South Africa's mining history, a look at this forbidding world might well provide an answer. One can only doff one's cap in salute to those men who went from Gold Fields to develop Black Mountain and who created a massive infrastructure in this desert wasteland. What Carleton Jones had once said about the early generation at Gold Fields still applied to the Class of 1977; he spoke of their 'burning optimism and tenacity of purpose'. At Black Mountain they established an oasis in a desert with these qualities. Aggeneys is said to mean 'a place of water' in Nama, but it needed the mining men to make it so. Making a mine and maintaining its existence in that dry environment depended on an adequate and continuing supply of water. At Pelladrift, where temperatures get up to fifty degrees and men and animals have been known to collapse and die, a water works and pumping station were established on the Orange River. A coffer dam, clarification works, balancing reservoir, high life pumping chamber and reticular pipeline were necessary to get the water fifty-two kilometres to Black Mountain. Water and much else that Gold Fields brought to Aggeneys have transformed the place. 'In the barren, sunbaked wastes of the North West Cape a new mining community has blossomed and is flourishing in this inhospitable area,' wrote the *SA Mining Journal* at the end of 1979 as Black Mountain was getting ready to start production. In a way Black Mountain compensated for Bank on the West Wits Line. At Bank a community had had to be dispersed because of the mining activity in the area. Mining at Black Mountain had done the opposite; it had created a community and transformed the environment in which it lived. In a couple of years the population of Aggeneys grew from 40 to 3 000. Before work started in 1977, Aggeneys had been a barren wilderness without water, power or housing. Moreover, the discomfort of the place was aggravated by having what is probably the highest diurnal temperature range in South Africa, up to seventeen degrees in a day. Within a couple of years brick houses with air conditioning had been built in lush surroundings and the Old Nama oasis had been turned into something worthy of the name. Black Mountain had fulfilled a social role in providing development and employment, particularly for the Coloured community, in a part of South Africa that badly needed it. At the same time Gold

Fields did not forget those who a century earlier had brought Western civilization into the area. These were not mining men but missionaries, from the Lutheran and then the Catholic Church, who had come to Pella on the Orange River in the 19th Century. The Catholic Church was the scene of great building activity in the 1880s. While Rhodes and Rudd were still at Kimberley, a group of French missionaries had trekked overland to the area of Black Mountain and under their leader, Father John Marie Simon, they built this church. The Pella Project, unlike that of Black Mountain, took seven years to complete. It was hard labour; 400 wagon-loads of stone quarried from the surrounding mountains had to be brought in and 200 000 bricks were made by hand on the river bank. One of the priests used to swim across the river to islands infested with baboons to collect wood for the interior of the church, for the pulpit and the pews. Such was the example that had already been set by the time Gold Fields arrived on the scene to make their contribution a century later. And when they did, they acknowledged those who had been there before, by donating R100 000 so that the decaying structure of Father Simon's Church might be restored and continue to serve the growing community that Black Mountain had created.

The *SA Mining Journal* at the end of 1979 had reported that all the elements were on target for production to begin at Black Mountain, 'thanks to thorough planning'. This was achieved despite the fact that 180 000 tons of equipment had to be brought by road or rail and then via poor gravel roads to the remote site. During this period Luipaardsvlei had been used as an assembly area for equipment going to Black Mountain, which was a thousand kilometres away. The convoys came and went and the traffic between the depot and the distant mine kept on until the job was completed and the man on the spot, the Mine Manager, D A Blair Hook, had got everything in place. At 75 Fox Street, Bernard van Rooyen, the project manager, had put together an outstanding team of experts whose skills were matched by their enthusiasm to tackle the extraordinary challenge that Black Mountain presented. They were as determined as Van Rooyen was that the target should be met, even if cutting corners sometimes caused raised eyebrows in the boardroom. After what he described as his 'Agonies at Aggeneys' were over, Van Rooyen set out the six Planners Precepts which he had kept in mind in the gestation of Black Mountain. These were:

1. Anything that can go wrong will go wrong. 2. Left to themselves things will go from bad to worse. 3. If several things can go wrong the one to go wrong will be the one that does most damage. 4. Nature always sides with the hidden flaw. 5. Nature is contrary. 6. If everything appears to be going well, you have overlooked something.

An all-important aspect of the project was getting Black Mountain products away to their destination. The Government, aware of the importance of the scheme for the country's development as a whole, had promised to help with rail and harbour facilities. As Richards Bay had fitted in with Gold Fields' coal operations, so Saldanha Bay, with its ore-handling facilities, might have been made to cope with the Black Mountain harvest. But in the beginning a 157 kilometre road had to be constructed from the mine to Loop 10 on the Sishen-Saldanha railway line to take the convoy of trucks working out of Black Mountain, to meet the trains.

The mine that its later manager, Kingsley Briggs, whose father had been manager of Sub Nigel for many years, took over, had been created by tremendous engineering skills. For miles around, the headgear rising like a steeple into the sky was a comforting sight, indicating the presence of 'Men at Work'. Below, a 400 metre shaft, 5,5 metres in diameter had been sunk. Fully automatic hoists, operating 10-ton skips for ore and waste were assembled and a large single deck fifty-man cage to move men and light material operated by a fully automatic service hoist. On 26 November 1979 trial milling began and on 29 February, in that leap year of 1980, the first overseas shipments were on their way. On 22 April that year Ian Mackenzie, chairman of the Standard Bank, a director of Apex Mines and a nephew of William Mackenzie, signalled once more his family connection with Gold Fields by performing the opening ceremony. A plaque records the historic occasion.

Gold Fields of South Africa entered the 1980s on a rising tide of success which looked as if it might carry it on in triumph towards the company's centenary in 1987. However, a company as cautious as Gold Fields has always been, seldom allows itself to be carried away by euphoria and will drink its health with watered wine. It even met calmly the exaggerated gesture of the gold price which saluted the New Year and the new decade by going to 850 dollars. However, as the president of the Chamber of Mines, R S Lawrence, was to say: 'Measured by any standards, 1980 was an outstanding year for the South African mining industry and for the country as a whole.' And in that outstanding year of 1980, Gold Fields was acclaimed as the outstanding company in the country. 'For Gold Fields of South Africa, the ride to the top is part of the history of the Witwatersrand and the discovery of the rich gold area known as the West Wits Line,' wrote the *Sunday Times*, when it announced that for the first time since 1975 a mining company had come out at the top of the *Sunday Times* earnings growth survey. 'In the 1980 ranking GFSA notched up an impressive 47 percent annual compound earnings growth over the previous four years.'

The distinction gained by the company in 1980 was a fitting climax to Ian Louw's own career, for in November that year, on reaching the age of sixty, he retired from the chairmanship of the company, though remaining a non-executive member of the board. As a mining man he had already been honoured, while on a visit to London, with the award of the gold medal of the Institution of Mining and Metallurgy. Barely eight years had gone by since Louw on the first anniversary of the new GFSA had announced boldly: 'We have now set ourselves the target of doubling the consolidated net profit over the next five years.' In July 1979 he was able to tell a Press conference in London that GFSA assets, starting from R225 million at the outset, were in sight of R1 000 million while profits had increased sevenfold from the R9,1 million of 1971. All this, said the London *Sunday Times*, showed that Gold Fields of South Africa had become the best mining company in Africa. At the same time the *Financial Times* in London gave its readers the benefit of its specialized information: 'A point that may not be generally realized about GFSA is that unlike most of the other mining finance houses, it has investment company status.' This was a reference to the fact that back in 1958 the company, then West Wits, had obtained a ruling to this effect in the South African courts. The *Financial Times* explained: 'This means that it pays no tax on profits from the realization of investments, provided that such profits are ploughed back into specified investments such as new mining ventures.' Gold Fields was beginning to make an impression in the financial centres of the world. In December that year Rowe and Pitman, leading City brokers, were advising their clients to buy GFSA; they referred to the company's major new investment in Black Mountain and Deelkraal that would soon be making their contribution to revenue.

Early in 1980 Deelkraal was ready to go and the Minister of Finance, Senator Owen Horwood, was there to see it off. By this time a new and unusual use for gold had been found, though no one ascribed this to the promotional activities of Intergold. The umbilical cord that had tethered the American astronaut, Edward White, to his Gemini spacecraft during his space walk was gold-plated to reflect thermal radiation. Horwood, addressing the distinguished assembly of guests at Deelkraal, said: 'When John Maynard Keynes described gold as a barbarous relic, he was living in another era. Little did he realize that gold's durability would result in its attaining a special position in the modern space age. I am not sure whether there is a connection between the critical part which gold plays in space travel and the speed at which its price moved in recent times.' Louw told Mrs Horwood that he would like to have given her a gold bar but he suspected shareholders might offer difficulties. Under the circumstances would she be content with a gold necklace instead? Quite clearly, the smiling Mrs Horwood was.

On a more serious note the Finance Minister voiced his fears about the effects of inflation on the mining industry, as well he might. 'I have noted that in 1979 the average working cost per ton milled at the gold mines was 2,9 times that which prevailed in 1973. These figures not only emphasize the eroding effect of inflation but also underline the difficulties which the entrepreneur has to face in taking decisions to invest in major capital-intensive projects which take five or more years to reach the production stage.' The Minister had put his finger on something that was to worry Gold Fields and the other mining houses as the 1980s advanced and inflation, unabated, played havoc with long-term planning of future operations. As time went on inflation, and other problems, made the year 1980 look increasingly like a false dawn.

When Ian Louw gave up the chairmanship towards the end of 1980, Robin Hope, his contemporary and fellow warrior during the Second World War, also decided it was time to go. Robin Plumbridge was appointed chairman. At forty-five he was the same age as Louw had been when he succeeded Bill Busschau fifteen years earlier. Busschau had died in 1976. There were vacant seats at the boardroom table. André Taute, the technical director, had gone in May 1979. Peter van Rensburg, a mining engineer whose thirty-four years service had given him a wide experience in various posts, including six years with Plumbridge in the gold division, joined the board to look after exploration and technical matters. Now another mining engineer, Colin Fenton, joined the board to take over from Plumbridge the gold operations for which a wide experience on the West Wits Line particularly equipped him. West Driefontein in that fateful year of 1962, Libanon, Kloof, Doornfontein and finally Deelkraal in the important planning stage, had all been his place of work over the years. Consulting engineer at 75 Fox Street, and a spell in the mineral economics division, had broadened the picture for him. In a way Fenton made up for Willie Malan who had departed for Anglovaal, for Fenton had swopped Anglovaal for Gold Fields back in 1956 after doing a spell of post-graduate work at Hartebeestfontein. It had happened almost by accident. 'I departed from Harties on my motorbike,' he said. 'I was now unemployed and thinking about another job. Well, the first mine you come to after leaving Hartebeestfontein is Doornfontein and it looked all right to me. So I joined Doornfontein which happened to be a Gold Fields mine.' Bernard van Rooyen also joined the board. Like Dru Gnodde who was already there, he had had a legal training, and had been building up an impressive track record, including the Black Mountain project. His years in London at 49 Moorgate had given him a wide grasp of the world of finance, which became his special interest and for which he was specially talented. However, arriving in the boardroom, he might for a moment have imagined himself back in the classroom at Jeppe High School for sitting at the table was his old history master. This was Dennis Etheredge, the Anglo American director on the Gold Fields Board. After leaving the wartime army, Etheredge had been a schoolmaster for a while. Then, having written an academic thesis on the early days of the Chamber of Mines which became a standard work, he transferred his interest permanently to mining where he rose to high places in the Anglo American Corporation, joint deputy-chairman at the time of his retirement in 1983. He had replaced John Shilling on the Gold Fields Board. It was Louw's custom to strengthen his board by bringing in outside directors distinguished in other fields. Dr J B de K Wilmot, a former deputy governor of the Reserve Bank, served for a number of years from 1970; D H Steyn, who had been Secretary of Finance, was another and he was followed by Gerald Browne who had also held that Treasury post. Like Hope and Plumbridge, Browne had been a Rhodes Scholar at Oxford and shared their strong convictions about gold; indeed, during his time at the Treasury, he had done much to expedite the appearance of the Krugerrand. Since Consolidated Gold Fields in London was the biggest minority shareholder it had two directors on the GFSA Board. In 1978 Gerry Mortimer, a mining engineer who had worked on GFSA mines, gave up his post of chief executive and deputy-chairman of CGF and, in addition, his place on the

GFSA board. His place, both in London and Johannesburg, was taken by Rudolph Agnew. Michael Beckett was the other director from London. Tommy Muller, Len Abrahamse and Jan Pijper had come in in 1971. If all the directors were to sit down together there would have been 13 at the table; however, the British company is always represented by one or other of its two directors, seldom by both at the same time, so a round dozen is the usual score.

The London company had acquired a new chairman in 1976 on the retirement of Donald McCall. This was Lord Erroll of Hale who had come to the Gold Fields board after a distinguished political career. He had been a member of the Macmillan Cabinet and served as President of the Board of Trade. For these services he was made a peer and so, for the third time in its history, the London company had for its chairman someone with a seat in the House of Lords. A man of many talents, proved as much in business as in politics, quick-witted and charming, he was to be severely tested by the unnerving experience that overtook him as chairman of Consolidated Gold Fields in the last days of 1979 and early in 1980. He was under the impression, he said, that a burglar was creeping up on him in the dark. Someone was after his company and no one knew who it was. Everyone, however, claimed to know why someone was after Consolidated Gold Fields. Fleet Street was saying with one voice that 'the jewel in the Gold Fields crown is GFSA'. Lord Erroll's burglar, whoever he was, was after the jewel in the crown. The British Press and the City of London kept up the guessing game for weeks: they talked about it over Christmas and into the New Year. Who was buying CGF shares? It was tantalizing.

At the annual general meeting of Consolidated Gold Fields' shareholders on 27 November 1979, Lord Erroll said that he wished to make a statement, before beginning formal business, about the rumours of a take-over 'to which the company has been subjected in the last few weeks. No approach has been made to us and the truth, if any, behind the rumour is extremely difficult to establish. A scrutiny of our registers has revealed nothing untoward but this cannot be conclusive. Whereas, under our company law, a shareholder is required to disclose his interest as soon as it reaches five percent of the total shares in issue, this rule, designed as a protection for existing shareholders, is in practice not enforceable against foreign investors. Furthermore, the abolition of exchange control means that an overseas purchaser of 10 percent or more of a British company's shares no longer needs to obtain Treasury consent and thereby agrees to abide by our laws and the regulations of the City take-over panel'. Lord Erroll then warned shareholders 'against the possibility of a creeping acquisition of your interests'. He also pointed to the probable reason for 'the raid on your company's shares', by describing the achievement of Gold Fields of South Africa, in which his own company had a forty-eight percent interest. The two Driefonteins, he said, produced fifteen percent of the Republic's total output and they were producing it at a cost of under fifty-five dollars an ounce. 'No other company produced at a cost lower than about 80 dollars an ounce. The weighted industry average was 115 dollars an ounce, the GFSA Group average 73 dollars an ounce.' He went on to say that 'in modern times the Group has an unparalleled record of success in exploration for gold; of the new capacity which the South African industry will have introduced between 1968 and the early 1980s, no less than two-thirds will have been developed by GFSA.

'Also in South Africa,' Lord Erroll went on, 'GFSA hold a 51 percent interest in the Black Mountain mine, which commenced production this month. The prices of its two major products, lead and silver, are currently very high and as the mine is among the lowest-cost lead producers world-wide, it could easily weather a severe market down-turn. It is situated in a highly mineralized area and there appears to be scope for other major developments in the vicinity.'

Such was the nature of the jewel in the crown. The buying of Consolidated Gold Fields shares went on. It was now January 1980 and still the mystery had not been solved. However, South Africa was involved and Fleet Street started to draw predictable conclusions. The Boer War had started again, this time on the economic front. Afrikaner interests were at work, they were saying. Having acquired General Mining and tumbled Union Corporation, they were marching on the GFSA fortress, hoping to enter by its accessible entrance in London. As late as 11 February 1980 *The Times*, Britain's traditional 'Thunderer', was thundering away. 'If the buyers of Gold Fields shares are Afrikaners, whether General Mining, Mr Anton Rupert, Sanlam or some combination, the target is more likely Gold Fields of South Africa. They may not care about Consolidated Gold Fields' other merits, just as they give little heed to the City's gentlemanly rules. The question Gold Fields and the city might ask is: What price Gold Fields of South Africa when the motivation to buy is partly the settlement of old scores against the English?' For a mining editor to beat a tribal drum in such jingo fashion was probably the measure of his frustration at not being able to unravel the mystery. If something nasty was going on in the British woodshed, the Boers were bound to be at the bottom of it. Another Fleet Street writer, Robert Tyerman, wrote: 'It's almost like the Boer War. That's how one leading London stockbroker described what he and a growing number of brokers both in the city and in Johannesburg suspect is behind the mystery buying of shares in CGF ... they see the steady purchase of between 10 and 15 percent of the mining finance house as the most recent round of a struggle that has been going on for more than 100 years in South Africa.'

Although it was predictable that the secret buying of CGF shares would be interpreted in London as a revival of Boer-Brit rivalry, no one was able to produce any evidence. The London brokers, James Capel, in their newsletter of December 1979 went into the matter and referred to that Afrikaner economic Long Tom – General Mining. That company, it said, had just about finished paying off the loans raised for the Union Corporation acquisition and 'the decks are therefore nearly cleared away for the next onslaught'. The London brokers then said there was luckily 'a policeman on hand who, if called soon, may put a brake on the predator's ambitions'. This policeman, it said, was Harry Oppenheimer who would not like to see 'the jewel in Gold Fields' crown (GFSA) fall into the hands of his greatest competitor'. It said much for the Oppenheimer image that he should have been cast in the role of 'the good guy', the policeman in the Punch and Judy Show. On 11 February Lord Erroll decided to ask the British Government to intervene. He requested the Department of Trade to appoint an inspector to investigate the ownership of the company's shares under section 172 of the Companies Act, 1948. This appeal to the British Government followed an announcement on 6 February that there had been a considerable increase in the number of unregistered share transfers. Forty million shares – twenty-seven percent of the equity – were in unknown hands. In the House of Commons members were putting down questions. 'The most popular City theory ascribes the buying which began before Christmas to Afrikaner interests in South Africa,' said the London Press. Things were getting serious. The Boers would be burrowing under the Bank of England next!

The following day it was all over. The mystery buyer realized that he would now have to break cover and run for base. Just after 9 o'clock on the morning of 12 February, David Lloyd Jacob was in his office when the telephone rang. It was Harry Oppenheimer, informing him officially that he had fifteen percent of the CGF shares and was about to go into the market for another ten percent. 'He sounded as if he were in a hurry,' said Lloyd Jacob afterwards. He probably was for the famous De Beers dawn raid had started. With the aid of the brokers, Rowe and Pitman, he acquired 13,5 million shares before Big Ben struck 10 o'clock. It was a masterly performance that proved Harry Oppenheimer to be a

Die Transvaler of 14 February 1980 had fun with the famous dawn raid by De Beers on Consolidated Gold Fields in London, its cartoon showing it as a game of cards in which Harry Oppenheimer acts the kingmaker and 'King takes all – Koning vat alles'.

chip off the old block. Eventually his companies had 29,9 percent of the shares of Consolidated Gold Fields which was as far as they could go without making a bid for the entire equity, which British regulations would have required of them. Later that day Ian Louw put out a statement from 75 Fox Street in which he said: 'Mr Oppenheimer has given me the assurance that his sole objective in acquiring a blocking holding in Consolidated Gold Fields is to maintain the present independent status of Gold Fields of South Africa Limited.' Louw himself offered no public comment on what had been presented as an amazing, and very expensive, act of altruism. But had the gamekeeper, self-appointed, been playing the role of gamekeeper or had the gamekeeper turned poacher? Long before it all started, the *Financial Mail* in September 1979, in the course of an article about the mining houses, had written about Anglo American ambitions and had said 'given the chance, it would grab control of GFSA through the off-shore acquisition of Consolidated Gold Fields. That may be a pipe dream …'

In London the British authorities were not very happy about what the *Financial Times* was to call 'a very murky affair'. They were concerned to find out if any British regulations had been broken. The London Stock Exchange appointed a committee of enquiry to go into the matter and in July 1980 it published its findings. The *Financial Times* called it 'a lame riposte to dawn raids' and said that it was clear that De Beers, with the active co-operation of members of the London Stock Exchange, ignored the spirit but not the letter of the United Kingdom law on the disclosure of share ownership. Sir Nicholas Goodison, chairman of the London Stock Exchange, said 'nothing nasty' had been discovered. The Anglo American-De Beers raid on a British company had been legal but may not have been cricket, he said. Cricket, however, had never been an accomplishment claimed by the Oppenheimer companies and was rather the distinction of Lord Harris's old company, the victim of the raid.

The whole episode had been an exercise in power, whether by a gamekeeper or a poacher depends on the way one looks at it. If Anglo American believed that Afrikaner interests wanted to get their hands on GFSA, a pre-emptive strike to prevent this happening was a step to preserve its own position of power in the South African mining industry. Nevertheless, the action of 12 February 1980 could not 'maintain the present independent status of GFSA', since in obtaining a dominating position in Consolidated Gold Fields, which itself had 48 percent of GFSA, the South African company could only be as free as the length of the Anglo American leash allowed it to be. The long shadow that had appeared in the early days of the West Wits Line had come to stay. That it had done so in 1980, at the very moment that Gold Fields of South Africa reached a pinnacle of success, only made the company more aware of it.

---

[1] This high grade was an inevitable consequence of the high pay limits forced on the mines by the fixed gold price and ever rising costs.

[2] It is expressed in metric terms since 1971 which was also the year that South Africa adopted the metric system.

CHAPTER TEN

In Sight of a Century – The 1980s

When in September 1981 Robin Plumbridge reviewed the affairs of the company for the first time since becoming its chairman, he was making his debut before the shareholders on the 10th anniversary of Gold Fields of South Africa as an independent company. He spoke of the dramatic change in the size and the profitability of the company in its first decade of independence. Whereas in 1971 there had been assets of R333 million, these had now grown to R1 736 million. Earnings, too, had grown in this period from R11,4 million to R166,6 million. To mark the anniversary in an appropriate manner, he announced profits up by no less than thirty-three percent on the record year of 1980 when Gold Fields had been named as South Africa's top company. There could be no doubt that ten years of running its own affairs had turned Gold Fields into a very fat cat. A substantial cash flow now gave it the wherewithal to finance new business without reducing strategic shareholdings. Its balance sheet, moreover, was impressive enough to support considerable short-term borrowings should these be needed for any major business opportunity. That such opportunities were surely coming there could be no doubt since the new chairman was determined to press on ever more vigorously with the policy of expansion that had already produced Kloof, East Driefontein, Black Mountain and Deelkraal. The previous year the *SA Mining Journal* had remarked: 'The feature of the GFSA gold quarterlies was the withholding of more than R100 million by five mines for their big capital spending programmes – an indication of the tremendous development now underway in the booming gold mining business.' When these new projects came to light and the public was made aware of what they would cost, it became clear how important that build-up of capital resources during the 1970s had been.

In 1985 Gold Fields, in announcing its Leeudoorn project, an extension to Kloof which amounted really to a new mine, said that it envisaged a capital expenditure of some R453 million in order to have it producing by 1990. No one blinked an eyelid at what to an older generation would have seemed an astronomical sum. That this was so was an indication of the extent to which the mining world had been changing in a South Africa that by the 1980s was itself in a period of rapid transition. In the run-up to its centenary in 1987, Gold Fields of South Africa was having to adapt itself to a new climate that was not merely economic but also social and political. Not only had the cost of launching a new mine reached unheard-of heights but the activity itself had become ever more challenging technically, transforming what had once been regarded as an ancient art into a modern science of many facets. Almost more important, however, was the new social climate that had been emerging and which demanded of a great mining company employing some 94 000 people an acute awareness of its social responsibility. Concern for its workers and for the environment in which they had to work had become over the years a prime consideration in company planning. This was heightened by the nature of the labour force which made it part of the racial complexity of South Africa, growing increasingly problematical and attracting more and more the attention, often critical and hostile, of the outside world.

André Taute, one of Gold Fields' most distinguished engineers, who had spent his career in evolving new techniques with new machines, admitted at the time of his retirement that man was the most important factor in the industry. 'The biggest single ingredient in any industrial enterprise, which of course embraces mining, is the individual – he is still the most important factor.' And in the South African context, he pointed to what he regarded as an encouraging development, the recognition of the black man as more than just 'a pair of hands'. It was significant that when Plumbridge took over the chairmanship of the company, he reserved for himself the personal responsibility for Manpower. As will be seen, it would grow in importance as the decade advanced and the political scene, both local and international, became increasingly disturbed by race relations in South Africa. Gold Fields, nor any other South African company, would be able to ignore the economic consequences of political pressures, both internal and external. And since Gold Fields of South Africa was the only mining house in Johannesburg whose biggest minority shareholder was a foreign company, Consolidated Gold Fields, based in London, its record in South Africa would be closely scrutinized by political groups in the British capital seeking to influence matters in the Republic. These would seek to make a point by rapping the knuckles of Consolidated Gold Fields, whose revenue was being largely provided by dividends coming from the successful gold mining operations being conducted by its associate in South Africa.

Even before Plumbridge presented his first chairman's review, stock exchanges round the world and financial journalists everywhere had become excited by the latest developments on the West Wits Line. Here a super mine had been created by the merging of the two Driefonteins, West Drie and East Drie, to which was to be added the mining lease of North Drie, still to be developed, the whole lot to become Driefontein Consolidated, the biggest gold producing company in the world. Plumbridge himself became its chairman. After all the ordeals that the Driefonteins had gone through together – sinkholes, flooding, fires – a masterpiece of mining engineering had appeared along the picturesque Gatsrante, in an area that covered some sixteen kilometres by ten kilometres. No mine in history had produced more gold than Driefontein; by the end of 1983 the 2 000 ton mark was passed. Of the world's large gold mines, it also had the

292

lowest cost per ounce produced. To get at a targeted 80 tons a year, enough gold to provide twenty million brides with a wedding ring, it is said, it needs to put some five million tons of ore through the mills. Other big mines, like Vaal Reefs and Harmony, process more rock but because the grades are lower, they do not turn out as much gold as Driefontein.

The merger scheme had been well thought out to express the Gold Fields *modus operandi* which is to have one company in which several mines cohabit. It meant that North Drie could be brought to production at a substantially reduced capital cost and within the tax structure of the merged operations. The East Drie area would be more rapidly exploited, while the surplus hoisting capacity and infrastructure of the older West Drie, employed for the benefit of East Drie and North Drie, thereby gave the old mine a further lease of life. In fact, being part of the larger complex, Driefontein Consolidated, whose life was put at fifty years or so, West Drie could expect to survive much longer than would have been the case if it had remained on its own. This was particularly so after North Drie became part of West Drie in due course. Even the removal of the inter-mine boundaries would be more than symbolic. It was reckoned to recover from the boundary pillars twenty-eight tons of gold worth at the time R350 million.

West Drie and East Drie did not, however, lose their separate identity by becoming part of Driefontein Consolidated. Each is exploited as a separate division under different management and in annual reports the contribution that each makes to Driefontein Consolidated results is listed separately. This seems sensible when one considers the sheer massiveness of an operation employing 27 000 people. Every day some 25 000 people at Driefontein Consolidated go down the various shafts to drill and blast the rock – twenty kilometres of face in 570 panels with 160 being blasted every day. Apart from the shafts that cover a distance of more than twenty-two kilometres, there are 900 kilometres of underground tunnels – about the distance from Johannesburg to Durban and half the return journey. There were at the time of the merger ten surface shafts going down to 1 500 metres. After that, sub-vertical shafts went down to where men were at work 2 700 metres below ground. These sub-vertical shafts even have their own underground winders. These underground headgears are a reminder of those strange medieval Churches of St Emilion and Aubeterre in France, where the entire Church, including the steeple, are sited in deep underground caverns. Driefontein had plans to go even deeper. In August 1983 a group of newspaper editors visiting the mine were told of a project in hand to sink three successive shafts, one below the other, to open up deeper levels of the property four kilometres below surface. The cost of doing this, including infrastructure, power supply, ventilation and refrigeration, was estimated at R360 million. The enormity of this project from which gold would not be recovered from these levels before the year 2000, endorsing Gold Fields' faith in gold, was not lost on the visitors.

If the enormous sums of money involved in making a mining giant like Driefontein Consolidated are placed within the scale of the mine itself, they are better understood. Whatever aspect of the mine one looks at, there is the same impression of massiveness. As at Deelkraal, the giant fans push 200 000 tons of fresh air through the mine every day. Driefontein also uses 35 000 tons of water a day to cool the workings, allay the dust and service the drills. Driefontein uses great quantities of service water but it is also obliged to pump out each day 150 000 tons of dolomitic water. It is because of the presence of this water in dolomite caverns that there are no working levels at Driefontein above the 1 000 metres below-surface mark. The mine uses vast quantities of electric power, 4 000 kilowatt-hours every day; this is enough current to light up a city the size of Pietermaritzburg. Much of this power goes into operating the giant winders. The big twin-motor Blair winder is capable of moving materials up and down the shaft at fifty-four kilometres an hour.

Driefontein also looks big on the Stock Exchange where its capitalization at some R5 billion puts this individual mining company just behind the giant conglomerates, Anglo American and De Beers. In 1985 it achieved for the first time a before-tax profit of R1 billion. In that year it had another achievement from which it draws no satisfaction. It was at the top of the list of tax-paying mines, contributing to the nation's moneybox no less than R618 million.

Behind Driefontein and its smaller colleagues of the West Wits Line, Kloof, Deelkraal, Doornfontein, Libanon and Venterspost stands always Gold Fields of South Africa. Like a submarine supply ship, it rides at anchor at 75 Fox Street, providing the administrative and technical talents that have made the mines the successes that they are. Its own rewards have been spectacular since these mines provide eighty percent or more of the mining finance house's investment income, amounting in 1983, for instance, to R140 million and enabling GFSA that year to mark up another record with a profit of R175 million. Two years later, in 1985, it went through the R200 million barrier.

Driefontein might have been a very comfortable set of laurels for Gold Fields to rest upon but in fact the task of exploring and prospecting has gone on interminably. Before long Plumbridge was devoting ten percent of his profit for this purpose. On taking over the chair at Gold Fields he had reorganized the duties of executive directors to give greater emphasis to 'New Business'. He declared: 'Our first priority is to find new projects as a result of our own exploration and metallurgical research efforts.' In saying this, he was once more underlining the fact that Gold Fields is above all a mining company. If another gold field were unlikely to be discovered, there was plenty of scope still for exploration from the existing fields.

By the mid-1980s it was clear that the West Wits Line, though older, could outlast the Orange Free State field, which had provided the excitement of the immediate post-war period. Gold Fields had already disclosed that it was moving northward into North Driefontein. But it was also busy going southward from Kloof with its investigations. Drilling programmes were going on, evaluations were being made. From time to time financial journalists would fly overhead in helicopters and, as one of them concluded: 'Investors bemused by the steadily increasing cash balances held by the operating mines can take comfort that funds are not simply being hoarded.' Gold Fields had to put up with criticism that it was being stingy with its dividends but it took no notice. New projects cost money and the company was making sure that there was plenty in the kitty when the time came to go ahead. Time was not always on its side. As Peter van Rensburg said, 'It's not really a question of speeding up the drilling because we have found something. Rather it's making best use of time available to us before the options expire.'

In June 1985 came news at last. It was 'the long-awaited Kloof extension', as one Johannesburg broker put it. Leeudoorn, for such it was, is likely to turn out to be a much more impressive development than is suggested by this description, however accurate. In effect, Gold Fields were announcing a new mine due to come to production in 1990 but they were doing so within their usual formula, for Leeudoorn was planned as a division of Kloof, adding 1 309 hectares or thirty percent to the Kloof mining lease. Kloof intended to double its milling capacity over twenty years from 180 000 to 360 000 tons a month. Kloof was already a very special mine, having the distinction of being the world's top mine on grades and the lowest cost producer. Gold Fields, in creating first Driefontein Consolidated and then Kloof/Leeudoorn, had sensibly strengthened the long-term future of the two mining companies that provided her with seventy-five percent of her earnings. Just how long-term may be judged by the reference in the Leeudoorn dossier to production plans for 2004! Going ahead with Leeudoorn, prepared to spend more than R400 million, was in itself an act of faith, not only in gold but in South Africa and in the world economy as a whole. But a company like Gold Fields has no option. A new shaft system in a major South African gold mine may take ten to fifteen years in planning and physical development before becoming operational. Plans, like prospecting, have to go on with an eye on the 21st Century. Everything being equal – however one may interpret the phrase – they will come to fruition in due time. But, as Peter Janisch, general manager in 1982 of the gold division at Gold Fields, has said: 'The gold mining industry of the later 1980s and the 1990s will be as different to that of the 1960s as today's collieries are to those of Victorian times.'

Collieries in Victorian times! Gold Fields' own collieries, Apex Mines, had started in the days of Queen Victoria. They were needed to serve the power-hungry gold mines of the Transvaal and a century later the mining sector was still consuming a considerable proportion, some thirty percent, of total electricity generated. By this time, however, South Africa's coal export trade had become the second largest in the world, in 1982 worth R1 132 million. Sixty percent of these exports were going to the countries of the European Economic Community for whom for a time South Africa was the main external supplier of coal. After gold, coal was the major earner of foreign currency for the country. Apex Mines had been one of the original companies taking part in the programme to supply low ash coal to Japan. When the energy crisis in Europe suddenly transformed the prospects for South Africa's coal industry, a number of new, mainly small, coal mining companies appeared on the scene. When the Government reorganized and expanded the coal export quotas some of the newer companies were favoured at the expense of older operators such as Gold Fields and JCI. Gold Fields, finding itself excluded, felt a sense of injustice and took steps in 1981 to have the situation remedied. The following year, under the revised Phase IV export allocations when the Government pushed up the quota from forty-eight million to eighty million tons, Gold Fields was given an allocation of 1 000 000 tons. This, it felt, was not good enough and quite unrealistic when it was considered that the company had helped to pioneer the export trade through Richards Bay, and also the amount that was needed to open up a new export colliery. Gold Fields again made strong representations and the quota was doubled.

By this time Gold Fields had decided to make an important new investment in coal in order to take advantage of the bright prospects for coal on the domestic market. Escom had plans that would double generating capacity over eight or ten years. By 1990 consumption of coal was expected to reach 100 million tons. Sasol was also busy with plans for expansion and Gold Fields, having taken up ten million shares in this great oil-from-coal industry, would be playing its part. This was later increased to fifteen million shares worth over R100 million. In 1984 Gold Fields bought Liberty Life's 49,9 percent interest in Clydesdale and then, in due course, increased this to 89,9 percent. Clydesdale was almost as old as Apex and had been a going concern for eighty years. The company had three important coal interests, the Coalbrook colliery, supplying coal to Escom, the New Clydesdale colliery which was providing high grade coal for the domestic market, and a fifty percent interest in the large Matla colliery, also supplying coal to Escom and reaching full production in 1985. GFSA, assuming control in July 1984, then set about a merger of its coal interests, bringing Apex Mines and Clydesdale together to form Gold Fields Coal. The plan, having been approved, went to the Supreme Court for official recognition but here ran into difficulty when some dissatisfied Apex shareholders raised objections which were upheld by the court. It was something of a blow to the prestige of Gold Fields and a setback in its effort to run its enlarged coal interests more efficiently. However, the matter was resolved and Gold Fields Coal became a reality in March 1986. With the Clydesdale and O'okiep acquisitions, Gold Fields enlarged its community significantly, pushing up the number of employees in the Group to 94 000.

Coalbrook colliery, some twenty kilometres from Sasolburg in the Orange Free State and conveniently close to the Taaibos and Highveld power stations, is a mine with a history, not all of which has been happy and one episode was tragic. On 21 January 1960 it was the scene of one of the greatest mining disasters in South African history, when 291 hectares of the mine collapsed and 435 miners lost their lives. The name Coalbrook was on the front page of newspapers round the world as desperate attempts were made to rescue any of the men who might have survived, but in vain. Five boreholes, including one big enough to haul up a man, were sunk into the workings and a shaft sunk alongside the collapsed area. It was clear, however, that there could be no survivors and it was believed that those who had been trapped must have died almost instantaneously.

The scale of the Coalbrook disaster led to an intensive investigation by the coal mining industry into the stability of mine workings and to the imposition of strict controls on every aspect of mine safety. An important part was played in these investigations by an expert who was a refugee from his native Hungary. This was Dr Miklos Salamon, who was destined to become one of the country's leading personalities in mining research and a prominent figure in the Chamber of Mines.

By the time Gold Fields came on the scene in the 1980s, Coalbrook had been performing well for some time and in September 1980 had reached its highest ever output of some 423 000 tons. With a bigger stake in coal, Gold Fields was now well placed to participate in South Africa's expansion in the field of energy, some forty-five percent of which comes from coal. In 1980 some stocktaking on coal reserves had been done and the official assessment put these at 110 billion tons, of which fifty-one billion were thought to be extractable. There was enough, in any case, for some 200 to 300 years.

Base metals and minerals had become an essential part of Gold Fields' mining activity and of its exploration programmes and was earning profits of nearly R100 million a year. But it was a different game from gold mining. Gold mining companies do not have to compete with each other in selling their product. There is only one customer, the South African Reserve Bank and one man's gold is as good as another's. The competition comes not in the selling of gold but in exploring for it. With base metals and minerals it is another matter. Markets have to be found and exploited. Commodity markets flourish or become depressed according to the state of the world economy. When this is in a period of deflation, the industrialized world reduces its demands and prices weaken. Gold Fields, through its group companies, felt the effects of these ups and downs in the market. Black Mountain, with its variety of products, zinc, copper, lead, silver, and in which so much capital had been invested, was feeling these strains in the early 1980s. The servicing of big loans made it important for Black Mountain to maintain profits and there were times when it was difficult to see how the loan obligations could be met. In 1983 special arrangements had to be made to tide the company over a difficult period. Fortunately the variety of Black Mountain's products enables it sometimes to pick up on the swings what it loses on the roundabouts. Copper may be out of favour while the world is asking for lead. Black Mountain held on and prospects improved so that by 1985 sales revenue had gone up from R35 million to R99 million, an impressive increase, even after taking into account the decline in the value of the Rand in relation to other currencies. Rooiberg Tin and Union Tin were other companies whose performance was affected by the state of health of the world economy. Zincor's problems in this respect were compounded by the effects in 1982 of South Africa's worst drought in living memory. Zincor provides sulphuric acid for agricultural fertilizers but what the farmers wanted was rain not fertilizers. The drought was a major worry for the gold mining companies, Gold Fields in particular. Its mining operations were using four percent of all the power generated by Escom. As Bodo Schmitz, chief consulting mechanical and electrical engineer at Gold Fields, has said: 'Every day we pump half a million tons of fresh air into the mines and shift 50 000 tons of water through a cycle which daily requires an additional 60 000 tons of fresh water.' A reduction in electricity supply to the mines, because of the drought, would have hit Gold Fields badly. However, the rains, like good times, came again and all was well once more.

Gold Fields exploration on the West Wits Line south of Kloof had aroused curiosity but perhaps even more interest was being taken in the company's persistent prodding for platinum. Consolidated Gold Fields had abandoned its platinum interest in South Africa in 1976, since when Gold Fields of South Africa had been taking a serious look at platinum, on its own account. In September 1983 shareholders were told that their company had a fifty-two percent interest in what Plumbridge described as a major exploration project. This was a platinum proposition which lay down dip of the Rustenburg company's Amandelbult mine, where diamond drilling had already produced encouraging results. To get at the platinum reefs, one would be starting at a depth of some 1 300 metres. The area had been identified some years earlier by a South African geologist, Dr Fred Collender, who had later gone to work in London as an adviser to the City stockbroking firm, Strauss, Turnbull, who took a particular interest in South African investment. In due course he persuaded them to take an interest in the Northam Amandelbult project, which Gold Fields was now prospecting. South Africa had become the world's biggest producer of platinum. Between 1979 and 1982 the United States, for instance, was getting most of its platinum group metals from South Africa. But as Consolidated Gold Fields had discovered in the days when it had a major part in Rustenburg Platinum, the metal has its ups and downs. But it remained an important sector in mining and GFSA, now that CGF was no longer involved, was keen to have its own share of the cake, particularly as production from existing mines was being stretched to the limits by the end of 1984 to reach a record 85 tons. In the way that the imminent demise of Union Tin has been reported over the years so, too, has the imminent birth of a new South African platinum mine, with GFSA cast by the Press in the role of midwife. 'All set for new platinum mine' was the big headline that enlivened Johannesburg at breakfast one Sunday in January 1985. 'South Africa on the brink of getting a new billion-dollar platinum mine,' announced the Sunday newspapers. However, perhaps the drills of GFSA, like the mills of God, grind slowly. Another 18 months would go by before Gold Fields was able to announce – on 11 June 1986 – that it was going ahead, that its by now 78 percent owned Northam Platinum subsidiary, proposed to create a new platinum mine in a consolidated area of 10 314 hectares between Northam and Thabazimbi. The mine on the Merensky Reef would have an initial milling capacity of 150 000 tons a month. It was reckoned that, in June 1986 money

298

values, it would cost R559 million to bring the project to the self-financing stage. With its investment in gold at Leeudoorn and in platinum at Northam, Gold Fields was declaring its faith in the future to the tune of a billion Rand, an act of remarkable courage since it was taken at a time of national difficulty and uncertainty.

In picking up the platinum baton laid down some years earlier by Consolidated Gold Fields, the South African company, GFSA, was re-establishing links that went back to Merensky himself in the 1920s and to the time when Carleton Jones had been called away from Sub Nigel to Fox Street to take charge of platinum operations. The way back to platinum had taken five years of careful preparation, an extensive drilling programme having finally confirmed that the Northam properties were underlain by payable platinum group metals on the Merensky Reef at mineable depth. Total reserves on the horizon down to 2 700 metres below surface were estimated at 163 million tons; at the same time the area was underlain to the same depth by an estimated 319 million tons on the UG-2 Reef.

Quite clearly, the evaluation of a great new mining venture sometimes takes longer than writing a big black headline in a Sunday newspaper. On the other hand, the acquisition of an existing mining venture is more quickly realized and here, too, Gold Fields had been busy.

The Black Mountain project had given GFSA a working relationship with the American company, Phelps Dodge and in October 1984 it had assumed the major role by buying a further 4,5 percent of the equity for R15 million. In 1983 there had been a further development with another American company, Newmont Mining, with which it had had a long association through Tsumeb in South West Africa. In 1983 it acquired from Newmont a further interest in Tsumeb which gave it forty-three percent of the equity. This was really an investment for the future since Tsumeb had been going through difficult times due to a feeble copper price. At the same time it acquired from Newmont a twenty-five percent holding in O'okiep, the historic copper mine in the North West Cape. Gold Fields was buying at a time when base metal prices were looking very sickly, having reached their lowest levels for several years. O'okiep struggled through 1984 but, with the aid of a Government loan, it reached better times in 1985.

GFSA's developing relationship with Newmont in Southern Africa was accompanied by that of Consolidated Gold Fields with Newmont in the United States where it had spent £400 million in order to get 28,6 percent of the American company. In due course both Rudolph Agnew, chairman of Consolidated Gold Fields and Robin Plumbridge of Gold Fields of South Africa joined the Newmont Board. The key figure at Newmont was the redoubtable Plato Malozemoff, chief executive for thirty years and chairman since 1966. He retired in 1986 and was succeeded by Gordon Parker, a South African and formerly managing director at O'okiep for six years. Newmont's interests in Southern Africa, apart from Tsumeb and O'okiep, also included a twenty-nine percent

Robin Plumbridge, chairman of Gold Fields of South Africa as it prepared to enter on its second century. At 45 he succeeded Ian Louw in 1980, the same age as Louw had been when he had become chairman 15 years earlier. Rhodes Scholar, mathematician, Rugby Blue, Plumbridge came to Gold Fields straight from Oxford, as William Busschau had done before him. Twice during the 1970s he was President of the Chamber of Mines, where he helped to launch Intergold and to promote the Krugerrand around the world. For his services to mining and to South Africa, in 1981 he was awarded the Decoration for Meritorious Service by the State President.

Rudolph Agnew, since 1983 chairman of Consolidated Gold Fields in London is also a director of GFSA and returns the compliment by giving the GFSA chairman, Robin Plumbridge, a seat on his board in London. Both are members of the board of Newmont Mining in the United States and take it in turns to attend board meetings in that country. Like others in the Gold Fields past, Rudolph Agnew came to mining from a crack army regiment, the King's Royal Irish Hussars.

301

holding in Palabora and an interest in Highveld Steel and Vanadium. The CGF investment in Newmont was particularly important for the British company which badly needed a success in the United States to compensate for two earlier disasters there, first with American Zinc in 1963 and again with Skytop Brewster, makers of drilling rigs, in the 1980s, which was a £87 million write-off. The relationship which CGF and GFSA have with Newmont requires that either Agnew or Plumbridge attend the board meetings. For Plumbridge, living in Johannesburg, these duties added a particular burden, involving five or six visits to the United States every year. That he performs them is an indication of their importance and the degree to which he is prepared to help his British colleague to whom the Newmont connection is particularly significant.

These visits to the United States by the chairman of Gold Fields of South Africa have helped to make the South African company well known there and by 1985 Americans had a one billion dollar stockholding. Americans have no trouble in identifying Gold Fields of South Africa. 'Isn't that that swell company that runs a string of classy mines out on the West Wits?' It has been rather the British company, Consolidated Gold Fields, that has had problems of identity in the United States, despite its big investments there. In August 1980 it took a full page in *Forbes Magazine* to make clear who and what it was. *Forbes* had published a list of the 100 largest foreign investors in the United States and failed to mention Consolidated Gold Fields. 'We at Consolidated Gold Fields,' the advertisement read, 'were sorry not to appear on the list in *Forbes* on 7 July. Our US sales of 750 million dollars, all in 100 percent owned operations would have put us about 50th. Investing in the US rather well is something in which we give a lot of time and effort. So we were upset not to be listed and asked *Forbes* why. It turns out that *Forbes* reckons that we are part of the Anglo American Corporation of South Africa. Wrong. Consolidated Gold Fields is a completely independent company. Anglo American has 12 and a half percent of our equity recently purchased and has said that it does not expect to buy more. Another major mining company, De Beers, also has 12 and a half percent of our equity. We have 38 000 other shareholders. We are working for all of them. Consolidated Gold Fields is alive and well and investing in the US. We'll try to be higher than 50th in your list next year, Mr Forbes. Leave space for us.'

That advertisement was not the end of the matter, for in March the following year Consolidated Gold Fields learned that De Beers and Anglo American had handed over to Minorco, the Bermuda-based company in the group, more than fifty-three million shares in their company. The chairman of Minorco, Julian Ogilvie Thompson, joined the CGF Board in London and Rudolph Agnew became a director of Anglo American in Johannesburg. Anglo American already had a director on the board of Gold Fields of South Africa. Of more immediate concern to GFSA was a development in May 1984 when the Old Mutual gave Anglo American its GFSA shares in exchange for Barlow Rand shares, enabling Anglo to increase its stake in GFSA by 5,6 percent. With just under thirty percent of Consolidated Gold Fields and some twenty percent of Gold Fields of South

Africa, the Anglo American Group had gone a long way towards realizing the ambitions of Sir Ernest Oppenheimer of fifty years earlier when the West Wits Line was opened up. This share swop was a further illustration of the old adage that a gentleman's agreement is not worth the paper it is written on! No one at Old Mutual seemed to remember that it existed and GFSA had not been forewarned of what was going on. And yet these were the shares that the Old Mutual, like Syfrets, had received from Consolidated Gold Fields in 1971 when Gold Fields of South Africa became an independent company and the British company had had to part with shares so that its shareholding in GFSA might be under fifty percent. There was a clear understanding that the shares would not be disposed of without first consulting GFSA. That they should have been handed over to the very company that had already made a sizeable and controversial inroad into the Gold Fields sphere only heightened the feeling that a trust had been betrayed.

Gold Fields, in building up a dominant position in the Tsumeb Corporation, had been unusually bold. This was a great mining enterprise whose future might well turn out to be as distinguished as its long past. Nevertheless it was a political risk since Tsumeb operated in the disputed territory of SWA/Namibia, which had become an international political football in a match in which South Africa was playing The Rest of the World. In increasing its investment in Namibia, Gold Fields was making a declaration of faith in the country's future whatever government might come to power there after obtaining independence. Gold Fields was not unaware of the evolving political situation in Southern Africa during the 1980s and had been exercising various choices. In August 1983 it had reduced its interests north of the Limpopo to little more than a presence. The country that had borne the name of the co-founder of the company and where he is buried in the Matopo Hills, had become another place, the Republic of Zimbabwe. Those who wished it well hoped that there was nothing significant in the fact that its new rulers had renamed the country after a celebrated ruin. Gold Fields felt that the neighbouring black State of Botswana offered better prospects and, in opening an office there, they hoped to be able to play a part in developing the mineral resources of that country.

Although it was Gold Fields of South Africa that was operating in Namibia, it was Consolidated Gold Fields in London who was getting the blame. Its share-holder meetings continued to be disrupted by members of political groups demanding independence for Namibia and objecting to a South African company, GFSA, exploiting its mines. CGF was not alone in having to deal with political activists disguised as shareholders. Rio Tinto Zinc with its big uranium mine at Rössing was as much the target of the anti-South Africa groups as it was of the environmentalists and the anti-nuclear lobby. Lord Erroll, as chairman of CGF, had been able to draw on his ministerial experience of the rough-and-tumble of the House of Commons, and handled the annual general meeting with skill. His successor, Rudolph Agnew, a former cavalry officer in the elite King's Royal Irish Hussars, added immense charm to a soldier's firmness and neutralized his opponents' fire. In any case, as he told the *Financial Times* on one occasion, 'We are no longer ambivalent on South Africa.' His company's assets in the Republic were just too attractive to run down.

Consolidated Gold Fields, after some of its sorties into diversification, one or two of which had ended in a cul-de-sac, had returned to its old function – natural resources. In 1984, for instance, nearly seventy percent of its assets were taken up by its forty-eight percent stake in GFSA and its direct holdings in Driefontein, Kloof and Deelkraal. Gold and South Africa were still important to the British company which was prepared to say as much. The time had passed when it could be made fun of by Julian Baring of the London brokers, James Capel who, in his newsletter in October 1979 commented on a CGF advertisement in the London Underground, which stressed the company's diversity. 'It makes no mention of the South African interests through GFSA which contributed nearly half of Consolidated Gold Fields' profits last year. Instead it gives the impression that Consolidated Gold Fields is a group which makes ladies' face powder, front door keys and operates a few gravel pits. Hardly surprising that Consolidated Gold Fields is the most ridiculously undervalued stock in the mining market!'

Consolidated Gold Fields had an investment in South Africa and, under Rudolph Agnew, was no longer prepared to hide it away. Nevertheless it made it quite clear that it was another company with a similar name, Gold Fields of South Africa, that administered gold mines in Southern Africa. As Agnew once told a shareholders' meeting made restless by the presence of political activists, his company did not employ black miners in South Africa. That was another company with a similar name. Political activists nowadays are too professional, too sophisticated, to be deterred by a statement of the legal position as to who is who and who owns what. The vulnerability of British companies invested in South Africa has been a continuing saga. At one stage the Church of England felt obliged to part with its shareholdings in South African mining ventures. The Catholic Archbishopric of Westminster at a certain period had conversations at 49 Moorgate. In 1975 they had R36 000 worth of CGF shares. A director of the London company, General Bowring, himself a practising Catholic, came to South Africa to visit the mines of the GFSA group and reported favourably on the working conditions of black miners. Had they been less than satisfactory, he would not have remained a director of CGF, the Catholic bishops were told. In 1975, as has been seen, Christian Concern for Southern Africa had produced a report that was highly critical of working conditions in GFSA mines. This was meant to be used against CGF which was the biggest individual shareholder in GFSA. And there were other similar reports from time to time. GFSA was bound to be involved since it was the only South African mining house still providing a British company with a large part of its income, forty-nine percent of Consolidated Gold Fields' operating profit in June 1984. The price that CGF had to pay for its South African connection was a disrupted annual general meeting. This was something that was likely to continue as long as the basic problems of

304

South African society remained unresolved and the world continued to judge the country in the way it did.

It is difficult to say to what extent awareness of social responsibility in a great company like Gold Fields has been sharpened by the critical attitudes of the outside world. Certainly they have had an effect in the same way that they have influenced attitudes in South Africa as a whole, leading in the 1980s to political and social reforms which would have amazed a previous generation. And yet these reforms had come nowhere near satisfying world opinion, which tends to be simplistic, nor indeed many of the aspirations of those who made up the overwhelming part of the country's labour force.

In the mining sphere, nevertheless, the scene has changed beyond all recognition in the generation that has passed since the end of the Second World War. There have been phenomenal improvements in social responsibility, in technology, health, safety and pay, and although pressure for these changes has come from many quarters, some of the strongest has come from the mining houses themselves. It may well be that mining houses regard these improvements as enlightened self-interest. That, after all, is the kind of comment normally made about businessmen. And yet the business community in South Africa, and not least the mining houses, have long been ahead, in their social attitudes, of the country's official administrations, whose rules and regulations provide the social order in which the economy has to work. Although Gold Fields has a conservative image, it has never lacked men who were prepared to speak out on the social issues that had a bearing on the company's activities. Back in 1947, at the time of Gold Fields' 60th anniversary, Peter Carleton Jones had said: 'Keep in front of you the problem of the colour bar. It is going to become a very important matter. Don't turn it to one side. ...' His successor, Spencer Fleischer, had written to London: 'The real solution is the abolition of the colour bar.' Bill Busschau in 1960, after Sharpeville, had led the delegation to Pretoria to see the Prime Minister to ask for a new deal for Black South Africa. Ian Louw regularly commented on the social and political issues when reviewing the affairs of Gold Fields or talking to the Press in London. In 1976, after the Soweto riots, he had said: 'It is not enough for equality of opportunity to be available in the Homelands only. Political institutions must be developed to permit Asian, Coloured and black urban communities to play a full and responsible role in society. I therefore urge the immediate implementation of initiatives directed towards the early provision of equal opportunities in employment, training and education in that order for all the peoples of the Republic.' Three years later, commenting on the Wiehahn and Riekert commissions that had investigated labour conditions, Louw told his shareholders: 'It is to be hoped that the Government will not be deterred by minority groups from implementing as speedily as possible the changes which are so essential if all are to have a proper opportunity to make their full contribution to all facets of the national life.'

When Robin Plumbridge took over the chairmanship in December 1980, he immediately pointed to what had become a serious structural imbalance in the economy, the fact that there existed at one and the same time an acute shortage of skilled and professional manpower and a high level of unemployment among the unskilled. Serving two terms as President of the Chamber of Mines during the Seventies had given him a wide grasp of the labour situation on the mines generally. During that decade for economic and social reasons there had been an enormous rise in the wages of black unskilled or semi-skilled workers, more than 800 percent. Yet on the gold mines productivity had increased by only four percent. The only way out of an apparent impasse was a non-racial approach to training and hence jobs. As he saw it, this called for 'the removal of the last entrenched elements of discrimination in the industry's employment practices, the determination of an equitable market-related wage curve which gives due cognizance to the level of skills of various categories of workers and a major increase in the training provided for all employees'. Two years later the head of his gold division, Colin Fenton, became President of the Chamber and he was asked if the training of blacks and the removal of barriers to their advancement were taking place satisfactorily. He replied that, although the number of opportunities for blacks to fill jobs was increasing, the process was hampered by deficiencies in basic education. This would have to be overcome if the mining industry were going to utilize all human resources effectively, irrespective of race.

Gold Fields by this time had been taking steps on its own initiative to tackle the problem of basic education. As it saw things, the day of the black mining engineer would be indefinitely postponed unless there was a dramatic improvement in basic education within the black community. After the traumas produced by the 1976 disturbances in Soweto and elsewhere, the Urban Foundation had come into existence to give practical expression to South African Business' sense of social responsibility. It was an initiative that Gold Fields fully supported. The company put up R500 000 for the Gold Fields Teachers Centre, which was itself part of the Urban Foundation's Funda Centre in Diepkloof in Soweto. Speaking at its inauguration in October 1984, Plumbridge said: 'The plaque we are about to unveil is symbolic of our investment in our people, our country and our future.' Soon after this Plumbridge was travelling to the Transkei for the opening of Gold Fields' Mechanical Workshops at Umtata which had been built at a cost of R750 000. He reminded those present that thirty percent of the labour force on the mines was provided by the Transkei and that the money brought back to the territory made the mines an important source of its revenue.

GFSA's concern with education and training and its recognition that this was an area where South Africa's economic and social future joined hands, was shared by Consolidated Gold Fields in London. Back in 1974 Donald McCall had announced that his company had set aside R4 800 000 for Black education in the Republic and in the former British Protectorates, Lesotho, Botswana and Swaziland. And when he came to Johannesburg he enabled *The Star's* Teach Fund to hit the R1 000 000 mark by handing the chairman of the Argus Company a cheque for R186 000. GFSA undertook to supervise in Southern

Africa the implementation of the various training schemes that the CGF money had made possible.

Up till July 1981 Gold Fields of South Africa had handled the financial side of its social responsibilities through a central Chairmen's Fund. However, it was clear that the Eighties in this sphere of social responsibility was going to be a very demanding decade. Social attitudes were changing fast and the potential for Business and Industry to play a social role in the national life had never been greater nor the need to do so more urgent. This was the background to the creation at 75 Fox Street in 1981 of The Gold Fields Foundation which would give a practical outlet for a new corporate activity. It was a question of giving something back. Robin Plumbridge had used that expression when he explained why he wanted to return to South Africa after having had the benefit of three years at Oxford on a Rhodes Scholarship. 'I felt I had a duty to put something back,' he had said. That he did so to no ordinary degree was recognized by South Africa itself when the State President conferred upon him the Decoration for Meritorious Service, not only for what he had done for mining but for the community at large.

The philosophy of putting something back had been imparted to the company but it had been Rhodes himself, the co-founder, who had set a precedent long ago. He used to speak of the two kinds of shareholder in a company that digs in the ground for gold. There was one kind who, when the hole was empty, would throw down his shovel and walk away. And the other kind, more socially sensitive and imaginative who, when the gold was exhausted, would fill up the hole. In modern times he would perhaps make an ornamental lake and donate the shovel to a museum for posterity. It was, perhaps, not altogether a coincidence that Gold Fields had been a pioneer in the grassing of abandoned mine dumps nor ever exercised its legal right to erect a slimes dam on a popular Johannesburg race course! The Gold Fields Foundation's concern with the environment and with conservation took on a much more practical application. In September 1984 Plumbridge was in Bophuthatswana, where in the presence of President Mangope and Dr Anton Rupert, chairman of the Southern African Nature Foundation, he opened the Gold Fields Resource Education Centre in the Pilanesberg National Park. It was, said President Mangope, 'a classroom in the wilds'. There was more of this the following year when Plumbridge opened the environmental centre in the Kruger National Park.

Not all Gold Fields classrooms were in the wilds, however. Some were in the universities. Gold Fields House, opened at Rhodes University in 1985, was not a set of classrooms, more a student residence, largely donated by the company. Gold Fields had long had a special relationship with the university named after its own co-founder. The Cory Library at Rhodes had since 1976 been the permanent home of the Gold Fields Collection, formerly known as the Rhodes Collection, which had been started in 1944 on the initiative of Carleton Jones. Everything that had to do with the early days of the company on the Rand and in particular with Rhodes and Rudd – documents, letters, both official and personal –

everything was painstakingly assembled by a Gold Fields mineralogist turned archivist, Charles Bawdon. Items were also collected for the Rhodes Museum in the university. In 1986, Stellenbosch University also received a grant of R1 million for a student hostel complex which would carry the names of gold mines of the GFSA Group.

Demands on The Gold Fields Foundation have increased as time has gone on. Sometimes as many requests as ten in a day will be handled. Grants and projects have increased in scope and variety. In 1985 a grant of R100 000 was made to 'Operation Hunger' and a similar amount went to the Free Market Foundation with whose free enterprise philosophy the company identifies. At the time The Gold Fields Foundation came into being in 1981, the company became a founder member of the Small Business Development Corporation, which had been formed by the private sector in co-operation with the State, and would help particularly the growing class of black entrepreneurs. Gold Fields committed itself to a payment of R5 million over five years.

The need for a charitable organization within the structure of a modern mining house, and particularly in a country like South Africa with its special problems, has been amply proved since The Gold Fields Foundation began to operate in 1981. However, even more important has been the recognition of the new realities of a South Africa moving towards the 21st Century. There was a realization that labour – white or black – however grateful for the helping hand provided by corporate charity would see it in the end as a form of paternalism. And paternalism, like patriotism, was not enough. The black labour force was beginning to organize the defence of its own interests through trade unions and other means. Changed attitudes on the part of government allowed the formation of black unions and gave the legal right to strike. Modernization of the machinery of industrial relations had become as necessary as the modernization of mining itself but would not automatically provide a panacea for all its problems. Nevertheless, the advanced technology that goes into the making of a modern mine is very much concerned with the welfare and the safety of those who day after day go up and down its shafts. It is a concern shared with the new trade unions who very soon began to make Safety one of their platforms.

Gold Fields takes pride in its achievements in mine safety. In the period 1938 to 1968 those stalwarts of the Group, Sub Nigel, Luipaards Vlei, Simmer and Jack, Vogelstruisbult and Rietfontein had between them won in no less than twenty-six years out of thirty the C S McLean Shield, the gold mining industry's top safety award. Of these Sub Nigel was outstanding with fourteen wins. During 1984 both East Drie and Kloof, two mines who have their fair share of sad memories of past accidents, announced more with thanksgiving than with pride, that they had achieved one million fatality-free shifts. Three years earlier West Drie had been awarded five stars in the International Mine Safety Rating Scheme and Apex Mines was the first colliery in the world to achieve that distinction. Commenting on the international scheme to improve mine safety, Dr Piet Smit, formerly head of Gold Fields' medical services, said: 'Maybe this is over-emphasized to a certain extent but it does play a part. Mainly because it keeps people aware of safety environments, keeps them aware of the dangers of malpractices and it does encourage top management to see that everything is provided so that they can get a rating, and of course they all try to rate for the five-star.'

The background history to the winning of safety awards and the sense of competition that exists between mines to win them, is sombre. In a ten-year period, from 1973 to 1983, no fewer than 8 209 people lost their lives in mine accidents in South Africa and nearly a quarter of a million were injured. Mining at great depths brings special hazards, particularly the danger of rock bursts caused by the build-up of pressure at depth. Methane gas is another. Gold Fields mines have not been spared and some of the worst accidents have taken place in the very mines that won safety awards, Kloof, East Drie and West Drie. When these emergencies occurred, they often produced some extraordinary acts of bravery and devotion and, among white and black miners alike, the crisis and the danger of the moment produced a remarkable display of that brotherhood of mining.

In March 1974 eleven miners were lost in a pressure burst at Kloof 2 000 metres below ground when thousands of tons of rock came tumbling down. Rescue attempts saved some; two miners trapped for forty hours were eventually rescued. It was nearly two months before the last body was found and brought to the surface. There were scenes of great bravery, notably that of the shift boss, Doors van Rensburg who, 2 000 metres below ground, braced his straining back against a collapsing roof and in constant danger of further rock falls, dug away until he had rescued a black miner trapped under the rubble. Kloof suffered another serious accident in November the following year when twelve black mineworkers, members of a tunnelling team, died in an explosion of methane gas. At the official enquiry into the accident the shift boss, Paul Grobbelaar, described how he had stopped to eat a sandwich before going in to mark up charge holes in the face. Had he not taken that snack, he too would certainly have disappeared in the explosion. That same year, 1975, the President of the Chamber, R S Lawrence, had gone out to East Driefontein to present the Chamber's award for outstanding bravery to Gary Peters, a stoper at the mine who had had himself lowered down an ore pass by means of a steel rope so that he could examine an injured Black machine operator, Alpheos Makhanya, who had fallen down the ore pass. Then, alone, Peters carried out a rescue operation which involved passing below the level of rock suspended in the other leg of the ore pass. Fifteen minutes after he had got Makhanya to safety, the rock fell filling the place where they had been.

In 1982 no fewer than eight Gold Fields men, two whites and six blacks, received the Chamber of Mines bravery awards following a dramatic rescue operation at West Driefontein on 30 July that year, when an earth tremor caused a rock fall. One of those who was so honoured was Dr Peter Lowe who, not long before, had become consulting medical officer at Gold Fields. Although having little experience of underground conditions, Lowe insisted on going down with

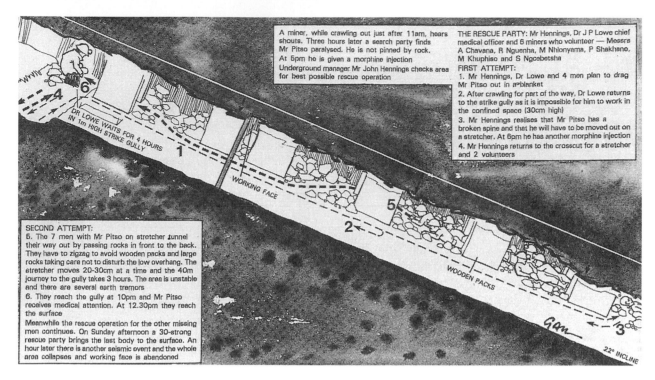

A miner, while crawling out just after 11am, hears shouts. Three hours later a search party finds Mr Pitso paralysed. He is not pinned by rock. At 5pm he is given a morphine injection Underground manager Mr John Hennings checks area for best possible rescue operation

THE RESCUE PARTY: Mr Hennings, Dr J P Lowe chief medical officer and 6 miners who volunteer — Messrs A Chavana, R Nguenha, M Nhlonyama, P Shakhane, M Khuphiso and S Ngcebetsha

FIRST ATTEMPT:
1. Mr Hennings, Dr Lowe and 4 men plan to drag Mr Pitso out in a blanket
2. After crawling for part of the way, Dr Lowe returns to the strike gully as it is impossible for him to work in the confined space (30cm high)
3. Mr Hennings realises that Mr Pitso has a broken spine and that he will have to be moved out on a stretcher. At 6pm he has another morphine injection
4. Mr Hennings returns to the crosscut for a stretcher and 2 volunteers

DR LOWE WAITS FOR 4 HOURS IN 1m HIGH STRIKE GULLY

WORKING FACE

WOODEN PACKS

GAM

22° INCLINE

SECOND ATTEMPT:
5. The 7 men with Mr Pitso on stretcher tunnel their way out by passing rocks in front to the back. They have to zigzag to avoid wooden packs and large rocks taking care not to disturb the low overhang. The stretcher moves 20-30cm at a time and the 40m journey to the gully takes 3 hours. The area is unstable and there are several earth tremors
6. They reach the gully at 10pm and Mr Pitso receives medical attention. At 12.30pm they reach the surface
Meanwhile the rescue operation for the other missing men continues. On Sunday afternoon a 30-strong rescue party brings the last body to the surface. An hour later there is another seismic event and the whole area collapses and working face is abandoned

The dramatic rescue of an injured miner at West Driefontein on 30 July 1982 in which Gold Fields' consulting medical officer, Dr Peter Lowe, took part, and which earned bravery awards from the Chamber of Mines for eight Gold Fields men.

MR JOHN HENNINGS   MR A CHAVANA   MR R NGUENHA   MR M NHLONYAMA

MR P SHAKHANE   MR M KHUPHISO   MR S NGCEBETSHA   DR P LOWE

310

the underground manager, John Hemmings, to the aid of Lebuajoang Pitso, who lay with a broken spine in an area that was likely to collapse at any moment. Six of Pitso's colleagues volunteered to go with them. Working only with the light of their headlamps, breaking their way through fallen rock, they could hear the earth moving all the time and in the darkness the sound of more rock falling. But they kept on and eventually reached Pitso who was given morphine. Many hours went by, however, before they could get him out of the mine on a stretcher. He was paralysed but his life had been saved. The names of his fellow mineworkers were entered on the list of brave men honoured by the Chamber of Mines – A Chavana, B Nguenha, N Nhlonyama, P Shakhane, N Khuphiso and S Ngcebetsha. And with these names were those of John Hemmings and Dr Peter Lowe.

It is not every day that the consulting medical officer will leave his comfortable rooms at 75 Fox Street to perform the kind of heroic act that Peter Lowe undertook that July day in 1982. Much of his time is devoted to the administration of what has become a highly sophisticated and modern medical service, with its three hospitals, 15 doctors and large nursing staff. Many doctors, such as L F Dangerfield and A T Halliday, built up enviable reputations in their hospitals. Lowe himself followed at head office in the footsteps of distinguished forerunners, Piet Smit for many years before him, and Dr E T Clifton before that. Perhaps the most celebrated of them all was Dr Leslie Williams, whose pioneering work in many fields, including the nutrition of mineworkers, is commemorated by the main Gold Fields hospital, located at Driefontein, the Leslie Williams Memorial Hospital. He was in his lifetime a legendary figure on the West Rand. He also had a remarkable resemblance to Buller Smart, his contemporary at Gold Fields where he was the senior consulting engineer. The physician and the engineer were sometimes mistaken for each other with disconcerting consequences. Arthur Stead was driving with Buller Smart through the West Wits mining area. They were on their way to visit the geologist Robert Pelletier, who was on holiday on the Vaal. A man in a van drove past them, glancing at them as he went by. Then he stopped ahead and walked back towards them. At the side of their car he suddenly dropped his trousers and lifted up his shirt to reveal a recent scar. 'That was a lovely job you did on my hernia, Doctor,' he said, 'I've had no more trouble.' Then, correcting his dress, he returned to his van and drove off again. 'What was all that about?', asked the Gold Fields consulting engineer. Stead explained that he had been mistaken for the Gold Fields medical officer.

Leslie Williams may have been a dab-hand at hernias; he would certainly have been surprised at the kind of surgery now being performed at the hospital that bears his name. Micro-surgery has almost become commonplace. A mineworker who may have the misfortune to have a limb severed in an accident underground, will very likely have it sown on again by such miracles of modern surgery. They became a source of wonder when they returned to their tribal home. On the other hand, as Dr Piet Smit has pointed out, times have changed.

Below, left, *Dr Leslie Williams (circa 1939), the Gold Fields doctor who became a legendary figure among the miners of the West Wits Line. He is commemorated by the Leslie Williams Memorial Hospital at Driefontein (above).*

Below, right, *Robin Plumbridge, chairman of GFSA, watching a student at the Gold Fields computer laboratory in the University of Cape Town.*

312

The tribal man is no longer a backward man. He is not a 'blanket man' any more. He comes to the mine in Western clothes and in most cases has had experience of Western medicine, though hardly of micro-surgery.

Going home for a black miner on the gold mines administered by Gold Fields will as likely as not mean going home to one of the tribal homelands within the Republic of South Africa. This was not always the case. In some earlier years the great majority of mineworkers on the Witwatersrand came from beyond the country's borders and were recruited by agencies of the Chamber of Mines. Since the political changes that took place in South Central Africa in the 1970s, this has changed. Whereas in 1974 some seventy-eight percent were foreign workers and only twenty-two percent came from within the Republic and its internal national states, by 1981 only forty percent were foreign visitors and sixty percent were black South Africans. The change had taken place as a result of a vigorous recruiting drive by The Employment Bureau of Africa, known as TEBA, and directed by Tony Fleischer, son of Gold Fields' former chief in Johannesburg, Spencer Fleischer. Having grown up in a mining environment at Sub Nigel in the 1930s, Tony Fleischer went on to fill important posts at the Chamber of Mines. One of the most remarkable changes that Fleischer detected in the 1980s was in the number of Zulus coming to work on the mines. From a mere 4 500 in 1974, their numbers had grown to 40 000 in 1981. Ten percent of Gold Fields' mineworkers were Zulus. 'It is most gratifying to see Zulus return once again to mining,' commented their leader, Chief Mangosuthu Buthelezi, chief minister of KwaZulu. To the many and varied sounds in the Wonderfontein valley was added the melody of the Zulus' lilting language and song.

The Zulus had arrived with the new times. The gold mining companies were having to take account of these. Men who were black South Africans and not foreigners from distant parts, preferred to work for shorter periods at a time nor did they wish to be separated from their families during the whole of their period of service at the mines. Gold Fields built a number of guest houses on their mines so that a mineworker could have his wife and family come and stay with him for up to a month at a time. It has been a way to mitigate the human hardship which is the inevitable effect of the migrant labour system. By the 1980s the authorities were beginning to show a greater readiness to listen to the arguments coming from the mining houses that with black mineworkers assuming to an increasing extent responsible duties as key workers, there was a need to house a bigger proportion of black workers with their families on mine property. This argument was enhanced when the proportion of black mineworkers of South African origin increased. These developments have led to a dramatic decline in the turnover of the black labour force. Gold Fields operated a bonus scheme which provided an added incentive for a mineworker to return after a spell at home to resume his duties at the mine. It certainly added to the efficient running of a mine to have a more permanent body of able and experienced men in the more demanding technical environment of a modern deep-level mine.

In June 1983 an historic event occurred in South African mining when, after almost a century of activity on the Rand, the Chamber of Mines recognized the National Union of Mineworkers representing black workers. The union conducted its first wage negotiation with the Chamber soon after and within three months it officially declared its first dispute. The Chamber had given the union permission to go recruiting on mines run by members of the Chamber and before long its organizers were visiting Kloof, Libanon, Venterspost and West Driefontein. Early the following year the NUM was claiming a membership of up to 70 000 among a labour force on the mines of some 600 000. Although the claim was not universally accepted, the NUM had nevertheless become a significant factor in the wage setting processes for the mining industry. However, by mid-year the industry was facing a problem. Traditionally, pay increases to black miners are made on 1 July. At the time the Chamber and the union had not been able to reach agreement on the scale of the wage increase. The Chamber had made an offer to the union which had rejected it. Most mining companies, including Gold Fields, felt it was their duty to go ahead and grant wage increases on the usual date because the majority of their black employees were not members of the union. Nor was it possible to identify who were members and who were not. The union objected to this action and called a strike for September. This became the first legal strike by black miners in South African history. Although it lasted only 36 hours it produced a number of scenes of violence and disorder on the mines. The strike was meant to affect only eight mines at which the NUM was recognized. Seven belonged to Anglo American and the eighth was Kloof, belonging to Gold Fields. In the event it spread to other mines. When it was over *Finance Week* in Johannesburg commented: 'Perhaps the greatest irony of the 36 hour strike is that all mining houses with the notable exception of GFSA were affected even though only GFSA and Anglo were in deadlock with the NUM. NUM decided against calling a strike on GFSA's Kloof where its members are only recognized in surface activities.'

A year earlier, in June 1982, Gold Fields, this time in company with Gencor, had had to cope with serious disturbances on some of their mines. They also had to meet strong criticism not only in the South African Press but in particular in the popular American magazine, *Time*. The disturbances, in which ten lives were lost, was the worst since the mid-1970s. When they were over and the dust had settled not only Gold Fields but the industry as a whole tried to determine why exactly they had taken place. But no clear picture emerged. 'The last time we had unrest we never found out at all,' said Colin Fenton, head of the gold division. There seemed to be a mixture of causes. One view was that different wage increases in different companies had caused dissatisfaction. There had been a lack of communication between management and the labour force and some genuine misunderstandings. All in all, it seemed to make it more urgent for black mine labour to be properly organized in unions. Gold Fields commented: 'The absorption of black employees into strong, responsible mine trade unions able to understand and interpret the wishes of all their members would undoubtedly take a great strain off management.' But even the formation of a black trade union would not in itself be an automatic panacea, it was felt. 'The development of trade unions fully representative of their members' interests is a feat not always accomplished even in mature industrial countries,' said Gold Fields.

The distressing events of 1982 had focused attention on the Mine Security organization which, since before the days of Colonel Trigger in the 1930s, had been a Gold Fields responsibility exercised on behalf of most, though not all, the mining companies. Its function has always been to see to the safety and security of mine employees and to safeguard mine property. Only in exceptional circumstances does it call in the help of the South African Police; this is a tactical decision which local managements make in the light of their circumstances and available resources. This occurred at Venterspost during the 1982 disturbances and provided the occasion for an extraordinary display of courage and diplomacy on the part of Krugersdorp's District Commandant of Police, Colonel M C Heunis. He went in unarmed and alone to talk to a crowd of 1 800 angry black miners some of whom had armed themselves with primitive weapons. He told them it was impossible to discuss their grievances with all of them and he asked them to appoint a committee so that he and the mine officials could go into their complaints with its members. They agreed to this and the crowd dispersed quietly. Usually, however, the Mine Security organization is able to handle its problems without calling in the Police. At its training centre on the West Rand both men and guard dogs go through a rigorous period of instruction.

The violent events of 1982 led to a reappraisal of the whole question of black labour on the mines. Lynne van den Bosch of Gencor, who had served with Colonel Fleischer in the Mine Engineering Brigade, spoke out in his capacity of President of the Chamber of Mines. 'There is a critical challenge facing us,' he said, 'in evolving industrial relations procedures that will match the requirements of the times and in stepping up progress towards a common wage structure.' Robin Plumbridge, speaking to shareholders that year, analysed the situation: 'One of the most complex problems relating to the removal of discrimination in the semi-skilled occupations is the establishment of appropriate market-related wage scales.' Some years earlier, he said, Gold Fields had tackled the problem by working out a unified wage curve that covered the whole spectrum of unskilled to skilled workers. This allowed workers to increase their earnings with their own abilities. Thus, where there was a gap in earnings these related only to skills and not race or sex. The problem, however, as Plumbridge explained, was that among black workers there were differing views as to the relative merits of different jobs. Traditionally, more importance was given to physical effort in a job than to skill or the responsibility of making decisions which in a modern economy produces greater rewards. 'It is clear that this was one of the main causes of the labour unrest which occurred on certain of the Group's gold mines at the time of the latest wage increases for black employees,' he said. Gold Fields made an effort to explain its point of view to its 69 000 black miners who had been caught up by the events of 1982. Of these, only 3 497 decided to sever their employment and return home.

As time has gone on, the organization of black mine labour has developed with the greater experience of its union leaders. At the same time, despite the unifying influence of the Chamber, the mining houses have not always shown an ability to act together in dealing with the black unions at times of dispute. Some houses have preferred to make their own arrangements, guided by the politics of the moment. Gold Fields has continued to hold the view that, while discrimination in wages must go, wages earned by miners must be related to their productivity. It has tried to hold the problem within economic boundaries, but in the increasing politicization of everything during the 1980s, such an approach has been difficult to sustain. By the mid-1980s, with widespread disaffection leading to the introduction, for the first time since 1960, of a state of emergency in various parts of the country, the conduct of industrial relations in the mining industry became ever more difficult and could not be separated from the political malaise in the country.

A great mining company like Gold Fields, which is the source of great wealth not only for itself but for South Africa, has been increasingly confronted with the problem of balancing one set of options with another. The act has become more demanding and more difficult as the decade has advanced, bringing with it the anxieties and uncertainties of a country trying desperately to construct a future in which there would be harmony between its peoples and a place for itself once more in the international community of nations. The puritan streak that has marked the activities of the company for a century and which reveals itself in such Victorian virtues as self-help, seems to offer a way forward. Having declared itself totally opposed to any form of racial discrimination, it also proclaimed that merit would be the criterion for advancement. However, since the conditions of life in South Africa are such that only a section of the population have advantages and privileges, while others are less fortunate, not everyone can assemble at the same starting line. Only education and training can compensate for this and Gold Fields, in spending some R35 million on training as opposed to R20 million on exploration, has given practical expression to this view. It may well be ahead of other groups in this way. Certainly it has been in the forefront of every new training programme developed in the industry. The first Black electrician coming out of apprenticeship in the gold mining industry was a Gold Fields man. Better trained people will produce more and when they do they will earn more and deserve to do so. It is an old-fashioned concept of equality derived from its Victorian beginnings. It might well have appealed to those Scottish shareholders who long ago provided the financial backbone of the company, and unwittingly perhaps, helped to form its character and influence its view of the world.

Meanwhile the technology of mining was being called upon to give increasing attention to the needs of the men involved in the industry. It was having to cope with the challenging problems of seeking gold three or four kilometres below the earth's surface while at the same time making the environment as tolerable as possible for those who had to go down there. Gold Fields, while continuing its own efforts to improve the underground environment, was also able to benefit from the Chamber of Mines' own research programme directed by Dr Miklos Salamon. High temperatures deep underground, they found, resulted in a reduction in safety standards mainly because of a reduced level of concentration and falling off in productivity. Sometimes temperatures at the rock face were as high as sixty degrees and had to be brought down, for instance, by the introduction of chilled water. The company's concern to reduce the number of people working at depth was illustrated by the research it conducted into what is known as slime-filling. This is a process that could reduce dramatically the number of people working underground. Instead of having men to put in the support system, a mixture of timber and concrete, slime-filling, piped directly from the surface to the working place, would substantially cut down the number of men formerly involved deep underground. This is but one item in a long Gold Fields record in research. Even before the First World War it had established research laboratories at Nelsonia, Booysens, which came to serve the industry as a whole. At Robinson Deep it had laboratories dealing specifically with ventilation problems and here the first primitive efforts at cooling the underground environment were attempted. The Investigations Committee at Gold Fields built up an enviable reputation for the work it carried out not only in the laboratories but also in the field. The company's mechanical engineers are remembered by such achievements as the cactus grab of the early 1950s, pioneered at Vlakfontein and later adopted by the industry as a major step forward in shaft-sinking, with mechanical lashing – removing the ore – replacing laborious hand-loading. Nearly twenty years later Gold Fields introduced the raise borer which they had investigated with Hubert Davies & Co to bore rock passes and later to supplement shaft-sinking techniques. Employed successfully on the Witwatersrand for the first time, at Doornfontein in 1969, it was adopted on a large scale by the industry as a whole. In 1975 André Taute was talking enthusiastically about the reef borer which could make it possible to do away with blasting.

The size and depth of the mines of the West Wits Line tell their own story of the achievement of the company's engineers – mining engineers, mechanical engineers, electrical engineers, computer specialists of the modern era. The enormous concrete-lined shafts of the company's mines today are a far cry from the old rectangular, timber-lined shafts of the past when, before the last war, hoisting 60 000 tons a month from 5 000 feet was considered an achievement. Computer techniques, pioneered at mine level at Kloof in the early days, and where the central control centre in the mill and reduction plant keeps an eye on everything, made this mine the most modern in the world. Apart from the facility which the computer provides for the storage and calculation of geological and engineering information, such as ore reserves and grades, rock stresses and displacements, heat flows and air flows, all of which are essential in designing a modern mine, they also help in assessing rapidly and at minimal cost the relative merits of mining methods and machines. The computer has become part of the equipment of the mining engineer, the mine manager, the metallurgist and the geologist, who can assess the amount of mineable ore in a particular area.

Those who in the 1980s have been responsible at 75 Fox Street for advancing the technological frontiers, whether in engineering, in metallurgy or geology, have never allowed the machine to replace either their own humanity or their sense of humour. One of the leading metallurgists of his time, D A Viljoen, until 1986 head of his department at Gold Fields, and a worthy successor there to distinguished predecessors such as W A Caldecott at the turn of the century, Andrew King, Harry Cross and others, admits that the most decisive factor in the exploitation of minerals today is specialized technology. 'More than a chemical formula, it is engineering know-how that holds the key to the future,' he maintains. On the other hand, in thinking of the role of the geologist and the modern tools now available to him, including satellite photography, he says: 'The human factor remains the most important, for mineral data must be interpreted and there is no substitute for keen eyes, well-shod feet and enthusiasm.' He recalled the answer that the veteran Gold Fields geologist Robert Pelletier gave when asked what he thought was the most useful geophysical instrument and he replied dryly, 'A pick!' His fellow geologist, Max Mehliss, commenting on the fact that the large budgets now devoted to exploration had transformed the status of the geologist's profession and even given them the grandiose title of earth scientists, said: 'Geologists hitherto looked upon as unnecessary evils, are now greeted as equals by shift bosses and chairmen!' Mehliss may well be that ideal mineral explorationist whom Viljoen defined as 'a subtle blend of optimist and cynic. He knows his chances of success are minimal for in no field of technical endeavour is the success rate so low. It is well known that only one prospect in several thousand turns out to be a viable mine by normal commercial standards.' If that other Gold Fields Viljoen, Dr Richard Viljoen, consulting geologist in the mid-1980s, looks back at the experience of his predecessors, Reinecke, Pelletier, De Kock, Truter, Cluver, Ben Weilers, he can have no illusions as to the challenge that his metier demands in the fiercely competitive exploration world of today.

If Gold Fields' team of metallurgists, now headed by Richard Beck, have been concerned with the future, they have not neglected the past; in fact they have set it to work again. The continuing activity of Vlakfontein after more than fifty years is the proof of their success. Nowadays a relatively small loss of metal in the recovery process could make the difference between a profitable enterprise and an unprofitable one. The early miners did their best with their primitive methods but these were wasteful and left a lot of gold behind in mine dumps and slimes dams. The modern metallurgist has devised ways of getting at the gold left behind by his mining grandfather. Although underground mining ceased at Vlakfontein in 1977, the mine had remained at work. Since that time it had operated a sand and waste rock reprocessing plant and by the time it celebrated its golden jubilee in 1984 had recovered another 5,8 tons of gold. The plant had a maximum capacity of 70 000 tons and Vlakfontein still offered work for some 443 employees. That compares with 6 000 in the heyday of the mine in the Algy

Cundill era. Still, it says much for modern skills that they have continued to squeeze worthwhile profits from an old mine like Vlakfontein, which has kept the Gold Fields flag flying on the East Rand and reminded nearby Dunnottar that the mine, not the flying school, is the reason for its existence. Brakpan, too, has reason to remember. Its mayoral chain in gold was Vlakfontein's gift in 1962.

Vlakfontein is one of the old properties that has been able to continue its mining activities though in a different way. Some of the other properties, more elderly still, Sub Nigel and Luipaards Vlei, had merged their identity in Gold Fields Property. In 1978 Gold Fields Property decided to part with the Luipaards Vlei mining title, thus disposing of its uranium reserves. West Rand Consolidated were to pay R3 million for it and agreed to GF Property having a twenty-five percent share of pre-tax profits arising out of the exploitation of the mining area. The arrangement seemed to satisfy the GF Property shareholders; it also finally brought peace between its chairman at the time, Dru Gnodde, and one of his persistent critics, the Johannesburg stockbroker Peter George. 'Burying the hatchet in a pile of uranium,' was how *The Star* described the incident. In ancient times metallurgy was part of the world of alchemy and astrology and at the shareholders' meeting at which the uranium announcement was made both Peter George and Dru Gnodde thought it appropriate to give their horoscopes an airing. Said George, reading out his message from the stars: 'You are reconciled with an old enemy and exciting times follow. A scheme which hangs fire now takes off. Friends arrange a surprise for you.' Gnodde, not to be outdone, read out his own horoscope: 'Your discovery about a close friend puts a different slant on the relationship. A windfall helps a disorganized friend out of trouble. A senior colleague creates new opportunities for someone you love.' It was a happy, if somewhat unusual conclusion to a shareholders' meeting.

There had always been shareholders who imagined that the best way to make money in the property business might be to have an interest in old mine property in and around Johannesburg. In their minds they saw high-rise dumps come tumbling down and high-rise flats going up in their place. In 1975 Bernard van Rooyen had warned that it was not as simple as it seemed. He told the South African Property Owners Association that of the 79 000 hectares held under mining title from Randfontein to Nigel, some twenty percent was unusable for development because it was undermined or occupied on the surface by dumps and other mining paraphernalia. Another twenty percent had already been developed for housing.

Shareholders in Gold Fields, however, did have a particularly valuable property. Like its old mines, it was situated on an historic site, in fact just a stone's throw from where Colonel Ferreira had found an empty parking spot for his wagon in 1886. The address is 75 Fox Street but the Gold Fields headquarters, for such it is, is very much bigger than the modest address suggests. No 1, London, was the famous address of the Duke of Wellington, but it gave no idea of the size and splendour of Apsley House where he lived at that address. It is rather like that with Gold Fields and 75 Fox Street. The building takes up a sizeable frontage on Fox Street, then creeps round the corner through Sauer Street, named after that Gold Fields pioneer, Dr Hans Sauer, into Commissioner Street, then takes a hefty bit out of that, too. Over the years Gold Fields buildings have come and gone but always on the same site. The great new modern ensemble assembled in time for the company's centenary is the work of the architect Louis Karol, who undertook to do the work in phases so that the life and activity of Gold Fields could go on in as orderly a fashion as possible. Gold Fields in setting aside at the start some R27 million for a new home in which to celebrate its 100th birthday, was at the same time making an architectural contribution to the City of Johannesburg, itself celebrating a centenary. It was an appropriate salute from its oldest mining house. The modern building that has risen on the ancient site of Gold Fields' past activity is somehow symbolic of the way that Gold Fields itself, as a company, has constantly renewed itself and ensured its survival, by taking new initiatives based on the firm foundations of past experience. It was very much in character when Gold Fields, with its strong sense of continuity and history, refused to follow the fashion and move from the central business area of Johannesburg. 'This is where we started, this is where we stay' has been very much the attitude of a company that continues to be what it was at the beginning, a mining house. So there it sits, astride Fox and Commissioner Streets.

The juxtaposition of these two streets had a special significance for one Gold Fields employee in particular. It reminded him of a crossroads in his career. This was Bok Odendaal, for many years a popular figure at Doornfontein mine where his mining colleagues knew him as 'the man with the jokes'. Before coming to Gold Fields he had been a railway policeman but felt his career as such was jeopardised by his inability to spell. The moment of truth had come when he had to write a report on an accident in Commissioner Street where a mule had been knocked down and killed. Not being able to spell Commissioner, he gave instructions for the dead mule to be dragged into Fox Street, the spelling of which gave him no trouble. Having transferred the scene of the accident to Fox Street, he thought in due course he might go there, too, and was soon on his way to Doornfontein.

Sir Ernest Oppenheimer is said to have told his architect that what he would like for the headquarters of his Anglo American Corporation was something between a bank and a cathedral. The evangelist who suddenly appeared one morning early in the 1960s at Gold Fields soon after the new Commissioner Street premises had been occupied, may well have mistaken the place for the Oppenheimer cathedral, since he proceeded to preach in a loud voice. From the Commissioner Street side, management and various other departments faced into the courtyard looking across to the original Fox Street building, which sported a small balcony on each of its floors. The evangelist, unannounced, appeared on the 8th floor balcony and began to deliver his religious message to the members of staff who, at work at their desks, were a captive congregation. Then he suddenly vanished and in his place stood the building superintendent,

320

Mr Ackroyd, who looked anxiously left and right. At that moment the evangelist appeared on the balcony of the 7th floor and went on with his sermon. Once more he vanished and in his place appeared the harassed Ackroyd. And so it went on from balcony to balcony, like a well-rehearsed game of hide-and-seek. Finally, completing his message, the evangelist disappeared for the last time into Fox Street. Work for the Lord, he seemed to be saying to the staff at Gold Fields. The pay is not very good but the fringe benefits are out of this world!

Those who spent their working lives with Gold Fields of South Africa in earlier times will say that it was not the money they earned which was the most memorable part of their service. If Gold Fields had a reputation in the past for being somewhat parsimonious with its pay, as it was, in the view of some of its shareholders, with its dividends, yet the fringe benefits commanded the loyalty and affection of those it employed. These were not material benefits. They consisted rather of those human advantages provided by an atmosphere of good company relations, which has long been the hallmark of the Group. The main fringe benefit is the simple fact of being a member of the Gold Fields community. Gold Fields people take a pride and pleasure in the achievements of their fellows, particularly on the sports field, whether it is Peter Ngobeni of West Driefontein who, running 100 metres in ten seconds, equalled the South African record, or his fellow Black athlete of an earlier period, Peter Reele, also of West Drie, who ran for his country in a marathon in Belgium in 1971. Or Peter Janisch, gamely running the Comrades Marathon five times after the age of forty. Those who may in the past have felt themselves underpaid in comparison with members of other houses, nevertheless stayed where they were because that was where they were happy to be. The bulging membership of the 25 Club, founded in that year of destiny, 1971, is proof of that, for to be a member of the club one has had to have completed twenty-five years. In 1984 the membership passed the 2 000 mark. With membership goes the traditional gold watch of the mining industry. Some have stayed for half a century. F R Pullock put in forty-three years at Simmer and Jack as part of his fifty with the Group. In 1985, John Boland marked up his 50th year and, during all those years, had sensibly never missed a pay day. A F 'Fergy' Lawson, first Secretary of the reconstituted Gold Fields of South Africa in 1959, retired in 1966 with fifty-two years of service behind him. But no one is ever likely to do better than John Sithole who, when he retired in 1979, had completed sixty-six years at Rooiberg and was reluctant to leave when the time came to go.

Gold Fields has always attracted men and women of a rather special calibre; the whizz kid's world has to be sought elsewhere. Conservative, austere even, but never lacking in inventive skills nor the ability to adapt to evolutionary change in the mining industry of which it is the doyen, Gold Fields has proved itself a survivor. And the welfare and prosperity of South Africa have been greatly enriched by its labours there for all of a hundred years.

The old shift ends.
Start of a new future?

Selected Index